# African American Connecticut
## EXPLORED

# African American
# Connecticut
# EXPLORED

Edited by Elizabeth J. Normen,
with Katherine J. Harris, Stacey K. Close,
and Wm. Frank Mitchell

WESLEYAN UNIVERSITY PRESS
Middletown, Connecticut

Wesleyan University Press

Middletown CT 06459

www.wesleyan.edu/wespress

© 2013 Connecticut Explored Inc.

Manufactured in the United States of America

First paperback edition 2016

ISBN for the paperback edition: 978-0-8195-7399-5

Designed by Katherine B. Kimball

Typeset in Galliard by Passumpsic Publishing

FRONT COVER IMAGE: Pharmacist Anna Louise James behind the
soda fountain in the James Pharmacy, c. 1909–1911. MC440-80-1
(detail). Schlesinger Library, Radcliffe Institute, Harvard University.

BACK COVER IMAGES: Amos Beman (Beinecke Rare Book and
Manuscript Library). Kente cloth (Amistad Center for Art & Culture).

The Library of Congress has cataloged the hardcover edition as:
African American Connecticut explored / edited by
Elizabeth J. Normen ; with Katherine J. Harris,
Stacey K. Close, and Wm. Frank Mitchell.
    pages  cm. — (Garnet books)
Includes bibliographical references and index.
ISBN 978-0-8195-7398-8 (cloth : alk. paper)—
ISBN 978-0-8195-7400-8 (ebook)
1. African Americans—Connecticut—History.  2. African
Americans—Connecticut—Biography.  I. Normen, Elizabeth J.
E185.93.C7A47   2013
974.6'00496073—dc23
2013031264

5  4  3  2  1

# Contents

Plates 1–9 follow page 236.

*Connecticut Explored*, founded in 2002, is a quarterly magazine dedicated to uncovering the state's cultural heritage with the aim of revealing connections between our past, present, and future. Our goal is to share Connecticut's rich and varied history, one good story after another. *Connecticut Explored* developed this book as part of its tenth-anniversary celebration in 2012. For more information about *Connecticut Explored* visit ctexplored.org.

The Amistad Center for Art & Culture owns and showcases a vital collection of nearly 7,000 items of art, artifacts, and popular culture objects that document the experience, expressions, and history of people of African descent in America. The Center's collection is housed at the Wadsworth Atheneum Museum of Art in Hartford, Connecticut. Founded in 1987, The Center developed this book as part of its twenty-fifth anniversary celebration in 2012. For more information about The Amistad Center for Art & Culture visit amistadartandculture.org.

# Preface

A book for a general audience that surveys the long arc of the African American experience in Connecticut is long overdue. *Connecticut Explored* and The Amistad Center for Art & Culture collaborated on development of this book; additional collaborators were the State Historic Preservation Office of the Department of Economic and Community Development and The Amistad Committee, Inc., the organization that administers the Connecticut Freedom Trail in cooperation with the State Historic Preservation Office.

As the magazine of Connecticut history, *Connecticut Explored*'s goal is to uncover the state's cultural heritage with the aim of revealing connections between our past, present, and future. We do this in a highly collaborative way, calling upon the tremendous talents and resources of the state's historians, curators, museums, historical societies, and archives. This book has been developed on the same model, and we owe a great thank you to our partners in this effort.

The idea for the book began with the more than two-dozen articles on African American history in Connecticut that had been previously published in the magazine over the last decade. Those articles, written for a general audience and no more than 2,500 words long, were like case studies that, when brought together, revealed a great deal about the African American experience in the state. The articles' strength was in the richness of the very personal and very human stories they portrayed—stories of real people who influenced history. Whether they lived lives that were ordinary or extraordinary, they told the collective story, too. And yet, gathered together, that collective story was incomplete. While a very rich trove of local histories, research reports, and essays on the subject of African Americans in Connecticut has been written and published, there has been no book-length treatment that allows for an interested reader to gain an understanding of the entire history from settlement in the 1630s through mid-twentieth century. Could we augment our two-dozen essays to offer such a book?

The editorial team of *Connecticut Explored*, represented by publisher Elizabeth Normen, The Amistad Center for Art & Culture, represented by executive director Olivia White, the State Historic Preservation Office, represented by Mary Donohue and Cora Murray, scholars Dr. Stacey Close, Dr. Katherine Harris, Dr. Frank Mitchell, and volunteer Constance B. Green, surveyed the available scholarship, both published and unpublished, and looked for additional essays that similarly focused on both the individual and the collective experience. Given the time frame we were working within, we did not commission new scholarship though some stories here are published for the first time. Some stories that we wanted eluded us, affirming that some of this history is lost or still to be uncovered.

Dr. Harris and Dr. Close were asked to write introductory essays that would provide broad overviews by era so that readers could place the topical essays into historical context. Dr. Frank Mitchell was asked to provide a photo essay that drew upon The Amistad Center's considerable collection of images, to write an essay on food culture, and to take on the Herculean task of summing it all up in a conclusion.

Our goal for this book is to tell this history as much as possible through the African American experience. You will not find in these pages, therefore, the story of the *Amistad* Affair with an emphasis on white abolitionists and celebrity lawyers but rather the response by the African American community to the *Amistad* captives' fight for freedom. You will not find the story of state heroine Prudence Crandall but will read instead about Crandall's student Sarah Harris's quest for an education and a professional vocation. You will read about nationally prominent black leaders such as Rev. Amos Beman and Rev. James Pennington, but will also read about local businessman William Lanson, Civil War soldier Joseph O. Cross, and World War II nurse Susan Freeman—individuals who represent the "everyman." Their stories convey their specific and personal experiences while illustrating the broader political and cultural challenges and opportunities of the times in which they lived.

More than thirty historians and scholars and several individuals writing personal recollections have contributed to this book. Dr. Harris's introductory essays cover the mid-seventeenth century to the Civil War, and Dr. Close covers the Civil War to the mid-twentieth century.

It is important to note that this book is not intended to be the definitive and complete history of the African American experience in Connecticut. There are many important people and developments only briefly touched on in the introductory essays that easily warrant their own essay or book. We invite readers to take this book as the beginning, a springboard to further reading and study. We hope it spurs further scholarship, particularly from the African American perspective. Dr. Harris comments briefly below on the scholarship currently available and a thorough review of the bibliography is also encouraged.

# Historiographical Notes

*Katherine J. Harris*

The African American experience in Connecticut has received cursory attention in surveys of African American history, texts on American history, unpublished micro histories, and published journal essays.[1] A historical synthesis of Connecticut's African American community similar to Graham Russell Hodges' *Root & Branch: African Americans in New York and East Jersey, 1613–1863* however, has yet to be published.[2]

Secondary published works such as William Dillon Piersen's *Black Yankees: The Development of an Afro-American Subculture in Eighteenth-Century New England*, published in 1988, have offered a glimpse of Connecticut's African American political and cultural traditions.[3] On the other end of the spectrum, Robert Austin Warner's *New Haven Negroes*, published in 1940, is a useful but very focused study of New Haven's African American socio-economic history as it evolved through the eighteenth to the first four decades of the twentieth centuries.[4]

Dr. Lorenzo J. Greene's 1942 study *The Negro in Colonial New England 1620–1790* examined the regional context of Connecticut's African American history. Greene's *history* remains the seminal scholarly treatment of African Americans in Connecticut, though like the Hodges volume, Greene covered a selected chronological period. Born in Ansonia, Connecticut in 1899, Greene lived and researched the Connecticut African American experience. He recognized its historical complexities.[5]

During the intervening decades since Greene published his study a comprehensive treatise on Connecticut African Americans has not been written. Hence this current exploration of Connecticut African Americans, in many ways, resumes where Greene's study ended. It is a starting point for a comprehensive history. But this volume based on primary, secondary, and other sources probes the richness and nuances of more than three hundred years of the Connecticut African American experience. Covering the foundational roots of African Americans in Connecticut to the early twenty-first century, this volume welds together topical historical essays and illustrations for the general readership and scholarly audience.

# Notes

1. John Hope Franklin and Evelyn Brooks Higginbotham, *From Slavery to Freedom: A History of African Americans*, ninth edition (New York: McGraw Hill, 2011 first published in 1947). Clayborne Carson, Emma Lapsansky-Werner and Gary Nash, *The Struggle for Freedom* (New York: Prentice Hall, 2007, 2011) combined volume one, second edition. David Goldfield, Carl Abbott, Virginia De John Anderson, Jo Ann E. Argersinger, William L. Barney, Robert M. Wier, *American Journey: A History of the United States* (Boston: Pearson, 2004/2011), volumes 1 and 2.

2. Graham Russell Hodges. *Root & Branch: African Americans in New York and East Jersey, 1613–1863*, (Chapel Hill and London: University of North Carolina Press, 1999).

3. William Dillon Piersen, *Black Yankees: The Development of an Afro-American Subculture in Eighteenth-Century New England* (Boston: The University of Massachusetts Press, 1988).

4. Robert Austin Warner, *New Haven Negroes: A Social History* (New Haven: Yale University Press, 1940).

5. Lorenzo J. Greene, *The Negro in Colonial New England 1620–1790* (New York: Columbia University Press, 1942). Lorenzo Johnston Greene Papers, A Finding Aid to the Collection in the Library of Congress, prepared by Joseph K. Brooks with the assistance of Patricia K. Craig, Lisa R. Madison, and Sheila R. Day, revised and expanded by Joseph K. Brooks (Washington, D.C.: Manuscript Division, Library of Congress, 2009), 3–4.

# Introduction

Where does this story begin? Start by imagining a person in his or her homeland somewhere on the continent of Africa, a person born free to a mother and a father in a community with a culture and history dating back thousands of years. Then step forward to the Connecticut colony in its earliest years. Dr. Harris writes that Africans were present there but their status was unclear. Were they free, indentured, or enslaved? Or possibly were some free, some indentured, and some enslaved? She notes that chattel slavery was legalized in Connecticut in 1643 under the Articles of the New England Confederation—as much as five years after the first African is said to be in the colony. So *we* begin the telling of this story with an assumption of Africans as people—though it's not clear and perhaps not likely that white Connecticans in that period did the same. Further, it is important to note that with the advent of legalized slavery comes the quest for freedom. It is not many years before we encounter an act of self-emancipation, in Hartford in 1658. So, too, the quest for equality and justice begins—at the beginning.

It may still be news to some readers that Connecticut was a slave state, that the institution of chattel slavery was legal here for 205 years, and that our economy was strongly tied to the institution. We are still learning about the nature of slavery in this state. There has been a notion that it was more benign here than in other areas of the country. We reject that idea, if simply because it is impossible to consider the ownership of one person of another and the denial of that person's free will to be anything other than cruel and morally wrong. But there is also evidence showing the treatment of enslaved people in Connecticut to be anything but benign. In an essay published in *Connecticut History*, for instance, Diane Cameron brings our attention to court records from November 13, 1654, regarding an enslaved African woman (not named, but referred to as Mr. Chester's "Blackemore") in which "Matthew Williams and John Lyley were accused of 'committing uncleanness with Mr. Chesters Blackemore.'" Three years later, this same woman bore a "second bastard" child. Cameron reminds us that because the historical record leaves gaps, we do not know the full nature of these incidents. But the accounts of this unnamed enslaved woman, other accounts Cameron documents in her essay, and evidence presented in this volume suffice to discredit any characterization of slavery in Connecticut as benign.[1]

We must also come to terms with the fact that Connecticut's economy was tied to the slave economy—though more on a national scale than as a useful economic practice on the rocky and limited agricultural land here. Connecticut companies insured slave owners against loss of "property," food grown here was shipped to Caribbean plantations to feed enslaved people, cotton came north to "feed" our textile mills, Ivoryton's ivory mills turned elephant tusks hauled to port by enslaved people in Africa into piano keys, New Haven's carriage makers catered to the Southern market—and Connecticut's shipping industry transported it all.[2] As Anne Farrow, Joel Lang, and Jenifer Frank note in *Complicity: How the North Promoted, Prolonged, and Profited from Slavery*, "Connecticut derived a great part, maybe the greatest part, of its early surplus wealth from slavery."[3]

And there is the misconception that Connecticut was a stronghold of the abolitionist movement. This is the birthplace of Harriet Beecher Stowe, after all, whose book *Uncle Tom's Cabin*—published only four years after slavery was abolished in Connecticut—did so much to raise awareness among whites of the cruelty and injustice of slavery in the south. This is the state that did so much to free the Amistad captives—whose case was adjudicated while slavery in Connecticut was still legal. This is the birthplace of radical abolitionist John Brown. These examples point perhaps to the source of the misconception. Though a full and detailed account of abolitionism here is yet to be told, several sources suggest that a very small minority of Connecticut's whites participated in abolitionist causes—though some of those that did so were influential, some on a national scale. In *Connecticut in the American Civil War: Slavery, Sacrifice, and Survival*, however, Matt Warshauer begins his work by disabusing us of the notion that Connecticut was broadly or predominantly abolitionist. He writes, "The simple truth is that in the 'land of steady habits,' one of the steadiest was a virulent racism. While New England was generally viewed as the national center of abolitionist thought, Connecticut stood apart. The famed abolitionist William Lloyd Garrison—outraged by attacks on Prudence Crandall's school for black girls and the decision by the town of Canterbury and the state to close the school—derisively referred to Connecticut as the 'Georgia of New England.'"[4]

It is in this context, then, that we read Elisabeth Petry's essay in this book about her mother Ann Petry's novel of black Connecticut, *The Narrows*, set in the 1940s. The title of the essay, a quote from one of the novel's characters, is "Just Like Georgia Except for the Climate." It brings us from William Lloyd Garrison right into the twentieth century. Readers should set aside any assumption that white Connecticans in any era were *predominantly* (there are notable exceptions) progressive in their thinking or tolerant of others different from themselves.

But this book does not dwell here. Our purpose is to show the evolution of life for African Americans in the state from a tenuous and dispersed existence to the development of vibrant communities with strong community institutions, from subsistence farming to skilled labor to business ownership and professional occupation. Throughout, African Americans in Connecticut utilized and participated in the political process. Even while denied the vote, they elected their own leaders, and petitioned the state for their rights—over and over, with persistence that would not be denied. Throughout, theirs was a culture rich with faith, music, art, and literature. It is our aim for this book to engender a better general understanding of the African American experience in Connecticut in all its complexity, to dispel long-held myths, and to bring to light the true nature of three centuries of lives lived in pursuit of justice, equality, and prosperity.

. . .

I wish to thank the editorial team of Dr. Katherine Harris, Dr. Stacey Close, Dr. Frank Mitchell, Olivia White of The Amistad Center for Art & Culture, Constance B. Green, and Mary M. Donohue and Cora Murray, both then of the State Historic Preservation Office of the Department of Economic and Community Development. The State Historic Preservation Office provided important grant support in Fall 2011 for the contextual essays by Dr. Harris and Dr. Close and access to research and resources of the Connecticut Freedom Trail. I cannot overstate the contributions of the editorial team. Their contributions shaped this book. I would also like to thank Dr. Frank Mitchell for his work as image editor. His extensive knowledge of the vast collection of The Amistad Center has enriched this book and enabled us to "put a face to a name" as often as possible.

We extend great thanks to our essayists whose participation made such an undertaking possible, to Jennifer Huget, whose editorial skills had a huge impact on the text, and Wesleyan University Press for taking on this project.

In addition to the State Historic Preservation Office, Department of Economic and Community Development, we thank the John and Kelly Hartman Fund for additional grant support.

It has been my immense honor to shepherd this book forward as part of the celebration of *Connecticut Explored*'s 10th anniversary and in honor of The Amistad Center's 25th anniversary.

August 2012                                                Elizabeth J. Normen,
                                              publisher of *Connecticut Explored*


. . .


We cannot change the history of Africans in America. Oh, that we could! But we can tell the story, start to set the record straight, and salute the people who individually and collectively made that history, allowed their stories to be our stories, and left Connecticut a better place.

The Amistad Center for Art & Culture and *Connecticut Explored*, with joy, pleasure, and pride, have partnered on this book to celebrate our respective anniversaries and the African American experience in Connecticut. I can think of no better way to mark our organizations' milestones.

This book is the result of extraordinary scholarship by Dr. Katherine Harris, Dr. Stacey Close, Dr. Frank Mitchell, and other contributors. It is the product of Elizabeth Normen's passion and the editorial team's dedication. I am grateful to them and to those whose stories are told in words and images on these pages to engage, enlighten, and encourage us all.


Olivia White, Executive Director,
The Amistad Center for Art & Culture, Inc.


Notes

1. Diane Cameron, "Circumstances of Their Lives: Enslaved and Free Women of Color in Wethersfield, Connecticut, 1648–1832," *Connecticut History* (Fall 2005): 249.

2. Anne Farrow, Joel Lang, Jenifer Frank, *Complicity: How the North Promoted, Prolonged, and Profited from Slavery* (New York: Ballantine Books, 2005), 49–51, 42, 193–205. See also Christopher Pagliuco, "Ivoryton," *Connecticut Explored* (Fall 2008).

3. *Complicity*, xviii.

4. Matthew Warshauer, *Connecticut in the American Civil War: Slavery, Sacrifice, & Survival* (Middletown: Wesleyan University Press, 2011), 2.

# PART I

## Settlement
## to
## 1789

# 1 Freedom and Slavery

The coexistence of freedom and slavery shaped the lives of people of African descent from their first arrival in the Connecticut colony. The seventeenth century is accepted as the period marking the entrance of the first Africans to the British colonies. For example, colonial Virginians date with reasonable certainty the time of Africans' arrival in British America in 1619. Historians Dr. John Hope Franklin, Dr. Alfred Moss, and Lerone Bennett used that documentation in preparing their African American histories. Franklin and Moss observed, "the twenty Africans who were put ashore at Jamestown in 1619 by the captain of a Dutch frigate were not slaves in a legal sense."[1]

Franklin, Moss, and Bennett's accounts offer a precise date of arrival and it underscores the fact that the African American experience in the thirteen, mainland British colonies did not begin with chattel slavery. Although New England had strong commercial interests tied to the transatlantic trade in Africans throughout the British Empire, dating the arrival of the first Africans in Connecticut and determining their exact status is not as straightforward as is the case with Virginia.

Scholarly research for this study has uncovered several dates for the initial presence of Connecticut's African residents and their status. Researchers for the Hartford History Project indicate that the first "Hartford Black" of whom they are aware was Louis Berbice from Dutch Guiana. In 1638 his master, the Commissary Gysbert Opdyck, brought him to the Dutch fort in a neighborhood that was to be known as Dutch Point. The record does not clarify whether Berbice was considered an indentured servant or enslaved, since the term "master" was also applied to the individual to whom the indentured servant was in service. However, "[f]or some reason, Louis was killed the following year by Opdyck."[2] In association with this date of the ill-fated arrival of the first African in Hartford, Franklin and Moss's research records that in 1638 a ship from Salem, Massachusetts, unloaded some Africans in Boston. The number was

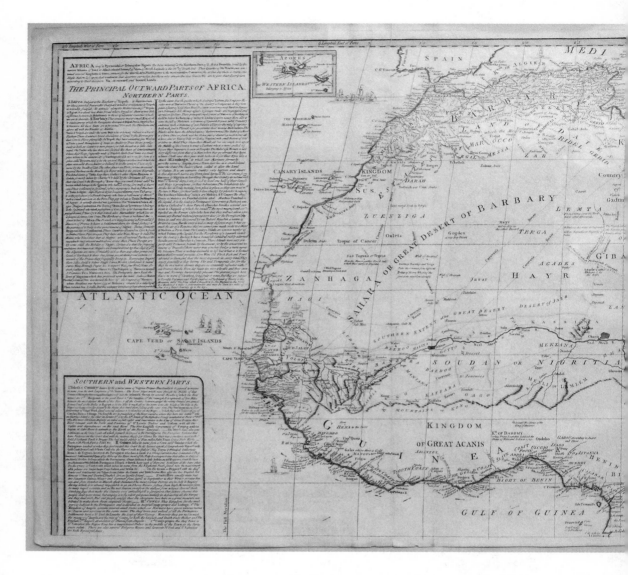

not specified, but the following year there were Africans in Hartford. Before the decade ended colonists were using Africans to build houses and forts in Connecticut.[3]

Elaborating on this observation, historian Douglas Harper's Web site about "Slavery in Connecticut" notes, "slaves were mentioned in Hartford from 1639 and in New Haven from 1644."[4] Yet in their voluminous resource book, James M. Rose and Alice Eichholz identify 1679 as the date of the arrival of the first Africans in the Connecticut Colony.[5]

Whether the first Africans, the ancestors of today's Connecticut African American communities, arrived in Connecticut during the

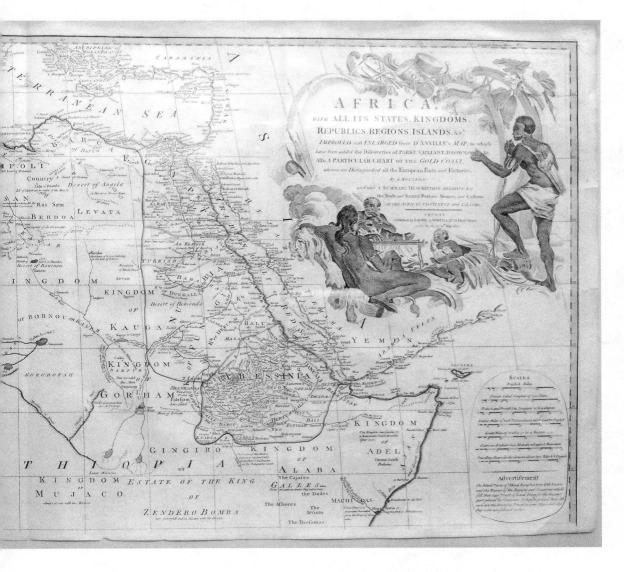

1630s, 1640s, or 1670s, there is no dispute that captivity dominated the African experience. Their legal definition as chattel, a designation by which a human being is considered property owned by another, and chattel slavery evolved in Connecticut over decades. From the early to mid-seventeenth century until the Connecticut state legislature abolished slavery in 1848, slavery and freedom—two contradictory conditions—formed the contours of the African American experience in the Connecticut colony and the state of Connecticut after 1788 and beyond.

It is vital to note that Africans were human beings not slaves or property when captured and taken from their families, towns, and

FIGURE I-I S. Boulton, "Africa with All Its States, Kingdoms, Republics, Regions, Islands, &c., 1787," Laurie & Whittle, London, 1800. *The Amistad Center for Art & Culture, Inc., 2000.2.1-5*

villages. They were from a multiethnic background that included the Hausa, Igbo, and Yoruba ethnic groups from what is modern Nigeria; the Fante and Ewe ethnic groups from what is now Ghana; the Wolof ethnic group from Senegambia (now Senegal and Gambia); the Mende ethnic group from Sierra Leone; and the Mandinka ethnic group who lived across much of West Africa. Plucked from their homelands, they endured the turbulent voyage of the Middle Passage from Africa to the Americas and the Connecticut colony.

Despite their ultimate condition of servitude, the status of Africans in Connecticut remained uncertain and ill defined. In parts of Litchfield County, some Africans were designated as indentured servants (with contracts binding them to work for a certain period in exchange for some form of compensation) and others were listed as "servants." The term could refer to an "indentured servant" or a euphemism for "slave." Only gradually did chattel slavery—in which a person is required to work without compensation—emerge in the New England colonies as a legitimate institution.[6]

For the Africans themselves, though, it was abundantly clear that others were enriching themselves and benefiting from their labor and that they did not live as free persons. British colonists legalized slavery in Connecticut when the colony was incorporated into the Articles of the New England Confederation in 1643. Deeply aware of the distinction between the free and unfree, in 1658 some Africans (and some Native Americans) in Hartford "decided to make a bid for freedom by destroying several houses of their masters."[7] But the revolt for freedom backfired.

Restrictions soon followed that barred Africans from many ordinary activities. In Connecticut in 1660, for instance, Africans were prohibited from serving in the military, although wartime necessity altered this prohibition. Discrimination against free black persons was more severe in Connecticut than in other New England colonies. In 1690, the colony forbade blacks and Indians to be on the streets after 9 p.m. Laws also forbade black "servants" to wander beyond the limits of the towns or places where they belonged without a ticket or pass from their masters or other authorities. A 1708 law cited frequent fights between the enslaved and white colonists and imposed a minimum penalty of thirty lashes on any black who disturbed the peace or who attempted to strike a white person. Speech, too, was subject to control. Under a 1730 law, any black, Indian, or mulatto slave "who uttered or published, about any white person, words which would be actionable if uttered by a free white was, upon conviction before any one assistant or justice of the peace, to be whipped with forty lashes."[8]

As early as 1717, citizens of New London in a town meeting voted their objection to having free blacks live in the town or own land anywhere in the colony. Although the General Assembly rejected the petition, that year the state legislature passed a law in accordance with this sentiment, prohibiting free blacks or mulattoes from residing in any town in the colony. It also forbade them to buy land or go into business without the consent of the town. The provisions were retroactive, so that if any black person had managed to buy land, the deed was rendered void, and a black resident of a town, however long he had been there, was now subject to prosecution at the discretion of the selectmen.[9] African American Robert Jacklin sold his property (in 1719) in New London in response to the community's hostility.[10]

Like the black codes that restricted movement, speech, and political rights of African Americans in the South and Midwest in the nineteenth century, enforcement of the prohibition against land ownership was uneven. The real value of the law seemed to be in harassment, discouragement of further settlement, and its service as a constant reminder to free blacks in Connecticut that their existence was precarious and dependent on white tolerance wrote historian Douglas Harper.[11]

During the first half of the eighteenth century New England traders thrived. New London, Connecticut, one of the colonies' major port cities, bustled with ships laden with rum, fish, African captives, sugar, and molasses.[12] By that time, New England slavery needed little legal recognition to continue growing and developing. Regularly, colonial records noted not the arrival of Africans but "the importation of slaves."[13] They were movable property, they occupied a heritable status, and they were liable to service for life. They had no contracts and they were salable chattels.[14] No other group of people from the colonial period through much of nineteenth century was subjected to such conditions.

The largest increase in the number of enslaved people took place between 1749 and 1774. By the end of that period, New London County had become the greatest slaveholding section of New England, with almost twice as many enslaved Africans as the county in Massachusetts that had that state's largest number of slaves. New London was both an industrial center and the site of large slave-worked farms; with 2,036 enslaved Africans, it accounted for almost one-third of all the blacks in Connecticut. The town of New

London itself, with 522 blacks and a white population of 5,366, led the state in number of enslaved Africans and percentage of black inhabitants.[15]

Enslaved Africans toiled primarily on small farms rather than large plantations and produced grains, onions, and other crops that were destined for other parts of the British Empire. They worked in the ports. Children joined adults in hard labor in all economic activities in Connecticut. Abuse of the African custom of axial loading—carrying loads on the head—led to fractured bones and caused enthesopathies, acute tears of muscles, tendons, and ligaments from the bones due to excessive lifting of heavy loads.[16]

Evidence indicates that merchants, ministers, politicians, military officials, physicians, lawyers, and a few small farmers owned enslaved people. Colonists also rented out their enslaved people. Sometimes the enslaved individuals received a portion of the money that they earned. More often the owners kept the money the enslaved persons earned.

Enslaved women experienced a special kind of victimization through sexual exploitation, rape, unwanted childbirth, painful separation from spouses, and the sale of infant children. Several cases of enslaved women in Wethersfield confirm the existence of such hardships. The cases include Reverend Gershom Bulkley's "Negro Maid Hannah," Elizabeth Williams's "faithful Marea," Ginny, who was beaten to death in the household of her owner, and Kate, "the enslaved woman of Captain Thomas Belding of Wethersfield," who was convicted of and executed for the death of her infant son born in April 1743.[17]

In the case of Elenor Smith Gomer, the trauma of enslavement was compounded by insecure freedom, lack of economic resources, and widowhood. In 1766 Elenor Smith, a free woman in her twenties, exchanged vows with Quash Gomer, an enslaved man originally from Angola. They struggled to survive. Their children were apprenticed at times to repay debts. Quash's death in 1799 further threatened Elenor's financial security. Her adult children in Hartford or Middletown took turns taking her in, but she died poverty stricken and ill on January 17, 1831.[18]

Despite such oppressive conditions, enslaved Africans in colonial Connecticut found ways to express their humanity. A key example of this was the election of Black Governors, the earliest evidence of which event exists in New London on the 1749 headstone of Floria, the wife of Hercules, "Governor of the Negroes," as the gravemarker identifies her. Still, slavery persisted in Connecticut for more than a century after that New London election—even as questions about the abolition of slavery intensified in Connecticut. The key issues surrounding the debate over abolition were whether slave owners should be compensated for the loss of their human property and whether the public safety would be imperiled by immediate emancipation of enslaved persons.

During the years leading up to the Revolutionary War, Connecticut considered a series of emancipation acts. The colonial legislature rejected emancipation bills in 1777, 1779, and 1780 and legislators rejected outright abolition of slavery in 1795. In 1774, Connecticut lawmakers passed the Nonimportation Act, a law to halt the importation of captive "slaves" to sell, dispose of, or leave in Connecticut. The ambiguous language did not prevent slavery, and the justification for the legislation was not based on humanitarian or moral grounds. Legislators emphasized the economic and social consequences by explaining "whereas the increase of slaves in this Colony is injurious to the poor and inconvenient. . . ."[19]

As the Revolutionary War era dawned, Connecticut had the largest number of enslaved Africans—6,464—in New England. Historian Jackson Turner Main surveyed Connecticut estate inventories and found that in 1700, one in ten inventories included enslaved Africans. All the principal families of Norwich, Hartford, and New Haven owned one or two enslaved Africans. By 1774, half of all ministers, lawyers, and public officials owned enslaved individuals, and a third of all doctors in the state owned enslaved Africans.[20]

In 1779, Africans in Fairfield County presented the first documented petition for the absolute abolition of slavery in Connecticut to the state's General Assembly.[21] But slavery persisted, as did resistance to it. Some enslaved Africans, such as Venture Smith in East Haddam, negotiated with their owners for a price to purchase their own freedom and that of family and friends. Other enslaved Africans, including Boston Nichols in Hartford, were emancipated by their owners. Others followed more complicated routes to freedom. For instance, the lives of enslaved Africans Cuff, Phebe, and their son Peter straddled the towns of Farmington, where 112 enslaved individuals lived in 1756, and Middletown, where 198 enslaved Africans lived in 1774. Isaac Miller owned Phebe, Cuff, and their son Peter. Deeds in the Connecticut state archives record Joseph Coe's purchases of Cuff in 1744 and Phebe in 1754. Cuff's aspirations for his freedom are evident in a notation in the deed for Coe's purchase of Cuff in 1744 and Phebe in 1754: "Cuff desires to have the Sir Name of Freeman annexed to his Name."[22]

The Revolutionary War presented opportunities for enslaved Africans to seek freedom. Peter, for instance, purchased his freedom from Coe on March 30, 1778. He may have received the funds to do so as partial payment for his service as a soldier, having enlisted in December 1777 and re-enlisted in March 1778.[23] Some enslaved men were promised freedom if they served in the war; such was the case of Tobias Pero of Derby. Others may have run away from their owners during the chaotic conditions of the war.

In the aftermath of the War of Independence, in 1784, advocates for abolition were able to garner support for gradual emancipation. Gradual emancipation did not confer freedom on any of the enslaved, but promised freedom to the children of the enslaved. The provisions of the gradual emancipation act detailed that black and "mulatto" children born after March 1 would become free at age 25. Legislators passed the bill without opposition. A supplementary Act in 1797 lowered the age to 21, thereby making the statute consistent with existing guidelines for apprenticeship, although enslaved African American apprentices did not receive money, clothes, or professional standing once their enslavement ended as other apprentices did.[24]

The number of enslaved persons in Connecticut declined due in part to gradual emancipation, which conferred freedom on the children of the enslaved. Connecticut ended the practice of converting free African Americans to enslaved. In the 1787 case *Wilson v. Hinkley*, the superior court affirmed the principle that a child born of a free African American woman was free. The case centered around Timothy Caesar, who was born to a free African American mother. He had been captured and enslaved as a "slave or servant" of Joseph Hovey in Mansfield, Connecticut.[25]

The essays in this section bring to light the lives of the ancestors of contemporary African Americans in Connecticut history from settlement to 1789, the year that the needed number of states ratified the United States Constitution. Despite accounts that purport to record the lives of African captives and enslaved African Americans, it is essential that readers recognize that these accounts are often reported in the words of the captors, slave owners, transcribers, or, in the case of Venture Smith, publishers. These accounts leave many unanswered questions. Archaeological investigations and historical research conducted by Dr. Warren Perry of Central Connecticut State University have sought to answer some of the questions regarding African descendant communities in colonial Connecticut. For instance, the discovery of Menkese Bundles that African Americans used to bridge the connection between the sacred and the material worlds unveiled the continuing presence of such African traditions during the oppressive period of enslavement, a phenomenon that is not well recognized because many writers of the time did not understand it.[26]

## Notes

1. John Hope Franklin and Alfred A. Moss Jr., *From Slavery to Freedom: A History of African Americans*, 7th edition (New York: McGraw Hill, 1994, 1947), 56. Lerone Bennett, *The Shaping of Black America* (Chicago: Johnson Publishing Company, 1975) 9, 13–16, 18–19.

2. Hartford Black History Project, Hartford, Connecticut. No published paper text accompanies the online version, Hartford Black History Project, A Struggle From The Start Exhibit, www.hartford-hwp.com/HBHP/exhibit/index/html.

3. Franklin and Moss, *From Slavery To Freedom*, 65–66.

4. Douglas Harper, "Slavery in Connecticut," slavenorth.com/author.htm.

5. James M. Rose, Ph.D., and Alice Eichholz, Ph.D., C. G., *Black Genesis: A Resource Book for African-American Genealogy* (Baltimore, Maryland: Gale Research Co. and Genealogical Publishing Co. Inc., 1978, 2003, 2005), 85.

6. See Litchfield Historical Society's list of Africans. Franklin and Moss, *From Slavery To Freedom*, 66.

7. Although Connecticut colonists enslaved Native Americans, the status of the Native Americans involved in the 1658 revolt is not clear. During the colonial era, after their defeat in war, British colonists imprisoned and enslaved Native Americans. Some were sent to the Caribbean, but they were not categorized as legal property, chattel, or declared enslaved for life. See Franklin and Moss, *From Slavery To Freedom*, 66. On the New England Confederation in 1643, see Edgar J. McManus, *Black Bondage in the North* (Syracuse: Syracuse University Press, 1973), 169–70.

8. Charles Hoadly, *The Public Records of The Colony of Connecticut From May, 1717, to October, 1725* (Hartford, CT: Case, Lockwood & Brainard, 1872) 390–91. Lorenzo Johnston Greene, *The Negro in Colonial New England, 1620–1776* (New York: Columbia University Press, 1942), 138.

9. The volume containing this act is missing from the series *The Public Records of the Colony of Connecticut* in the Connecticut State Library. See reference to a similar statute in Connecticut Archives, Miscellaneous Papers 1635–1789, Index (Hartford, CT: Connecticut State Library, 1923), 214.

10. Dominic DeBrincat, "Discolored Justice: Blacks in New London County Courts, 1710–1750," *Connecticut History*, vol. 44, no. 2 (Fall 2005): 189–90. See also Douglas Harper, "Slavery in Connecticut," slavenorth.com/connecticut.htm.

11. Douglas Harper, "Slavery in Connecticut," slavenorth.com/connecticut.htm.

12. Franklin and Moss, *From Slavery to Freedom*, 65–66.

13. Ibid., 58.

14. Michael L. Conniff and Thomas J. C. Davis, *Africans in the Americas: A History of the Black Diaspora* (New York: St. Martin's Press, 1994), 127.

15. Greene, 74–75.

16. Numerous examples of such injuries have been documented in the skeletal remains of Mr. Fortune. Dr. Warren Perry dignifies the life of Mr. Fortune by addressing him formally in his work. Dr Perry's archaeological and anatomical study identified multiple enthesopathies that suggest that Mr. Fortune was worked to death when enslaved by the Porter family in Waterbury, Connecticut.

17. Diane Cameron, "Circumstances of Their Lives: Enslaved and Free Women of Color in Wethersfield, Connecticut, 1648–1832," *Connecticut History* (Fall 2005): 250–51.

18. Ibid., 249–52.

19. David Menschel, "Abolition without Deliverance: The Law of Connecticut Slavery 1783–1848, *The Yale Law Journal*, 3 (September 24, 2001): 183, 189, 193.

20. Jackson Turner Main, *Society and Economy in Colonial Connecticut* (Princeton: Princeton University Press, 1983), 177, see table 5.1.

21. The 1779 Emancipation Petition of Prime and Prince from Fairfield County submitted to the General Assembly of the State of Connecticut, see Elizabeth Hubbell Schenck, *The History of Fairfield, Fairfield County Connecticut* (New York: J.J. Little and Company, 1905), ii, 325.

22. Anne J. Arcari, "Freeman in Name Only: The African American in Colonial Farmington, Connecticut" (Master of Arts thesis, Trinity College, Hartford, Connecticut, 1998), 35, 36. Arcari appended copies of original deeds, emancipation papers and enlistment papers. A copy of the thesis is in the library of the Connecticut Historical Society. Also see David O. White, *Connecticut's Black Soldiers 1775–1783* (Chester, CT: Pequot Press, 1973), 58. Peter served 1777–1783, and Cuff 1777–1782. Greene, *The Negro in New England*, 92–93.

23. Arcari, "Freeman in Name Only," 35, 36.

24. On the Gradual Abolition Act of 1784, see Menschel, "Abolition without Deliverance," 215; and The Gradual Abolition Act of 1784.

25. Menschel, 183.

26. On African cultural and herbal remedies, gris-gris, and Menkese (Minkisi) Bundles, see Franklin and Higginbotham, *From Slavery To Freedom*, 74, 75, 76, 81.

# 2 Venture Smith, from Slavery to Freedom

Out of almost twelve million African captives who embarked on the Middle Passage to the Americas, only about a dozen left behind first-hand accounts of their experiences. One of these was Venture Smith, whose *A Narrative of the Life and Adventures of Venture, a Native of Africa: But Resident above Sixty Years in the United States of America. Related by Himself* was published in New London, Connecticut in 1798.[1]

Smith's brief, dramatic account is a powerful reminder of colonial Connecticut's diversity, shaped by networks of migration and trade that extended not just to England but also to the West Indies and West Africa. His story is a reminder that alongside the war over political principles and national autonomy waged by Revolutionary New Englanders there was another, bitterly fought struggle over slavery, freedom, and equality.

## *A Child Named Broteer*

Around 1730, in a place called Dukandarra in the savannah region of West Africa, a family named its new child Broteer. According to the narrative, his father, a local leader, exercised authority with honor and generosity. His mother was one of several wives. In time, young Broteer worked tending large herds of sheep. Their world was turned upside down when a marauding army threatened, betrayed, and ultimately overwhelmed their people. Broteer looked on as the army tortured and killed his father for refusing to disclose the location of his treasure. Broteer was taken captive and marched to the coastal slave-trading center Anomabo (in present-day Ghana) for sale.

As Broteer later recalled, an officer on a Rhode Island slaver commanded by a "Captain Collingwood" purchased him for "four gallons of rum and piece of calico cloth." The vessel was probably the *Charming Susannah*, which departed Newport in late 1738 and returned in September 1739. Renamed Venture by his captors, Broteer survived the smallpox epidemic that ravaged the ship during the Middle Passage, and while most of the surviving captives were sold in Barbados, he was brought to New England.[2] In Newport, where the slave traders landed Venture, and in the fertile New York and Connecticut farmland along the eastern end of Long Island Sound where he spent the next three decades, as many as one in five people were of African origin.

### A Man Called Venture

Smith's account of slavery emphasized two things: the system's violence and injustice and the bargaining power he gained through his extraordinary physical strength and self-discipline. During the 1740s and early 1750s, George Mumford owned Venture. Mumford rented Fisher's Island from members of the Winthrop family. Venture was one of more than a dozen enslaved people and indentured servants who worked the 3,000-acre property as a large, commercial farm, raising mostly sheep and dairy cows.

In his mid-twenties, Venture married a fellow slave named Meg. Soon thereafter, he made an unsuccessful runaway attempt. A newspaper advertisement placed by his owner in April 1754 confirms this account and offers the only contemporary physical description of Venture: "he is a very tall Fellow, 6 feet 2 Inches high, thick square Shoulders, Large bon'd, mark'd in the Face, or scar'd with a Knife in his own Country."

Shortly thereafter, Mumford sold Venture to a farmer named Thomas Stanton II in Stonington, Connecticut. Venture convinced his new master to purchase his wife Meg, but Venture's relationships with the Stantons were marked by betrayal and violence.

At one point around 1760, Venture intervened in a conflict between his wife and Mrs. Stanton. His master retaliated by clubbing him brutally and stealing the money he and Meg had been saving up to purchase their freedom. Venture complained to a local justice of the peace to no avail. Ultimately, Venture was sold to Oliver Smith, a small-scale Stonington merchant, and they reached a deal whereby Venture earned the money to purchase his freedom through various kinds of work, including cutting vast amounts of cordwood. It was in honor of the one master who did not betray or cheat him that Venture adopted the surname "Smith."

## Freedom Brings Success and Struggle

As a newly free man, Venture Smith set out earning money and investing it so that he could reunite with and support his family. Thomas Stanton still owned Meg and their two sons, and a member of the Mumford family owned their eldest child, Hannah.

Smith worked as a sailor on a whaling expedition, fished, and cut cordwood in various places around Long Island Sound. He also invested in land. In 1770, he bought a twenty-six-acre parcel that bordered the farm of his former master Thomas Stanton. (That area is now part of the Barn Island Wildlife Preserve.)

In 1775, he used proceeds from the sale of this land to purchase a small piece of land on Haddam Neck, Connecticut, where he cut lumber. Within a few years, his land in Haddam Neck grew to more than 100 acres. There, he reunited his family and pursued a variety of entrepreneurial activities—farming, lumbering, fishing, and working as a small-scale trader along the Connecticut River and the east end of Long Island Sound.

Recent archaeological excavations of his homestead, now owned by the Connecticut Yankee Utility Company, uncovered the remains of a house and barn as well as ancillary storage buildings, a blacksmith shop, and a dry dock for repairing boats. But Smith's account makes it clear that as proud as he was of his successes, he was also conscious of the obstacles that had been placed in his path. Long after he became free, unscrupulous and sometimes openly racist men continued to cheat him in business transactions. And the courts could not be relied upon to give him equal justice.

## The Story He Told

By the time Smith prepared his life story for publication in 1798, he was showing the signs of his old age: His strong, tall body was bowed, and he was going blind. Since he was not literate, he must have had help getting his story written down. That help may have come from Elisha Niles, a local schoolteacher, but no contemporary evidence has surfaced to support this attribution. The narrative was published by a very politically active newspaper publisher. Nonetheless, there is good reason to believe that the *Narrative* as published in 1798 reflects Smith's own distinctive voice. In many cases, specific details he mentions can be corroborated with contemporary evidence. But more importantly, the tone of his narrative and his emphases are distinctive and unusual and therefore unlikely to reflect the influence of others. Smith emphasized continuities between life in West Africa and in North America; he emphasized the violence of slavery in New England, and he described his struggle for freedom and equality as a lop-sided series of struggles rather than as a simple consequence of the spirit of freedom and revolution that swept the new nation.

Venture Smith died in 1805. He was buried in the graveyard of the First Congregational Church in East Haddam. Alongside him are buried his wife Meg, who died several years later, and other members of their family. Smith's gravestone, carved by John Isham, a well-known carver in the region, can be seen there to this day. It describes him as "Venture Smith, African. Tho the son of a King he was kidnapped and sold as a slave but by his industry he acquired Money to Purchase his Freedom." Since then, he has been widely remembered in the region for his industry, integrity, and successes.[3]

## Notes

This essay was originally prepared for connecticuthistory.org.

1. Smith, Venture. *A Narrative of the Life and Adventures of Venture, a Native of Africa: But Resident above Sixty Years in the United States of America* (New London, CT: Charles Holt, 1798). For a reliable edition of Venture Smith's *Narrative* and the latest scholarship about him, see James Brewer Stewart, ed., *Venture Smith and the Business of Slavery and Freedom* (University of Massachusetts Press, 2010). Venture Smith's *Narrative* was first published 1798, and several editions have been published since his death, some with significant omissions or additions. The 1835 edition omits a sharply worded passage at the end about his children. The 1896 edition, published by H. M. Selden of Haddam, Connecticut, includes a series of "reminiscences" that emphasize Smith's physical prowess rather than his mental fortitude and entrepreneurial savvy. The most authoritative twentieth-century edition of the *Narrative* is in Dorothy Porter, ed., *Early Negro Writing, 1760–1837* (1971). A good online edition is available through the University of North Carolina's Web site at http://docsouth.unc.edu/neh/venture2/venture2.html.

2. For details about Captain James Collingwood, the *Charming Susannah*, and Anomabo, see the Trans-Atlantic Slave Trade Database available at www.slavevoyages.org.

3. James Brewer Stewart, *Venture Smith and the Business of Slavery and Freedom* (Amherst, MA: University of Massachusetts Press, 2010).

*Peter Hinks*

# 3 Caesar and Lois Peters

Caesar and Lois Peters were enslaved African Americans who lived in Hebron, Connecticut, in the late eighteenth century, and though they and their children became free, the story of how they gained their freedom reveals much about transformations in popular thinking about race, slavery, and liberty during the era of the American Revolution.

Caesar apparently arrived in Hebron when he was eight or nine years old in about 1758. He was at that time the slave of Mary Peters, who was the mother of the Reverend Samuel Peters, the local missionary from the Anglican Church. About ten years later, Mary Peters transferred ownership of Caesar to her son Samuel. In September 1774, Rev. Peters fled town because both his Anglicanism (in Congregational Connecticut) and his loyalty to the British crown had alienated him from the community and jeopardized his security. He eventually journeyed to London.

While townspeople had known Caesar for many years—one as far back as 1758—and all applauded the virtue and industry he had displayed before Samuel Peters's flight, none had questioned his enslavement in the 1760s and the 1770s. In 1774, the citizens of Hebron, like most white colonial New Englanders, existed in a context of near axiomatic racial understandings: They believed that Africans were absolutely inferior to Europeans and their presence and labor would not be viable in the colonies without firm white regulation and guidance.

One correspondent writing anonymously in a Connecticut newspaper that year articulated these assumptions bluntly: "I beg . . . to silence those writers who insist upon the Africans belonging to the same species of men with the white people, and who will not allow that God formed them in common with horses, oxen, dogs, etc. for white people alone, to be used by them either for pleasure or to labour with their other beasts in the culture of tobacco, indigo, rice and sugar."

"Those writers" to whom the correspondent refers were the anti-slavery writers whose ideas were just beginning to challenge precisely the racial model he describes. Although some enslaved people in Connecticut did have complex, interpersonal relationships with their owners that softened the stark dichotomy of subordinate and master, the essential belief that Africans were placed in the world by God to be subject to white authority, and that slavery was thus the appropriate natural condition for them—pervaded the thinking of whites in late colonial America, north and south. The numbers reinforced these assumptions: In 1770, there were about 50,000 slaves in the North, with a few hundred free blacks scattered throughout.

The Revolution, however, would begin to undermine these assumptions and alter the numbers at their root. Assertions of the centrality of individual liberty and freedom to human dignity and meaning by philosophers John Locke, the Baron de Montesquieu, and Jean-Jacques Rousseau loomed large in the Revolutionary era. At the same time, the religious anti-slavery of Anthony Benezet, Jonathan Edwards, Jr., and Samuel Hopkins argued for the essential unity and fellowship of all humans under God and began to meld with the egalitarian and democratic currents of the Revolution.

Others began to ridicule the notion that the physical differences between whites and Africans were signs of Africans' moral inferiority. These ideological transformations were enormously important in helping to undermine prevailing racial assumptions. But at the more ordinary, every day level, another development was unfolding that would be every bit as important in eroding racial preconceptions as were the ideological trends: Blacks were seeking freedom, were becoming free, and were living valuable, meritorious lives wholly outside of white supervision. The tumult and social dislocations of the Revolution provided an unprecedented opportunity for people of African descent to highlight their dedication to freedom, to demonstrate that they were not the degraded, unruly chattel described routinely in colonial stereotypes, and that they were capable of using their freedom responsibly and productively.

Caesar and Lois provide a powerful example of this emerging reality and its impact on whites. From legal depositions taken in 1787, we know much about Caesar's life in Hebron after the flight of Rev. Peters and the outbreak of the Revolutionary War. As the war began, Caesar had married Lois (about whose earlier life little is known). In the months after Peters fled, Caesar, Lois, and their growing family continued to live and work on Peters's large estate. Yet with war in full swing by 1776, the newly appointed state's attorney of Connecti-

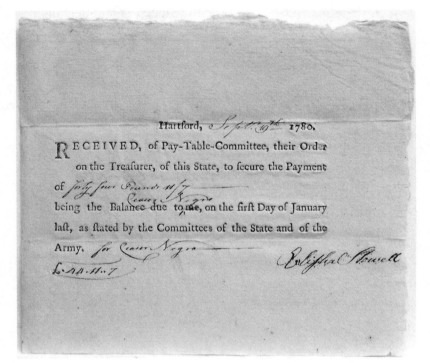

FIGURE 3-1 Some of Connecticut's enslaved men earned their freedom through service for the Patriot cause, as evidenced by this pay voucher for a man named Cesar, 1780. With a loyalist owner, Caesar Peters took a different path to freedom. *The Amistad Center for Art & Culture, Inc., Simpson Collection, 1987.1.2151*

cut confiscated Peters's property as abandoned and converted it to public property to be used for the support of the state.

Caesar and Lois were summarily turned out from Peters's land, and the farm was rented to white tenants, even though Caesar's working of the farm had been commendable. It is worth noting that no members of white Hebron intervened to protect Caesar and secure his tenancy. Caesar and Lois were abandoned to fend for themselves at a time of enormous insecurity; the captive couple's resourcefulness during this period of duress clearly impressed several of the deponents deeply.

The family squatted on marginal lands immediately adjacent to the Peters estate. One townsman marveled that they had "supported themselves comfortably for about five or six years, without any assistance from said Master, or his estate, except the privilege of firewood, although at that time sd. Caesar had a number of small children unable to do any business towards their own support." Another remarked that, "by good economy and close application to business [they] did procure a very comfortable living [for] some years." None of these deponents indicated that they or any other Hebronites had sought to help Caesar and Lois in any way during these years.

With the war's end, none of the townspeople mounted any op-position to having Caesar, Lois, and their several children re-occupy the Peters estate. In fact, it appears they were very glad to have Caesar and Lois replace the former tenants. One deponent illuminated the situation for the justices: "After the national peace, sd. Caesar returned to one of his sd. masters houses and cultivated the farm which was much damaged by tenants." He continued: "By industry and frugality [he] supported his family, and at the same time was at no small cost in repairing the fences and buildings, and he has given his family good schooling, and has been at considerable expense by sickness, AND I understand that he has paid all the taxes that have been called for; he lived in a comfortable, thriving situation."

Those sentiments prevailed, the deponents indicated, until September 1787, when the citizens of Hebron witnessed a horrible sight. Six heavily armed men approached the Peters house. Two of them were agents appointed by Peters, who by 1787 had long lived in London; the other four were men from South Carolina who had come to take possession of Peters's slaves. While Peters had indicated in correspondence some wish to free the slaves, the agents John & Nathaniel Mann, whom Peters had empowered to act on his behalf, determined to sell them to cover some pressing debts.

After dismounting their horses and wagon, the men forcibly entered the house, violently seized Caesar, Lois, and their children, dragged them to the wagon, and threw them in. They quickly slapped heavy and chafing irons on Caesar. As one white eyewitness of the event recounted, "Their cries and shrieks were shocking to human nature." When the white neighbors of Caesar approached the men and asked them with what justification they seized this family, the agents' power of attorney and the deed of sale were thrust in their faces. Far more daunting was the young Carolinian who "held a drawn sword in his hand and by his words and gestures fully indicated that he would make use of it upon such as made the least attempt to relieve the sufferers." The six men, weapons brandished, galloped away with their captives.

The townspeople of Hebron were outraged. One recalled that, "the whole transaction exhibited such a scene of cruelty as was unparallel to anything I had ever seen." Another later asserted in a deposition that "this scene left such an impression on his mind as is not worn out to this day."

A large posse of men convened and launched an action that was unprecedented for eighteenth-century Connecticut. A deponent testified: "A number of persons moved with compassion under the colour of lawful authority pursued and overtook them 20 miles from this place and within one mile of a vessel bound to South Carolina . . . [the pursuers] retook them and brought them back to the place from where they were taken." Yet Caesar and Lois were not out of danger. Despite their rescue, "the agents of Mr. Peters manifest a determination to sell and disperse the family which [continues] to render their condition very miserable and unhappy." This painful uncertainty would continue for them for two more years, but throughout that time the townspeople protected and fought for the family.

Many Hebron residents were willingly deposed as they pursued various legal recourses to secure the freedom of Caesar and his family once and for all. By January 1789, their petitions and depositions reached the General Assembly. In that same month, after much struggling and anxiety, Caesar, Lois, and all of their progeny were designated by the state forever free.

While information is scant about their remaining years, we do know that Lois died in Tolland, Connecticut on December 18, 1793. Caesar later remarried a woman named Sim. They left Hebron for a few years but returned by 1803. Caesar remained there with his family until his death on July 4, 1814.


Note

This essay was originally prepared for connecticuthistory.org.

*Ann Y. Smith*

# 4 Fortune's Story

Fortune was an African American enslaved in the household of Dr. Preserved Porter in Waterbury, Connecticut in the eighteenth century. He died in 1798, but his remains were not buried. Instead, his skeleton has been studied for two centuries, offering insights into medicine, science, and history. Currently in the custody of the Mattatuck Museum in Waterbury, the skeleton continues to provoke debate about our past and his future.

Fortune and his wife Dinah lived with their three children and Fortune's older son Africa in a small home owned by Fortune on Dr. Porter's property. He probably worked on Dr. Porter's seventy-five-acre farm, running the farm operations while Porter concentrated on his medical practice and real estate speculation.

Porter was a physician who specialized in the treatment of bones, as did three generations of Porter physicians before him. In the 1780s, when Fortune and his family were part of the Porter household, Dr. Porter was in his fifties, raising young children of his own. One of Porter's younger children, his son Jesse who was born in 1777, studied medicine with his father when he came of age late in the eighteenth century, and continued in the family business, serving as a physician in Waterbury until his death in 1860.

In the eighteenth century, colonial medicine was evolving from the traditional practices of midwives, folk healers, and herbalists to a science based on anatomical knowledge derived from dissection and the direct observation of the human body. Trained by Scottish physicians immersed in the perspective of the Enlightenment, advocates of this new approach began offering anatomical lectures in Newport and Philadelphia by the middle of the eighteenth century. The first American medical school was established in Philadelphia in 1764 to promote these new techniques.

Even rural physicians who did not have the resources to study in colonial cities or European colleges were eager to establish their connections with this more modern approach to medicine. They acquired books about anatomy and, when possible, anatomical specimens. To demonstrate his up-to-date credentials in 1783, for example, a Rhode Island doctor announced the opening of his practice by inviting the public to visit his office and see his wired skeleton, prepared from the body of an "executed Negro."[1]

Porter was a believer in this new scientific approach. He was a founding member of the Medical Society of New Haven County in 1784, a select association that testifies to his interest in professional medical practices and his status as a recognized practitioner.

Acquiring anatomical materials to support this new kind of study, however, was problematic. In the seventeenth and eighteenth centuries, English law in most colonies prohibited the digging up of bodies—a protection against witchcraft, with obvious implications for medical studies. At the same time, common law in colonial New England allowed the bodies of executed criminals to be made available for anatomical study. Some state legislatures specifically permitted judges to sentence those convicted of capital crimes and other offenses to be dissected as further punishment beyond death.[2]

Yet there continued to be a shortage of bodies available for medical study, and physicians and medical students sought cadavers wherever they could be found. These bodies typically belonged to those whose position in society placed them among the disenfranchised in life: Native American prisoners of war, people hanged for capital offenses, prostitutes, suicides, and enslaved people.

Connecticut lawmakers grappled with the demand for corpses for medical research and the competing public outrage over the use of bodies for this purpose. In 1810, the state prohibited grave robbing for medical dissection, but the practice continued. Riots broke out in New Haven in 1824 when it was learned that students at the medical school had taken the body of a recently deceased young woman from her grave in West Haven. The Governor's Foot Guard was called out to control the violence when her remains were found in the cellar of the medical school.[3] When the Connecticut legislature passed an act permitting the dissection of unclaimed bodies in 1833, public protest led to the repeal of the act in 1834.

At the time of Fortune's death in 1798, Porter would have been sixty-nine years old and probably retired from the active practice of medicine. However, his twenty-one-year-old son Jesse was just beginning his medical practice and would have benefited from the opportunity to study a skeleton. Fortune's skeleton was valuable, priced in the doctor's estate at $15, higher than the value of Fortune's surviving widow Dinah, who was valued at $10.[4]

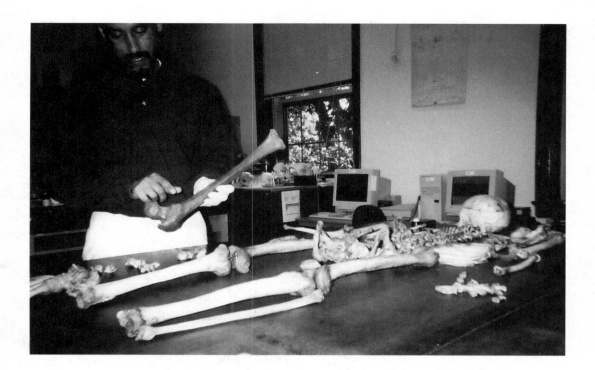

FIGURE 4-1 The skeleton of Fortune being examined at Howard University, c. 1997. *Private collection*

Nineteenth-century historians report that Porter prepared the skeleton for use in his School of Anatomy in Waterbury. While there is no evidence that such a school existed, the bones were indeed preserved and cleaned. Several were labeled in a fine eighteenth-century script. Subsequent generations of Porter family members recalled early anatomy lessons aided by study of the skeleton. One of Porter's descendants wrote to the director of the Mattatuck Museum that she had received her first medical instruction as a child, when her father taught her the names of the bones using Fortune's skeleton "just as the Porters were taught in the ages gone before."[5]

Given Fortune's status as a slave, Porter may have felt entitled to the use of his body in death as in life. Apparently, Porter was not dissuaded from using the skeleton by his relationship with Fortune or his ongoing relationship with Fortune's wife and children, who continued to live as members of the Porter household until the elder Porter's death in 1803. Nor is there evidence of any negative reaction from the community, who seem to have been aware of the slave skeleton's presence throughout the nineteenth century.

The skeleton remained in the possession of subsequent generations of Porter physicians until 1933, when Sally Porter Law McGlannan, a descendant of Preserved Porter and one of the earliest female graduates of Johns Hopkins Medical School, donated it to the Mattatuck Museum.

In the 1990s, the museum worked with a team of community advisors and scholars to understand Fortune's life and its broader implications. The museum's African American History Project Committee, led by Maxine Watts, guided these activities. Scholars included the late Gretchen Worden, former director of the Mutter Museum in Philadelphia, Susan Lederer, Yale University School of Medicine Section of the History of Medicine, and Toby Appel of the Yale School of Medicine historical archives. Anthropologists Dr. Warren Perry of Central Connecticut State University and Leslie Rankin Hill of the University of Oklahoma assisted in the analysis of the skeleton. Based on the findings of anthropologists, forensic artists, and historians, the museum's permanent exhibition about Fortune's story presents an image of the eighteenth-century world of African Americans, enslaved and free, in Waterbury. Connecticut Poet Laureate Marilyn Nelson was commissioned to write *Fortune's Bones: The Manumission Requiem* (Front Street, 2004). Dr. Ysaye Barnwell transformed her moving poem into a cantata that was performed in Waterbury and at the University of Maryland.

Fortune was laid to rest at Riverside Cemetery in Waterbury on September 12, 2013. Additional research and curriculum materials are available on the project's Web site, www.FortuneStory.org, created by Raechel Guest. Research is ongoing.

Notes

This essay originally appeared in the Spring 2007 issue of *Connecticut Explored*.

1. 1773 *Providence Gazette and Country Journal*, quoted in Michael Sappol, *A Traffic of Dead Bodies* (Princeton: Princeton University Press, 2002)

2. Ibid.

3. Rachel Engers, "Anatomy of an Insurrection," *Yale Medicine* (Spring, 2002).

4. Preserved Porter's estate inventory, 1804. Collection of the Connecticut State Library, State Archives.

5. McGlannan files, Mattatuck Museum Collection Records, Waterbury, Connecticut.

*David O. White*

# 5 Revolutionary War Service, Path to Freedom

The largest battle fought in Connecticut during the American Revolution, the Battle of Groton Heights, took place in 1781 at Fort Griswold in Groton, which overlooked the entrance to the Thames River. Seeking to free up this obstacle, on September 6 a contingent of British soldiers attacked the fort, which was defended by local militia. Many of the Connecticut men died during this battle, including two African Americans defenders Lambert Latham and Jordan Freeman. One of the few markers installed to note the experiences of Connecticut's African American Revolutionary War soldiers shows Freeman during the battle using a spear to kill the British officer Major William Montgomery. Both Latham and Freeman were enslaved at the time and likely did not have to accompany their owners to the fort, or at least did not have to participate in the battle. Yet, these two men represent several Connecticut blacks who fought for American freedom without any apparent promise that by doing so they would themselves be free afterward.

Connecticut's colonial records show that African Americans fought in most of the colony's wars prior to the American Revolution. Some of these black soldiers were free and some owned by whites. An example of one man who was free is Prince Goodin, who lived in Canterbury. In 1757 he joined a company of men formed by Israel Putnam to fight in the French and Indian War (1754–1763). Rev. James Cogswell, Canterbury's minister, urged Putnam's unit to fight against the French forces threatening the British colonies "for our Properties, our Liberties, our Religion, our Lives."[1]

During a battle at Lake George, Goodin was taken prisoner and sold as a slave in Montreal. Three years later he was freed by British led forces and returned to Connecticut. Goodin petitioned Connecticut for money to cover the three years he spent enslaved in Montreal, and the General Assembly agreed with his request. He was paid ten pounds.[2] Goodin married in 1761 and bought a house and land in Canterbury, but for some reason he soon sold this property and disappeared from the town's records.[3] His experiences note that before 1770 an African American man could serve in the armed forces of the colony, marry, and own property. His case, however, does not reflect the experiences of most blacks living in Connecticut at that time.

When the Revolutionary War began in 1775, blacks responded to the call for troops, and many of them were among the militiamen who converged on eastern Massachusetts. Lemuel Haynes of West Hartford, whose father was an African, was no longer living in Connecticut, but he did serve with Minutemen who fought in the first engagements at Lexington and Concord. Haynes later saw duty at Fort Ticonderoga. After the Revolution, he entered the ministry and served Congregational churches in Torrington, Connecticut, Vermont, and New York. Several of these churches were predominantly white.[4] Timon Negro of Wethersfield was one of the few black soldiers from Connecticut to march to Massachusetts on April 20, when the Lexington alarm was given. Cash Affrica of Litchfield served with Connecticut's First Regiment.[5]

Blacks were not re-enlisted in 1776 because the Continental Army and many state regiments closed their ranks to them. In the latter part of 1775, George Washington held several war councils which decided to exclude slaves from the army and "to reject negroes altogether." Connecticut's representatives to these councils agreed with the decisions.[6] When they were announced in November, free blacks voiced such strong disapproval that Congress, fearful that they might join the British, ordered in January that those free blacks who had served at Boston could re-enlist, but no others.[7] Cash Affrica did serve again from 1777 until the war ended in 1783.

Enslaved men could have been motivated to enlist in the army for several reasons, but for many the major reason was that such service often meant that they would be free at the end of the war. Free blacks were motivated to serve for much the same reasons as were the whites: adventure, conviction, or for the bounty.[8]

Some African American soldiers from Connecticut were already free when they joined their countrymen in opposing the British during the war, though it is not easy to determine which men fit this category. When a black soldier is identified in state records as "a free Negro," it sometimes means he was given his freedom to enlist with the army. One soldier who was free prior to the war was Ebenezer Hill. Hill was born enslaved in Stonington around the year 1740, but he had achieved his freedom before the start of the Revolution. Hill fought at Saratoga, New York in 1777 and saw the British army surrender there to the Americans.[9] Samuel Bush enlisted from the town of Stamford and served under the command of General George Washington. According to Elijah Huntington's 1868 *History of Stamford*, Bush insisted after the war was over that Washington sign his discharge in 1783 with the words, "take this and keep it with care, it may someday be of use to you."[10] And several descendants of Robert Jacklin, a free Connecticut black in 1717, enlisted with Connecticut's troops and served in the war.[11]

Connecticut's Revolutionary War records and some local town histories generally identify the black men who served as soldiers for Connecticut with the promise of freedom when the conflict was over. Some were actually freed before they enlisted, while others had to wait until their enlistment was over to be considered free. Some owners required their slaves to pay a portion of their salary as soldiers to purchase their freedom. A few of these owners did not follow through on their promise of freedom and several blacks went to court to win a decision in their favor. An example of this is the case of Jack Arabas of Stratford, who was signed up for the army by his owner, Thomas Ivers. Arabas served six years in the war, from 1777 to 1783, but Ivers tried to reclaim him when the conflict was over. Arabas fled, was caught by the authorities, and was sent to jail in New Haven. Arabas sued Ivers, and the court awarded him his freedom, concluding that since he fought for the country's liberty, he should have his own liberty as well.[12]

An unusual situation involved a man named Titus who asked his owner for permission to enlist in the military. The owner refused because he had several sons already in the army and needed Titus at home. For agreeing to stay back, the owner gave Titus his freedom from slavery when the war ended.[13]

Some white men who were drafted into the army were allowed to pay someone else to serve in their place. When Linius Bishop of Guilford was told he was to be part of that town's quota of soldiers, he offered his slave, Gad Asher, freedom to serve in his place. Asher agreed, was injured during the war, and eventually went blind.[14] He had a number of children, including a grandson named Jeremiah. Jeremiah Asher, who later was a minister, wrote in his 1862 *An Autobiography* that as a child he heard so much about his grandfather's exploits that he felt he had "more rights than any white man in the town."

Among those enslaved in Connecticut who joined the army and won their freedom for doing so was Bristol Baker of New Haven. Like many of the white soldiers, Baker's enlistment was for six years

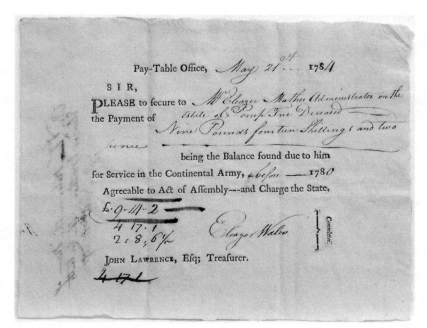

FIGURE 5-I Pay Voucher
to Pomp for service in
the Revolutionary War,
1784. *The Amistad Center
for Art & Culture, Inc.,
Simpson Collection,
1987.1.2153*

(1777–1783). In 1784 he was emancipated by his owner, who noted
that Baker was a "good Soldier . . . and capable of Business Equal
to most white men. . . ." This last statement likely was to assure
town officials that Baker would not become a financial burden on
the community. Baker died in 1793 and left a small estate that included the bounty land the government gave him as part of his salary as a soldier.[15] A copy of Bristol Baker's discharge paper signed
by George Washington was printed in William C. Nell's 1855 book
*Colored Patriots.*

Samuel Orcutt's 1874 history of Wolcott notes that Prince Duplex, who was owned by Reverend James Chapman, served with
Connecticut's troops from 1777 to 1780, and upon his freedom
bought land in the town of Wolcott.[16] And Charles Davis's 1870 history of Wallingford describes how Chatham Freeman was freed by
Noah Yale to take the place of Yale's son in the war. When Freeman
returned after the war he agreed to work for Yale for seven years in
order to gain the freedom of a woman Yale owned. At the end of
this time the two free blacks married.[17]

Some black soldiers did not fare too well during the war. Pompey Dore, who entered the service under that name, was discharged
six years later as Pomp Edore. He received his liberty before going
into the service, but spent the last two years of his enlistment in the
Invalid Corps. When Edore was discharged he was a sick man and

had to turn to his former owner for help. He soon died without having the chance to truly live as a free person.[18] Another case is that of Joseph Sackett, who joined Connecticut's Seventh Regiment in March 1778. His owner freed him the following month, but Sackett grew ill by September and died in November.[19] Sackett was owed money from the government at the time of his death. A list was later published noting such persons and the amount each was owed, but Sackett's former owner, Joseph Wadsworth, either did not know about this money or had moved out of Connecticut. In 1793 John Sedgwick petitioned the Connecticut government for this pay and received it. There is no record that Sedgwick had once owned Sackett, but the amount was paid to him anyway.[20]

It isn't clear exactly what duties black soldiers in the American Revolution performed. Their status as soldiers in their units is difficult to determine because black soldiers did not write about their experiences, and the records are generally silent on this issue. It seems that most Connecticut blacks in the military were on a basis equivalent to white soldiers. Often, it appears, soldiers, white and black alike, cooked their own meals and waited on themselves rather than having these services provided by others. And, black soldiers suffered death and injuries while fulfilling their military duties from 1777 to 1783 just as whites did.[21]

Another aspect of interest in the development of Connecticut's military forces and the use of African Americans was the creation in 1781 of an all-black company within the Fourth Regiment. Most units before 1781 were integrated. A Hessian officer fighting with the Americans noted that in New England every American unit he saw had blacks as members and that they were "able bodied, strong, and brave fellows."[22] Benjamin Quarles wrote in *The Negro in the American Revolution* that whites and blacks were so integrated in the American forces that it was not at all unusual to see mixed-race units. Why Connecticut formed a separate company of black soldiers in 1781 is unclear. An *aide-de-camp* to George Washington, a white officer David Humphreys led the company. All of the officers in this company were white, and all of the black soldiers were privates. While most of the companies in Connecticut's Fourth Regiment consisted of thirty-five men, the all-black company held forty-eight.[23]

This all-black unit might have been formed because of racism, but there is no direct evidence supporting this. There were still forty black soldiers serving with whites in other Connecticut units from 1781 to 1783. Further, when Connecticut reorganized its army in

1783, all of the state's units were integrated again. It is possible that Connecticut's all-black company served with an all-black unit from Rhode Island. Colonel Humphrey's duties with General Washington kept him from personally leading the men under his charge. Two European officers observing the military action spoke highly of these soldiers' appearance and placed the number of blacks in the Rhode Island unit to be more than Rhode Island's records suggest were actually there. The presence of Connecticut's all-black company alongside the Rhode Island unit might be the reason for this appearance of more African Americans.[24]

It appears that the inequality between white and black soldiers so prevalent in later conflicts such as the Civil War and in World War I and World War II did not exist in Connecticut during the American Revolution. There is little information on this subject, and one would assume some white officers would have held prejudices. Yet, army life has a way of making private soldiers see themselves as equals while serving together. Further, as former slaves for the most part, asserting independence and demands for equal rights might not have been a goal for the black participants. With freedom in view for many of them, black soldiers might well have been willing to endure anything while serving in integrated units. It does appear that the blacks received the same pay and the same provisions as the white soldiers did. And, when the war was over, records show that black veterans received government benefits along with the white participants.

The government pensions that some former black soldiers received reveal something of their financial condition after the war. Few had wealth of any kind or land of any amount. The federal government authorized pensions in 1818 for those veterans who needed financial help. Fourteen years later all of the Revolutionary War veterans qualified for assistance.[25]

Gad Asher received a disability pension in 1783 because he was unable to remain on active duty because of blindness. When Asher died in 1835 he left an estate of $104.96, which included four acres of land.[26] His grandson Jeremiah received a lot more by listening to his grandfather's stories about service during the war; he wrote in his autobiography that such teachings "gave his parents much trouble." "Neither my father nor my mother could persuade me that white boys were allowed to insult me because I was colored," Jeremiah Asher wrote, "I invariably felt justified in defending myself."[27]

And, when James Mars lived in Hartford in the 1840s he attempted to get his elderly mother a pension based on his father's war service. Connecticut's veterans, black and white, usually collected their allowances at banks located at large centers such as New Haven and Hartford. An officer of the bank at New Haven who paid these pensions for the government said of the blacks who collected them each month, "the correct deportment and good appearance of the colored pensioners was a matter of frequent notice and remark, by all those attached to this institution."[28]

Connecticut's African Americans continued to suffer discrimination and racism after the war was over, just as Jeremiah Asher noted. European travelers to the United States during the first half of the nineteenth century described some of the difficulties blacks faced. Regarding blacks he saw in the North, Henry Wansey wrote in 1794, "nor do they yet seem to feel their importance in society; this is a position of inheritance reserved to the next generation of them."[29] Wansey may have been right. It was the children, and particularly the grandchildren, who made gains in Connecticut, although they were still saddled with sometimes-unbearable hardships. Cesar Beamont (later Beman) had a son and grandson who became Christian ministers in Connecticut (Jehiel and Amos Beman), and both were active in opposing injustices shown toward African Americans. Prince Duplex's grandson, Cortland Creed, became the first black physician in the city of New Haven. Creed also served in the Civil War as acting assistant surgeon of Connecticut's all-black Thirtieth Regiment.[30] And Holdridge Primus, another grandson of Gad Asher, spent many years in Hartford working for a store in the city. Holdridge's son Nelson became an artist in Boston and California, and his daughter, Rebecca, taught freed slaves in Maryland at the end of the Civil War.

Frederick Williams Seymour was an unusual black citizen of Connecticut. Born in 1866, he was the great grandson of a white Connecticut soldier of the Revolutionary War. Proud of this fact, he applied for membership to the Connecticut Society of the Sons of the American Revolution and was accepted as a member in the 1920s. He was one of the few (if not the only) black members of that organization.[31] Yet, today there must be living thousands of descendants of Connecticut's 289 documented black soldiers who served in the Revolutionary War. It is difficult to find many of these descendants. Still, the lives of a few immediate descendants of several of these soldiers offer a glimpse of contributions that they made in Connecticut and elsewhere.

# Notes

1. James Cogswell, *God, the Pious Soldier's Strength & Instructor: A Sermon Deliver'd at Brooklyn in Promfret, to the Military Company, Under the Command of Capt Israel Putnam, on the Thirteenth Day of April, 1757* (Boston: Draper, 1757), 24.

2. Petition of Prince Goodin to the Connecticut General Assembly, Colonial Wars, 1675–1775, French War, 147–148, Connecticut Archives, Connecticut State Library

3. Births, Marriages, Deaths, I, 1706–1840, Canterbury Town Hall; Canterbury Land Records, Book 7, 19, 127.

4. Timothy Mather Cooley, *Sketches of the Life and Character of the Rev. Lemuel Haynes, A.M. for Many Years Pastor of a Church in Rutland, Vt., and Late of Granville, New-York* (New York: J.S. Taylor, 1839), 45–46; N.A.A.C.P., *Black Heroes of the American Revolution 1775–1783* (New York: N.A.A.C.P., [n.d.]), 8.

5. *Record of Service of Connecticut Men in the War of the Revolution, War of 1812, Mexican War* (Hartford: Adjutant-General's Office, 1889), 41, 196, 361; Alain C. White, comp. *The History of the Town of Litchfield, Connecticut 1720–1920* (Litchfield: Enquirer Print, 1920), 152.

6. George H. Moore, *Historical Notes on the Employment of Negroes in the American Army of the Revolution* (New York: C.T. Evans, 1862), 6–7.

7. Moore, 7–8.

8. Benjamin Quarles, *The Negro in the American Revolution* (Chapel Hill: Institute of Early American History and Culture, 1961), 78–80.

9. *Record of Service of Connecticut Men . . .*, 151, 49; William C. Nell, *The Colored Patriots of the American Revolution* (Boston: R.F. Wallcut, 1855), 136.

10. Nell, 160, 135; Elijah B. Huntington, *History of Stamford, Connecticut from its Settlement in 1641 to the Present Time, Including Darien, Which Was One of its Parishes until 1820* (Stamford: self-published, 1868), 234.

11. Stamford Genealogical Society *Bulletin*, XIII (September 1970), 9–10; Connecticut Archives, Miscellaneous, II: 33.

12. Connecticut Historical Society collections, XII, 58; *Record of Service of Connecticut Men . . .*, 207, 339; Jesse Root, *Reports of Cases Adjudged in the Superior Court and Supreme Court of Errors, from July A.D. 1789 to January A.D. 1798 . . . with a Variety of Cases Anterior to that Period . . .*, I (Hartford: Hudson and Goodwin 1798), 92.

13. Norman Litchfield and Sabina Connolly Hoyt, *History of the Town of Oxford, Connecticut* (N. Litchfield, 1960), 42.

14. Jeremiah Asher, *An Autobiography, with Details of a Visit to England, and Some Account of the History of Meeting Street Baptist Church . . .* (Philadelphia, the author, 1862), 1–5; National Archives Pension S17244.

15. Brister Baker Probate, 1793 #532, Connecticut State Library

16. Samuel Orcutt, *History of the Town of Wolcott* (Waterbury: American Printing Co., 1874), 74.

17. Charles H. S. Davis, *Wallingford, Conn., from its Settlement in 1670 to the Present Including Meriden and Cheshire* (Meriden: Charles H.S. Davis, 1870), 344.

18. Connecticut Archives, Revolutionary War, II, V: 163–68; National Archives Service of Pomp Edore.

19. Thomas Sackett Emancipation Certificate, 4/14/1778, Connecticut Historical Commission; National Archives Service of Thomas Sackett.

20. Connecticut Archives, Revolutionary War, III, III: 66–68; National Archives, Service of Thomas Sackett; Edward C. Starr, *A History of Cornwall, Connecticut: A Typical New England Town* (New Haven: Tuttle, Morehouse and Taylor, 1926), 201, 362–63.

21. David O. White, *Connecticut's Black Soldiers 1775–1783* (Chester, CT: Pequot Press, 1973), 30–31.

22. George Washington Williams, *History of the Negro Race in America*, vol. I (New York: G.P. Putnam's Sons, 1882), 343.

23. Connecticut Archives, Revolutionary War, II, IV: 101–2. Revolutionary War Pay Book, Fourth Connecticut Regiment, 9–10/1782, New Haven Colony Historical Society.

24. Alain C. White, 32–33; Marquis De Chastellux, *Travels in North America in the Years 1780, 1781, and 1782*, 2 vols, Howard C. Rice, Jr., Trans., II (Chapel Hill: University of North Carolina Press, 1963), 229; Evelyn M. Acomb, ed., *The Revolutionary Journal of Baron Ludwig von Closen* (Chapel Hill: University of North Carolina Press, 1958), 89, 91–92.

25. Charles Knowles Bolton, *The Private Soldier under Washington* (New York: C. Scribner's Sons 1902), 245.

26. Connecticut Archives, Revolutionary War, II, IV: 1a. National Archives Pension S17244.

27. Asher, 5–6.

28. Ebenezer Baldwin, *Observations on the Physical, Intellectual, and Moral Qualities of Our Colored Population. With Remarks on the Subject of Emancipation and Colonization* (New Haven: L.H. Young, 1834), 31.

29. Henry Wansey, *The Journal of an Excursion to the United States of North America in the Summer of 1794* (New York: Johnson Reprint Corp., 1969), 56.

30. *New Haven Directory 1856–1857*, 58; *New Haven Directory 1890*, 593. *Connecticut War Record*, June 1864.

31. Letter from Charles Jacobs, The Connecticut Sons of the American Revolution, to the author, November 23, 1971.

*Katherine J. Harris*

# 6 In Remembrance of Their Kings of Guinea

*The Black Governors and the*
*Negro Election, 1749 to 1800*

As early as 1749, throughout Connecticut and other New England colonies, the African and African American community—including enslaved and free people alike—maintained a custom of electing its own leadership through an institution they established and called the "Black Governor." (The terms "Black Governor" and "Black King" were both used, though the latter was more common in areas with stronger ties to the British Crown.) The first Black Governor in Connecticut, Hercules, was elected in approximately 1749 to represent New London. The date is imprecise because the single reference located to date is the inscription on the 1749 headstone of Floria, "wife of Hercules, Governor of the Negroes," in the Antientest Burial Ground in New London, Connecticut located on Hempstead Street. The tradition of electing Black Governors continued until 1855 or 1856.

This essay takes an introductory look at the Black Governors during the period of the settlement of the Connecticut through the formative period of the state of Connecticut. A second essay on this topic appearing later in this volume explores the 1800s. Although a variety of sources are used and they are mostly from white Americans, African Americans also documented the election festivities of the Black Governors. They were Ebenezer Bassett, son of Black Governors Eben Tobias and grandson of Tobias Pero, and Nancy Freeman, widow of Black Governor Roswell Freeman.

Historian William Fowler described the election he observed in 1820 of Caesar, the Black Governor of Durham, as having been "In remembrance of their Kings of Guinea."[1] But Fowler, his contemporaries who also reported on the "Negro elections," and present-day historians have varied in their interpretations of the tradition. Fowler wrote that in mounting their own elections, "the Negroes" were simply imitating their white owners, having accompanied them as they participated in colonial elections. Connecticut's United States Senator Orville Platt and Derby's local historian Jane Shelton are among those who have subscribed to this interpretation. In their contemporary studies of this Connecticut African American tradition, historians Clayborne Carson and co-author Emma Lapsansky wrote that the Negro elections imitated white political elections, but added that these elections fused African and European traditions. The 2011 edition of the late John Hope Franklin's *From Slavery to Freedom*, co-authored with Evelyn Higginbotham, notes that African Americans adapted and inverted New England's white electoral celebrations. One would not see the traditional electoral process as it existed among whites (where a test of strength to determine who would be governor would not pass muster); rather, the Black Governor candidates might dress in comical garments—though they were very serious about the role.[2] The Black Governors' elections emerged within the context of the political discourse in colonial society, the exclusion of the small numbers of free Africans from the political process, and African agency that asserted their right to freedom using their own political culture.

Reports of the Connecticut tradition of electing Black Governors (and Kings) appear in local histories and articles from the eighteenth, nineteenth, and twentieth centuries. Those often-overlooked local histories provide brief and incomplete biographies of the Black Governors, along with useful information about the election process and the duties of a Black Governor. But from what context did the tradition of the Black Governor emerge?

African captives arrived in the Americas with an understanding of their political culture. In what is now Angola, a title of leadership was *ngola*. In Yoruba speaking areas of what is now Nigeria one of the titles of leadership was and is *oba* for a male or female ruler. African captives, the ancestors of contemporary African Americans in Connecticut, were seized from Angola, Nigeria, Cameroon, Ghana, and other areas where intricate systems of checks and balances prevailed. Despite their captivity in the Americas, enslaved Africans reclaimed this political heritage and transformed it using the language of English-speaking America. They used the titles "Governor" and "King" to identify the position of leadership for their elected official.[3]

The research places the narrative of Connecticut's Black Governors within the larger context of African American empowerment and participatory politics beginning in the colonial African American community. Denied the official right to participate politically as part of the emerging nation, African people in the Americas used the Black Governors' and Kings' elections as a form of political empowerment.

Political traditions were similar among African communities and also unique to particular societies. For example, virtually all the polities included a council of elders. Northern Nigerians adopted the political system of emirates and sultanates, while the Asante in Ghana organized an elaborate political system of the Queen Mother, the Asantehene (king or chief executive), and the Nsafohene (provincial governors), along with the council of elders. Throughout Africa, women held prominent roles in political and economic structures. In Igbo-speaking areas of what is now Nigeria, the Queen's Council regulated economic activities. Africans from the Hausa Emirates of what is current-day Northern Nigeria brought with them the traditions of Islamic political and economic systems.[4]

In addition, African parliaments and assemblies such as the *Ngongo* in Cameroon and the Council of Elders in most parts of Africa based decisions on consensus or mutual agreement rather than majority rule. The heads of households elected members to the Council of Elders on the basis of their wisdom and character. Regular citizens—men, women, and children—could attend council proceedings. Retrieving an African practice, the black community in Connecticut held its public processions and council meetings in open space, near natural settings. In Connecticut, such places as the South Green and the Connecticut River in Hartford or Hawkins Point and the Ousatonic (or Housatonic) River in Derby served as sites for the Governors' elections and meetings. African connections ran deep among New England's Black Governors and Kings. William Piersen, in *Black Yankees: The Development of an Afro-American Subculture in Eighteenth-Century New England*, counted eleven such leaders who were likely born in Africa, such as King Pompey, who was elected Black Governor in Lynn, Massachusetts in the 1740s. Connecticut Black Governors born in Africa include Boston Nichols of Hartford, London of Wethersfield, and Boston Trowtrow of Norwich. Quash Freeman, Black Governor of Derby, was stolen from Africa as a child and enslaved in Derby.[5] Governor Roswell Freeman, sometimes called Roswell Quash, son of Quash Freeman, would have been the first born of the generation in the Americas.

Boston Trowtrow's Akan name, probably a playful name "trowtrow" for slippery, suggests his African birth. Cuff, or Coffe, seems to be from Kofi, a traditional Akan name for a male child born on

Friday. Quaw, generally spelled Kwa, is derived from the name for a male child born on Wednesday. Quash, or Quosh, may be from Kwasi or Kwesi, a male child born on Sunday.

It is not safe to assume, though, that those with traditional African names were in fact born in Africa. For example, Broteer Furro, born in Dukandarra, Guinea and captured and enslaved in Connecticut in the 1700s, named the son he had with his wife Margaret Cuff, a version of "Kofi," though the child was born in Connecticut.[6]

Still, Piersen notes, using African-derived names was one way in which African captives in America paid tribute to their heritage. Similarly, aspects of the logistics surrounding the election of Black Governors paid homage to African origins. The locations chosen for holding elections were reminiscent of the African context, Piersen notes, and ceremonial processions associated with those elections were also very much in keeping with African praise traditions that were invoked for significant events. Colonial settlers interpreted these expressions of praise as noise and disorder, but the processions captivated them nonetheless. Fowler witnessed one such celebration and recorded it in his account of Durham's election of Governor Caesar. Historian Frances Manwaring Caulkins vividly described the procession and installation of Black Governor Samuel Huntington in Norwich in 1800.

New England and parts of the South were not the only places in which Africans asserted their political customs. In parts of South America and the Caribbean, for instance, the tradition of electing Black Kings or Governors spanned more than a century. In Brazil, on the *quilombo*, or settlement of Africans who had run away from plantations, Africans established *Palmares* as a virtual black state that survived until the 1690s.

Drawing data from documents in the Connecticut State Archives and the Connecticut Historical Society, Billie Anthony, a teacher at Hartford's Fox Middle School, worked with her students from 1995 to 1997 to compile a list of twenty-two individuals who had served as Black Governors in Connecticut.[7] This essay adds to that list five more Black Governors identified since Anthony and her students completed their project: Hercules, Deptford Billings, and Ira Tossett from New London County, Will from Litchfield, and Lyman Homer from Plainville (which was part of Farmington until 1869).

The election of a Black Governor was considered central to the political tradition; when Governor Cuff of Hartford appointed his successor John Anderson without an election in 1776, for instance, the local African American community did not approve. Moreover, no Black Governor could rule as an autocrat. The New Haven community removed Black Governor Quash Piere in 1832 when it seemed that he had violated the trust of the office. (That mistrust stemmed from an incident in which his cane was found in a chicken house; the assumption was that he had stolen chickens, though there is no evidence that he actually did so.) Though the elections themselves were vital to establishing trust between the Black Governor and those he represented, the election process varied from locale to locale. According to Ebenezer Bassett, the son and grandson of Derby governors, sometimes Black Governors were elected by consensus through a simple voice vote. According to Samuel Orcutt, co-author of *The History of Derby*, on one occasion the election of a Black Governor was decided at Hawkins Point in Derby by a test of strength.

The research on the Black Governors intersects with multiple histories and themes. It links the histories of Connecticut, Africa, and the African Diaspora in the Americas and the rest of the Atlantic world. The history of Connecticut's Black Governors is also connected to that of Native Americans. Derby's Black Governor Eben Tobias's wife Susan Gregory Bassett was a woman of Native American heritage. The fact that the tradition of Black Governors emerged during slavery refutes the idea that slavery had completely squashed the spirit of enslaved people.

While, as noted at the start of this essay, many viewed the Black Governors as autocrats or imitators of white politicians, another view interprets the experience of Connecticut's Black Governors as an example of the concept of African agency or resistance to enslavement. Research places the narrative of Connecticut's Black Governors within the larger context of African American empowerment and participatory politics beginning in the colonial African American community.

Research on Black Governors has been challenging because information is incomplete. Despite consulting census records, newspapers and secondary sources for this essay, for instance, the family records for London, John Anderson, Peter Freeman, Samuel Huntington, Thomas Johnson, Quash Piere, Wilson Weston, and Nelson Weston remain incomplete. Society did not consider African Americans as people; official documents for African Americans, whether enslaved or free, often did not record their dates of birth or list the names of their parents, siblings, wives, and children. In spite of those omissions, the historical record provides for a fairly solid understanding of the Black Governors in Connecticut.

The criteria for the election of Black Governors were not codified in a specific document, though documents from Bassett and other observers do reflect the desirable traits and the duties of the Black Governors. Good character, commitment to the community, advocacy for educational opportunities, voting rights, and economic self-determination were among the qualities sought in these governors. It has been suggested that the Black Governors were chosen because they appeared to be surrogates for white authority. Commentaries indicate,[8] however, that the governors were elected for their strength of character, importance within the African American community, and contributions to the nation, not for their money or their connection to a good family. Several were Revolutionary War veterans, and Black Governors William Lanson and Lyman Homer helped build the Farmington Canal.

Events during the Revolutionary War era demonstrated the seriousness of the Black Governor's election in the African American and Euro-American communities. When it appeared that loyalists were involved in selecting John Anderson as Black Governor in 1776, both the white and black patriot communities became outraged.

In New Haven in the early nineteenth century, events challenged assumptions expressed by such historians as Charles Burpee that the Black Governors represented white authority or served as go-betweens among whites and blacks. Public officials harassed Black Governor William Lanson, who was elected King or Governor in 1825, and he was fined for alleged infractions. Lanson owned property on the fringes of New Haven. As that land became desirable to city officials, their harassment of Lanson increased. He was accused of "keeping a loud house" and allowing inappropriate people to stay in his residences. Newspapers leapt into the fray, attacking Lanson's character. In 1814, Lanson petitioned the Connecticut legislature for either the right to vote or exemption from taxation for African Africans in the New Haven area.[9] In apparent retaliation, town officials levied fines against him, arrested him (often without formal charges), and ultimately stripped him of his property. New Haven Black Governors Thomas Johnson and Quash Piere were tarnished as well. Johnson was charged with violating an antiquated law against playing cards in 1837. Quash Piere was accused of theft based on circumstantial evidence that his cane was found in a chicken coop in 1832.

It has been suggested that Black Governors imitated whites by wearing their owners' cast-off clothing, but there is not much evidence to support this or to suggest that the practice of wearing one's

**Table 6-1**
*Connecticut's Black Governors, 1749–1800*

| Name and status | Town | Date |
| --- | --- | --- |
| Hercules<br>based on inscription on wife Florio's headstone | New London | 1749 |
| London<br>owner Thomas Seymour, Esquire | Hartford | 1755 |
| Quaw<br>owner George Wyllys, Secretary of the Colony | Hartford | 1760 |
| London<br>owner John Chester | Wethersfield & Simsbury | 1760 |
| Cuff<br>status as enslaved or free unclear | Hartford | 1766–1776 |
| Boston Trowtrow<br>owner Jedediah or Jabez Huntington | Norwich | 1770–1772 |
| Samuel Huntington<br>owner Samuel Huntington, Governor of the State | Norwich | 1772–1800 |
| John Anderson<br>owner Philip Skene, British prisoner of war, son of<br>former Lt. Governor, Ticonderoga and Crown Point | Hartford | 1776 |
| Peleg Nott<br>owner Jeremiah Wadsworth, Congressman | Hartford | 1780 |
| Peter Freeman | Farmington | 1780 |
| Will*<br>owner Moses Seymour | Litchfield | before 1793 |
| Boston Nichols<br>owner James Nichols | Hartford | 1800 |

*Black Governors identified by Katherine J. Harris, 2002

owner's clothing was anything more than a matter of convenience. Peleg Nott was described as wearing garments his former owner Jeremiah Wadsworth gave him and riding a horse supplied by Wadsworth. Samuel Huntington also rode a horse supplied by his former owner. These are the only accounts thus far to have linked the Black Governors to their owners' or former owners' garments.

Were the Black Governors largely the slaves of prominent men? In fact, several of the Black Governors were enslaved by important Connecticut public and religious officials. London was owned by prominent Hartford attorney Thomas Seymour. Quaw's first owner, Reverend T. Worthington, was pastor of Center Congregational Church in Hartford; his second owner, George Wyllys, was secretary of the Connecticut Colony and secretary of state for Connecticut. London Chester, also known as London Wallis, was enslaved by the wealthy John Chester family in Wethersfield. Peleg Nott and his family were purchased by Jeremiah Wadsworth, the

Connecticut financier. Boston Trowtrow was enslaved by Jedediah and Jabez Huntington, the nephew and brother of Samuel Huntington, Connecticut governor from 1786 to 1796 and president of the Continental Congress. Juba Weston was enslaved by members of the Judge John Humphreys and General David Humphreys family of Derby. Quash Freeman was enslaved by prominent Derby landowner Agar Tomlinson.

Yet other Black Governors were freemen; some gained their freedom by running away from slavery or indentured servitude, as was possibly the case of William Lanson. Peter Freeman and Ira Tossett purchased their freedom, while others, including Boston Nichols and Peleg Nott, were freed by their owners. Tobias Pero was freed in return for military service, and Eben Tobias, Lyman Homer, Roswell Freeman, and Wilson Weston and Nelson Weston were born free.

The specific month during which the elections occurred and whether they occurred in only in one town at a time is another open question. Platt wrote:

When the custom originated, it is impossible to determine. That it prevailed before the Revolution is clear, . . . Negroes increased rapidly between 1730 and 1750 . . . Many of them came with their masters to the election in Hartford, and it is probable that the first elections of [N]egro governors were held in Hartford by the votes of those who had come with their masters to the election ceremonies [of white colonial officials].[10]

It is clear, nevertheless, that Black Governors functioned in the eighteenth and nineteenth centuries within black communities that were rooted in the human tragedy of enslavement. Slavery was legal in the United States until December 1865, when the Thirteenth Amendment, which abolished the practice, was ratified. Although Connecticut enacted gradual emancipation laws in the late eighteenth century, resistance to slavery took place on many levels.[11] Laws and customs in Connecticut dating from the colonial period (as noted in the introductory section about slavery and freedom) prohibited African Americans from assembling in mass gatherings; they did so, anyway. Laws and customs in the state restricted blacks' movement from place to place. Yet election records note that people from Waterbury gathered to attend the election in Derby, for example. Laws and customs prohibited African Americans from owning weapons. But at the ceremonies surrounding the election of Black Governors, participants reportedly carried swords. And at the funeral for Boston Nichols in 1810 in Hartford's South Congregational Church, Nichols's sword was laid across his coffin. At the 1830 election of Roswell Freeman in Derby, gun salutes were fired. For enslaved and free communities of African descent, the elections of the governors asserted their humanity. Later, the elections of the Black Governors were to serve as vehicles to organize for the abolition of slavery.[12] Denied the official right to hold elective office or participate in politically in the United States, African people in the Americas used the elections of the Black Governors and Kings as a form of political revolt and self-determination.


## Notes

1. The tradition began in New Hampshire in the 1600s. William C. Fowler quoted in Orville Platt, "Negro Governors," *Papers of the New Haven Colony Historical Society*, VI (New Haven: Tuttle, Morehouse and Taylor Co., 1900), 325.

2. Platt, "Negro Governors," 318. Jane De Forest Shelton, "The New England Negro, a Remnant," *Harper's New Monthly Magazine* (March 1894): 536.

3. Michael L. Conniff and Thomas J. Davis, *Africans in the Americas: A History of the Black Diaspora* (New York: St. Martin's Press, 1994), 53–54. William D. Piersen, *Black Yankees: The Development of an Afro-American Subculture in Eighteenth-Century New England* (Amherst, Massachusetts: University of Massachusetts, 1988), 118, 128.

4. Cheik Anta Diop, *Precolonial Black Africa: A Comparative Study of the Political and Social Systems of Europe and Black Africa, from Antiquity to the Formation of Modern States* (New York: Lawrence Books, 1987), 43–86; 89–111. Joseph E. Harris, *Africans and Their History* (New York: Penguin Books, revised edition 1987), 119, 121. Shane D. White, "It Was a Proud Day: African Americans, Festivals, and Parades," *The Journal of American History* 81: no. 1 (June 1994): 50.

5. Lorenzo Greene, *The Negro in Colonial New England 1620–1776* (New York: Columbia University Press, 1942), 255; Piersen, *Black Yankees*, 135; Judge Sherman Adams and Henry R. Stiles, *The History of Ancient Wethersfield, Connecticut* (New York: The Grafton Press, 1904), 702. Shelton, "The New England Negro," 536. Samuel Orcutt and Ambrose Beardsley, *The History of the Old Town of Derby, Connecticut, 1642–1880: With Biographies and Genealogies* (Springfield, MA: Press of Springfield Printing Company, 1880), 182.

6. Venture Smith, *A Narrative of the Life and Adventures of Venture A Native of Africa, But Resident Above Sixty Years in the United States of America Related By Himself* (New London: 1798/Middletown, Conn: J.S. Stewart, Printer and Bookbinder), 4, 31; on his son Cull in Arna Bontemps, ed., *Five Black Lives* (Middletown, Connecticut: Wesleyan University Press, 1971 and 1988).

7. Teacher Billie Anthony and students at Fox Middle School in Hartford, Connecticut documented five Black Governors in the Hartford area. On New London County, see James M. Rose and Barbara W. Brown, *Tapestry, A Living History of the Black Family In Southeastern Connecticut* (New London, CT: New London County Historical Society, 1979), 37. Conniff and Davis, *Africans in the Americas: A History of the Black Diaspora*, 98. John S. Bassett, "Antislavery Leaders in North Carolina," *Johns Hopkins University Studies In Historical and Political Science*, Series XVI: 6 (June 1898): 7–11.

8. Shelton, "The Negro in New England," 537–38. Orcutt and Beardsley, *The History of Derby*, 549–50. Platt, "Negro Governors," 331.

9. William Lanson and Bias Stanley's Petition to General Assembly for the right to Vote, 1814, Connecticut State Library, Hartford, Connecticut.

10. Platt, "Negro Governors."

11. Overt revolt occurred as early as 1658 by enslaved Africans with Native Americans in Hartford. Franklin and Moss, *From Slavery to Freedom*, 76. Slave revolts in Hispaniola in 1522, Barbados in 1692, New York in 1712 and 1741, South Carolina in 1739, Antigua in 1736, Jamaica in 1760, and Haiti in 1791 are listed in Conniff and Davis, *Africans in the Americas*, 64, 84, 139.

12. John E. Rogers, *Inner City Bicentennial Booklet 1776–1976* (West Hartford, CT: University of Hartford, 1975), 49. For reprints of the 1779 petitions from Fairfield county's African community presented by the Black Governors, according to Rogers, see Elizabeth Hubbell Schenck, *The History of Fairfield, Fairfield County Connecticut* (New York: J.J. Little and Company, 1905), ii, 325.

# 7 Ancient Burying Ground

## *Monument to Black Governors*

From 1995 to 1997 students Andriena Baldwin, Christopher Hayes, and Monique Price from Hartford's Fox Middle School led research and fund-raising efforts to honor the 300 or more African Americans interred in unmarked graves in Hartford's Ancient Burying Ground. They discovered that five of Hartford's Black Governors were likely buried there. The students used primary sources—census, probate, church, and land records—to uncover and document the African presence. With the assistance of the Ancient Burying Ground Association and a committee of students, parents, and representatives from the Center Congregational Church and the Historical Commission, the African Americans interred in the Ancient Burying Ground, including the five Black Governors, were commemorated in 1998 with a unique hand-carved black slate memorial.

In the Connecticut State Library archives the students found the bill of sale for London, elected governor in 1755. He was purchased for £60 on September 11, 1725, by Thomas Seymour, the grandfather of Hartford's first mayor. Governor Quaw, elected in 1760, was owned by Colonel George Wyllys, secretary of the colony and later the state. Governor Quaw's election party was held at Amos Hinsdale's tavern, which stood near present-day South Park. Governor Cuff was elected in 1766 and resigned from office in 1776. John Anderson, the personal slave of Major Philip Skene (a British prisoner of war being held in Hartford), succeeded him in 1776.

The announcement that Anderson was the new "Governor of the Slaves" and that a good sum of money had been paid for his election party at Knox Tavern aroused great suspicion, as there hadn't even been an election! An immediate investigation found no evidence of conspiracy, but a document signed by both Governor Cuff and John Anderson states that Cuff had resigned because he was "weak and unfit," and that he had appointed Anderson in his place. Six Africans or African Americans are listed as witnesses. Not long after they

FIGURE. 7-1 Monument to Black Governors, Ancient Burying Ground, Hartford, 2013. *Photo: Billie M. Anthony*

signed the document, Major Skene escaped from the Americans and John Anderson disappeared from history.

One of the most interesting Black Governors was Peleg Nott, owned by Colonel Jeremiah Wadsworth, a Hartford businessman and representative to Congress, and the richest man in Connecticut. Nott participated in the American Revolution, driving a provisions cart. He was a man of considerable reputation, entrusted with money, goods, and later farmland in what is now West Hartford. He was elected governor in 1780 and celebrated the election in the African custom of a grand parade. An eyewitness places him on a "frisky horse." Wadsworth eventually freed Nott and his wife, and they probably lived somewhere near where the Wadsworth Atheneum now stands.

Boston Nichols of Hartford, described as a "stable and respectable man," was married to a woman named Rose. In 1774 Captain James Nichols freed them, and in 1783 he granted Boston some land and a house for five pounds. This site was near the old Charter Oak tree, on what is now called Wyllys Street. According to accounts pieced together by the student researchers, the place on the 1790 map of Hartford identified as "Negro house" was where the couple lived. In 1800 Nichols was elected Governor of the Blacks. When he died in 1810, he was buried in the Ancient Burying Ground with his "cocked hat" and his sword in his coffin. The exact whereabouts of his grave are unknown, but his life is memorialized on the ledger stone of the African American monument.

In recent years, the stories of the Black Governors and their families have begun to be recovered and restored to Connecticut's history. Inspired by the students' work, others have organized to further the research and tributes. In 2001, the Connecticut General Assembly, through the Connecticut Freedom Trail, commissioned Dr. Katherine Harris of Central Connecticut State University to conduct research on Connecticut's Black Governors. In addition to bringing the total of known Governors to twenty-seven, Dr. Harris uncovered myriad personal stories and fascinating details. The John E. Rogers African American Cultural Center was one of the first historical groups to honor the Hartford students for their work; that organization has held Black Governors Balls and circulates an exhibit on The Black Governors.

. . .

The Ancient Burying Ground is located at Main and Gold streets in Hartford, adjacent to Center Congregational Church.

Note

This essay originally appeared in the Aug/Sept/Oct 2004 issue of *Connecticut Explored*.

# PART II

1789
to the
Civil War

*Katherine J. Harris*

# 8 The Rise of Communities and the Continued Quest for Freedom for All

The early nineteenth century saw the rise of distinct African American communities as the number of freemen in Connecticut increased and the number of those enslaved decreased. Fleeing slavery or simply searching for economic opportunity, African Americans migrated and established unique African American communities.

Although in the early twenty-first century the largest concentrations of African communities are in Connecticut's major cities of Hartford, New Haven, and Bridgeport, an exploration of Connecticut's residential patterns reveals that in the seventeenth, eighteenth, and nineteenth centuries an African American presence could be found throughout the state's cities, hamlets, and towns. A circa 1820 map of tiny, rural Burlington, for example, includes a "Negro house." This may have been where Farmington's Black Governor Peter Freeman lived after his move from Farmington until his death in 1826. Years earlier he had been among the families of African Americans who lived, farmed, and conducted business in the Scott Swamp area of Farmington. London Chester (the former Black Governor of Wethersfield, also known as London Wallis) in the 1780s lived with his family in the Indian Hill section of West Simsbury and in New Hartford. The Litchfield hills were home to a few African American families whose descendants still live in Connecticut.[1] Although small numbers of enslaved African Americans lived in Deep River and New Haven in the eighteenth century, their numbers increased by the 1830s. Unpublished research on such towns as Bristol, Granby, Griswold, and Lisbon has uncovered information about African American residents who owned land and businesses, founded organizations, and built small communities in those towns. Although no sudden shift occurred from farming to small business ownership, African Americans owned plots of land and established groceries, thrift shops, churches, and boarding houses.[2]

The Freeman and Hawley families were part of this phenomenon when they formed part of the nucleus of a new community on Long Island Sound in the south end of Bridgeport. During the 1820s and 1830s they purchased lots and built homes. The community soon boasted a grocery store, an African Free School, a library, and two centers of African Methodism: the Bethel African Methodist Episcopal Church and Walters African Methodist Episcopal Zion Church. The families named their community "Little Liberia." Eliza and Mary Freeman left instructions for the construction of an obelisk to mark their burial site in nearby Derby. The obelisk was an indication of their self worth and a symbol for future generations of African American accomplishments.[3] The obelisk still stands in Derby's Uptown Cemetery.

Another example of an African American enclave that formed in the early nineteenth century is the Birches, also known as Birchville, or Governors Island, the community in Plainville where Lyman Homer was the Black Governor.[4] Still, it was in Deep River and New Haven that African Americans built rare—and, in New Haven, controversial—communities.

### Deep River

Public records date the earliest African American presence in the area that would become the municipality of Deep River to the 1700s. In Saybrook's villages of Winthrop, Essex, Chester, Westbrook, and Deep River, the Murdock family in the western part of Saybrook (now Westbrook) owned enslaved African Americans. According to Daniel Connors's history of Deep River, enslaved persons labored on many of the stone-wall constructions in the area. The Lays, Chapmans, Spencers, and Posts also owned enslaved persons. Despite the benign term "Negro Servants" used in advertisements for runaway slaves and Negro servants, documentation on the Lay family's purchase of Africans confirmed that these "Negro Servants" were in fact enslaved.[5] These families' listings in the 1790 census index suggest that that they had emancipated their enslaved persons, as the space for listing the number of enslaved people in their households is left blank.[6] The passage of Connecticut's 1784 Gradual Emancipation Act encouraged slave owners to release the enslaved from bondage. But slavery remained legal, and Connecticut businesses continued to profit from the institution.

These circumstances remained the parameters within which white Americans and legally free African Americans conducted their lives in Deep River. The village attracted a number of black families around the mid-nineteenth century, as documented in Barbara W. Brown and James M. Rose's *Black Roots in Southeastern Connecticut*. They include the mariner Henry and his wife Sarah Ann (Taylor) Condol,[7] Asaph and Sabra (Billings) Carter,[8] and the family of musician Sawney and Clarissa Freeman.[9]

Deep River's free African Americans would not likely have wanted to trade places with those still enslaved. But life outside of slavery in this small town could be quite harsh. Still, African Americans continued to arrive in Deep River, albeit in small numbers.

The first enslaved person that most of the townspeople knew of in Deep River was a man who had run away from slavery in Maryland during the 1820s. Daniel Fisher (who later changed his name to William Winter) made his way north via the Underground Railroad. Eventually his sister Nancy and other family members joined him in Deep River. Kinship ties also connected other families to Winter. He became related by marriage to several Deep River families, including the Beale, Mitchell, Sturgis, and Williams families, who arrived after the Civil War.

Just a few weeks prior to his death in 1900 (some accounts list 1899), Winter recounted his early life in slavery and escape (when he was known as Daniel Fisher).[10] He was born into slavery in Westmoreland County, Virginia, around 1808. He had five brothers and two sisters. Though he doesn't mention his parents' names in the interview, he does note that his owner's name was Henry Cox. "When I was about twenty years of age my master was obliged on account of heavy losses, to sell me, and I was sent to Richmond to be sold on the block to the highest bidder."

Fisher went on to describe his flight from slavery to freedom, a journey on which he was joined by another young, enslaved man. They traveled to Richmond and finally reached Fisher's old plantation home. Fisher pleaded with his former owner to purchase him. Cox replied that he was now poorer than he was when he initially sold Fisher and advised Fisher to stow away on a vessel. This he did. Fisher recounted the aid he received from "some Philadelphia colored people" who took him to New York. In New York, Fisher met members of the Abolition party. His journey continued as he traveled via steamboat to New Haven. There "a colored man took me to the Tontine Hotel, where a woman gave me a part of a suit of clothes. I was fed and made comfortable, and then directed to Deep River: with instructions that upon arriving there I was to inquire for George Read, the station agent for the Underground Railroad, or Judge Warner."[11] Fisher walked from New Haven to Deep River and arrived there about 1828.

George Read suggested that Fisher disguise himself and change his name. Because Fisher arrived during the winter months in Deep River, he chose the surname Winter and thereafter called himself William Winter(s). Winter worked for various employers, but he was also a skillful entrepreneur. He purchased property in what was called Williams Hill on Main Street. He experimented with growing cotton and tobacco and had pastures, gardens, and apple orchards. That property, now on Winter Avenue, was registered in the Deep River land records, and deeds recorded the sales of his land to a number of individuals during his lifetime and after his death. These reveal that he sold plots to Edwin Fisher (a family member), Felicia Bollman (an African American citizen of Deep River), Henry Johnson, and Isidor Fox. Some of Winter's property was bounded to the east by land owned by other African Americans, including the Charles Mitchell family. The Bollman family owned the land to the west.[12]

Winter also had culinary skills; newspaper articles announced festivities that he catered. He also prepared succulent dishes at the Oyster River House in Old Saybrook. According to a local newspaper account dated March 3, 1882, Mrs. Charlie Mitchell played the piano at a wedding that Winter catered at a location called Riverview.[13] Photographs of Winter show him shopping and participating in town activities.

Other African Americans included the Williams and Simonton families. Some families listed in Deep River town records as African American had blended heritages. The Randalls and Scudder families were Native American and African Americans. The Booma family was African American and Euro-American. While some of the families had roots in southeastern Connecticut, as Brown and Rose research in ample detail, the Fishers, the Mitchells, Beales, and Williamses had Southern roots in slavery.

Having survived enslavement and the long journey north, African Americans began rebuilding their lives in Deep River. Their activities in church, at work and school, as property owners, and in military service are memorialized in Deep River's streets, houses, and cemeteries. Some members of Deep River's African American community in the twentieth century left to join the military. Henry M. Scudder was a U.S. Marine in World War II. He is buried in Deep River's Fountain Hill Cemetery.

At a time when *de facto* and *de jure* segregation existed in the post-slavery world of the nineteenth and twentieth centuries in much of the United States, photos and documents show that in Deep River, African Americans and white Americans did not live a segregated existence. They worshipped at the same Deep River Baptist Church.[14] African American Jennie Floyd was depicted in an 1895 photograph with her white American co-workers with whom she apparently worked side by side at the Acme Steam Laundry.

Similarly at Pratt, Read & Company, which opened in 1809, photos of African Americans Charles and Thomas Mitchell, Frank Booma, Stephen Beale, Robert Sturgis, and others depict them seated along with their white co-workers as they manufactured piano keys and actions and processed ivory. Their employment generated the income they needed to support their families. George Read's enterprise importing and processing ivory supported Deep River's economic growth and promoted links with such towns as Ivoryton. Regrettably, that employment was linked to the processing of ivory, the devastation that the ivory trade wrought on the elephant population in Africa, and the harsh use of forced labor there. This has only been acknowledged in the twentieth and twenty-first centuries. During World War II, Pratt, Read, & Company ceased producing piano products and converted its factory works; African American and white Americans manufactured gliders there.

Nor was education segregated in Deep River. Throughout the decades of the 1900s, the children of the town, African American and white American, attended grammar school and high school together. Photographs show young African American girls and boys in the same grammar-school classes with their white American classmates.[15] Two young African American men posed with their baseball and track teammates in photos taken during the 1920s.

Children in the Mitchell and Sturgis (starting with Robert Sturgis in 1899) families were among the first African Americans to graduate from Deep River High School. African American students attended Deep River Schools throughout the 1930s to 1950. By the 1960s, many descendants of the nineteenth-century community of African Americans had left Deep River. But Florence Sturgis was among the few African Americans who made Deep River her permanent home. In 1962, Sturgis, a 1908 Deep River High School graduate, celebrated the seventy-fifth diamond jubilee of her graduation with some of her former classmates.[16]

While racial confrontations occurred fairly frequently in Hartford and New Haven in the nineteenth and twentieth centuries, such conflicts appear not to have taken place in Deep River. But there were reminders that Deep River's African American community could not escape racial conflict entirely. State legislation denied all African Americans in Connecticut the right to vote until the Fifteenth Amendment to the Constitution was passed in 1870. Even then, African Americans who chose to run for elective office found they had no support base. Voting issues aside, employment opportunities for African Americans seemed limited to rank-and-file laboring jobs rather than management or administrative positions. In a move that put the town decades ahead of Connecticut's major cities, however, Deep River hired African American Stephen Beale as a firefighter in 1896.[17]

In a postscript to the storied history of Deep River's African American community, some family members moved to other places. The Clarkes in New Haven and the Beatty Family in Wallingford, for instance, are descendants of the Mitchell, Williams, and Winter families. Others remained in Deep River: Robert Sturgis, for example, stayed there until his death in 1955. Winter's grandniece Florence Sturgis lived in Deep River until she passed away in 1964.[18] Two streets are named in honor of African American citizens—Winter Avenue for William Winter and Mitchell Lane for Charles Thomas Mitchell.

### New Haven

Deep River and New Haven shared a number of common characteristics with regard to the African American community. For one, both of their black communities dated from the colonial era. By the early nineteenth century, a small influx of African Americans from other parts of the state and the south added to those communities' populations. New Haven, however, had a much larger African American community: Deep River's African Americans numbered fewer than 100, while in New Haven they numbered around 600 in the 1830s.[19]

In New Haven, a number of factors offered both greater possibilities for improvement in the lives of African Americans and greater limitations. New Haven tended to be a more activist community—and suffered the consequences. William Lanson's life, as described in a later chapter, illustrates this well—especially in the 1830s. A twentieth-century description of Lanson acknowledges his leadership within the African American community. "New Guinea was the local name for the vicinity of Chapel and Franklin Streets presided over by William Lanson; tenanted chiefly by the African race. . . ."[20]

He was often at the center of events involving the African American community. His businesses enabled him to support himself, his family, and other African Americans—and yet he became the target of the white community's resentment and ended his days penniless.

Receipts from 1832 for Isaac and William Lanson's livery stable indicate that they, their family, and their friends were surviving the waves of European immigration and the new political order of Jacksonian America. But the Jacksonians tightened the grip on political democracy and the rights of citizenship for Africa Americans. Evidence of this came in the form of the refusal of city officials to support a Negro college and the passage of the so-called black laws to prevent young female students from entering the state for the purpose of attending Prudence Crandall's school in Canterbury (see essays 21 and 22). Although controversies in the lives of the Lansons were not over, in the early 1830s Lanson and his family prospered from their various enterprises and extended assistance to their local community.

Lanson was a small business owner with multiple businesses in New Haven, including a construction company that worked on extending New Haven's wharf and the Farmington Canal. He owned two livery stables that held forty horses, carriages, and harnesses.[21] He built a hotel and owned real estate, including houses he rented to more than twenty small families. Access to housing was a major problem for New Haven's African Americans because most white property owners would not rent to them. While Lanson derived income from his rental property, he also provided a needed social service for citizens who may have been forced out into the streets. In his brother Isaiah's words, Lanson also owned a "good store in the basement of the hotel; and he had a large barn, livery stable, eight or ten horses, and all kinds of carriages, and he told me he put $1,000 worth of furniture in his hotel."[22]

Despite these fortunate circumstances, life for Lanson and other New Haven African Americans was never secure. Freedom was fragile as long as slavery existed, and racial discrimination imperiled the exercise of the full rights of citizenship. Mob violence and racial attacks on African American communities occurred in the 1830s with great frequency throughout the United States. Some scholars connect this violence to animosity from displaced unemployed white Americans who felt threatened by the growing sense of autonomy and self-sufficiency of African Americans.[23] Riots erupted in the New Liberia and New Guinea sections of New Haven in 1831.

One example of white backlash against the African American

community was this account that read: "This was known as the center of vice and prostitution where blacks and whites illicitly mixed. It was raided by a white mob in 1831. Whites were dragged out and arrested, but Negroes were ignored."[24] The riot occurred along what was called Negro Lane (now State Street).

Contrary to this negative description of the New Guinea section of New Haven, authorities did not produce evidence of prostitution, and policeman Jesse Knevals testified in court that he had not seen any bad conduct in Lanson's houses. The testimony was to no avail; William Lanson became the target of legal attacks and assaults on his character; a topic examined in detail in an investigative monograph.[25]

During the early 1800s, New Haven's black population actively agitated for reforms. New Haven was a station on the Underground Railroad despite a 1793 federal law authorized federal marshals to cross state lines to retrieve fugitive slaves. Members of the extended Lanson family, including Laban, Harriet, Elizabeth, and Nancy signed petitions on behalf of escaped enslaved persons in 1838. The petitions were submitted to the state legislature. The petitioners began with the words: "We the undersigned colored inhabitants of the town of New Haven Respectfully pray your honorable body, immediately to pass a law securing a Trial by Jury, to all persons claimed in this State as fugitive slaves."[26] William Grimes was an example of someone to whom the Lansons gave assistance. He escaped slavery from Savannah, Georgia, and made it to New Haven. He wrote in his 1825 biography *The Life of William Grimes, The Runaway Slave* about his work for Isaac Lanson and Able [Abel] Lanson, "son of [Isaac] Lanson," in their livery stable. Grimes also worked with Able [Abel] quarrying stone.[27] The legislature denied the petition for a jury trial for those alleged to be fugitive slaves, but the petition and others like it reflected the growing determination of African Americans to advocate for themselves. Though the New Haven African American population remained small, such petitions went to the heart of the fears of New Haven's elite that the city was attracting too many African Americans. The Lanson family's and the New Haven African American community's association with the antislavery cause and the assistance they gave escaped fugitives was one cause of white people's animosity.

William Lanson was a member of the African Ecclesiastical Society and the African Improvement Society. He supported the two societies' efforts to provide educational opportunities for African American students. Prominent African American civic leaders, including Reverend Amos Gerry Beman, Prince Duplex, Bias Stanley, and Scipio Augusta worked with Lanson in these organizations. Lanson, Stanley, and Beman campaigned for voting rights.[28] They met at the Temple Street African Church that moved later to Dixwell Avenue and was the predecessor to the current-day Dixwell Congregational Church. The African American community that existed at the time of Lanson's election as Black Governor or King in 1825 was scattered in various pockets throughout the city.[29] Several areas marked the residences of African Americans: Negro Lane (now State Street), Samaritan Street, and "Sodom Hill." By the 1820s and 1830s, African Americans lived in the section known as Mount Pleasant, well on the fringe of the original colony.[30]

Simeon Jocelyn conceived the idea of turning this area into a model community of interracial harmony called Spireworth. (It was later named Trowbridge after a prominent New Haven merchant who built most of the houses there.)[31] The site replicated the nine-squares concept of the original New Haven settlement, with eight geometric squares surrounding a town green in the center.

In the first decades of the nineteenth century, African American communities in New Haven, Hartford, and across the state were coming together and forming institutions that would support their aspirations. They established churches and abolition and temperance societies, along with schools to more effectively educate their children. People petitioned for voting and other legal rights. African Americans were creating close-knit and mutually supportive communities in the face of increasing white resistance.

Notes

1. Database of African Americans in Farmington compiled by Dr. Charles Leach, Anne Arcari, Barbara Donahue, and other members of the Farmington Historical Society. Anne Arcari, "Freeman in Name Only," 38. In Hartford a small interracial community along the Hog River fell to nineteenth-century urban renewal and construction of Bushnell Park. U. S. Census 1800, 1810, and 1820. Sherman W. Adams and Henry R. Stiles, *The History of Ancient Wethersfield, Connecticut* (New York: The Grafton Press, 1904), 702. *Simsbury, Connecticut Births, Marriages and Deaths*, transcribed from the Town Records and published by Albert C. Bates, (Hartford: 1898), 196. *Register of the Inhabitants of the Town of Litchfield, Conn.*, (Hartford: The Case Lockwood & Brainard Company, 1900), 157. Steve Grant, "Sisters Trace Black Ancestors to 1700s in Litchfield County," *Hartford Courant*, Sunday, March 3, 2002, H8.

2. On Bristol, see Barbara Hudson, "Connecticut Freedom Trail Documentation for Bristol, Connecticut," Bristol Historical Society (2012); on Granby, see "Peter White an African by birth who died owning a $200 to $300 estate," *Public Records of the State of Connecticut*, Box 7, doc. 56, (1826); on Lisbon, see "land owner Pero Moody 1823"; and on Griswold, see "business and land owner Isaac Glasko 1823" in *Public Records of State of Connecticut*, Box 2: Folder 3.

3. On the Freeman sisters, see C. Brilvitch, *National Register of Historic Places* for Mary and Eliza Freeman's House in "Little Liberia" of Bridgeport, 1. The church history was dedicated to Alice G. Farrar, November 28, 1893–April 18, 2002. She was the oldest member of Walters Memorial AME Zion Church. *History of Walters Memorial African Methodist Episcopal Zion Church* (Bridgeport: Walters Memorial African Methodist Episcopal Zion Church, 2002), 3.

4. Henry Allen Castle, *The History of Plainville 1640–1918* (New Britain: Hitchcock Printing and Distribution Services, 1966), 22–23, 73, 81. Mrs. Ruth Hummel and Mrs. Gail Johnson Williams pointed out these documents to me in the Archives of the Plainville Historical Society.

5. Daniel J. Connors, *Deep River, The Illustrated Story of a Connecticut River Town* (Stonington: Pequot Press Inc. and The Deep River Historical Society, 1966), 31. "Niantic History," www.dickshovel.com/nian.html. The Nehantic (Niantic) and other Native American communities of the Algonquian language cluster negotiated and fought to hold onto their lands while European settlers and merchants challenged each other in the area of Fort Saybrook around the town of Saybrook in the 1600s.

6. Connors, *Deep River*, 31; Barbara W. Brown and James M. Rose, *Black Roots in Southeastern Connecticut, 1650–1900* (New London: New London County Historical Society, Inc., 2001), 522 on the Lay family and their purchase of enslaved African Americans.

7. The Condol family: Henry Condol married Sarah Ann Taylor in Deep River, October 10, 1847. He was from Lyme, and she was originally from Colchester. They lived in Deep River where Henry found employment as a mariner. They had two children. Mary was born in July 1848 in Deep River, and Henry was born the following year. Sarah died in Deep River November 18, 1853, at the age of 39. Henry was fatally shot December 5, 1857, by Elisha Miner in a story of intrigue involving Miner, a white fellow from Lyme, and Miner's wife. Connors, *Deep River*, 82, *Norwich Aurora*, December 19, 1857, Brown and Rose, *Black Roots in Southeastern Connecticut, 1650–1900*, 81–83.

8. Asaph and Sabra (Billings) Carter Family: Asaph was the son of Aaron and Rachel (Bolles) Carter. Asaph married Sabra Billings in Chatham on June 21, 1796. Between 1810 and the late 1820s, they resided in Chatham and Lyme. Their daughter Sally was born ca. 1810. Her place of birth is not listed, but apparently between the late 1820s and 1830 the family moved to Saybrook. Sally married Eli Bailey on January 30, 1826, in Saybrook. Brown and Rose state that Sally Bailey died just two years later, August 11, 1828, in Saybrook. Sally's mother, Sabra Carter, is in the 1830 census for Saybrook with six members in the household listed. Brown and Rose, *Black Roots in Southeastern Connecticut, 1650–1900*, 65. "Sally Bailey, colored wife of Eli, 18, the 8/16/1828 consumption," *Vital Records Book*, Deep River Historical

Society. This entry indicates that Sally Bailey died of tuberculosis (often called consumption) at the age of 18. Brown and Rose, *Black Roots in Southeastern Connecticut, 1650–1900*, 65, 149.

9. The Sawney and Clarissa Freeman Family: Sawney was a well-known musician throughout the area of southeastern Connecticut. He played violin and a special type of organ instrument. This was the same Sawney Freeman who entertained guests at the Black Governor's inaugural election celebrations for Caesar in Durham, Connecticut, in 1820. Clarissa and Sawney had seven children. Their first daughter, Polly, was born September 17, 1794, in East Haddam. The other six children were born in Saybrook. They were Nancy, born August 10, 1796; James, born June 15, 1798 (died March 7, 1821); Clarissa, born October 12, 1800; Mason, born January 31, 1803; William, born June 21, 1805; and Sarah, born May 19, 1815. Brown and Rose, *Black Roots in Southeastern Connecticut, 1650–1900*, 149; William Chauncey Fowler, *History of Durham, Connecticut* (Hartford: Wiley, Waterman and Eaton, 1866), 162.

10. "Billy Winters Dead," the *Deep River New Era*, November 22, 1900.

11. See also Maria Hileman, "A Former Slave's Odyssey," the *Day*, December 24–29, 2000: A 5–6.

12. Daniel Fisher/William Winters plaque on the side of the 1922 building on North Main and Winter Avenue. Deep River Land Records 44/256–8/20/1898: William Winters to Edwin Fisher–land only–bound north & east by Winters, south by Bollman & west by Winter Avenue–the grantee agrees to build a dwelling house within 2 years. See also Deep River Land Records 43/281–5/25/1899. DRLR 48/280–5/17/1919-Isidor Fox to Andrea Giardini–10 acres m/1 excepting 4 parcels sold–$2300.00–bound north by Bollman & estate of William Winters, east by Charles Mitchell, Williams, Duggan & La Place, south by Bollman's homelot & west by Winter Avenue. Deep River Land Records 48/279–5/17/1919: Estate of Henry Johnson to Isidor Fox–land & buildings–same description. Connors, *Deep River*, 32. See Winter's "Scrapbook" at the Deep River Historical Society on his property transactions. Beginning Saw Mill Southworth Property approx landing Connecticut River.

13. Connors, *Deep River*, 32. The Coulter House may be the site where Winter worked. "A Grand Christmas Entertainment, *The New Era*, IV, December 30, 1876: 30. Mrs. Charlie Mitchell played piano at the March 3, 1882 wedding at Riverview. William Winter catered the event. Mrs. Charlie [Theresa] Mitchell was the wife of Charles T. Mitchell after whom Mitchell Lane is named. See Winter's Scrapbook at the Deep River Historical Society.

14. Deep River Baptist Church, *Sketch of The Baptist Churches in Saybrook, Connecticut with the Summary of Belief Covenant, and Catalogue of Members of the Deep River Baptist Church* (Hartford: Press of Case, Lockwood & Brainard, 1870), 35, 36, Connecticut State Library Hartford, Connecticut.

15. Franklin and Moss, *From Slavery to Freedom*, 290, 445, 452. See photographs at the Deep River Historical Society.

16. *Deep River High School Alumni Association 75th Anniversary 1887–1962* (Last class graduated in 1950) and Deep River Historical Society Archives from list compiled by curator E. M. DeForest.

17. See list of Deep River Fire Department Members, Deep River Historical Society.

18. Daniel Sturgis's headstone in Fountain Hill Cemetery, Deep River, Connecticut. Daniel Sturgis was born in Snow Hill, Maryland. He died April 27, 1938. Sarah [Beale] Sturgis and Daniel Sturgis had three children. The children were Emmaline, who died Feb. 4, 1890; Florence, who died January 14, 1964; and Robert, who died March 27, 1955.

19. Rollin G. Osterweis, *Three Centuries of New Haven, 1638–1938* (New Haven: Yale University Press, 1953), 288.

20. Arthur Hughes and Morse S. Allen, *Connecticut Place Names New Haven* (Hartford: Connecticut Historical Society, 1976), 364. John Hope Franklin and Evelyn Brooks Higginbotham, *From Slavery to Freedom*, 67. Although Franklin and Higginbotham state that the election served as a way to secure obedience and loyalty, Lanson's experience does not support this conclusion.

21. See Isaiah Lanson, *Isaiah Lanson's Statement and Inquiry Concerning . . . William Lanson* (1845), 6; 1832; a list of Lanson's property including his livery stables is available at New Haven Museum and Historical Society.

22. Lanson, *Isaiah Lanson's Statement and Inquiry Concerning . . . William Lanson*, 11. U. S. Population in 1830: 12,866,020: black population: 2,328,842 (18.1%) including 319,599 free African Americans. Census data for New Haven's African Americans: Free 566; enslaved 4; total 570; Connecticut Free 8,064; enslaved 23; total 8,087, Robert Austin Warner, *New Haven Negroes* (New York: Arno Press, 1969), 201.

23. Emma Lapsansky, "Since They Got Them Separate Churches, Afro Americans and Racism in Jacksonian Philadelphia," *American Quarterly*, 32 (Spring, 1980): 54, 75.

24. Description of the riots in 1830s, excerpted from Warner's *New Haven Negroes*, 58. Gary Highsmith, "New Haven's African King," Yale Teacher's Institute. See Lanson, *Statement of Facts*, 6.

25. Katherine J. Harris, *William Lanson: The Triumph and Tragedy Entrepreneur, Political and Social Activist, Black King (Governor), Contractor on Long Wharf and the Farmington Canal Projects*, (New Haven: The Amistad Committee Inc. of New Haven, 2012), 60–63.

26. Petition for Trial for fugitive slaves, from New Haven to Legislature of the State of Connecticut, July 1838, Connecticut State Library.

27. William Grimes, *Life of William Grimes The Runaways Slave written by himself*, in *Five Black Lives*, ed. Arna Bontemps (Middletown, Connecticut: Wesleyan University Press), 107, 108, 116, [59–128].

28. Charles W. Burpee, *The Story of Connecticut* (New York: American Historical Co. Inc., 1939), 507. Warner, *New Haven Negroes: A Social History*, 46, 47, 80, 82, 85. Bias Stanley and William Lanson of New Haven, "Petition for Tax Exemption to Compensate for lack of Franchise, 1814, Connecticut State Library. The Assembly rejected the petition. Amos Gerry Beman of New Haven, "Petition to the General Assembly for the Franchise," 1841, Connecticut State Library. The Assembly rejected the petition.

29. Platt, "The Negro Governors," 333, 324. Warner, *New Haven Negroes: A Social History*, 46, 47, 80, 82, 85. Burpee, *The Story of Connecticut*, 508. Fowler, *History of Durham*, 170. Orcutt and Beardsley, *History of Derby*, 537, 550.

30. Warner, *New Haven Negroes: A Social History*, 30–31.

31. Paul Arougheti, project leader, Cristina Change, student fellow, Michael Haverland, faculty, *Trowbridge Square: Creating an Urban Village*, prepared for Trowbridge Renaissance by Yale Urban Design Workshop, (New Haven, Connecticut, 2001), 29.

*Katherine J. Harris*

# 9 Colonization and Abolition in Connecticut

The words freedom, emancipation, abolition, manumission, emigration, and colonization were sometimes used interchangeably in the long debate over solutions to the slavery crisis. In the chambers of the national government and the state of Connecticut this debate consumed much of the eighteenth and nineteenth centuries.[1]

The discussion of abolition took a number of forms. They ranged from gradual emancipation and immediate abolition to compensated emancipation. The compensated emancipation formula would support payments to slaveholders for their "property." Connecticut's Elihu Burritt endorsed this formula. As debates continued over the dilemma of abolition and freedom, however, groups of Northerners and Southerners embraced another strategy: colonization, a strategy Thomas Jefferson had proposed in his *Notes on Virginia* published in 1782 and suggested by James Monroe in 1800. Both were slaveholders and presidents of the United States.

African Americans viewed colonization as a means of defrauding them of the rights of citizenship and a way of tightening the grip of slavery.[2] For Southern pro-slavery supporters, colonization was a means to strengthen slavery by removing free African Americans who, they argued, made enslaved persons restless. Meanwhile, Northern pro-colonizationists supported colonization because they feared the activism of free African Americans and their insistence on full citizenship rights.[3]

The tragedy was that African Americans began to view their ancestral home with disdain. They dropped the use of "African" in names of their organizations with the exception of the African Masonic Lodge, the African Methodist Episcopal Church, and African Methodist Episcopal Zion church and used instead "The Colored American," the name of African American Charles B. Ray's newspaper. Tragedy and irony also lay in the colonizationists using the model of Massachusetts-born Paul Cuffe, a man of African and Native American descent and a merchant and political activist whom

Connecticut African Americans cited in their voting rights petitions to strengthen their call for the right to vote. Cuffe demonstrated that it was possible to organize and transport diasporan Africans to Africa. In 1815 Cuffe used his own funds to transport thirty-seven African Americans to Freetown, Sierra Leone, the settlement British government officials and abolitionists established to receive African American loyalists and Africans from the British Caribbean.[4] The following year, the U.S. Congress chartered the American Society for the Colonization of Free People of Color, commonly called the American Colonization Society (ACS). With a membership roster of pro-slavery advocates including Bushrod Washington (George Washington's nephew), James Monroe, Thomas Jefferson, Henry Clay, Andrew Jackson, and anti-slavery advocates John Quincy Adams, Francis Scott Key, and others, all reached a consensus that colonization or deportation would solve American racial problems.[5]

With a $100,000 appropriation and the endorsement of President James Monroe, U.S. Naval Lieutenant Robert Fieldhouse Stockton embarked upon the voyage to West Africa with twenty-eight free African Americans. Citing the benevolent intent of colonization, some Connecticut colonizationists joined the local state auxiliary of the ACS. In 1824, colonizationists named Connecticut's Jehudi Ashmun the Provisional Governor of Liberia.[6]

Colonizationists maintained that African Americans could help regenerate Africa and they would be better off there. The Reverend Leonard Bacon of New Haven was among this group. Bacon's colonization interests were not exclusive. Bacon and Theodore Dwight Woolsey, a moderate antislavery supporter, also spearheaded the formation of the African Improvement Society. They believed that African Americans should receive benevolent attention here in Connecticut. Despite the paternalistic attitudes of Woolsey and Bacon, the society was somewhat radical for the times. Membership was open to white and black citizens, men, women, and children. The board of managers included black and white members.[7] This private voluntary organization devoted its activities to civic activism, education, spreading evangelical missions, and abolition. In the meantime, Connecticut's local colonization auxiliary petitioned the General Assembly for funding. The legislature rejected the petition; however, the colonization debates intensified.[8]

White American colonizationists suggested Haiti, Central America, and Canada as possible alternative sites to residence in the United States. Hartford's African American daguerreotypist Augustus Washington suggested Mexico, which had abolished slavery in 1820. Washington himself remained in Hartford and worked with abolitionists, but he subsequently emigrated to Liberia in 1853.[9] Black American interest in emigration dimmed as colonizationists continued to advocate removal of free African Americans. Anti-colonizationists in the African American community argued that leaving the United States would mean abandonment of their rights as citizens and desertion of enslaved friends, kin, and the fight to end slavery. Maria Miller Stewart of Hartford, Connecticut, addressed a Boston audience on the subject in 1833. In what was reportedly the first public address delivered by an American-born woman, she identified herself as a "daughter of Africa" but rebuked the colonization movement.[10]

Although the abolitionist movement was still in its early phase in 1833 when Stewart gave her address, white and black abolitionists often viewed situations differently. For example, William Lloyd Garrison started his social activism as a colonizationist and supported gradual rather than immediate abolitionism, but the abolitionist cause in Connecticut received a boost in the mid 1830s from the African American religious community, which advocated more rapid change. Ministers such as James W. C. Pennington at the Talcott Street Congregational Church, those at the "Freedom Churches," as the African Methodist Episcopal Zion churches were known, the African Methodist Episcopal Church, and other African American religious and civic groups embraced abolitionism more forcefully than others in the abolition movement.

Ministers who served at Bridgeport's Walters Memorial African Methodist Episcopal Zion Church were all abolitionists. From the pulpit they rallied their congregations to worship while fighting racism and oppression. Rev. D. Vandevere [or Vanderere], Rev. I. W. Hood, Rev. John Taylor, and Rev. Leonard Collins served in the Bridgeport church and worked throughout the Pennsylvania, New York, and New England conferences to promote the abolition of slavery. Their strong sermons and defiant strategies lent the abolitionist movement an air of importance. The ministers' actions further developed the abolitionist movement and the Underground Railroad. Strategies included the organization of a speakers' bureau through which formerly enslaved persons would talk about their slave experiences to sympathetic white Americans. Among the best known of these speakers was Frederick Douglass. An early minister of Walters Memorial African Methodist Episcopal Zion Church Rev. William Serrington met Douglass fresh out of slavery while Serrington was serving as pastor in New Bedford, Massachusetts, at the Second Street A.M.E. Zion Church in 1838.[11]

The abolitionist movement in New England gave a safe haven to runaway enslaved persons who found refuge in Bridgeport's "Little Liberia," at least until the Fugitive Slave Law of 1850 authorized fines and arrests of individuals who aided fugitives and reinforced the authority of slave owners and federal marshals to cross state lines to apprehend alleged fugitives. Meanwhile, abolitionists kept the pressure on government officials. In 1844, Connecticut Governor Roger Sherman Baldwin proposed legislation to abolish slavery. The General Assembly opposed the law. But legislators introduced the abolition bill again in 1848. Connecticut's business community still reaped profits from slavery's cotton destined for Connecticut mills, and slavery's corollary commercial transactions in banking, shipping, insurance, and federal tariff policies. By the 1840s, though, there were few enslaved African Americans in Connecticut, and the abolition law passed. The legislation did not end the abolition and colonization debate in Connecticut or the nation. That debate continued into the 1860s. Nevertheless, when Connecticut's last enslaved person, Nancy Toney of Windsor, died in 1857, her death marked the end of an era of more than two hundred years of slavery in Connecticut.[12]

## Notes

1. On Connecticut and profits from the slave trade and slavery see, Anne Farrow, Joel Lang, Jenifer Frank, *Complicity: How the North Promoted, Prolonged, and Profited from Slavery*, 34, 51, 54, 51–65, 78, 114–15. Constitution of the United States, Fifth Amendment, 1789.

2. Thomas Jefferson, *Notes on the State of Virginia*, 1782.

3. Franklin and Higginbotham, *From Slavery to Freedom: A History of African Americans*, 180.

4. On Cuffee, emigration, and colonization, see Franklin and Higginbotham, *From Slavery to Freedom*, 124–25, 179, 181.

5. *National Intelligencer*, December 24, 1816, December 31, 1816 and January 3, 1817 (Rare Book Room, Cornell University, Ithaca, New York).

6. Samuel John Bayard, (ed), *A Sketch of the Life of Com. Robert F. Stockton with Appendix . . .* (New York: Derby & Jackson, 1856), 42. Copy of "Treaty between Robert F. Stockton and Eli Ayres, and chiefs of Mesurado," December 15, 1821, Jehudi Ashmun's Papers. Ministry of Foreign Affairs, Republic of Liberia. Documents researched between 1978 and 1979. After a protracted exchange with local Dey, Bassa, and other African sovereigns of what was known in 1821 as the Ducoh Corridor, Stockton secured at gunpoint the concession of land that formed the nucleus of the United States' informal colony of Monrovia, Liberia.

7. Warner, *New Haven Negroes*, 46, 47, 80. Randall K. Burkett, "The Reverend Harry Croswell and Black Episcopalians in New Haven 1820–1860," *The North Star*, 7: 1 (Fall 2003): 4–5.

8. Prof. Benjamin Silliman at Yale College, Seth Terry Esq., of Hartford, and the Treasurer, Honorable John S. Peters of Hebron, the Honorable Ebenezer Young of Killingly, Reverends Joel H. Linsley of Hartford, Samuel Merwin of New Haven, Thomas H. Gallaudet, and Honorable Seth P. Beers of Litchfield were among the founding members of the Connecticut Colonization Society in 1828. *Report of The Joint Select Committee on African Colonization*, 130A-130H Connecticut General Assembly, (Connecticut State Library, Hartford, Connecticut). On voluntary associations, see *International Encyclopedia of the Social Sciences* (New York, 1968), VI: 362–63. Warner, *New Haven Negroes*, 80. Burkett, "The Reverend Harry Croswell and Black Episcopalians in New Haven, 1820–1860," 4.

9. Franklin and Higginbotham, *From Slavery to Freedom*, 178–80, 181–97. Washington emigrated in 1853, see George Sullivan, *Black Artists in Photography 1840–1940* (Dutton, New York: Cobblehill Books, 1996), 23–37.

10. Franklin and Higginbotham, *From Slavery To Freedom*, 179–80, 181–97. Bert James Loewenberg and Ruth Bogin, *Black Women in Nineteenth-Century American Life* (University Park and London: The Pennsylvania State University, 1976), 196–97.

11. For the relationship between Douglass and Serrington, see William Jacob Walls, *African Methodist Episcopal Church: Reality of the Black Church* (Charlotte, North Carolina: A.M.E. Zion Publishing House, 1974), 149 and 150. *Church History of Walters Memorial African Methodist Episcopal Zion Church* (Bridgeport, Connecticut: Walters Memorial African Methodist Episcopal Zion Church, 2002).

12. Connecticut Abolition of Slavery 1848. On Toney, see Connecticut Freedom Trail: www.ctfreedomtrail.org/trail/concept-of-freedom/sites/#!/palisado-cemetery.

*Katherine J. Harris*

# 10  The Black Governors, 1780 to 1856

For African Americans, the late eighteenth and nineteenth centuries brought renewed battles for the abolition of slavery and the rights of citizenship. The struggle for these twin goals coincided with the continuation of the Black Governor elections. These became the staging ground for African American assertiveness and a symbol of political leadership. An earlier essay in this volume on the topic traced African political traditions and the origins of the elections of the Black Governors from 1749 to 1780, with commentary on the nineteenth century. This essay resumes the exploration of this ceremonial African American leadership position from the late eighteenth century to 1856, with a selective look at several of Connecticut's Black Governors.

Black Governors' advocacy for the right to vote and other rights of citizenship, along with their participation in the fight to abolish slavery, distinguishes them from their white American political counterparts who, among their other duties, were bound to protect slavery as a constitutional right. Slavery had been a legal institution in Connecticut since the colonial period. The U.S. Constitution legalized slavery in the entire United States under the property provision of the Fifth Amendment—enslaved African Americans were legally defined as property. While there was no explicit provision in the state constitution that required Connecticut state governors to protect slavery, they were obligated to uphold Connecticut's proslavery statutes and the U.S. Constitution. Connecticut Governor Roger Sherman Baldwin introduced legislation to abolish slavery in 1844. It failed. Furthermore, during the early republic and leading into the Jacksonian era of the 1820s and 1830s, legislatures across the country constricted the provisions for the right to vote for African Americans. These provisions extended the right to vote to all white American men age twenty-one or older regardless of property ownership. In Connecticut, African Americans were excluded from voting by law. It is in this context that the Black Governors elections continued until 1856.[1]

Research on the life of Farmington's Black Governor Peter Freeman, who lived from 1752 to 1826, reveals a detailed picture of his enslavement, freedom, land ownership, military service, retirement, and election in 1780. As noted in the introductory essay on the Black Governors, Peter Freeman was the child of enslaved parents Cuff and Phebe Freeman, who were originally from Middletown.[2] Peter and his father Cuff made several land transactions that resulted in their owning some 94 acres of land located along the Farmington, Plainville, and Bristol town lines. Peter and Cuff raised such crops as wheat and traded rye and other products with their white American and African American neighbors.

A February 22, 1851, article in a supplement to the *Connecticut Courant* offered a view of Freeman and his prominent role in the community. The author is thought to be William S. Porter, who recorded Farmington and Hartford's local history.

I would add the name of Peter Freeman, well remembered by persons of middle . . . and old age. Cuff and Peter Freeman were owners of a large farm in the west part of Farmington and were good . . . citizens, but the decision of Judge Judson . . . [has] denied them that title. Peter Freeman was for several years elected governor of the blacks . . . a man [with?] more than common intelligence and well versed in history. He served honorably through the Revolutionary war; and keenly felt the dishonor and injustice put upon him when, after fighting side by side with his white brother . . . he was denied the privilege of going up with him to the ballot box.[3]

Although Porter's commentary was vague as to Freeman's specific duties as Governor of Farmington's African American community, the commentary, nevertheless, offers an important description of Freeman when his memory was still fresh in Porter's mind. He highlighted Freeman's intelligence and military service and the denial of his right to vote. This circumstance may have compelled him to use his leadership position as Black Governor as an opportunity to express a political voice within his community even as he continued to pursue the franchise.

Freeman served as mediator in matters involving Farmington's African American members and the white community, possibly dealing with land and economic transactions. He also presided over ceremonies for special occasions. The research thus far has not uncovered any specific occasions, but African Americans in Farmington may have celebrated the U.S. Constitutional provision that ended the transatlantic slave trade in 1808. This first annual holiday, specifically for the African American community, was initiated by African Americans in Boston, New York, and Philadelphia.[4] Since William S. Porter recorded that Freeman was elected Governor several times, not only once in 1780, he may have led celebrations for this important occasion.[5]

Freeman was also Governor in Farmington at the same time as Peleg Nott served as Governor in Hartford. While the process of rotating the elections from town to town receives fleeting attention in available records, it appears that Farmington, Wethersfield, and Hartford were not the only sites at which those elections were held. For a time, Derby served as the location for the elections and associated festivities, beginning with Quash (or Quosh) Freeman in 1810.

Quash was the enslaved man of Agar Tomlinson at Derby Neck. Tomlinson owned a large estate and a number of enslaved persons. Quash, "a native African,"[6] was stolen when he was a boy and sold to slave traders. The name Quash/Quosh is possibly derived from the Akan name "Kwasi," the name given in Ghana and the Ivory Coast to a male child born on Sunday. As he grew to manhood, Quash became a man of great size and Herculean strength, according to descriptions of him in Orcutt and Beardsley's *History of Derby*. Another local historian in Derby, Jane Shelton, writes that the enslaved persons on Tomlinson's estate were under Quash's immediate control.[7] This description of Quash also appeared in Orcutt's history, but he added that Quash "bossed" his master.[8]

Tomlinson emancipated Quash in 1800. Quash's wife, Rose, was enslaved by a Reverend Mr. Yale. The record is not exactly clear on the date, but Rose was emancipated as well. Quash received a little house on a tract of land in town, a barn, a yoke for oxen, a cow, and farm implements.[9] After his emancipation, he gave himself the name "Freeman."

Maps point to the site of what is now Osbornedale State Park as the location of the Freeman household. Information on Governor Quash's date of birth, death, and burial site has not been located. The 1810 U.S. census listed a Quash Freeman of Derby. His age was not recorded; the notation of his race as "Black" with five people in the family is all that the census records reveal.[10] (We do know that Quash and Rose had one son, Roswell. In 1830, he too was elected Black Governor of Derby.)

Apparently Quash served for five years as Derby's head of state for the African American community. This description affirms the seriousness and significance of Derby's elections of this Black Governor. Quash was no longer enslaved when elected in 1810. According to Shelton's article "The New England Negro," reprinted in *The Valley Drummer*, "The Negroes did not consider their pageant, their military drill, and the election as essentially humorous. It was one of their few symbols of dignity. Quash, the slave of Agar Tomlinson, was rendered so proud by his elevation to office that the local saying was that Uncle Agar (Quash's master) lived with the Governor."[11] A description of one of Quash's assistants notes, "Little Roman (his wife's name was Venus), who was so short that his sword dragged on the ground, was Lieutenant Governor under Quash."[12]

In 1815, Tobias (or Tobiah) succeeded Quash Freeman as Governor. Our information about Tobias comes from his grandson Ebenezer Bassett. Tracing briefly the family's history, Bassett wrote: "My father, Eben the Elder was the great-grandson of an African Prince. His father Tobias, or Tobiah was "raised" in the family of Capt. Wooster of Derby, fought in the war of independence, and was recognized as a man of tact, courage and unusual intelligence for a person of his time and condition."[13]

Several entries for the name Tobias or Tobiah appear in the U.S. census records. It is not definitively clear that the entries are for the Tobias who was a Derby Black Governor, but David O. White's *Connecticut's Black Soldiers 1775–1783* contains a brief reference to Tobias Pero of Derby. According to White's research, Pero was granted his freedom to serve in the War of Independence by the selectmen of Derby. Pero's brief biography matches Ebenezer Bassett's description of his grandfather, which is cross-referenced in Lorenzo Greene's *The Negro in Colonial New England 1620–1776*.

Tobias or Tobiah, a "governor" who was the slave of Captain Wooster of Derby, fought in the patriot army and his son, Eben Tobias, the property of Squire Bassett of Derby, also held office.[14]

Information regarding Tobias's parents, his wife, and his residence and burial site has not been located. He had a son, Eben Tobias, who was also a Black Governor.

Roswell Freeman served as the Black Governor of Derby from 1830 to 1837. Often called Roswell Quosh, he was Rose and Quash Freeman's only son. Roswell was very tall, very thin, and very dark, according to contemporary descriptions. Shelton's article contains an 1894 interview with Nancy, Roswell's widow, which adds a humane touch to the piece. But even as she noted that Roswell was a skilled fox hunter, the author did not resist the opportunity to degrade African Americans: She surmised that Roswell's skill as a hunter was "because the Negro is not as far removed from primitive life as the white man that he seems to have more comprehension of the animal creation."[15] Still, Shelton described Roswell and Nancy as "marked figures in the colored ranks. No one of higher standard of right, better principles, kinder instincts as friend and neighbor was more respected in his position worthy of good esteem."[16]

Nancy was born free, but her parents were enslaved. Her father was Daniel Thompson, and her mother was Tamar Steele. Nancy said that when she was nine years old she went to live with Truman Coe on Coe's Lane on Derby Hill. She stayed there until she was eighteen years old. When she was sixteen, she later recalled, "Roswell came and asked if I would accept of his company, and I accepted of it."[17] She waited two years to marry. "I was awful proud to marry the Gov'nor's son."[18] Nancy was a devoted churchwoman but was forced to worship in the gallery. Her dignity and status as the Black Governor's wife did not save her from this stigma of segregation.

Freeman emphasized the significance of the celebration of May Day, training day, and the Governor's election. The elections were on occasion held in Humphreysville and Oxford, but generally they took place at Hawkins Point in Derby. The site, near water and open space, recreated the setting of an African tradition of holding such important events in a natural setting rather than behind closed doors. Orcutt described Roswell Freeman as being less popular than other governors, "for he was opposed to 'treating' on election day."[19]

A newspaper notice published around 1820 or 1830 publicized the election:

ATTENTION, FREEMEN!
There will be a general election of the colored gentlemen of Connecticut, October first, twelve o'clock, noon. The day will be celebrated in the evening by a dance at Warner's tavern, when it will be shown that there is some power left in muscle, catgat [sic], and rosin.

By order of the Governor,
From Headquarters[20]

The vote was sometimes taken *viva voce*, Ebenezer Bassett notes in his letter to Platt. The notice above refers to an election of "colored gentlemen of Connecticut" not just of Derby."[21] The notice does not specifically mention women. Whether women voted always, sometimes, or not at all has not been documented.

Roswell Freeman served as Black Governor for seven years. He died on October 6, 1877 at age seventy-four. Nancy was ninety-one when she gave her 1894 interview to Shelton. The Freeman family name appears in the U.S. census records throughout the nineteenth century. An approximate location of the Roswell and Nancy Freeman homestead has been located in Derby in what is now part of the Kellogg Environmental Center. Both Roswell and Nancy Freeman are interred in Bare Plains Cemetery in Ansonia, Connecticut.[22]

Warner's Tavern, the scene of many of the Black Governor festivities, no longer stands in Derby, but memories passed down through the generations relay the history of Derby's Black Governor. To flesh out that information, teams of researchers are investigating the site of the Freeman homestead, where descendants lived until 1911.

During the decade between the end of Roswell Freeman's term as Black Governor and the election of Derby's next governor, New Haven's black community elected three governors, William Lanson, Quash Piere, and Thomas Johnson. They served during tumultuous years characterized by racial rioting, an interracial alliance of activists and abolitionists who called for the establishment of a black college, an influx of European immigration, urban expansion, and the hardening of New Haven's Protestant commercial elite's control over New Haven society. As discussed in essay 8, all of these governors were tarnished. Authorities arrested Lanson repeatedly (see also essay 14), levied frequent fines upon him, and charged him with keeping a loud house, or allowing men and women to fraternize inappropriately at his boarding houses and businesses. He was arrested and stripped of his property.[23]

New Haven officials enforced antiquated laws in their dealings with Quash Piere, a person of blended heritage, or, as one account describes him, "a mulatto from the West Indies, [who] was brought to New Haven by Captain William Pinto."[24] The African American community elected him while he was enslaved; as the criteria for the Governor were based on character, he must have exhibited some special quality that his supporters respected. Piere was so elated with his election that he had a gold-headed cane made and inscribed "Quash Piere, Governor of Connecticut." His elation did not last long. New Haven officials accused Piere of theft, their accusation based on evidence that could easily be considered circumstantial. They arrested him and levied fines against him.

Despite the less than solid case against Piere, New Haven's black community took the matter seriously. Orville Platt's article "Negro Governors" contained an excerpt from a letter that described the African American community's response: "the negroes called a convention and deposed him and elected Thomas Johnson of New Haven, in his place."[25] Johnson was a "car man" or stagecoach driver in the employ of merchants Timothy and Stephen Bishop on State Street. Johnson remained in office for four years. Platt's article is the only known source of information about Johnson's unhappy demise as Governor. He too was brought to court and charged with violating an antiquated law that prohibited poker playing. New Haven officials arrested Johnson, and the magistrate fined him four dollars. Platt quotes from a letter written by Mr. C. S. A. Davis, the presiding magistrate in Johnson's case, to the Honorable N. D. Sperry.[26] The letter read:

In the year of 1837, when I was trying magistrate of New Haven, there were eleven negroes brought before me for playing poker. They all pleaded guilty and I fined them four dollars each and costs, as the statute required, and they all paid the fine costs, among the number was Governor Johnson, and I think he was the last Governor that was elected by the negroes as the custom was given up about that time.[27]

Johnson's arrest marked the end of his term as Black Governor. The arrest also ended the elections in New Haven. Given the growing uneasiness of New Haven's commercial and political elite over African aspirations for political rights as expressed through numerous petitions submitted to the General Assembly, interracial cooperation to build a black college, and interracial cooperation and leadership in voluntary associations such as the African Improvement Society and the African Ecclesiastical Society, it's not clear whether the demise of the Black Governor elections in New Haven was the desired outcome of the arrests and harassments of Lanson, Piere, and Johnson. However, the elections did not cease altogether; they moved back to Derby in 1840 with the election of Eben Tobias.

Eben Tobias was sometimes called Black Eben or Eben the Elder. He was the son of Tobias Pero, a Black Governor of Derby. A biographer of Eben Tobias also recorded his name as Tobias Bassett. Black Eben was sometimes called by his father's first name, just as Roswell Freeman was sometimes called Roswell Quash. Eben Tobias was married to Susan Gregory Bassett, a Native American of the Schaghticoke branch of the Pequot ethnic group. The couple

**Table 10-1**
*Connecticut's Black Governors, 1800–1856*

| Name | Town | Date |
|---|---|---|
| Boston Nichols | | |
|     owner James Nichols | Hartford | 1800 |
| *Deptford Billings | New London | 1804 |
| Quash Freeman | Derby | 1810 |
| Ira Tossett* | Norwich | 1811? |
| Tobias Pero | Derby | 1815 |
|     Capt. Wooster, owner or guardian | | |
| Caesar | Durham | 1820 |
| Juba Weston** | Derby | 1825 |
|     enslaved or free, status is unclear | | |
| William Lanson | New Haven | 1825 |
| Lyman Homer | Plainville | 1830 |
| Roswell Freeman | Derby | 1830–1837 |
| Quash Piere | New Haven | 1832 |
|     owner Captain William Piere, West Indies | | |
| Thomas Johnson | New Haven | 1833–1837 |
| Eben Tobias (Bassett) | Derby | 1840 |
| Cuff | Woodbridge | 1840 |
| Nelson Weston | Seymour | 1850 |
| Wilson Weston | Seymour | 1855 or 1856 |

* Black Governors identified by Katherine J. Harris, Ph.D., 2002
** Juba Weston is listed as a Black Governor on the list compiled by Greene in *The Negro in New England* and as being a slave of the David Humphreys family. Juba Weston lived on the property of Humphreys's uncle Judge John L. Humphreys.

moved to Litchfield, where their son Ebenezer Bassett was born on October 16, 1833. He came to Derby as an infant with his parents.[28]

Ebenezer Bassett provided a biography of his father in a letter to Platt. Bassett wrote: "My father was a mulatto, born in the family of Squire Bassett of Derby, the day of the battle of Trafalgar, October 21st, 1805." According to his son Ebenezer Bassett, Eben was a descendant of an African prince, but the rest of his lineage was less clear. The term "mulatto" was used to describe persons of mixed African and Native American descent and those of mixed European and African ancestry. Writing about his father, however, Bassett explained:

He inherited somewhat more than his father's natural intelligence, and was of the very finest physical mould, being over six feet tall and admirably proportioned. He was besides, ready of speech and considered quite witty . . . within the two years I have heard them used by speakers at the reunions of our Republican League in New Haven.[29]

Eben Tobias was one of five candidates who met in the area of the Old Point House (Orcutt and Beardsley's *History of Derby* does not record the date) to decide the election on the test of strength. Tobias was the victor and became Derby's next Black Governor. Orcutt wrote that the Black Governor lent an imposing character to the ceremony. Orcutt also described the feathers, flowers, and ribbons of red, white, and blue that the Governor wore as "most laughable."[30] This was apparently the point. Ebenezer Bassett stated that a farcical military display was sometimes a part of the festivities for the Black Governor's election. Bassett described additional details about his father and his election:

Under the circumstances herein referred to, it is altogether natural that he should be, as he actually was, brought forward and "elected" one of the so-called "Negro Governors" of Connecticut. I remember that he held the office two or three terms, and I remember, too, how Sundays and nights he used to pore over books on military tactics and study up the politics of the State.[31]

Orcutt commented that the method of choosing or electing the governor changed to meet the wishes of the candidates. "They had no ballot stuffing, returning boards, or corrupt and civilized practice of buying votes." The descriptions also reflect the merging of aspects of African political traditions, such as *viva voce* voting and holding festivities near water, and the American tradition of balloting.

The previous paragraphs synopsize a longer inquiry into the tradition of Connecticut's Black Governors. Those officials served not only in the towns mentioned in the preceding passages but also in Litchfield, Norwich, Durham, Humphreysville, Plainville, Woodbridge, and Seymour.

Nelson and Wilson Weston were the last of the Black Governors. They were the sons of Juba Weston, who also served as Black Governor in Derby. Details about Weston's term as Black Governor, the location of elections, and his exact residence have been difficult to pinpoint because of the municipal changes in the area. Names and jurisdictions changed from Chusetown, to Derby, Ansonia, Shelton, Humphreysville, and finally Seymour. Recent discoveries of birth and church records have filled in some of the gaps.

Available records do not state why the elections ended in 1855 or 1856. It is possible that the rising tide of antislavery/proslavery conflict interrupted the continuation of the election of the Black Governors and the Civil War between 1861 and 1865 disrupted the tradition entirely. After the war the African American struggle in Connecticut to obtain full voting rights as citizens overtook the election of the Black Governors. The long tradition of symbolic political participation, however, had sustained a sense of political empowerment throughout a period when African American humanity was often under siege.[32]

## Notes

1. See the essay in this volume "In Remembrance of Their Kings of Guinea."

2. For details on the life of Peter Freeman and his family, see Anne J. Arcari, "Freeman in Name Only: The African American in Colonial Farmington, Connecticut," 35, 36. Copy of the thesis is in the Connecticut Historical Society. Arcari appended copies of original deeds, emancipation papers and enlistment papers. David O. White, *Connecticut's Black Soldiers 1775–1783*, 58. Peter served 1777–1783 and Cuff served 1777–1782. See Greene, *The Negro in New England*, 92–93. *War Pensioners* lists, 61, copy in Arcari files. Frank Landon Humphreys, *The Life and Times of David Humphreys 1752–1818 Diary of David Humphreys* (New York: G.P. Putnam, 1917), I: 192.

3. "Black Governors," *Connecticut Courant*, February 22, 1851.

4. On the U. S. Constitution's provision abolishing transatlantic slave trade and African American celebrations, see Franklin and Higginbotham, *From Slavery to Freedom*, 112. For more on the Freeman family and Farmington, see Arcari, "Freeman in Name Only," 38. U. S. Census 1800, 1810 and 1820.

5. "Black Governors," *Connecticut Courant*, February 22, 1851.

6. Shelton, "The New England Negro, a Remnant," *Harper's New Monthly Magazine* (March 1894), 536. Greene, *The Negro in Colonial New England 1620–1776*, 252

7. Shelton, "The New England Negro," 536.

8. Orcutt and Beardsley, *History of the Town of Derby, Connecticut 1642–1880*, 548.

9. Orcutt and Beardsley, *History of the Town of Derby, Connecticut*, 548. Shelton, "The New England Negro," 536. Dr. Lorenzo Greene confirmed these details and wrote: "The first 'governor' of Derby, Connecticut, was Quosh, the slave of Agar Tomlinson of Derby Neck, where a branch of the Tomlinson family (1941) still resides." Greene, *The Negro in Colonial New England 1620–1776*, 252.

10. Orcutt and Beardsley, *History of the Town of Derby, Connecticut*, 548. United States Census 1810 in the Connecticut State Library, Hartford, Connecticut.

11. *The Valley Drummer* (Derby, Connecticut; Archives of the Derby Historical Society, January 15, 1987); Shelton, "The New England Negro" 536. Warner, *New Haven Negroes*, 9–10.

12. Shelton, "The New England Negro," 536.

13. Bassett's letter was quoted in Platt, "Negro Governors," 331.

14. See Greene, *The Negro in Colonial New England 1620–1776*, 252. See also David O. White, *Connecticut's Black Revolutionary War Soldiers*, 44.

15. Shelton, "The New England Negro," 537.

16. Shelton, "The New England Negro," 537. On Roswell Freeman 1803–1877, the year of Governor Roswell Freeman's birth was calculated based on the genealogy of Derby that records Roswell's death in 1877. Orcutt and Beardsley, *The History of Derby*, 548–550.

17. Shelton, "The New England Negro," 537–38. Nancy did not describe her work at Mr. Coe's. She said she stayed with Mr. Coe another year to work to get a cow and the following year a feather bed, perhaps a sort of trousseau for her marriage. Nancy described the wedding, dress, and cake. Roswell and Nancy had thirteen children. Orcutt and Beardsley, *The History of Derby*, 548–50.

18. Shelton, "The New England Negro," 537–38; Orcutt, *The History of Derby*, 549–50.

19. Orcutt and Beardsley, *The History of Derby*, 550.

20. This notice appeared in Orcutt, *The History of Derby*, 550. Orcutt wrote that the notice was printed more than fifty years ago. He published his book in 1880, so the notice may have been for elections in the 1820s or 1830s.

21. Platt, "Negro Governors," 332.

22. Platt, "Negro Governors," 548. Shelton, "The New England Negro," 537. Roswell Freeman of Derby was listed in the 1840 census as age 24, black, and with 9 members in the family. He was listed also in the 1850 census in Derby age 45 with nine in the family.

23. Katherine J. Harris, *William Lanson: Triumph and Tragedy: Entrepreneur, Political and Social Activist, Black King (Governor), Contractor on Long Wharf and the Farmington Canal Projects* (New Haven: The Amistad Committee Inc., 2010), 60–63.

24. Platt, "Negro Governors," 334. The term "mulatto" is used to refer to a person with African and European parents. But caution is urged because the term was often arbitrarily applied to persons based on complexion in the eighteenth and nineteenth centuries.

25. Warner, *New Haven Negroes*, 124.

26. Platt, "Negro Governors," 334.

27. Platt, "Negro Governors," 334.

28. Rayford Logan, and Michael R. Winston, *Dictionary of American Negro Biography* (New York and London: Norton and Co., 1982), 32. Platt, "Negro Governors," 331. Orcutt and Beardsley, *The History of Derby*, 550. "Tobias, the elder alias Black Eben was the father of E. D. Bassett our Haytian Minister [Ambassador]." Platt, "Negro Governors," 550.

29. Platt, "Negro Governors," 550.

30. Orcutt, *The History of Derby*, 550: "In the area of the Old Point House well, five candidates participated in contest to be the first to ascend a steep sand bank that reach down into the Ousatonic turnpike." Bassett's letter quoted in Platt, "Negro Governors," 332.

31. Platt, "The Negro Governors," 332.

32. For more on these points, see Warner, *New Haven Negroes*, 34–35, 94–95, 122–23.

# 11 James Mars

James Mars (1790–1880), a religious leader, activist, farmer, and writer who was born into slavery, analyzed the social and political challenges facing nineteenth-century Connecticut through the dramatic story of his family's escape from slavery and his years of public service. His observations were documented in the *Life of James Mars, a Slave Born and Sold in Connecticut. Written by Himself* (Case Lockwood Company, 1868), a copy of which is held in the collection of The Amistad Center for Art & Culture. That book is excerpted here.

Mars proved a faithful witness to and a prescient commentator on issues of equality, racial privilege, faith, and citizenship. Born into slavery in Connecticut, he gained freedom in his early twenties through the gradual emancipation law enacted by the state in 1784. His defiance in supporting independent black churches, facilitating the escape and legal defense of an enslaved southerner living in Connecticut, advancing petitions to the legislature, and writing an autobiography defined Mars as an engaged critic on the issues of his day—many of which are now critical issues for ours. These issues—inequality in the experience of black and white youth, the fight for full citizenship, and the struggle to retain one's humanity while fighting or surviving injustice—are reflected in the excerpts reprinted here.

Although there are other Connecticut-based slave narratives (Venture Smith, James Pennington), the drama and compassion of Mars's story, his skillful portrayal, and his good luck in being a portrait subject combined to make him a recognizable presence and his life an American parable. He survived the horrors of slavery and went on to live a productive life influenced by religious teachings. Mars fought against slavery but was able to forgive those who held slaves. For Mars that meant reconciling with Mr. Munger, who kept him until he was an adult, but with whom he later became and remained friends. Of the varied labors Mars performed, both as a slave

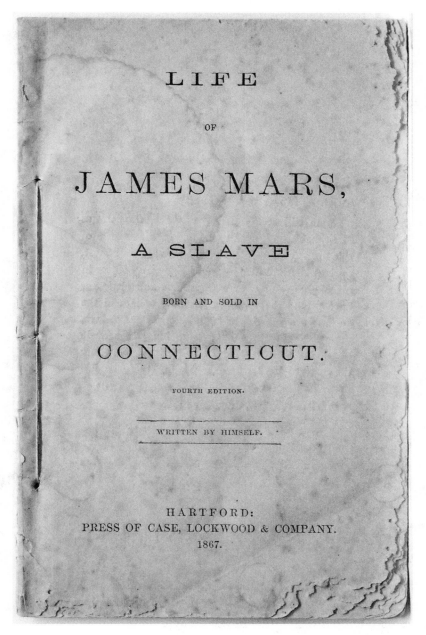

FIGURE II-I James Mars, *Life of James Mars, A Slave Born and Sold in Connecticut Written by Himself,* 1867. *The Amistad Center for Art & Culture, Inc., Simpson Collection, 1987.1.3172*

and as a free man, it is the totality of his life's work as recounted in his autobiography that draws us back for repeated readings, references, and interpretations.

I soon found that I was to live or stay with the man until I was twenty-five. I found that white boys who were bound out, were bound until they were twenty-one. I thought that rather strange, for those boys told me they were to have one hundred dollars when their time was out. They would say to me sometimes, "You have to work four years longer than we do, and get nothing when you have done, and we get one hundred dollars, a Bible, and two suits of clothes." This I thought of . . . I had now got to be in my sixteenth year, when a little affair happened, which, though trivial in itself, yet was of consequence to me. It was in the season of the haying, and we were going to the hayfield after a load of hay. Mr. Munger and I were in the cart, he sitting on one side and I on the other. He took the fork in both of his hands, and said to me very pleasantly, "Don't you wish you were stout enough to pull this away from me?" I looked at him, and said, "I guess I can;" but I did not think so. He held it towards me with both his hands hold of the stale. I looked at him and then at the fork, hardly daring to take hold of it, and wondering what he meant, for this was altogether new. He said, "Just now see if you can do it." I took hold of it rather reluctantly, but I shut my hands right. I did as Samson did in the temple; I bowed with all my might and he came to me very suddenly. The first thought that was in my mind was, my back is safe now. . . .

. . . Although born and raised in Connecticut, yes, and lived in Connecticut more than three-fourths of my life it has been my privilege to vote at five Presidential elections. Twice it was my privilege and pleasure to help elect the lamented and murdered Lincoln, and if my life is spared I intend to be where I can show that I have the principles of a man, and act like a man, and vote like a man, but not in my native State; I cannot do it there, I must remove to the old Bay State for the right to be a man. Connecticut, I love thy name, but not thy restrictions. I think the time is not far distant when the colored man will have his rights in Connecticut.[1]

## Notes

This essay originally appeared in the May/June/July 2004 issue of *Connecticut Explored*.

1. *Life of James Mars, a Slave Born and Sold in Connecticut. Written by Himself* (Hartford: Case Lockwood Company, 1868). The complete text of *Life of James Mars, a Slave Born and Sold in Connecticut. Written by Himself* can be accessed on line at http://docsouth.unc.edu/neh/mars/menu.html. Also, Mars's grave in Norfolk's Center Cemetery is a site on the Connecticut Freedom Trail.

*Cora Murray and
Whitney Bayers*

# 12  Black Abolitionists Speak

As previous essays have noted, blacks had resisted slavery and fought for its abolition even before the formation of the Union in 1776. In 1779, 1780, and 1788 blacks petitioned the Connecticut General Assembly for "the abolition of Slavery in Connecticut." Here we feature the words of some of Connecticut's leading black abolitionists, spoken and written as they strove to be front and center in all aspects of the struggle for their human rights.

Three generations of Middletown's Beman family played leadership roles in championing the causes of anti-slavery and temperance. Jehiel and his son Amos were ministers. Jehiel's daughter-in-law Clarissa Beman established a chapter of the Colored Female Anti-Slavery Society in Middletown.

I am one of those who believe that colored men best know their own wants and grievances, and are best capable of stating them. Let our white friends, if they wish to help us, give us their countenance and money, and *follow* rather than *lead* us.

—AMOS G. BEMAN, letter to the editor of *Colored American*,
March 23, 1841. Beman Collection, the Yale Collection of American
Literature, Beinecke Rare Book and Manuscript Library.

[T]o think that my father faced the cannon's mouth for this country's liberty, and I and my brother [are] still bound.

—JEHIEL C. BEMAN, letter to the editor of an
unknown African-American publication, August 10, 1844.
Beman Collection, the Yale Collection of American Literature,
Beinecke Rare Book and Manuscript Library.

Who would be free, themselves must strike the blow—the rights of no people are safe in the hands of their political enemies.

—AMOS G. BEMAN, date unknown.
Beman Collection, the Yale Collection of American Literature,
Beinecke Rare Book and Manuscript Library.

Reverend Dr. James W. C. Pennington, a fugitive slave, made his escape from Maryland by way of the Underground Railroad to Connecticut in 1827. He became a minister at Fifth (Talcott Street) Congregational Church in Hartford and traveled to Europe, where, in 1849, the University of Heidelberg, Germany presented him with an honorary Doctorate of Divinity. Pennington was also pro-emigration and helped organize missions to Africa.

To the Declaration of Independence. That Declaration places personal liberty among the inalienable rights of all men. If personal liberty be thus the inalienable right of every man, then *no* power on earth can alienate it—not even the Constitution which is twelve years younger than the Declaration. And we must need assume that the Declaration was written, adopted, and signed, under circumstances far better calculated to secure a correct decision upon the matter in hand, than those under which the Constitution was brought into being.

—JAMES W. C. PENNINGTON, *Covenants*
*Involving Moral Wrongs are not Obligatory Upon Man*,
sermon delivered at the Fifth (Talcott Street) Congregational
Church, Hartford, Thanksgiving Day, November 17, 1842.
University of Detroit Mercy Black Abolitionist Archive.

Maria Stewart, a Hartford native, was one of the first female public speakers in America and is one of the few black female abolitionists for whom any records survive.

The unfriendly whites first drove the native American from his much loved home. Then they stole our fathers from their peaceful and quiet dwellings, and brought them hither, and made bond-men and bond-women of them and their little ones; they have obliged our brethren to labor, kept them in utter ignorance, nourished them in vice, and raised them in degradation; and now that we have enriched their soil, and filled their coffers, they say that we are not capable of becoming like white men, and that we never can rise to respectability in this country. They would drive us to a strange land. But before I go, the bayonet shall pierce me through. African rights and liberty is a subject that ought to fire the breast of every free man of color in these United States, and excite in his bosom a lively, deep, decided and heart-felt interest.

—MARIA STEWART, "African Rights and Liberty,"
Stewart's third public speech, delivered at the
American Masonic Hall, Boston, February 27, 1833.

Though you should endeavor to drive us from these shores, still we will cling to you the more firmly; nor will we attempt to rise above you: we will presume to be called your equals only.

—MARIA STEWART, "African Rights and Liberty,"
Stewart's third public speech, delivered at the
American Masonic Hall, Boston, February 27, 1833.

The work to be done is not to be completed in a day or a year; it will require a long time to remove the evils which slavery and habit have so deeply engraven upon the very foundation of everything.

—AMOS G. BEMAN, letter to the editor of
the *Weekly Anglo-African*, September 6, 1862.

## Note

This essay originally appeared in the May/June/July 2004 issue of *Connecticut Explored*.

*Tamara Verrett*

# 13  From Talcott to Main Street

*Hartford's First African American Church*

In 1819, a group of African Americans in Hartford grew weary of being assigned seats in the galleries and in the rear of churches and decided to begin worshipping on their own in the conference room of the First Church of Christ, now Center Church, in Hartford. This would become the first black Congregational Church in Connecticut, the third oldest in the nation. The congregation moved its services to a building on State Street in 1820. That same year, the congregation established itself as The African American Religious Society of Hartford and resolved to build a house of worship where all would be welcome and no one would have assigned seating. In 1826 the congregation purchased property at the corner of Talcott and Market streets, where they built a stone-and-brick church.

The church became a key institution in Hartford's black community and a center for abolitionist and social activity. Noted lecturers including Arnold Buffman, former president of the New England Anti-Slavery Society, and abolitionist Rev. Henry Highland Garnet helped establish the church as an anti-slavery meetinghouse.

Realizing that members could not prosper without an education, the founders established a district school. For many years this was the only place in Hartford where black children could learn to read and write. Having become a religious and educational beacon, the church changed its name to the First Hartford Colored Congregational Church in 1839.

The church had several pastors in its early years. Among them was Rev. Dr. James W. C. Pennington, who is remembered as an eloquent orator, preacher, and freedom fighter. A fugitive slave, he escaped from Maryland through the Underground Railroad. For years, Pennington feared that he would be dragged back into slavery, until Harriet Beecher Stowe's brother-in-law, John Hooker, purchased him for $150. Pennington received his freedom papers on June 3, 1851.

In 1860 the church was renamed the Talcott Street Congrega-

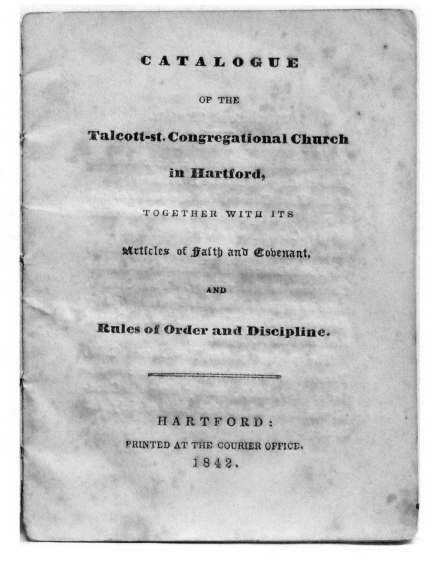

FIGURE 13-1 *Catalogue of the Talcott Street Congregational Church in Hartford, together with its articles of Faith and Covenant,* 1842. *The Amistad Center for Art & Culture, Inc., 1993.1*

tional Church. In the years that followed, the church had several pastors. By 1886, the congregation was in search of stability, and Rev. Robert F. Wheeler was named pastor. Under the leadership of Rev. Wheeler, the congregation eventually outgrew the original building. The old single-story church had to be torn down to make room for a new two-story building. At the farewell service in 1906, Rev. Wheeler said, "Although the name of this organization has changed at different times, the property has belonged to the same people and has been used for the same purpose."

In 1916, the arrival of Rev. Dr. James A. Wright, one of the most distinguished ministers in Hartford, ushered in a vibrant era for the church through two world wars and the beginning of the civil rights movement. The Baltimore native received degrees from Howard University, Andover Theological Seminary, and Harvard University and served as pastor for forty-three years. Rev. Wright oversaw the merging of the Talcott Street Congregational Church with Rev. Samuel Gilbeau and the congregation of Mother Bethel Methodist Church on November 19, 1953. The new Faith Congregational Church created a congregation of 500 people and spurred the need for a new church home.

Faith Congregational Church moved in 1954 to the former Windsor Avenue Congregational Church, built in 1871 at 2030 Main Street in Hartford, where it stands today. Within a year after that move, the former church on Talcott Street was demolished after 128 years of service.

Just five years after the church moved to its new home, in January 1959, a three-alarm fire began during a choir rehearsal and caused extensive damage. Ministers and community leaders quickly rallied to raise funds to restore the church, and on Easter Sunday the following year, the church celebrated a beautifully restored sanctuary. Unfortunately, Rev. Wright died less than a month before the re-dedication. The church retains many of his important papers and books.

Today, Faith Congregational Church maintains its rich history. In 2004, the church celebrated its 185th anniversary with the theme "A Strong Foundation, A Challenged People, A Dedicated Spirit" in recognition that Faith Congregational Church—no matter what the name—is still the same people with the same purpose.

Note

This essay originally appeared in the Summer 2005 issue of *Connecticut Explored*.

*Mary M. Donohue*
*and Whitney Bayers*

## 14 Fortresses of Faith, Agents of Change

### *AME and AME Zion Churches in Connecticut*

Black churches have long been at the forefront in the battle for social progress and equality. Since the end of the eighteenth century, African Americans worked to organize Christian congregations that would afford them full membership, often splitting away from white congregations. In addition to serving the spiritual needs of their members, African-American churches served as social and political platforms, boldly condemning slavery, organizing abolitionist societies, serving as stations on the Underground Railroad, starting schools for black children, and hosting nationally known speakers such as Frederick Douglass and William Lloyd Garrison. As African-American churches emerged in urban areas, they became social centers for the surrounding neighborhoods—safe places to worship, discuss issues, and hold meetings. Issues of great importance to these congregations throughout the nineteenth and twentieth centuries included suffrage, lynching, the Ku Klux Klan, and access to fair housing and education.

Two of Connecticut's earliest black churches were Talcott Street (now Faith) Congregational Church in Hartford and Dixwell Avenue Congregational Church in New Haven. In a long and complex history, Faith Congregational Church traces its roots back to 1819, when Hartford's African Americans rejected seating in the galleries of white churches and began to worship in a meeting room of the First Church of Christ. In 1820 a white abolitionist Simeon Jocelyn and twenty-four former slaves founded Dixwell Avenue Congregational Church as the African Ecclesiastical Society.

Among black congregations in Connecticut, two particular denominations stand out. At a time when the Underground Railroad was heavily traveled, congregations of the African Methodist Episcopal (A.M.E.) and African Methodist Episcopal Zion (A.M.E.Z.) churches had conductors standing by to send freedom-seeking passengers on toward liberty.

The A.M.E. denomination stemmed from St. George's Methodist Church in Philadelphia. Amidst rising tension between black and white members and the segregation of black worshippers into an upper balcony, member and former slave Richard Allen and others gathered fellow congregants and left St. George's to form a new church in 1794. In 1816, the African Methodist Episcopal church officially departed from the Methodist church and became the first independent black denomination in the nation.

Little Bethel A.M.E. Church, 44 Lake Avenue, Greenwich, established in 1882, was the first African-American church in Greenwich. Local contractor A. N. Meilinggaard built the current structure in 1921, in the church's original location.

In a separate movement in 1796 in New York City, African-American parishioners left the congregation of the John Street Methodist Church and organized a separate African chapel, which they named Zion. Black Methodists were rarely allowed to preach and were restricted from becoming members of the Methodist Conference. After two decades of continued affiliation with the Methodist Church, the group voted to make a separation to become the African Methodist Episcopal Church. In 1848, Zion was added to the name in order to distinguish their denomination from the Philadelphia group and to honor their mother church.

The earliest of this denomination in Connecticut is the Varick Memorial A.M.E. Zion Church in New Haven. Named for James Varick, the first black ordained bishop of the A.M.E. Zion church, Varick Memorial Church was organized in 1818 when more than thirty African Americans left the Methodist Church to form their own congregation. In 1820, it officially became affiliated with the A.M.E. Zion church movement of James Varick. By 1841, the church had a building on Broad Street, but it relocated in 1872 to Foote Street. In 1908, the present building was constructed, and it was here that Booker T. Washington made his last public speech before his death in 1915.

Cross Street A.M.E. Zion Church, 160 Cross Street, Middletown, became known as the Freedom Church for its abolitionist activity in the nineteenth century. The Cross Street A.M.E. Zion Church of Middletown originated in 1823, and a building was erected in 1830, under the leadership of Reverend Jehiel Beman. Beman, the son of a Revolutionary War soldier and the father of Amos Beman, led the congregation in the antislavery cause. Women of the church, under the leadership of Clarissa Beman, created one of the first women's abolitionist societies, known as the Colored Female Anti-Slavery Society of Middletown. Its goal was not only to bring an end to slavery but also to improve the condition of free African Americans. The church continued to be a community leader during the Civil Rights movement of the late 1950s and 1960s. The congregation participated in protest marches and was witness to numerous visits and speeches by Dr. Martin Luther King, Jr. In 1965, to help black students go to college, the church's Reverend William Davage founded the Greater Middletown Negro Youth Scholarship Fund. The church was rebuilt in 1867, moved about a quarter mile in 1929, and demolished in 1978. A new church building was constructed in 1978 and later sold to Wesleyan University. A building at 440 West Street now houses the congregation.

Metropolitan A.M.E. Zion Church in Hartford is directly descended from the first African-American church in Hartford. When the African Religious Society separated into two churches in the early 1830s, one became the Talcott Street (now Faith) Congregational and the other the Colored Methodist Episcopal (now Metropolitan). The first pastor of the Methodist church was Hosea Easton, an early African American protest writer, who raised funds to replace the church building when it burned in 1836. The new structure, on Elm Street, also provided a school for African American children. By 1856, the church was located on Pearl Street and associated with the African Methodist Episcopal Zion movement of New York. In 1924, the church building was sold to the City of Hartford. The congregation relocated to Main Street in 1926 and was later incorporated as the Metropolitan African Methodist Episcopal Zion Church.

Over the years, A.M.E. and A.M.E.Z. churches have been bastions of community activism. With community centers at home and missions in countries around the world, these denominations continue to strive for equality and share their message of acceptance and faith.

## Note

Dr. Katherine Harris conducted much of the original research for this article for the State Historic Preservation Office. This essay originally appeared in the Summer 2011 issue of *Connecticut Explored*.

*Katherine J. Harris*

# 15 William Lanson

*Businessman, Contractor, and Activist*

For multitudes of eighteenth- and nineteenth-century African Americans such as William Lanson, documenting vital years of their lives is not a simple process.[1] It is difficult to piece together, for instance, Lanson's date or place of birth and other details of his early life, because the births and deaths of African Americans, particularly those who were enslaved or indentured, were not regularly recorded. Yet for all we do not know about him, Lanson emerges as an important figure. Despite the tumult that accompanied him for much of his adult life, Lanson prevailed for a time as a successful businessman, leader, and advocate for his community against the rigidity of race and class. The following passages offer glances into Lanson's life of some sixty-plus years.

A December 5, 1799, advertisement in the *Connecticut Journal* for a "runaway servant named Lanson about 20 years old," may very well refer to William Lanson and would suggest his birth in or around 1779.[2] His brief 1850 *Statement of Facts Addressed To The Public* and his son Isaiah's 1845 publication *Isaiah Lanson's Statement and Inquiry Concerning The Trial of William Lanson, Before The New Haven County Court* offer nothing about Lanson's life prior to 1803 or 1807.[3] Neither Lanson nor his son recorded his place of birth. In this same *Statement of Facts*, however, Lanson wrote: "I have been in this town [New Haven] 47 years this spring . . ."[4] This confirms that Lanson traveled from another place and arrived in New Haven in 1803.

In 1807, Lanson acquired property outside of New Haven's colonial-era Nine Squares city boundary in the area that later would become the posh neighborhood of Wooster Square. When Lanson purchased it, though, it was an open field used for plowing contests, according to New Haven Historic Preservation Trust. The deed, dated March 2, 1807, listed Mary Wooster as the grantor or seller.[5] Throughout the first three decades of the 1800s, Lanson purchased more property, a sign of business success and social and political standing.

During the period of the early republic (roughly 1789 to 1825), New Haven municipal officials procured funding to make the city's harbor more commercially viable. William Lanson found a solution to the problem of the shallow harbor. James Hillhouse, the Farmington Canal project superintendent and an abolitionist, hired Lanson to implement his vision, building a 1,500-foot extension to the stone wharf from East Rock. Lanson quarried the stone, loaded it onto scows from a jury wharf, and placed it in position. Lanson's section of the wharf formed part of the last quarter of the structure. He built it entirely of stone, in contrast with the rest of the wharf that was constructed from wood and earth.[6] At low tide, remnant stones from Lanson's portion of the wharf are still visible.

Lanson's extension enabled merchants to unload cargo directly onto the wharf instead of transferring cargo to smaller boats and rowing it to and from the ships. While New Haven still had to compete with rival ports at Boston and New York, the city's trade networks strengthened with Europe, the Caribbean, and the southern United States. Connecticut's manufactured products now could be shipped more efficiently. This stimulated the demand for Connecticut carriages, clocks, wool cloth, rubber boots, arms, and hardware. Demand for these products in turn provided employment for many New Haven residents.[7]

In 1811, New Haven's Reverend Timothy Dwight, President of Yale College, commended the achievements of Lanson and his brothers. Dwight applauded them and described them as "honourable proof of the character which they sustain, both for capacity, and integrity, in the view of respectable men."[8]

When Long Wharf, as it came to be known, was completed in the 1820s, it extended 3,500 feet into the harbor and emerged as a commercial and maritime hub for the city. Business offices, sail lofts, ship chandlers, rope walks, blacksmith shops, bars, and boarding houses all found a place on the wharf.[9] Lanson's son Isaiah published a brief account that described his father's work on the Long Wharf, East Haven Bridge, and the steamboat wharf.

Mr. Lanson . . . built nearly all the East Haven Bridge and the steamboat wharf, with his own hands; and also long wharf, which he built, when there was no way of getting to the pier without going in boats. Mr. Lanson's earning on that wharf amounted to about $25,000; there is also the basin wharf, with two walls, six feet thick, and one thousand feet long.[10]

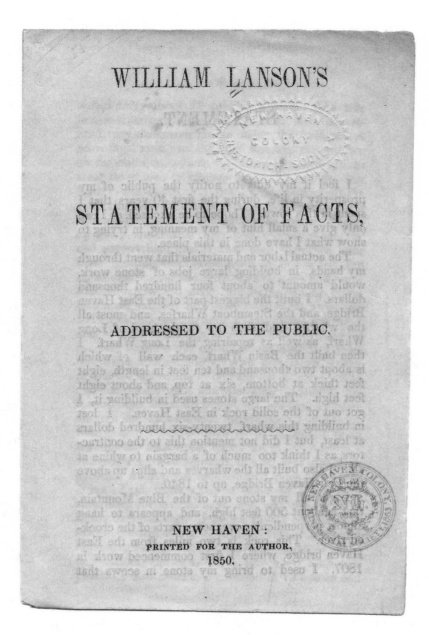

In Isaiah's words, "These and a great many other pieces of work-
manship which he has mastered, show him to be an industrious and
hard-working citizen."[11]

Lanson obtained more building contracts from private individuals and corporations for projects such as the Farmington Canal. He
purchased more property with the proceeds from his work. At the
time, his status as a property owner allowed him the right to vote.

While voting was reserved for the political and social distinction accorded a "freeman," there were no restrictions based on race until 1814 and 1818.[12]

It appears Lanson exercised this important civic right; in a petition he filed with African American compatriot Bias Stanley, the men identified themselves as being of African descent. They petitioned the Connecticut General Assembly in 1814 to oppose the denial of suffrage to "men of colour."[13] Lanson and Stanley asked to be relieved of the requirement to pay taxes if the General Assembly did not acknowledge their right to vote. The General Assembly denied the petition, and it did not alleviate their tax burden. Lanson and Stanley's petition, however, was only the first of several presented by African Americans from cities throughout Connecticut.

Lanson's activism and continuing business enterprise attracted both apprehension and approval from New Haven's elite. But approval overshadowed apprehension when Lanson became a member of the African United Ecclesiastical Society and worked on the Farmington Canal project in the 1820s. William Lanson, along with white abolitionist Simeon S. Jocelyn, was working with black parishioners to establish an African Union Church. He and the members of the African United Ecclesiastical Society, a local group, joined together, and on October 24, 1824, Lanson became one of the founding members of the society in New Haven. Its members were mainly African Americans, although Simeon Jocelyn served as an inspirational co-founder. The organization's membership rolls included Revolutionary War veteran Prince Duplex, who served as clerk, Bias Stanley as treasurer, and Scipio Augustus as representative to the national conventions.[14] They laid the foundation for the twentieth-century Dixwell Avenue Congregational Church, the successor of the African United Ecclesiastical Society.

As Lanson and the African United Ecclesiastical Society developed their plans for religious and educational outreach, new prospects in the commercial sector opened up for Lanson with the city of New Haven. The successful completion of the Erie Canal motivated Connecticut merchants' interest in building a canal to transport goods. Hoping to replicate the success of the Erie Canal, in May 1822 proponents for a canal, led by the Honorable Timothy Pitkin, chartered the Farmington Canal Company. The route selected ran north from New Haven Harbor through Hamden, Cheshire, and Southington, across the Great Plain to Farmington, Plainville, New Hartford, and Colebrook. The artificial waterway then connected to the Connecticut River at Northampton, Massachusetts. Supporters of the Farmington Canal planned to connect it to the canals in Massachusetts that crossed the Connecticut River at Brattleboro, Vermont.[15]

The canal project organizers selected prominent politician and abolitionist James Hillhouse as the project's director or superintendent. According to researcher Amy Trout, Hillhouse was always dedicated to aiding African Americans, and he hired William Lanson to build the New Haven section of the canal. Construction started in 1825. Lyman Homer, Black Governor of Plainville, was also hired to help.[16]

In 1827 Lanson began construction on the walls of the canal basin in New Haven Harbor. Lanson described the basin walls: "each wall . . . is about two thousand and ten feet in length, eight feet thick at bottom, six at top, and eight feet high."[17] He quarried his own stone from Blue Mountain in East Haven. Lanson hired other free African Americans, possibly as many as twenty to thirty men, to help construct the canal basin. He reportedly compensated each worker in full, although he was never fully paid for his own work. Lanson estimated that the canal project cost him $2,600. He avoided drawing attention to this fact because, as Lanson stated, ". . . I think too much of a bargain to whine at all."[18] Trout explained, "Lanson, like the Irish canal diggers, had little power to protest the slow delinquent payments."[19]

When completed, the Farmington Canal was 86 miles long, with 28 locks in Connecticut. Connecticut businesses used the Farmington Canal for several decades to import and transport such products as coffee mills, oysters, French lace, imported silks, spices, and newsprint for the burgeoning newspaper industry. Despite this auspicious beginning, the canal project did not yield the profits the investors anticipated. The canal closed in 1847.[20] The canal builders abandoned the project in 1852 and investors lost one million dollars.[21] But Lanson's efforts and those of others associated with the canal project—investors, engineers, surveyors, and laborers—had helped to set a course for New Haven's commercial development.

In addition to his construction and engineering projects, Lanson accrued income from other business enterprises. He owned two livery stables that consisted of forty livery horses, carriages, and harnesses.[22] Isaiah Lanson estimated that his father's worth circa 1832 was $20,000. Lanson's apparent prosperity extended to other aspects of life as well, including the recognition of his community.

In 1825, he was elected Black Governor; black New Haven called him "King Lanson." He served until 1830. Connecticut's United

States Senator (1879–1905) Orville Platt took note of his prominence, listing Lanson in his research about the "Negro Governors." (That research was based on original investigations, eye-witness accounts, and correspondence with United States Minister Resident, or Ambassador, to Haiti from 1869 to 1877 Ebenezer Bassett, a son and grandson of Derby Black Governors Tobias Pero and Eben Tobias.[23])

Neither Platt nor Greene recorded specific activities from Lanson's years as governor or king of New Haven's African American community, but it is likely that he conducted the standard duties of the office. Those typically included making occasional tours of inspection in Derby and New Haven, appointing justices of the peace to function as a local court and constable, and appointing a lieutenant governor.[24]

Lanson clearly served as a community leader. He supplied lodging and employment for people working on his construction projects. He offered shelter and other assistance to runaway enslaved persons and arranged for Parson Jocelyn to conduct religious services with them; the same Simeon Jocelyn who championed the cause of the Negro College and who, with the aid of interracial cooperation of citizens from Hartford, New Haven, and Farmington, secured legal assistance and sanctuary for the Amistad captives.

But for all Lanson's contributions to society, a series of events occurred in the 1830s and 1840s that turned Lanson's life upside down. By the mid-1830s, William Lanson was being hauled into court with some frequency; he wrote, "I didn't know why."[25] Public officials in New Haven began accusing Lanson of harboring people of ill repute. He endured many arrests. The courts levied fines against him for alleged infractions such as "keeping a loud house" or serving alcoholic beverages without a license, although neither proved to be the case. His residence was under surveillance for months at a time, watched closely by policeman Jesse Knevals,[26] who made Lanson his personal project.

Authorities attached fines to his estate. A review of available court documents and newspaper accounts does not provide a clear timeline for Lanson's alleged infractions. But an examination of petitions submitted to the Connecticut Legislature might provide some insight into the larger controversies taking place in New Haven and a possible reason that William Lanson was targeted.

Lanson built a hotel called King Lanson's Liberty Hotel or the Liberian Hotel around 1825. He wrote long articles about his efforts to maintain an orderly clientele and obtain the necessary licenses for his establishments.

But New Haven tax collector Gardiner Morse, a major foe of Lanson's, wrote an 1887 article about him. The article identified Lanson as "king of the colored race."[27] Morse acknowledged Lanson as the Black King, but defamed him as well. As Morse described it: "William Lanson who was known as the king of the colored race of the town, and part or principal owner of premises occupied by his color on Franklin street, was induced to dispose of his real estate interests on Franklin street, and establish a settlement on the water front, at the foot of Greene street, on the lot then occupied by a barn-like building, known as the old slaughter-house, which he converted into a house of resort and entertainment for guests of his kind, and surrounded it with, buildings and barracks for the accommodation of tenants of color of a low and unfortunate condition of life and character."[28]

In response to this series of attacks, Lanson wrote: "I was very well through this 40 years, . . . I was doing all this extra work in order to accumulate something for my old days, and was prospered in all my undertakings."[29] And yet, he spent some of his earnings fighting court charges and paying fines. He used the rest of his money to sustain his family and his community. Eventually ill health struck Lanson and his wife Nancy. During the economic instability of the Jacksonian era between 1837 and the 1840s, Lanson went through a bankruptcy.[30] In a tragic end to his life, Lanson was separated from his community and passed away in an almshouse. The last years of his life stood in painful contrast with his earlier life of accomplishment. Despite Lanson's personal losses, some of the institutions he helped to establish remain a part of New Haven's African American community. In the end, the Dixwell Avenue Congregational Church and the Farmington Canal Heritage Greenway remain part of his twenty-first-century legacy.[31]

## Notes

1. William Lanson, *William Lanson's Statement of Facts Addressed To The Public* (New Haven: Printed for the Author, 1850), 7. He wrote in his 1850 *Statement of Facts* "If I should live to see the 16th day of June next, I should be 68 years old . . ." This would suggest 1782 or 1783 as the year of his birth (Lanson, *William Lanson's Statement of Facts*, 3). Since the month of the publication is not indicated, it is unclear whether Lanson was referring to June of 1850 or June of 1851.

2. *Connecticut Journal*, December 5, 1799, p. 1, v. XXXII, No. 1675.

3. William Lanson, *William Lanson's Statement of Facts Addressed To*

*The Public* (New Haven: Printed for the Author, 1850) New Haven Museum and Historical Society. Isaiah Lanson, *Isaiah Lanson's Statement and Inquiry*, 15.

4. Lanson, *William Lanson's Statement of Facts*, 3.

5. Town of New Haven *Register of Deeds*, vol. 55 1804–1807 (Microfilm Connecticut State Library, Hartford, Connecticut). U. S. Census 1790; U.S. Census 1800. Osterweis, *Three Centuries of New Haven, 1638–1938*, 288. Lanson File, New Haven Museum, New Haven, Connecticut.

6. Warner, *New Haven Negroes*, 21–22; Lanson Papers, New Haven Museum. Platt, "Negro Governors," 334. Patricia Gaffney Ansel, "Looking at History Through Architecture," 1 (yale.edulynhtil curriculum units/1983/1/83.01.04), 5. George Foote and Richard Silocka "Maritime History and Arts," Yale University Teachers' Institute, New Haven, Connecticut. T. R. Trowbridge, "History of Long Wharf in New Haven," *Papers of the New Haven Historical Society*, 1, 86.

7. Patricia Gaffney Ansel, "Looking at History Through Architecture," 5.

8. Dwight quoted in "The Attack on Black Citizenship in Connecticut," Historic Transcripts, The Gilder Lehrman Center for the Study of Slavery an Resistance, 2007, cmi2.yale.edu/citizens all/stories/Module3/documents/lanson_statement.html.

9. Steve Grant, "William Lanson: The Slave Who Helped Build New Haven," *The Hartford Courant*, Sunday September 16, 2001 H5, HI. Ansel, "Looking at History Through Architecture," 5. *Historical and Archaeological Survey: Long Wharf Pier Structure*, New Haven, Connecticut, March 2008.

10. Isaiah Lanson, *Isaiah Lanson's Statement and Inquiry*, 4.

11. Ibid.

12. In the William Lanson files at the New Haven Museum, the name William Lanson [or Lamson] appeared on the Register of "Freemen." It has not been definitively established that this was the William Lanson that is the subject of this study. Town of New Haven *Register of Deeds*, vol. 55 1804–1807 (Microfilm Connecticut State Library, Hartford, Connecticut). C. J. Hoadly, *Records of the Colony and Plantation of New Haven, from 1638 to 1649 transcribed and edited in Accordance With A Resolution of The General Assembly of Connecticut, With Occasional Notes and An Appendix by Charles J. Hoadly, M.A.* (Hartford: Case, Tiffany and Company for the editor, 1857). For an explanation of the terms free planters and Free Burgesses see "Free Man's Charge," *New Haven's Settling in New-England And Some Lawes For Government: Published for the Use of that Colony* (London: Printed by M.S. for Livewell Chapman, at the Crowne in Pope-head-Alley, 1673), 9, 13, 17, 100. "1807 List of Freemen of New Haven," New Haven Museum.

13. *Petition of William Lanson and Bias Stanley 1814*, Connecticut State Library, Hartford, Connecticut.

14. These groups shared several traits. Membership was voluntary not compulsory; private donations funded the associations. A voluntary association defined in *International Encyclopedia of the Social Sciences* (New York, 1968), VI: 362–63. Warner, *New Haven Negroes*, 80. Burkett, "The Reverend Harry Croswell and Black Episcopalians in New Haven, 1820–1860," 4.

15. Castle, *History of Plainville*, 30, 80. "The Farmington Canal," *Connecticut Herald*, September 20, 1831, vol. 28, no. 43, whole no. 1456, 2.

*Farmington Canal National Register Nomination*, Connecticut Historical Commission, Hartford, Connecticut, 1985.

16. Amy Trout, "The Story of the Farmington Canal," reprinted in *Yale Alumni Magazine*, October 2001, 2. Warner, *New Haven Negroes*, 21–22. Ellsworth S. Grant, "The Ill-Fated Farmington Canal," *Hog River Journal*, 6, no. 2 (Spring 2008): 24–31. Ruth S. Hummel, *The Farmington Canal in Plainville, Connecticut, New England's Longest Canal's in One of Connecticut's Smallest Towns Circa 1828–1848* (Plainville Historical Society, Inc., 2007), 10–17, 60–61, and 75 on the workers, including Lyman Homer, Black Governor of Plainville).

17. Lanson is quoted in Amy Trout, "The Story of the Farmington Canal" (New Haven Colony Historical Society), 8. Castle, *History of Plainville*, 30, 80. Lanson's article in the *Columbian Register*, Saturday, March 14, 1829, 1.

18. Lanson quoted in Amy Trout, "The Story of the Farmington Canal," 8.

19. Lanson quoted in Amy Trout, "The Story of the Farmington Canal," 8. See Farmington Canal Daybook (Hillhouse Family Papers, Manuscripts and Archives, Yale University). William Lanson, *William Lanson's Statement of Facts Addressed To The Public*, 3. Lanson's article in the *Columbian Register*, Saturday March 14, 1829, 1. *Historical and Archaeological Survey: Long Wharf Pier Structure*, New Haven, Connecticut, March 2008.

20. The canal, however, brought as many liabilities as benefits. Rain caused breeches in the Farmington Canal. Each time there was a break in the bank due to flooding, farmers who lived in the area had to be paid for the loss of their crops and livestock.

21. Hummel, *The Farmington Canal in Plainville, Connecticut*, 76–77. Grant, "The Ill-Fated Farmington Canal," 28.

22. *Isaiah Lanson's Statement and Inquiry Concerning . . . William Lanson*, 6.

23. Greene, *The Negro in Colonial New England, 1620–1776*, 255. Warner, *New Haven Negroes*, 46, 47, 80, 82, 85. Platt, "The Negro Governors," 318.

24. Platt, "The Negro Governors," 324. Warner, *New Haven Negroes*, 46, 47, 80, 82, 85. See also Lanson Files at the New Haven Museum for Lanson's article in the *Columbian Register*, Saturday March 14, 1829, 1. Burpee, *The Story of Connecticut*, 507–8. Fowler, *History of Durham*, 170. Orcutt and Beardsley, *History of Derby*, 537, 550. Warner, *New Haven Negroes*, 46, 47, 80, 82, 85.

25. Lanson, *William Lanson's Statement of Facts*, 6.

26. On Knevals, see A. E. Costello, *History Of The Police Department of New Haven From the Period of the Old Watch in Colonial Days to the Present Time. Historical and Biographical. Police Protection Past and Present. The City's Mercantile Resources Illustrated* (New Haven: The Relief Book Publishing Co., 1892), 37, 39. William Lanson, *William Lanson's Statement of Facts*, 6.

27. Gardiner Morse, "Recollections of New Haven," *Papers of the New Haven Colony Historical Society*," V (New Haven: New Haven Historical Society, 1887), 98, 100, 102.

28. Morse, *Recollections of New Haven*, 98, 100, 192.

29. William Lanson, *William Lanson's Statement of Facts*, 2.

30. For more on these events see, Katherine J. Harris, *William Lanson: The Triumph and Tragedy*. Edward Pessen, *Jacksonian America Society, Personality,*

*and Politics* (Champagne, Illinois: University of Illinois Press, 1969), 50–70. Frederick M. Binder, *The Color Problem in Early National America As Viewed by John Q. Adams, Thomas Jefferson, and Andrew Jackson* (The Hague: Mouton, 1968). Lanson responded to charges that his "tenements were houses of ill-fame," *Columbia Register*, March 14, 1829, ADDITIONAL NOTICE (New Haven Museum and Historical Society). William Lanson, *William Lanson's Statement of Facts*, 6.

31. Dean Sakamoto, Greenway Preliminary Research Inventory Study, July 2009 (New Haven, Connecticut).

# 16 The Ruggles, Norwich, and Abolitionism

David Ruggles (1810–1849), a native of Norwich, Connecticut, came from humble stock but rose to become one of the nation's foremost warriors against slavery and racism during the antebellum period. Ruggles coined the phrase "practical abolitionism" for the common-sense argument that self-emancipated enslaved people had the right to resist unto death. Ruggles was the first black bookseller and magazine publisher (in New York City), a key Underground Railroad operative, and a doctor of hydrotherapy. His boyhood in Norwich was the stimulus for his accomplishments and his grievances against slavery.[1]

Born on March 15, 1810, in Lyme, Connecticut, Ruggles was the eldest of six children of David, Sr., a woodcutter and blacksmith, and Nancy, a renowned caterer. The family soon moved to Bean Hill, a small village at the northern outskirts of Norwich. There the family lived in a tiny house on a miniscule plot of land that was owned by Nancy's mother Sylvia, who had been freed by Aaron Cleveland, a local abolitionist and grandfather of future president Grover Cleveland.

The Ruggles family was part of a mixed-race community of wealthy whites and black servants in Bean Hill. Governor (and former President of the Continental Congress) Samuel Huntington had lived nearby, and so did his nephew and adopted son, Samuel H. Huntington, later governor of Ohio. One servant of that family was Samuel Hun' ton who, along with Sutton, another Bean Hill resident, was a Black Governor elected by fellow slaves and freed people to this honorary but socially significant post. Other neighbors were less respectable. Close by the Ruggles's home lived Caesar Reynolds, a black youth with whom David Jr. got into several scrapes with the law. After Reynolds was sent to prison, where he murdered a guard and thereby earned the death penalty, David Jr. replaced him as coachman for a wealthy man. These experiences may have prepared him for his future bouts with racist coachmen and railroad conductors who refused him service.

David Jr. prospered in this intimate community of Bean Hill, benefiting particularly from his mother's close business relationships with the elite of the state and village and from the political and moral examples he was exposed to there. The state had initiated gradual emancipation in 1784, and efforts to finally extinguish slavery produced lively debate for many years. Young David could learn about these controversies through the newspapers and the public lectures of Aaron Cleveland and other abolitionists. Telling lessons also came from fugitive slaves who slipped through town before boarding coastal and oceanic ships.

His daily routines in Bean Hill exposed young David to shops on the green and several print shops. Every year brought the highlight of General Training Day, at which his mother, Nancy, sold cakes along with Aunt Nancy, the wife of Governor Sutton, who peddled tasty root beer. It was at one Training Day that young David and Caesar Reynolds stole a horse and took it joy riding. That nearly landed both in prison, a fate that Reynolds suffered and that ultimately brought him to the hangman's noose.

Above all, David Ruggles benefited from local schools and from the friendships of his classmates. Evidence of David's childhood education appears in "The Freedmen of Sixty Years Ago," an article by Erastus Wentworth that appeared in March 1876 in the *Ladies' Repository*, a Methodist magazine published in Cincinnati from 1841 to 1876. Wentworth, a native of New London, Connecticut, and the magazine's publisher, displays much of the paternalist racism of the day in his article about Connecticut's freed people, but his article is uniquely valuable for detail on Ruggles's early family and school life as well, offering forgotten insights into Norwich's free black community.[2]

Wentworth spends several pages describing free blacks he knew as a child from an unidentified neighborhood in Connecticut, though most references suggest that it was Bean Hill. He identifies Governor Sutton and his wife, Aunt Nancy, Jason Brown, and his wife, Dimmis Brown, another root beer and cake purveyor. Another resident was Will Tracy, a black Revolutionary War veteran whose "wretched fiddle and worse fiddle playing" grated on the author's ears.

Wentworth recalled Nancy Ruggles with some reverence as the "factotum" of the neighborhood. In his recollections, Nancy Ruggles "officiated at births, parties, marriages, and deaths; made cakes, waited on table, washed and ironed almost every day of the week;

and in the absence of daily papers, interviewers and reporters, gathered news from all quarters, and peddled it from door to door, usually affecting great mystery, and enjoining listeners to keep what she had told a great secret, yet carrying the same story to every house in the neighborhood." According to Wentworth, if Nancy Ruggles did not know about something, it was not worth knowing. She advocated for her own rights. Wentworth credits Nancy as a great Methodist who firmly rejected the "Negro pew," the practice in which Protestant churches forced black congregants to sit in a rear loft during church services. James W. C. Pennington, the famed black Hartford Congregational minister, complained that the "negro pew" made "getting right" with God impossible.

Wentworth had less kind things to say about David's father. Had David, Sr. not been such a drunkard, argues Wentworth, "the family might have been well-clothed, well-fed, and well-housed, instead of wallowing in filth and rags." Notwithstanding this nineteenth-century precursor to the Daniel Moynihan theory of blaming the shiftless black father, the description of Ruggles's parents sheds light on his own determination to demand public equality, his own struggles with the bottle and eventual allegiance to the temperance movement, and his fondness for fine clothing.

Wentworth praises young Ruggles as the "smartest black we were ever acquainted with." According to Wentworth, David, or "Dave," as the writer called him, was proficient in arithmetic, geography, and grammar and "even commenced the study of Latin, under the tutorship of a little preacher who had been to Yale College." Ruggles was the leader of the local boys in "all sports and mischief's and scrapes." His "wit, shrewdness, and resources were endless." He led the other students in charivari, or parades designed to taunt their elders.

Ruggles himself wrote fond memories of his time in Norwich. In a pamphlet published in 1834 when he was twenty-four, he recalled his "by-gone days in New England, the land of steady habits where my happiest hours were spent with my playmates in her schools and in her churches." Ruggles remembered ice-skating and playing with balls and hoops in Connecticut. He happily noted that he and his friends "walked and swam her beautiful streams—when we climbed her tall pines and elms and oaks—when we rambled thro' all her fine orchards." Ruggles clearly remembered his early upbringing with happiness and was quick to point out that his childhood days were racially integrated. Unlike virtually every other African American memoirist, Ruggles did not recall a terrible day when racial prejudice intruded on childhood friendship. Rather, the lessons he learned in Connecticut were about racial equality. Ruggles quoted from English poet William Cowper's widely circulated poem "The Negro's Complaint" to affirm this egalitarian message:

> Fleecy locks and black complexion
> Did not forfeit nature's claim,
> Skins did not differ, but affection
> Dwelt 'in black and white the same.'

School presented a mixed message for the young scholar. His later erudition indicates good pedagogy with sound preparation in logic, literature, and debate. But his teachers did not envision an activist life for him in America. One of his teachers at the Second Norwich Congregational Church was Lydia Huntley Sigourney, the daughter of a prosperous Norwich shipping family who later became a famed essayist and poet. In the tenor of paternalism similar to Wentworth's, Sigourney recalled her black pupils as obviously grateful for common attention, given that most of them were quite young and intellectually untrained. She also recalled that school anniversary celebrations raised money for a library in Liberia, which according to Sigourney "was just lifting its head above the surrounding darkness." This was an early reference to the American Colonization Society's efforts to convince free blacks to abandon life in America and migrate to Africa, a plan that Ruggles and other free blacks angrily rejected. However disquieting it may have been to hear his beloved teacher recommend that he find a future in Africa, Ruggles otherwise benefited from the school. As his career indicates, he came out of the Norwich schools highly literate and versed in classical and sacred literature. He was at home with the sayings of great writers and had a penchant for logic and ethics. Ruggles believed his school days taught him morals and virtue, elements that enabled him to stand up to the debilitating racism he would later face.

Not all of Ruggles's school experiences were joyful. One moment surely contributed to his sensitivity toward racial injustice. Wentworth observed, "Schoolmasters in those days were tyrannical and cruel and resorted to the most barbarous devices to punish derelict boys." After one incident involving Ruggles's mischievous behavior, the teacher seized the frisky lad and tied one of his feet high up on a post in the middle of the room. Ruggles was compelled to stand for a long time on one leg in this torturous position. As it happened, a classmate had recently returned from New York City with a pocketknife. Slipped through many hands, the knife was used to sever the rope. Ruggles then staggered out the schoolhouse door in the manner of a drunken man "so cleverly and ludicrously as to set the whole school in a roar of laughter," despite the schoolmaster's unsuccessful attempt to pursue the miscreant scholar.

Ruggles moved to New York City in 1825 at age fifteen, toiled as a mariner, and in 1827 opened a grocery shop with help from Norwich residents who had also moved to New York. At first he advertised the sale of fine wines and spirits, beverages that appealed to working-class New Yorkers and perhaps reflected the influence of his father and of the sailors he had encountered in his voyages. Under the influence of Samuel Eli Cornish and perhaps of his mother, Ruggles abruptly became a temperance advocate and a radical abolitionist. He joined a black church, either the Dey Street Presbyterian Church or the African Methodist Episcopal Church. There, according to Wentworth, he became superintendent of a large and flourishing Sunday school.

On a return visit to Norwich, Ruggles visited one of its larger churches. Wentworth reported that a teacher handed Ruggles a "Testament and offered to hear him read. Surprised at the fluency and eloquence with which he read (he was a natural orator like his mother)," the teacher said:

"Who are you"?

"I am a native of this town but reside in New York now. You have a nice Sunday-school here, but it is not quite one-third as large as the one I have charge of in New York City."

In this exchange and in the classroom incident, Ruggles encountered authority figures who doubted his brilliance and who were willing to torture or taunt him. He responded with cool anger or exaggerated ridicule. His mother was undoubtedly influential in his responses. These incidents suggest that Ruggles's childhood experiences prepared him for the insults and condescension that he received as an adult abolitionist in New York City and beyond. His intense sense of injustice when refused service on stage coaches and railroad cars perhaps derives from his days as a coachman, from his powerful sense of equality with whites, and from his mother's insistence on equal rights. A fervent learner, Ruggles did not back down to educated whites who regarded him as an intellectual inferior; rather, he put them in their places. He did so with a cool, rational anger that tied his life experience with the demands of his emerging practical abolitionism that confronted the daily inequities of slavery and discrimination.

Ruggles maintained contact with his Norwich family and friends. In 1834 he opened the first African American bookstore in the nation (in New York City). His advertisements listed some of the titles available for purchase at the store or that could be borrowed through his circulating library including *A Sermon by Reverend Mr. Dickinson of Norwich, Ct* and the *Address of the New York Young Men Antislavery Society, To Their Fellow Citizens.* Delivered on the Fourth of July, 1834, at the establishment of the Norwich Antislavery Society, Reverend Dickinson's speech combined temperance with pleas for equal justice and the right of literacy of enslaved and free blacks. Dickinson refuted claims by the American Colonization Society and by Southern slaveholders that the extinction of slavery could not be immediate. Anything less than abolition now was, in Dickinson's view, sinful and un-Christian. In his sermon, Dickinson refuted the claim that not all slave masters were cruel by arguing that the "system [of slavery] which occasionally leads to outrage, and which affords the slave no protection against it, is most cruel." Dickinson also recanted his lifetime membership in the American Colonization Society. Because of his recognized brilliance and reputation, abolitionists across the country reprinted and sold Dickinson's sermon many times.

Ruggles had to be pleased that the pastor of his home church now demanded the immediate end of slavery. His sale of the minister's antislavery sermon indicates that he was in contact with his hometown. Dickinson was one of many New England Congregationalists who had become dominant players in the antislavery movement by the 1830s. Descended from a distinguished Montreal family and graduated from Yale College in 1826, Dickinson was considered to be among the most brilliant young clerics of his time. His acceptance of the pulpit at the Second Congregational Church of Norwich was a coup for the city. This was the church where Ruggles family had worshipped at times and where its children, starting with David, were educated. Dickinson served the church between 1832 and 1835, before abruptly resigning to serve as a missionary to Singapore, where he remained until 1839.

David Ruggles remained in New York City, running his shop, writing letters to antislavery and other newspapers, and helping fugitives from Southern slavery such as Frederick Douglass find succor in the Northern cities and Canada. One of Ruggles's protégées, James W. C. Pennington, became a prominent Congregational pastor in Hartford. Ruggles aided James Lindsay Smith, later a prominent Norwich political figure, in his burst to freedom.

In addition to helping freedom seekers, Ruggles strived to make Connecticut a headquarters for black abolitionist activities in 1841 when he called for a national convention to be held in New Haven that year. The split in 1840 in the national antislavery movement had convinced many blacks that independent efforts were necessary. The planned convention soon became controversial because it would include only blacks and would compete with another convention scheduled in Albany at the same time. The Albany convention included many of the black abolitionist luminaries, many of who would offer luster to Ruggles's plans, except that the Albany convention emphasized political party alliances with whites. History showed, Ruggles observed, that any oppressed group had to act on its own behalf as long as it was not wholly emancipated. Race was a factor, a "badge to our condition as *disenfranchised* and *enslaved* Americans."

Because slavery had reduced blacks in the eyes of the whites:

We have no right to hope to be emancipated from thralldom until we honestly resolve to be free. We must remember that while our fellow countrymen of the south are slaves to individuals, we of the north are slaves to the community, and ever will be so, until we rise, and by the help of Him who governs the destiny of nations, go forward, and like the reformed inebriates, ourselves strike for reform, individual, general, and radical reform, in every ramification of society.
—NATIONAL ANTI-SLAVERY STANDARD, October 1, 1840

Ruggles initially met with extraordinary success in his call. More than one hundred black activists from all over the eastern United States signed an announcement for the convention, to be held on the first Monday of September 1840 in New Haven. Problems soon emerged, however, regarding the proposed convention. Even Ruggles's protégée James W. C. Pennington retracted his support to join the Albany convention. Undaunted, Ruggles repeated his call for the convention in the same issue of the newspaper. In-fighting raged among black abolitionists as even New Haven antislavery activists declared that Ruggles could not be trusted and had maligned the people of New York and New Haven by not inviting whites. The meeting drew only five delegates and twenty observers. Despite the poor turnout, it did succeed in creating a new organization, the American Reform Board of Disenfranchised Commissioners. Undeterred, Ruggles convinced Isaac L. Dimond, a New York entrepreneur with New Haven roots, to donate a plot of land for a black vocational school, a plan much bruited about in the abolitionist press but one that unfortunately never materialized.

In the next few years, David Ruggles lived in Northampton, Massachusetts, where he operated a hydrotherapy hospital based upon use of cold-water treatments to cure ailments, a practice that was widely respected at the time. Ruggles garnered a national reputation for his work in hydrotherapy while continuing his abolitionist activities before his untimely death in 1849 from a severe bowel infection at age thirty-nine. He is presumed buried in the Yantic Cemetery in Norwich. Efforts are now underway to confirm the presence of his remains. The gravesite is recognized on the Connecticut Freedom Trail.

## Notes

1. This essay is based on Graham Russell Gao Hodges, *David Ruggles: A Radical Black Abolitionist and the Underground Railroad in New York City* (University of North Carolina Press, 2010; paperback edition, 2012).

2. [Erastus Wentworth], "The Freedmen of Sixty Years Ago," *Ladies' Repository: a monthly Periodical, devoted to Literature and Religion* 36 (March 1876): 244–51. The journal is available online in several places. All subsequent quotations are from this source.

# 17 A Family of Reformers

## *The Middletown Bemans*

More than a century before the Civil Rights movement of the 1960s, the Bemans of Middletown, Connecticut were activists devoted to the struggle for equal opportunities for African Americans in the job market, schools, and the voting booth. Jehiel Beman, his second wife Nancy, his sons Amos and Leverett, and his daughter-in-law Clarissa were among the intellectual elite of the black middle class in Connecticut in the decades before the Civil War.

Jehiel Beman came to Middletown in 1830 from Colchester with his wife Fannie (Condol) and their seven children. Both were born free but were the children of slaves. Jehiel's father, Caesar, was the slave of John Isham of Colchester, who freed him in 1781, probably in exchange for his service in the American Revolution. Oral tradition has it that Caesar chose the surname Beman to emphasize his right to "be a man."

Although the state's gradual manumission of slaves began in 1784, slavery was not fully abolished in Connecticut until 1848. At the turn of the eighteenth century, Connecticut's black population, both enslaved and free, was concentrated in agricultural areas. Beginning in the 1820s and 1830s, African-American families from Colchester, Lyme, and East Haddam began to migrate to Connecticut cities, especially Norwich, New London, and Middletown. The recent migration by young white men to the western frontier (Ohio and western New York) created an acute labor shortage throughout Connecticut. Unskilled workers were needed on farms and in river port towns such as Middletown, and also in cities, where opportunities were available for those free men and women who had trades, such as shoemakers, dressmakers, and carpenters.

According to the 1820 federal census, Middletown had 211 African American residents (208 free; 3 slaves), most of whom were newcomers to town. No doubt this was a time of optimism and hope for the black community in Connecticut; in Middletown, Jehiel Beman exemplified this sense of optimism. In 1830 he accepted the call to be pastor for the African Methodist Episcopal (A.M.E.) Zion Church, established in 1822, which was the third of its kind in the United States. The church had recently built a house of worship (originally located near the current southeast corner of Church and Pine streets). In 1830, Beman's two eldest sons, Leverett Castor and Amos Gerry, were twenty and eighteen years old, respectively. They had attended the Colchester Colored School before moving to Middletown.

In 1830, Amos attempted to enroll at Wesleyan University, but the administration of the Methodist institution bowed to pressure from Southern representatives on the school's board of trustees and blocked his admission. He would have been the institution's first African-American student. Undaunted, Amos engaged a willing Wesleyan student to tutor him in private, but white students who opposed his participation in the college community threatened violence. Heeding his father's advice that "the role of the black minister could be [pivotal] in the life of the black community and in movements for the elevation of the race," Amos enrolled in Oneida Institute in upstate New York, and in 1841 he was appointed pastor of New Haven's Temple Street African Church, where he served for almost twenty years.

Amos is by far the best known of the Beman reformers. He was active in New Haven during the Amistad trials and worked with nationally known abolitionists and civil rights leaders, including Reverend James W. C. Pennington, Simeon Jocelyn, Lewis Tappan, Charles Ray, and Henry Highland Garnet.

Less is known about his older brother Leverett, and though his contributions were more local, they made history nonetheless. He lived in Middletown until his death in 1883 and earned his living as a shoemaker, the trade his father also practiced (in addition to his ministry). Leverett and his father rented a shop for $10 per year on Court Street, just down the hill from the family home on Church Street.

In the spring of 1847 he walked into the town clerk's office in Middletown and filed a survey map of land he owned on the edge of the city in a low-lying area known as Dead Swamp. Leverett had paid to have the land surveyed and divided into eleven house lots. His plan was to sell the house lots and develop a neighborhood where middle-class black families could own their own homes. Presumably, he may have offered the lots for sale to the general public, but he was primarily interested in selling property to some of the 200 or so African Americans then living in town—and turning a profit.

FIGURE 17-1 Portrait of Amos G. Beman. *Scrapbook of Amos G. Beman, 2, front paste-down, Yale Collection of American Literature, Beinecke Rare Book and Manuscript Library*

Leverett's simple but radical plan for a black residential community represented the hopes and dreams of Connecticut's black population in the mid-nineteenth century for homeownership and the other rights it conveyed on their long, hard road to full equality. Only a few decades before, the nation's founders had argued over whether voting rights and full citizenship should hinge on one's status as a property owner. Housing available to African Americans often was substandard; moreover, few blacks were able to own property even years after slavery officially was abolished. The organization of Beman's free black community was, therefore, highly unusual. It may be unique in Connecticut.

Today Leverett's development is known as the Leverett C. Beman Historic District. This small triangle of land, bordered by the current Vine and Cross streets and Knowles Avenue, covers a mere four acres. Between 1830 and 1865, African Americans built ten houses

in the neighborhood; five of the original buildings are still standing. Leverett built his house at the corner of Vine and Cross streets
in 1843, where the Neon Deli stood in 2009. Some of the houses
in the neighborhood predate the development, built by the African
Americans who helped established the A.M.E. Zion Church in the
mid-1820s, among them George W. Jeffrey and Ebenezer Deforest.
Some of the residents were newly freed or escaped slaves who made
their way north from Southern states. Others were families who had
relocated from the eastern part of the state and who made up the
majority of Middletown's black population.

Isaac B. Truitt bought 11 Vine Street in 1864 after renting it for
several years. A seaman in 1860, he and his wife Eliza were born in
Cedar Creek, Sussex County, Delaware about 1820. Around 1853
they came to Middletown, where their five children were born. A
veteran of a black Connecticut regiment in the Civil War, by the
mid-1870s Truitt was employed at Wesleyan College as a chimney
sweep, cleaning out the stovepipes in student rooms and classrooms.

Amster and Emily Dingle, married in Hartford in 1855, bought
Lots E and F in 1861 from Beman for $100 and built their house,
which is today located at 170 Cross Street. Dingle was born in 1831
in Delaware, probably in New Castle County. Emily Peters, his wife,
was born about 1833 in Chatham (East Hampton), Connecticut.
Her grandfather had been a slave in Hebron. Dingle enlisted in
the Twenty-ninth (Colored) Regiment Infantry, Company F, in
December 1864, a few years after they built their house and their
daughters Elizabeth and Mary were born. Dingle died from disease
within a month at the muster camp in Fair Haven.

Many of the families illustrated the complex interrelationships
among the small populations of Connecticut African Americans.
Families intermarried within the Triangle and took in the relatives of
their neighbors. Herod and Abigail Brooks, who came to Middletown from Lyme in 1828, built 9 Vine Street about 1840. Abigail
was the sister of Asa Jeffrey, who already lived in the Triangle. Eu-
nice Brooks, a relative, owned the house by 1835, and when she
remarried in 1855, she lived there with her new husband, John Cambridge, and James and Orrice Brooks, both nineteen, the children
of Herod and Abigail Brooks. James grew up, married John Cambridge's daughter, and continued to live in the house. His sister Orrice married George O. Smith, who lived in the neighborhood at
what is today 10 Knowles Avenue.

Patriarch Jehiel Beman saw his role as much more than a spiritual
guide to his congregation. The church provided him a pulpit from

which to encourage the social, political, and economic advancement of the black community in Connecticut. The efforts that Jehiel Beman and other reformers undertook during the mid-nineteenth century were nothing short of a full-fledged civil rights movement. Their goal was to end slavery and make African Americans full members of American society. They formed organizations, circulated petitions, wrote essays, and engaged in activities to oppose slavery. Jehiel was a founding member of the Middletown Anti-Slavery Society in 1834. Nancy Beman, Jehiel's second wife, and Leverett's wife Clarissa organized the Colored Female Anti-Slavery Society in the same year; the society was only the second of its type in the country. The goal of the anti-slavery societies, which had both black and white members, was the immediate abolition of slavery. National leaders of the anti-slavery movement, including Boston's William Lloyd Garrison, were regular visitors to the Beman home in Middletown. Jehiel wrote many articles for Garrison's *Liberator* newspaper and for the *Colored American*. He also helped establish the A.M.E. Zion's first national publication, *Freedom's Journal*, in 1827.

The going was not easy, however. The activities of the local abolitionist groups were frequently met with violence, including a proslavery riot on Cross Street in 1835. Many moderate whites supported emancipation of American slaves but were comfortable only if the newly freed blacks were sent back to Africa, an idea encouraged by the American Colonization Society as early as 1816. Not surprisingly, most African Americans, including the Bemans, rejected the plan. The Bemans, with Amos as the group's secretary, led an organized response to the colonization movement in 1831. In the group's minutes, Amos articulated their views: "Why should we leave this land, so dearly bought by the blood, groans and tears of our fathers? Truly, this is our home, here let us live and here let us die."

Members of the Middletown community, whites and blacks alike, actively participated in the Underground Railroad. Evidence confirms that Benjamin Douglas, a local white industrialist, opened his house at the head of the South Green to fugitive slaves. In an 1854 letter to Frederick Douglass, at the time the most prominent abolitionist in the United States, Jehiel assured him that, "The Underground Railroad . . . is in good repair . . . and open for business . . . at all hours of the day and night." Henry W. Foster, who lived on Cross Street in 1860, is also recorded as being an agent of the Underground Railroad in the 1850s when he resided in Hartford. The Fugitive Slave Act of 1850, which made it a crime to aid an escaped slave, put Middletown's participants in serious jeopardy.

Reformers of the nineteenth century emphasized moral reform as a way of uplifting the black community in the eyes of the white populace. The Bemans felt that if African Americans lived sober lives and learned trades that made them industrious, contributing members of their towns, they would be accepted as complete participants in American society. In 1833, Jehiel founded the Home Temperance Society in Middletown. The primary directive of the organization was to promote complete abstinence from spirits, but the group also debated ways to make political gains for African Americans. Jehiel emphasized that education was the gateway to a better life for the next generation. After their move to Middletown, Jehiel enrolled his younger children at the Lyman C. Camp School in Middletown. Jehiel also helped recruit students for Prudence Crandall's school in Canterbury, Connecticut in the 1830s. Later, Leverett created the Mental Improvement Society in 1870 to encourage education. Like Booker T. Washington, Jehiel encouraged African Americans to develop trades and practical skills to become productive contributors to the labor force. Through the state temperance group, Jehiel established an African-American employment agency to help men find work.

The Home Temperance Society increasingly became a venue for political debate and action. State and national conventions of temperance groups in the 1830s eventually segued into Colored Conventions that organized at local, state, and national levels. In 1849, the first Connecticut Convention of Colored Men met in New Haven. Amos represented Middletown at subsequent state and national conventions and brainstormed ways to use political means to gain equal opportunities. The conventions' primary efforts eventually focused on attaining basic rights: equality under the law, due process, including trial by jury, and the right to vote. For a very brief time at the beginning of the nineteenth century, Connecticut's freed blacks were allowed to vote, a right taken away by the General Assembly in 1814. As leaders of the black abolitionist movement, the Bemans led a successful petition drive in 1847 for black suffrage, which was passed by the General Assembly. This time the right to vote was defeated by Connecticut voters in a state-wide referendum. Although appeals for suffrage were made time and again, African Americans in Connecticut were not granted suffrage until 1870 with the passage of the Fifteenth Amendment.

Middletown's black population steadily declined after 1850. There were only seventy-three African Americans there in 1910. African Americans competed for jobs with the increasing number of immigrants, and the black middle class virtually disappeared. Few of the remaining blacks in Middletown lived in Leverett's neighborhood. Those who worked in the service industry—housekeepers, servants, and chauffeurs—often lived with their employers. Others lived closer to where work was available for African Americans, either at the riverfront where men worked as stevedores and laborers or in rental housing in rural areas where many worked as farm laborers. By 1920, the neighborhood along Cross Street was predominantly home to white immigrants, first- and second-generation Swedish Americans and later Italian immigrants. Only five black individuals remained in Beman's development, all on Knowles Avenue. By the time Middletown's African-American population hit an all-time low of fifty-seven in 1920, European immigration had begun to decline, and job opportunities in New England increased. Middletown saw an influx of Southern blacks, brought here in the late 1920s and early 1930s, primarily to provide labor for Middletown's brick industry.

Wesleyan University presently owns all but two of the properties in the Triangle, including the A.M.E. Zion's former church. Students live in the historic residences. The A.M.E. Zion congregation adapted to meet the needs of an ever-changing community and is now located at the northeast corner of Wadsworth and West streets a half mile away. Wesleyan is taking the lead in continuing the research and exploration of this neighborhood by establishing an archaeology program in the Triangle to learn what artifacts can teach us about the rise and fall, the aspirations and frustrations, of Middletown's nineteenth-century black community.

## Note

This essay originally appeared in the Winter 2009/2010 issue of *Connecticut Explored*.

# 18 Rev. James W. C. Pennington

## *A National and Local Voice for Freedom*

In 1827 James Pembroke, an enslaved man of African descent who would eventually take the name James William Charles (W. C.) Pennington, managed to escape to freedom in the North. According to his narrative, he experienced an early childhood of parental separation. His father, Brazil Pembroke—whose last name was that of his owner—resided on the land of one slaveholder, while his mother lived with another slave owner. His life changed after his mother's owner agreed to purchase his father. Consequently, both parents were able to physically live with their family.[1] Even with parents present, James quickly discovered that the condition of slavery carried few exemptions from torture on the small farm, even for children. While his owner's children were cruel, the actions of the overseer, Blackstone, chilled his soul. James made the horrible mistake of playfully picking up one of the hickory switches that Blackstone kept to whip the enslaved that broke his rules. When the overseer saw James riding the long switch like a horse, the man flew into a rage and savagely beat the child with another piece of hickory that he kept handy. The level of fear in the child reached a point where he decided to seek refuge for hours in the woods or some other hiding place for fear of being beaten by Blackstone.[2]

The feudal system of chattel slavery had little use for idle hands; consequently, his owner tendered the nine-year-old to a stonemason. His brother, also a mere child, received training with a pump-maker. The owner no longer had to house or feed the children, while in return he would soon receive the services of a skilled craftsman. The pump-maker offered to purchase his brother, and James's owner agreed to the sale. The two brothers remained separated thereafter. They were no closer in distance than six miles. After two years learning the work of a stonemason, his owner sent him to work as a mason in the blacksmith shop where James grew up. The blacksmith, an enslaved man, had also learned his trade as a young apprentice. When he finished his assigned duties as a mason, he transitioned to learning the trade of the blacksmith. James worked at that trade for nine years.[3]

The desire to be free of the brutality of slavery eventually led James to take flight from Maryland. The violent beating of his father, a shepherd who cared for the owners' and his own Merino sheep, at the hands of the slave master for appearing to eyeball the white master forced him to make the dash for freedom. Coupled with vicious racial tirades from the owner, he never forgot the dozen blows with the cane that his owner delivered to his body, which left him aching for a long periods.[4] With a small morsel of bread and a bundle of clothes, James struck out for freedom, heading for Pennsylvania or some Northern state.

Although he was captured and detained by whites during his flight, he was allowed to continue on his way after he lied about being part of a smallpox-infected slave gang about to be sold in Georgia. Although this was clearly untrue, he knew the impact the statement would have and fear it would generate. In 1827 Pennington managed to meet a sympathetic "Christian woman," who informed him that he was in Pennsylvania, a free state. She also sent him to the home of a Quaker, William Wright. Quakers were known for their active role in the anti-slavery movement. The local members of the Society of Friends sheltered and educated their runaway friend.[5]

Through their connections and aid, he eventually made it to New York. While his friends on the Underground Railroad aided in his freedom, their devotion to Christ played a role in his conversion to Christianity. This conversion set him on the road to abolitionism, teaching, and the ministry. His newly seized freedom gave him the opportunity to choose a new last name, Pennington. Over the years, he would consider among his friends William Lloyd Garrison, Simeon Jocelyn, and Lewis Tappan, leading abolitionists of the day.[6] A decade after acquiring his freedom, Pennington became an ordained minister and studied at Yale University. One of the highlights of duties as a minister was conducting marriages, particularly of fugitives. In 1838 David Ruggles, an abolitionist and friend, informed him that a fugitive named Frederick Douglass and a woman named Anna Murray wanted to be married. Although Douglass and Murray had no money to pay for the nuptials, Pennington still graciously agreed to marry the couple.[7]

When Pennington finally made the move to Hartford, he became part of a highly organized and engaged African American community. African Americans, after segregated treatment, formally organized a church in 1826, which eventually became the Talcott Street Congregational Church and later Faith Congregational Church. The church's quest for Pennington's services as pastor began in 1838, but he declined the offer. In 1840, though, the determined Hartford congregation managed to persuade the talented minister to relocate. Once installed in the pulpit in Hartford,[8] he pastored the church and taught in a local school for African American children. Although Hartford's regular school system technically accepted all children, in 1830 African American parents, who disliked the treatment of their children in the regular system, requested a separate school for their children. Parents established the North African and South African schools. They housed the first school at Talcott Street, while African American Methodists provided space for the other school.[9] Amos Beman served as the best known of the early teachers; however, he moved on to pastor the Temple Street Church in New Haven. Politically and socially, James Mars, Henry Foster, and Ann Plato, faithful members of the church, were already formidable leaders in the community. Deacon Mars was a member of the executive committee of the Connecticut Anti-Slavery Society, while Foster led the efforts to develop a state temperance society for African Americans. Mars joined a coalition that fought to free Nancy, an enslaved woman brought from Georgia by her owner. In 1843 Pennington served as one of the Connecticut Anti-Slavery Society's delegates to the world anti-slavery convention. At the September 2, 1840 meeting of that organization, Pennington accepted the group's presidency. In 1844 the talented Plato taught students in the Elm Street School.[10]

Although his eight years as pastor included a trip to England and two years on leave, Pennington plunged headlong into building up the educational and cultural life of African Americans. He knew that he was part of burgeoning leadership class. His writings for the well-respected *Colored American*, a leading African American newspaper published in New York, revealed his concern and passion about improving quality of the education and facilities. Members of the state temperance society considered the newspaper "vital" to the empowerment of African Americans. In its pages Pennington chastised parents and school committees for their failures. He urged parents to not be satisfied with the mere rudiments of education, while he suggested that school committees needed to upgrade buildings, equipment, furniture, and instructional materials.[11]

When Augustus Washington, a Dartmouth College–trained student and future daguerreotypist, came to Hartford, Pennington and his wife taught and served as administrators at a school in two rooms in his church's lower level. Washington also became a teacher of African American children in Hartford. Although he only taught two years, he impressed Thomas Robbins, a visiting clergyman, with his skills as an educator.[12] When Ann Plato published a collection of her writings, Pennington proudly wrote the foreword. He used her writings as proof that African Americans were capable of intellectual pursuits, not simply the drudgery of slave labor. The minister suggested that African Americans should purchase the book.

The publication of Pennington's *Textbook of the Origin and History, Etc. Etc. of the Colored People* in 1841 served as a further challenge to notions of African American inferiority. He challenged assumptions about the curse of Ham on Africans and also responded to Thomas Jefferson's arguments about African inferiority.[13] According to historian Donald Spivey, Pennington spent a great deal of his time condemning racism in Hartford. Pennington found whites in the city to be apathetic or hostile toward African American residents. For a short time, the minister published two anti-slavery newspapers (the *Northern Star* and *Clarksonian*). The decline of the *Colored American* and need for African Americans to have a voice of their own in the struggle against slavery and racism prompted his move into publishing.[14] While Pennington understood the importance of the *Liberator*, published by William Lloyd Garrison, he knew that freedom came with the ability to do for self. Both papers played important roles in the struggle, though both suffered from financial difficulties.

His struggle was not one simply against the masters of slavery. He joined with other leaders to demand that people live upstanding lives. On September 2, 1840, Pennington was among a group of delegates of the Connecticut State Temperance Society who resolved to work to foster a culture of high morals and character.[15] Temperance organizing had been a part of his work since his days in New York.

African American and white allies in the city also organized efforts to aid in the support of the Amistad captives. Pennington was at the forefront in forging the Union Missionary Society, which became the American Missionary Society. The society played an instrumental role in funding the Amistad freedom fighters' travel back to Sierra Leone. A May 1841 public meeting of African Americans addressed concerns about the safe return of the Mendi people to Sierra Leone and the need to send missionaries to Africa. Pennington saw efforts to return the Mendi safely to Africa as divinely inspired. On November 21, 1841, the minister led prayers at services at the Broadway Tabernacle in New York for departing group. Included were two members of his church, Henry and Tamar Wilson. Henry, who formerly worked as a tailor, and his wife would serve as teachers. The couple decided that they wanted to be part of the missionary group to proselytize among the people of Sierra Leone.[16]

While living in Hartford, Pennington boldly continued to champion the cause of runaways and ending slavery. He continued his earlier work with the New York Vigilance Committee. Throughout the North, vigilance committees used their networks to ensure that runaways had an opportunity to seek freedom. When a family of seven fugitives arrived at Pennington's door, he welcomed and sheltered them in his home. A dwelling nearby served as their new home. Other people, with his help, filtered into Canada by way of Massachusetts. Pennington, still a runaway at this time, would not know legal freedom until Rev. John Hooker, a friend and fellow minister, negotiated his purchase from his Maryland slave owner.

In 1847 Pennington and Amos Beman represented Connecticut at the National Convention of Colored People. Pennington presented a commerce resolution that argued for people of African descent to collaborate internationally to improve their economic lives.[17]

When he decided to take a two-year absence for "classical studies" and higher education training, his travels outside the country to the Caribbean and British Isles provided Pennington an opportunity to appeal to supporters for financial assistance in his freedom cause. Even as he remained deeply concerned about re-enslavement and the sale of family members, throughout his time in Hartford he remained vigilant about the lack of voting rights for African Americans in Connecticut. Although the Whigs and the Liberty Party seemed more amenable to aiding the cause of African American voting rights, both parties failed to lead on the issue of enfranchising African Americans. African American leaders argued that should not pay taxes unless they received representation.[18]

On June 25, 1847, the schoolroom at Talcott Street Church served as the meeting place for a discussion on suffrage. Pennington was part of an appointed three-member corresponding committee. The members at the meeting joyously supported efforts in the legislature to amend the state Constitution to allow African American men to vote. They also urged that representatives in the legislature offer detailed discussions about the issue without prejudice.[19] The state legislature refused to pass a suffrage bill.

Although the struggle for the right to vote failed in the 1840s,

Pennington considered it his duty to confront and criticize ministers about racism within the abolitionist movement and clergy leadership. He reported that it was not unusual for white abolitionists to sit down beside him at meeting, only to move to another seat once they recognized the color of his skin. As for white ministers in Connecticut, he chastised them at a Middletown meeting for their failure to accept African American ministers fully in the brotherhood of ministers. In 1843 his criticism appears to have led to his acceptance in the Hartford Central Association, an organization of congregational institutions run by ministers. By 1844 Pennington presented a sermon outline in West Avon and later preached in the Farmington Congregational Church. Rev. Noah Porter, D.D. and pastor of the Farmington church, delivered the sermon at Pennington's church. Porter also served as the leader of the anti-slavery convention at which Pennington leveled his criticisms. Pennington eventually received more than ten offers from white ministers to preach from their pulpits.[20]

Three years later, in 1847, the First Colored Presbyterian Church in New York, whose pastor had recently died, inquired to see if Pennington might relocate to their church. He declined the offer and returned to lead the congregation at Talcott Street. Pennington felt an allegiance to the little church in Hartford, at least for the moment.[21] The church members in New York refused to take no for an answer, though, and eventually Pennington accepted their offer. His new church had a congregation of more than 400 members, three times larger than that of the Fifth Congregational Church on Talcott Street.[22]

While the move provided an opportunity to pastor a larger congregation, earn a larger salary, meet more frequently with national leaders of abolition, increase membership, and publish his narrative, Pennington's new pastorate of a Presbyterian congregation came with a legacy that posed significant challenges to him as an abolitionist. Unlike the anti-slavery Congregational Church in New England, the Presbyterian Church, with close ties to the South and history of supporting slavery, refused to publicly condemn slave owners. In addition, most of the congregation no longer lived near the church. The parent church body decided to sell the church, pay off its debt, and obtain a new church facility. In 1850 the U.S. Congress passed a new fugitive slave law that allowed slave owners to receive help from northerners in retrieving runaway slaves. When he did return to Hartford in 1856, he remained there for less than a year. He cited health concerns that forced him to leave the city.[23]

Pennington spent a portion of the following decade traveling in the ministry. The coming of the Civil War tested his pacifism. He eventually decided to add his voice to the list of powerful African American leaders such as Frederick Douglass who recruited African American soldiers.[24]

While the North's victory ushered in freedom from slavery, it also gave Pennington an opportunity to once again establish solid ties with the Presbyterian Church, this time in Florida. Although the freedmen of Florida lived far from Pennington's former homes in New York and Connecticut, among African Americans his name and reputation remained revered. He eventually had the opportunity to conduct missionary work in Florida for the Presbytery. Sadly, his work ended with his death in 1870. Although he never received the acclaim afforded to Frederick Douglass or Martin Delaney, he was one of the giants of African American leadership.

Like Douglass, Pennington spoke with an authentic and powerful voice against slavery and for the dignity of humanity. Like Douglass, he respected the power of education, self-empowerment, and alliances with white abolitionists. Guided by his religious convictions, he gave a national voice to major local issues of the day and a local voice to the greatest national issues of the day.

## Notes

1. James W. C. Pennington, *The Fugitive Blacksmith; or, Events in the History of James W.C. Pennington Pastor of the Presbyterian Church, New York* (London: Charles Gilpin, 1850, third edition), 2. Available on Google books. In the most recent biography on Pennington the author uses the year 1808 found in the Clergy Registry of the Third Presbytery of New York. Christopher L. Webber, *American to the Backbone: The Life of James W.C. Pennington, the Fugitive Slave Who Became One of the First Black Abolitionists* (New York: Pegasus Books, 2011), 27. One of the best articles on Pennington written by a Connecticut resident is by David O. White, "The Fugitive Blacksmith of Hartford: James W.C. Pennington," *Connecticut Historical Society Bulletin*, XLIX (1984): 5–29. *The Colored American*, September 19, 1840. See also David E. Swift, *Black Prophets of Justice: Activist Clergy Before the Civil War* (Baton Rouge and London: Louisiana State University Press, 1989), 205. Swift puts the date of birth in 1807.

2. Pennington, 3.

3. Ibid., 4–5.

4. Ibid., 8.

5. Ibid., 16–41. See also Swift, *Black Prophets of Justice*, 205.

6. Pennington, 49–54.

7. Webber, *American to the Backbone*, 113.

8. *The Colored American*, August 8, 1840.

9. Webber, *American to the Backbone*, 143.

10. *The Colored American*, August 8, 1840. Swift, *Black Prophets of Justice*, 202, 205, 219, 226–27. See also Webber, *American to the Backbone*, 162, 181. See *Hartford Courant*, July 1, 1847, *The Colored American*, September 19, 1840, *The Colored American*, May 15, 1841.

11. Swift, *Black Prophets of Justice*, 173, 212, 217.

12. Webber, *American to the Backbone*, 146.

13. Steve Courtney, "Ann Plato Showed Talent Was Colorblind," *The Hartford Courant*, August 4, 2002. See also Webber, *American to the Backbone*, 162. Swift, *Black Prophets of Justice*, 222–23.

14. Donald Spivey, "Point of Contention: The Historical Perspective of the African American Presence in Hartford," in *The State of Black Hartford*, ed. Stanley Battle (Hartford: Greater Hartford Urban League, 1994), 50–54. See also Manuscript Records in Connecticut Historical Society. See also *The Hartford Courant*, October 27, 1985, and February 3, 1991

15. *The Colored American*, September 19, 1840.

16. Ibid., August 8, 1840, Swift, *Black Prophets of Justice*, 202, 205, 219. See also Webber, *American to the Backbone*, 162, 181. See *Hartford Courant*, July 1, 1847, *The Colored American*, September 19, 1840, *The Colored American*, May 15, 1841, and *Hartford Courant*, December 21, 1841.

17. Swift, *Black Prophets of Justice*, 235, 238–39. Webber, *American to the Backbone*, 235, 242–43.

18. Swift, *Black Prophets of Justice*, 234–35. His method of record keeping on financial assistance resulted in a chafed relationship with Lewis Tappan. Webber, *American to the Backbone*, 235, 242–43.

19. *Hartford Daily Courant*, July 1, 1847.

20. Swift, *Black Prophets of Justice*, 233.

21. Ibid., 219.

22. Ibid., 240.

23. Webber, *American to the Backbone*, 249, 387–88.

24. Ibid., 410–11.

*Jessica A. Gresko*

# 19 Coming to the Aid of the *Amistad* Africans

On the morning of August 26, 1839, a mysterious ship drifted in the waters off Long Island. The long, black schooner rode low in the water, its sails in tatters. A U.S. Navy ship patrolling the waters moved in to investigate. What the sailors found was a story that would intrigue the nation for the next two years.[1]

The ship, the *Amistad*, was a Spanish vessel far away from its homeport in Cuba. It had been transporting a group of recently enslaved Africans purchased at the slave market in Havana, Cuba, to the city of Guanaja when the captives rebelled. They killed the ship captain and commandeered the ship. Using gestures to communicate, the Africans demanded that their former captors, two Spaniards, return them to Africa. But the Spaniards purposefully made little headway across the Atlantic, eventually drifting into the Long Island waters where the ship was found. Now that the U.S. Navy had intervened, the Spaniards asked for the United States' help in returning to Cuba with "their slaves" in chains.

Sending the thirty-five men and four children back to a life of slavery was a complicated matter of law. Spain and America had treaties governing ships and returning property. But slavery was a controversial subject in the United States of 1839, a union divided into slave and free states. For the next two years, heated legal wrangling pitted abolitionists and other supporters of the Africans against the Spanish and United States governments. The protracted battle eventually landed in the United States Supreme Court, forcing the country to confront the institution of slavery some twenty years before the Civil War.

Existing scholarship on the case of the *Amistad* captives largely focuses on the white abolitionists that helped the group and the celebrity aspect of the trial, most notably seventy-three–year-old former president John Quincy Adams's impassioned defense of the Africans before the U.S. Supreme Court. Missing from these accounts has been any serious study of how African Americans responded to the case.[2] Newspaper articles, letters and other contemporary records show that African American communities—including Connecticut's —were keenly interested in the *Amistad* case and the plight of the Africans. Black communities were some of the first to donate money to help the captives and were among the most generous donors to their cause throughout their stay in America. They turned out in large numbers to see the men at church fundraisers and followed the case's progress in frequent articles in a prominent black-run news-paper, *The Colored American*. At every step of the captives' journey, the black community was involved.

When the *Amistad* appeared off Long Island in 1839, Martin Van Buren was in his third year in the White House and struggling to pull the country out of a depression. The union consisted of twenty-six states and slightly more than 17 million people. It was also a time of change for the nation's free black population.

The 1840 census found nearly 378,000 free blacks living in the United States (though some guessed the number might be closer to 500,000 with many escaped slaves hiding from census takers), including more than 8,100 in Connecticut.[3] At the same time, the early nineteenth century saw the rise of black churches and a stron-ger abolitionist movement with a growing number of black aboli-tionists. One of the biggest events of the 1830s in the abolitionist movement was the founding of the American Anti-Slavery Society in Philadelphia. The society called for the emancipation of slaves and their acceptance as equal citizens. While the society started with fifty-nine white and three black abolitionists, by 1838 there were 1,350 local chapters.[4] Anti-slavery groups formed in Connecticut cities such as Middletown, where members of the Beman family helped found abolitionist organizations.

It was against this backdrop that the *Amistad*'s capture became big news in the summer of 1839. Reports of the capture of the strange schooner appeared in papers from Connecticut and New York all the way down to South Carolina.[5] One newspaper that took particular note was the *Colored American*, a New York paper that at the time was the only paper in the country published by a black pro-prietor and circulated among a mostly black audience.[6] The paper's editor and sole writer, Charles B. Ray, took an immediate interest in the case, no doubt reflecting the interest of his readership, which in-cluded subscribers in big cities like Boston and Philadelphia but also in cities such as Massillon, Ohio, and Hartford, Connecticut.[7] Dur-ing the two years the *Amistad* Africans were in the United States, Ray's four-page weekly paper published more than eighty original articles about the group, updating readers on the status of their trial and helping raise money for their cause.[8]

While the paper's first articles were little more than reprints from other newspapers, on September 14, 1839, Ray reported on a development no one else took note of. With the Africans being held captive in a small jail on New Haven's green, two black self-improvement societies in New York decided to sponsor a concert at a black church for the prisoners' benefit, raising $84.08. The money was donated to the *Amistad* Committee, a group of white abolitionists that became the main group coordinating the legal defense of the Africans and donations to their cause.[9]

New York's black community wasn't the only one immediately intrigued by the Africans. New Haven's sizeable black community also became interested in their fate. According to the 1840 census, New Haven's total population was approximately 14,000, and about seven percent of residents were black. Of the 987 black residents, all but 43 were free citizens.[10] Furthermore, by 1839, New Haven was home to a well-established black church, the Temple Street Colored Congregational Church. [11]Records show that by October 1841 the three African girls found on board the *Amistad* had been attending "Sabbath school and public worship in the African church" for "some time."[12]

Early evidence of the church's involvement in the case is difficult to document, however. At the time the Africans arrived, the church was in a period of transition. Its pastor, the Rev. James W. C. Pennington, who would later figure in preparations for the Africans' return, had just left for another congregation in Hartford.[13] Amos Beman, who served as the church's pastor for the next twenty years, did not take over formally until late 1841, just as preparations were being made for the Africans to return home.[14]

Still, the church's parishioners and their future pastor were no doubt aware of the drama unfolding in their city. The church was just four blocks from the jail where the group was being held.[15] There, visitors lined up by the thousands to pay twelve and a half cents each for the chance to gawk at the Africans.[16] The same scene later repeated itself at the jail in Hartford, where people of all "colors, sexes, and sizes" came to see the men.[17] Meanwhile, a scrapbook Beman kept shows he was not only writing for the *Colored American* but also following the *Amistad* case. Among his papers is a copy of the Supreme Court argument in the case.[18] His later writings note he "had a personal acquaintance with Cinque and the *Amistad* Africans."[19] And in late 1841 Beman became involved with the Union Missionary Society based in Hartford, which was involved in preparations for the Africans' return home.[20]

New Haven's black community had one additional connection to the *Amistad* group. Once the Africans were jailed in the city Yale University professor and linguistics expert Josiah W. Gibbs visited the group and learned to count in Mende, the language most of the group spoke. Gibbs then went to New York and began walking the docks, counting in Mende to any black man he saw. In this way, Gibbs found James Covey, a young formerly enslaved man from Sierra Leone employed on the British Ship *Buzzard*, who returned with Gibbs to New Haven to serve as interpreter.[21] Through Covey, the Africans were able to tell their side of the rebellion story, and Covey quickly became a friend. In a short letter printed in the *American and Foreign Anti-Slavery Reporter* in November 1840 Covey noted he had become a member of one of the city's two black churches. "I now member of the church two months, and very happy in my soul," he wrote.

With their side of the story finally able to be told, the Africans traveled to Hartford for their first trial in Circuit Court on the charges of murder and piracy. The trial lasted for a few days in mid-September 1839, and the group then returned to New Haven where they stayed through the winter of 1839. Their second trial in District Court, on the matter of property and salvage, took place in New Haven and lasted for a week in January 1840. The end result of both hearings was that the captives were free men. Despite the favorable rulings, there was little celebration. There was no doubt the U.S. government would appeal the case to the U.S. Supreme Court.[22]

A little more than a year passed between the lower courts' rulings and the beginning of the Supreme Court trial in February 1841. During the wait, black communities' interest in the case did not wane. If anything, it grew.

The *Colored American* continued to report on the Africans, and editor Charles B. Ray hired a correspondent in Washington to cover the Supreme Court case for the paper. "The doings also of the [S]upreme [Court] in the *Amistad* case, before which court that case is to come . . . will be well worth the price of the paper," Ray wrote in announcing the correspondent, who would write under the pen name "Libertas."[23]

Black communities also continued to send money to the *Amistad* Committee, which was providing defense lawyers for the Africans and taking care of their physical needs. By October 1840, these costs were mounting. Anticipating additional expenses as a result of the upcoming Supreme Court trial, the *Amistad* Committee solicited donations through advertisements in several papers including the *Colored American*. Black communities quickly responded.[24] In December the *Colored American* reported that a benefit on behalf of the *Amistad* men at the Colored Baptist Church in Cincinnati raised $50.[25] In January it reported that black citizens of Wilmington, Delaware, donated $35.[26]

A more complete record of black contributors comes from the *Amistad* Committee itself. As part of its October appeal for money, the group promised to acknowledge all donations with lists in two different newspapers.[27] Each of the resulting four donor lists acknowledges black citizens' contributions. In January, for example, the "Colored Citizens of Cincinnati" were recognized again, this time for a $90 contribution, while the "Colored people in the Little Wesley Church" in Philadelphia gave $40.39. In February the "Colored people in Columbus, O[hio]" sent in $20.50, and the "Colored People of Philadelphia" donated $30.24.

Individuals donated too. Philadelphia resident Hannah Hicks identified herself as "a poor colored woman" when she sent in her donation of fifty cents in November 1840, with the very first group of donors.

At the other end of the spectrum from Ms. Hicks stood wealthy black men such as Robert Purvis, the Philadelphia cotton broker and abolitionist.[28] In December 1840, he and three others were appointed to a committee to solicit donations for the *Amistad* men. But he went further.

Late in 1840 Purvis commissioned a painting of Cinque, the leader of the *Amistad* Africans, from Nathaniel Jocelyn, brother of *Amistad* Committee member and Temple Street Church founder Simeon Jocelyn, at a cost of $260.[29] Purvis had big plans for the portrait, in which Cinque was portrayed not as a slave but as a "tragic hero" in a classic white toga.[30] When the work was finished in early 1841, Purvis had an engraver make copies and then donated the copies to Philadelphia's American Anti-Slavery Society, which sold them at a dollar apiece, with the proceeds benefiting the organization.[31]

Purvis's motives for commissioning the painting likely were more than philanthropic. Art historian Richard J. Powell has argued that the painting was part of a "well-timed, carefully orchestrated publicity campaign" to help the *Amistad* men, one that attracted attention just before the Supreme Court justices adjourned to reach their decision in the case.[32]

On March 9, 1841—eighteen months after the Africans arrived on U.S. shores—the Supreme Court announced its decision in the case. The *Colored American*'s correspondent in Washington announced, "Justice is satisfied, and the *captives* are free!"[33]

While a great deal of excitement followed the Supreme Court's verdict, anyone following the trial closely realized that the *Amistad* affair was not over. Though the Supreme Court had freed the Africans, it had not ordered the government to send them back to Africa. As a result, the *Amistad* Committee and other supporters began to collect money for their return voyage. One of the ways the committee raised money was by bringing members of the *Amistad* group to speak at churches, charging admission and soliciting donations.

The first of these meetings took place in New York City in May 1841.[34] Though the *Amistad* Committee coordinated the meetings, some of the most fruitful stops were at black churches. *Colored American* editor Charles B. Ray attended the New York meetings for both black and white audiences. Of the meeting at the A.M.E. Zion Church on Church and Leonard streets, he told readers:

The audience was principally made up of colored people, and we do not recollect of ever having seen a larger assemblage of our people on any occasion . . . the Africans were more interesting, we thought than at any of the previous meetings. [One of the Africans] in giving a history of his being taken from his own country . . . stated "you are my brethren, the same color as myself."[35]

Dramatic differences between meetings organized for black and white audiences were also evident in Philadelphia, where the Africans traveled after their appearances in New York. Samuel D. Hastings, a white minister who coordinated the Philadelphia appearances, quickly discerned that black audiences were more supportive. Reporting on at least five meetings specifically for white audiences, Hastings was discouraged. After a dismal turnout at one church at which the committee charged admission, Hastings and his fellow organizers decided to hold a free meeting, hoping to raise more money through a simple collection. But a meeting whose target audience was black was much more successful. That meeting raised $60 to $70, while meetings for white audiences had raised only $40 and $50. On May 27 Hastings wrote a fellow abolitionist, "The colored people of [Philadelphia] will do more for the [Africans] than the whites."[36]

In addition, Philadelphia's abolitionist newspaper the *Pennsylvania Freeman* noted that three meetings at the First African Presbyterian church netted $283.87, a little more than half of the total reported collected in Philadelphia. Smaller but no less important was another donation the paper acknowledged—$2.01 collected by the "pupils of the colored Public School."[37]

Meetings were not the only place where free blacks showed their support for the *Amistad* Africans. Just weeks after the Supreme Court's decision, a black community in Buffalo, New York, reported holding a packed celebration at a local hall.[38] And the black residents of Columbus, Ohio, sent a public letter to John Quincy Adams, reported in the *Colored American*, thanking the former president for arguing the case in front of the Supreme Court. The letter said the community was "deeply touched with the result of the trial."[39]

While black communities celebrated the Africans' release, the men themselves settled into a fairly routine life in Farmington, a small town of 2,000 just outside of Hartford and a short distance from New Haven. Though small, the town's black population included a stonemason, a blacksmith, and several farmers and their families. A black woman ran a boarding house where the Africans briefly stayed. And they also attended the city's church, which had both black and white parishioners.[40] A letter about the group written by a local (most likely white) abolitionist during the time notes that a "colored man" was "one of their best friends."[41]

Two visitors to Farmington during this time also suggest that the black community was deeply involved with the *Amistad* men. Philadelphia minister Samuel D. Hastings visited the men in August 1841 and, in a letter, passed along a message from Cinque: Would Robert Purvis, the black Philadelphia cotton broker and abolitionist who had commissioned Cinque's portrait, send him a hat?[42] A few months later, William P. Johnson, one of the organizers of the original concert on behalf of the group at New York's First Colored Presbyterian church, also visited the *Amistad* men and reported on the visit to the *Colored American*.[43]

In nearby Hartford the *Amistad* men found more supporters. There, in 1841, the Rev. James W. C. Pennington[44] organized the Union Missionary Society, a society founded and run by free blacks for the purpose of sending black missionaries back with the *Amistad* Africans. The group held its first meeting in August 1841 and drew forty-three delegates, most of them black, from half a dozen states. Five of the *Amistad* Africans also took part.[45] The society quickly gained financial support from the black community and ultimately was able to pay two black missionaries to accompany the Africans on their journey home.[46]

By November 1841 preparations had been made for the Africans' voyage back to Africa. Both blacks and whites participated in final goodbye ceremonies in New York: one at a white church on November 21 and another at a black church the following evening. Only the meeting at the black church, however, was called "immensely large," a fitting sendoff by a community that had been engaged with the Africans' quest for freedom from the very beginning.[47]

## Notes

This essay is adapted from Gresko's 2005 thesis for Columbia University, "Black Americans and the *Amistad* Case."

1. For a full account of the capture of the ship, see Howard Jones, *Mutiny on the Amistad* (New York: Oxford University Press, 1987), 4–7. The account is primarily based on John Warner Barber's *A History of the Amistad Captives*, written during the trial, and the trial testimony of Lt. Richard W. Meade and another crew member.

2. Jones's 1987 work, *Mutiny on the Amistad*, largely considered the definitive work on the incident, does not mention the black community's reaction to the case. Other, earlier works, including Mary Cable, *Black Odyssey* (New York: Viking, 1971) and William Owens, *Slave Mutiny: The Revolt on the Schooner Amistad* (New York: Plume, 1997 reprint of New York: Dutton, 1953) are similarly silent. In fact, currently, the black community's reaction to the case is confined to one or two pages in works on black history such as Benjamin Quarles's excellent book *Black Abolitionists*, 2d ed. (London: Oxford University Press, 1977) or similar space in autobiographies of prominent black men at the time such as Julie Winch's *A Gentleman of Color: The Life of James Forten* (New York: Oxford University Press, 2002), which profiles the prominent Philadelphia sail maker. However, even Winch, who covers the trial on pages 324–25 and says, "James Forten and his family followed with avid interest the fate of the *Amistad* captives," cites Jones's book as a place to go for further information and a description of the trial.

3. Phillip S. Foner, *History of Black Americans: From the Emergence of the Cotton Kingdom to the Eve of the Compromise of 1850* (Westport, CT: Greenwood Press, 1983), 251. Online Historical Census.

4. Helpful accounts of the growth of the abolitionist movement and black involvement in it can be found in James Brewer Stewart, *Holy Warriors: The Abolitionists and American Slavery* (New York: Hill and Wang, 1976), chapters 2–4, and in Benjamin Quarles's *Black Abolitionists*.

5. "The Slaver," *New York Morning Herald*, August 28, 1839. "The Low Black Schooner Captured," *New York Journal of Commerce* (evening edition) August 28, 1839. "The Low Black Schooner Captured," *Charleston Courier*,

September 2, 1839. "The Suspicious Looking Schooner Captured and Brought Into This Port," *New London Gazette*, August 28,1839. Reprinted in the *Emancipator*, September 6, 1839.

6. Foner, 257.

7. The only reference describing circulation numbers seems to be in Jesse Mae Wyche's 1930 Columbia dissertation "The *Colored American* and Its Editors." Wyche does not explain how he comes up with his circulation figures, however, so I have omitted them. See letters on December 11 and December 25, 1839 for Boston and Buffalo, March 30, 1841 for a letter from Hartford.

8. The only comprehensive biography of Ray is *Sketch of the Life of Rev. Charles B. Ray* written by his two daughters Florence and Henrietta in 1887 after their father passed away. Other accounts of Ray's life are in Benjamin Quarles's *Black Abolitionists* and Gerald Sorin's *The New York Abolitionists*. Another helpful summary is Ray's brief biography in *American National Biography*. This summary of Ray's activities is gleaned from a compilation of those sources.

9. A report on the amount of money the concert raised, its organizers, and where it was held is in *The Colored American*, September 28, 1839. The program of the upcoming concert appears in the September 14, 1839 issue of the paper.

10. Robert Austin Warner, *New Haven Negroes: A Social History*, 2nd ed. (New York: Arno Press, 1969). Slavery did not completely end in Connecticut until 1848. In 1784 the state enacted a gradual emancipation act whereby the children of slaves would be freed when they reached a certain age. Their parents, however, remained slaves. These 43 men and women were not affected by the gradual emancipation act.

11. The church was founded in 1824. Among its founders was Simeon Jocelyn, a white abolitionist who became one of the heads of the *Amistad* Committee, further evidence for a likely connection between the church and the Africans. Additional information about the church can be found in Kurt Schmoke, "The Dixwell Avenue Congregational Church 1829 to 1896" *New Haven Colony Historical Society Journal* 20, no. 1 (1971). It is also important to note that the church went through several name changes. It was first called the Temple Street Colored Congregational Church and was located on Temple Street but later moved to Dixwell Avenue and became known by that street's name.

12. Quote is from Amos Townsend to Lewis Tappan October 3, 1841, *American Missionary Association Papers*. Same is confirmed by another letter of James Birney to Lewis Tappan, October 2, 1841, *American Missionary Association Papers*.

13. David O. White, "The Fugitive Blacksmith of Hartford: James W.C. Pennington." *The Connecticut Historical Society Bulletin* 49, no. 1 (1984): 9.

14. The best source on Beman is Robert A. Warner, "Amos Gerry Beman: 1812–1874; a Memoir on a Forgotten Leader," *The Journal of Negro History*, 22, no. 2 (April 1973): 200–221.

15. See the 1830 "Buckingham Map" in Dean B. Lyman, Jr., *An Atlas of Old New Haven or "Nine Squares" as shown on various early Maps* (New Haven: Chas. W. Scranton & Co., 1929).

16. Jones, 65.

17. The *Morning Herald*, New York. October 4, 1839, quoted in "Amistad—A True Story of Freedom" at the Connecticut Historical Society.

18. Papers of Amos G. Beman. Beinecke Rare Book and Manuscript Library, Yale University.

19. Amos Beman, *Weekly Anglo-African*, from Portland, Maine, March 1, 1859, quoted in David E. Swift, *Black Prophets of Justice*, 186.

20. "Abstract of the Proceedings of the Missionary Convention," the *Colored American*, September 4, 1841.

21. Jones, 43.

22. Accounts of both trials can be found in several places. Jones, 62–135; Cable, 37–75. A shorter account appears in Samuel Flagg Bemis, *John Quincy Adams and the Union* (New York: Knopf, 1956), 390–93 and 397–99.

23. "Correspondent at Washington," the *Colored American*, November 14, 1840.

24. Another appeal appears in the *Pennsylvania Freeman*, November 5, 1840.

25. "Brother Ray—please acknowledge," the *Colored American*, January 2, 1841. The paper reports the sum as $90.

26. "Meeting in [*sic*] Behalf of the Amistad Africans," the *Colored American*, February 6, 1841.

27. The two papers were the *New York Journal of Commerce* and the *American and Foreign Anti-Slavery Reporter*.

28. Basic biographical information on Purvis is available through *American National Biography*.

29. Cinque's name has been spelled various ways over the years: with or without an accent on the "e," as Cinquez or Jinqua, and also as Sengbe. Also complicating matters is the fact that Ruiz and Montes gave Cinque the name Joseph as his Spanish name, and so his name also appears as Joseph Cinque. Scholars now believe the most correct translation of Cinque's name from Mende into English is Sengbe Pieh. I have chosen to spell Cinque's name as it appeared most often in the papers of the time: Cinque. Where authors and historical sources have used other spellings I have preserved their language. Information about the cost of the painting is in Richard J. Powell, "Cinqué: Antislavery Portraiture and Patronage in Jacksonian America" *American Art* 11, no. 3 (Autumn 1997): 57.

30. It is unclear who decided how Cinque should be portrayed. Richard Powell seems to suggest the conception was all that of the artist Nathaniel Jocelyn, brother of *Amistad* Committee member Simeon Jocelyn. I believe, however, that if Purvis had larger aims for the work, then he had some input on the finished product. Powell discusses the imagery of the painting in the same article. The painting itself is in the New Haven Colony Historical Society's exhibit "Cinque Lives Here." Text accompanying the painting states, "Jocelyn is credited as the first American artist to depict an African as more than just a slave."

31. The best source on the Purvis painting is Richard J. Powell, "Cinqué: Antislavery Portraiture and Patronage in Jacksonian America," 48–73. Additional information on it is in Julie Winch, *A Gentleman of Color*, 324–25. Sources conflict on whether Purvis donated the plates or sold them to the society. It is improbable that Purvis needed the society's money, however, and seems more likely that they were given to the group or sold at a nominal fee.

32. Powell, 62.

33. "Postscript," the *Colored American*, March 13, 1841.

34. No official travel schedule for these meetings exists, and even scholarly histories are vague about where the Amistad men stopped and when. Using the Lewis Tappan papers and accounts in the *Colored American*, however, a rough schedule can be charted.

35. "Meetings of the Liberated Africans," the *Colored American*, May 22, 1841.

36. Letters from Hastings to Tappan are written on May 20, 1841 and May 27, 1841. They can be found in the Lewis Tappan Papers at the Library of Congress, reel #6. Quote is from a letter of May 27, 1841. Though a third series of meetings was held in Boston during the approximately second week of November 1841, this meeting is much less well documented. The *Liberator* reports on the meeting (19 November 1841), but this account, its largest, is pulled from another paper, the *Lynn Record*. It is unclear whether or not meetings were held at black churches in Boston or how black communities may have responded.

37. The *Pennsylvania Freeman*, July 16, 1841.

38. "A Meeting of Congratulation," the *Colored American*, April 17, 1841.

39. "Very Interesting Correspondence," the *Colored American*, May 22, 1841.

40. Barbara Donahue, et. al., *Speaking for Ourselves: African American Life in Farmington, Connecticut* (Farmington, CT: Farmington Historical Society, 1998), 22–32.

41. Austin F. Williams letter to Lewis Tappan. August 18, 1841. Farmington Abolitionist Papers.

42. "Amistad Freemen," the *Pennsylvania Freeman*, August 18, 1841.

43. "For the Colored American," the *Colored American*, November 20, 1841.

44. Herman E. Thomas, *James W. C. Pennington: African American Churchman and Abolitionist* (New York: Garland Pub., 1995). One of the best mini-biographies, however, is David O. White, "The Fugitive Blacksmith of Hartford: James W. C. Pennington." Helpful information on Pennington is also in Robert Austin Warner, *New Haven Negroes: A Social History*, and in Quarles, *Black Abolitionists*. Pennington's own biography, *The Fugitive Blacksmith*, in which he revealed for the first time that he was a fugitive slave, came out in 1845. The book, however, is more concerned with his own escape from slavery and does not mention any of his activities related to the *Amistad*.

45. Notices and minutes of the meeting appear in several places. A short notice appears in the *Colored American*: "Abstract of the Proceedings of the Missionary Convention," the *Colored American*, September 4, 1841. The most complete account is from the *Union Missionary Herald*, "Preparatory Convention," January 1842, 4–21.

46. Because of the short time in which the Union Missionary Society had to raise money—from August to November 1841—the group effectively borrowed $500 from the *Amistad* Committee and promised to pay the money back within the year. Clara Merritt DeBoer, *Be Jubilant My Feet: African American Abolitionists in the American Missionary Association, 1839–1861* (New York: Garland Publishing, Inc., 1994), 89.

47. "The *Amistad* Africans. Farewell Meetings and Embarkation," the *Colored American*, December 25, 1841.

# 20  In Search of an Education, Seventeenth to Nineteenth Centuries

Public schooling in the United States throughout the nineteenth century was by modern standards appallingly inadequate.[1] In Connecticut, by the 1830s, schoolhouses typically were dilapidated, the methods and materials of teaching primitive, and teachers more often than not untalented and untrained. Most boys and girls by the age of twelve or fourteen had left school for productive work on the farm or in the factory. Except in the dozen or so larger cities where clusters of African-American families made separate schools possible, the few black children in one-room school houses were treated with disdain, isolated, and inculcated with convictions of their own inferiority. How did this entrenched and virtually universal racism affect the education of Connecticut's small black population?

Most African-American children in antebellum Connecticut received little or no benefit from the common schools. Their parents were not welcome at district school meetings and were systematically excluded from the schools. In 1817 a group of black parents in Norwich protested an initiative by the town to collect poll taxes, which they had not previously paid, nor heard that blacks had ever paid in any town they knew of. The basis of their protest was that "if we must pay taxes the same as white people our request is that we might have the same Privilege granted us as the white people." The particular deprivation they complained of was "the use of the Publick School Money." The General Assembly, which they had petitioned, ordered Norwich either to admit the black students to the public schools or stop taxing their parents. The white town fathers chose to stop taxing them. Nevertheless, black children, forty-one of them, continued to attend Norwich's common school, though apparently taught in separate rooms from white children at the time of the petition.[2]

Under the labor laws of 1813 and 1873, children could be excused from attendance if they lacked suitable shoes or clothing to wear to school.[3] The compulsory attendance law was loosely enforced in general and with regard to black juveniles not at all. Thus the poorest children—those whose parents could not afford shoes or warm clothes for them, who needed their ten-year-olds at home to take care of the three-year-olds, who needed the income of their twelve-year-olds, those who faced the greatest impediment to education generally—were Connecticut's nineteenth- and twentieth-century black families. Henry Barnard pointed this out in 1838 when in his annual state-wide student enumeration of those least likely to attend school he listed black children—for whom he urged the establishment of separate schools and the enforcement of truancy laws. That would cost less, he declared, than the expense of the prosecuting and incarcerating all the black criminals apprehended in the state. Negroes' education, he said, "would be cheaper to the community than their crimes and vices, which are the offspring of neglect and ignorance." Barnard's suggestion was widely and deeply unpopular, and he didn't repeat it in subsequent annual reports.[4]

Nevertheless, in the early nineteenth century, some African-American parents sent their children—at least until the age of nine or ten—to the district common schools. For instance, James Mars, a ten-year-old enslaved boy, attended a district school in Litchfield sometime around 1800, and enslaved children are known to have attended the district school in Colchester before the Revolution. Black and Native American children attended schools in Griswold, Haddam Neck, Colchester, and Norwich, sometimes with greater regularity than whites. In the last of these towns a segregated building, denominated a "high school," was established for black children when the town gave up an old district school building in 1803, but when that facility was closed in response to public pressure in 1840, black students were barred from the public high school.[5]

Even where local custom permitted it, few black parents had the heart to compel their children to attend the district schools. As William W. Ellsworth—who later became Connecticut's governor—pointed out in 1833, "Of every age and in every district school [black children] are to other pupils, but hewers of wood and drawers of water . . . the objects of taunt, contempt, and ridicule." In Rocky Hill, a teacher customarily punished his students by making them sit next to the single black child in his school. A black girl's sitting among white girls in Clinton was cited as an unusual occurrence. As a six-year-old attending a district school in Hampton in about 1809, Theodore Weld, later a great abolitionist leader, found a sin-

FIGURE 20-1 Students and Teacher at Center School, Farmington Village, Kellogg Studio, 1885. *Farmington Library, Farmington, Connecticut*

gle black boy in the one-room building. The boy was seated alone at the back, isolated from all other contact. The boy recited by himself and the teacher "generally sent him back to his seat with a cuff or a jeer." When Weld, in sympathy, asked to be seated next to him, the teacher "burst out laughing and exclaimed, 'Why, are you a nigger, too?' and, 'Theodore Weld is a nigger,' resounded throughout the school."[6]

Indeed, the anti-slavery—but racist—Connecticut Colonization Society warned in 1828 that if you educate the Negro, "you have added little or nothing to his happiness—you have unfitted him for the society and sympathies of his degraded kindred, and yet you have not procured for him and cannot procure for him any admission into the society and sympathy of white men." One white commentator said in 1833 that in Connecticut's district schools "the colored class sit on the lowest bench. They cannot go to these schools—as soon as their minds become expanded, they must retire from them." He challenged his audience to point out to him a single instance "where any black had continued to attend, for any length of time, and derive benefit," apparently wholly unaware of the irony in his statement.[7]

This school-house racial persecution drove African-American children out of the common schools—called "common" because they were intended to mix together future citizens of all classes and religions, but apparently not races. Black Connecticans early sought remediation. By the mid-nineteenth century the state's largest cities included small black ghettoes in which towns and districts could erect schoolhouses to serve small neighborhoods of wholly black children. For many African-American parents, these schools were a relief, free of racial discrimination and demeaning isolation.

A quick survey of Connecticut's major cities reveals this pattern. In New Haven, for instance, as early as 1792 three young women, daughters of the city's most prominent and best-respected families, established, as a private philanthropy and in the face of considerable local opposition, a primary school for African-American children. That school's duration is described as "many years." Schools for blacks were set up in 1811 and 1825 as part of New Haven's common school system.[8]

In 1851—two years after *Roberts v. Boston*, in which the Massachusetts Supreme Court upheld segregated schooling—the New Haven school committee voted "that in as much as schools are organized and in successful operation for colored children, it is inexpedient to admit any into the schools of the white children." In 1850, out of New Haven's black population of 7,693, 1,264 were in school. But black children were not admitted to the embryonic public secondary schools such as the one provided by private philanthropy in New Haven in the 1830s. In 1860, there were three primary schools for African-Americans in New Haven; attendance, however, was irregular. But in 1870, because of the anti-segregation state law of 1868, they were closed down by the New Haven Board of Education—perhaps out of spite, as the Board declared, "the law stepped in and virtually said there are no longer any colored people in the State. It seems now, to the Board, that no course was left to them except to get rid of the School as quickly as possible."[9]

In Hartford a separate school for black children was set up at least as early as 1809 but had disappeared not later than the mid-1820s. In 1833, in association with the establishment of the Talcott Street Church a few years earlier, a primary school was conducted in the little church.[10] At about the same time the African Methodist Episcopal Church organized a school in its church on Pearl Street. This school was probably better than most country district schools—even those within the Hartford system. In 1857 it enrolled eighty-six students who attended in much larger proportions than did their white neighbors. In 1859 a new building was put up on Pearl Street—described "as a model building, without any superior of its kind in the country."[11]

Not so well known as those in Hartford and New Haven, the black school in Bridgeport was perhaps the longest lived, established in its own building in 1841 and continued after 1871 in one ungraded room of the Prospect Street School. When segregation was forbidden in 1868 under state law, the black students in the Prospect Street School were distributed according to age throughout the school—but not until 1880.[12]

In 1861 the Middletown board of education suggested "that the interests of the District would be promoted by the establishment of a small school exclusively for colored children." Such a school was set up in the basement of the high school, and though at first few were willing to attend there, it shortly became a success with attendance rates higher than those of many other primary schools. Within a few years its graduates were going on to the district high school. Four African American students applied for admission in 1864, and none of the white students "have passed a better examination or proved themselves more worthy of advancement," the district visitor reported.[13] In 1874, the secretary of the state board of education, Birdseye N. Northrop—who opposed forced integration—reported that "mixed" schools had "long been maintained in Connecticut." "With two or three exceptions of separate schools maintained on a liberal plan acceptable to all, the races mix freely in our [common primary] schools."[14]

Indeed, by the mid-nineteenth century, Connecticut's major cities all supported—though marginally—at least one school for African-American children. Most youngsters, of course, were still consigned to the ill-kept and ill-attended one-room schoolhouses across still largely agricultural Connecticut. Typically these schools served twenty to forty students with no black students or perhaps only a couple. It is a telling irony that, while public-school advocates and supporters extolled the common schools as incubators of the republican principles of liberty and equality, they would have those principles inculcated in segregated schools. You could meld city kids and rural kids, German kids and Yankee kids with Irish-Catholic kids; different nationalities, languages, even religions could be enveloped in a common democratic ethos—but not different races.

Connecticut's nineteenth-century black citizens, like others across the North, were divided in their opinions as to the content and objectives of these segregated schools. Some wanted to emulate the white common schools; others believed training in the trades would be more appropriate. One who promoted a curriculum of parallel tracks, the traditional three Rs and training to practice a trade or profession, was Rev. James W. C. Pennington. Pennington, who had escaped slavery in Maryland, was trained as a blacksmith and self-educated in traditional common school courses and then the classics with help from sympathetic white men he encountered along the way. Pennington taught in black schools in the 1830s and 1840s in Newtown, on Long Island, and in New Haven. While there, he studied theology and was soon called to fill black pastorates in Hartford and New Haven, teaching in segregated schools associated with his pastorate in each town. The schools in Hartford, where Pennington taught from 1840 or earlier to 1847, were part of that city's common school system, but Pennington had to beg the school society for his school's share of the state school fund and local school taxes. Connecticut's common schools were always under-funded, and black schools more so than the others.[15]

Pennington saw the hazards in restricting the education of black children to the common schools, where not only the teachers and students were racially derogatory but the textbooks as well. Schooling in that physical and intellectual environment would continue to mis-educate African American children, inculcating and reinforcing beliefs that blacks were inferior, as Carter Woodson would point out in the twentieth century. Nevertheless, the Hartford African schools taught the traditional skills and subjects.[16]

Despite the burden of their race, a few extraordinary black Connecticans leveraged formal education to lift themselves into the classically trained intellectual elite. We have already met James Pennington, and David Ruggles (1810–1849) is written about elsewhere in this volume. One other such Connecticut-educated intellectual was Edward Bouchet (1852–1918).

Edward Bouchet attended one of New Haven's primary schools for African American children; he excelled there and was admitted to the prestigious Hopkins School founded in New Haven in 1660, graduating first in his class. He was admitted to Yale, became the college's first black graduate, and was elected to Phi Beta Kappa. He was America's first black recipient of a Ph.D. degree (from Yale, in chemistry). Bouchet spent most of his adult life as a teacher at the Institute for Colored Youth in Philadelphia. His colleague there was Ebenezer Bassett, who was educated in New Haven's colored district schools, studied at Yale, and became, in 1857, the first—and for a while the only—black graduate of the Normal School at New Britain. After a year of very successful teaching in New Haven, Bassett, too, found a friendlier acceptance in Philadelphia, where he entered politics and earned appointment by Ulysses Grant in 1869 as minister to Haiti. He served there until 1877 and remained for the rest of his career in the U.S. counselor service.[17]

Another Connecticut-educated teacher was Amos Gerry Beman

FIGURE 20-2 Edward A. Bouchet (*second row, third from right*), Yale University Class of 1874 Reunion Portrait, Pach Brothers Studio, 1914. *The Amistad Center for Art & Culture, Inc., Simpson Collection, 1987.1.1414*

(1812–1874). He grew up in Colchester, where there was an active primary school for African American children. Beman's father became the pastor at Middletown's African church. An ugly racial incident at Wesleyan inspired a student there to make amends by tutoring Beman. After only a few months that project's participants came under threat of physical harm, and their work together ended. But Beman had learned enough to proceed with a classical education on his own. He studied for the ministry and in 1839 succeeded Pennington as pastor of the Temple Street Church in New Haven. Like Pennington, Beman conducted a school for children of his congregation and remained not only a much respected pastor and teacher, but also a civic leader and major force in the temperance movement. Perhaps more meaningful was his participation in the effort to enfranchise Connecticut's black males (which was accomplished two years after his death) and, of course, in anti-slavery movements.[18] The success of these men is attributable to their extraordinary—even heroic—character and intellect, not to their local schooling. "We may safely assume," writes one qualified scholar, "that two to three times as many colored as white adults lacked command of literacy and arithmetic and the basic intellectual orientation to their world." For those who did succeed, "we must look elsewhere than the schools."[19]

Racially segregated schools had never been required by law in Connecticut. Where they did exist, it was by local district policy, usually a matter of unwritten tradition. In still-rural Connecticut, perhaps twenty districts out of about 1,600 had rooms or buildings set aside for African American students. In Hartford, the "model school" on Pearl Street was a good one and open to blacks only. But much of Hartford was still thinly populated, and black children who lived on the outskirts continued to go to the regular district schools. In 1864 the Hartford School Committee said that either all black children should attend the black school, or that school should be disbanded and the black children integrated into the "mixed" schools. A Hartford town meeting, however, voted that no "colored children should attend the District Schools." This was in April 1868, when the Radical Republicans had gained control of the General Assembly. In May they quickly passed a law forbidding such discrimination—explicitly requiring every public school in the state be "opened to every child between the age of four and sixteen, residing in the district, without regard to race or color." The Pearl Street school, however, remained open for a time "for any who wished to attend."[20]

The statute of 1868 outlawing compulsory segregation, though inspired by the action of the Hartford town meeting, applied throughout the state. Thus all the schools set up specifically for African American children, often at the request of their parents, were either shut down or opened to students of any race. Segregated public schools nevertheless continued to function in Connecticut for eight years after they had been declared illegal by the General Assembly.[21] They were worse than an anomaly: In a state that boasted of its common schools as guarantors of egalitarian republicanism, racial segregation in those very schools profoundly degraded and disgraced the state and its citizens—many of whom by the end of the Civil War knew better, but let it happen.

By the turn of the twentieth century most Connecticut residents lived in cities. In 1920, three out of every ten Connecticans lived in Hartford, New Haven, or Bridgeport—and blacks were even more concentrated in urban centers than whites.[22] In 1915 about 2 percent of the students in New Haven schools were black; and in 1930, 3.5 percent (1,047 students), which appears to show some improvement. But when we know that six years later there were only 284 black high-school graduates resident in that city, a rather dismal picture appears. Just as large numbers of African Americans were about to migrate into Connecticut from the South, the educational context of the black community was thin, indeed. During World War I, as black migration out of the South to northern industrial cities increased, Hartford's African American population rose from about

1,500 to 4,000. A subterranean movement, perhaps inspired by the racist and much-viewed film *The Birth of a Nation* (1915), created a groundswell of pressure to set up separate schools for black immigrants—but not white ones, of which there were tens of thousands in the city. Counter-pressures convinced Superintendent of Schools Thomas Weaver to withhold the segregationist plan, and the proposal died. But Rev. Richard Randolph Ball of the A.M.E. Zion Church put forth a plea, poignant in its prophetic sentiment: "Where there is segregation," he declared, "there is no equality in school appropriations, length of school term and character of buildings and there is unequal pay for teachers." Separate schools would not be equal, and in the end, they were not established.[23]

Between 1940 and 1970, when the first wave of black migration began to recede, another, much greater wave—associated with Connecticut's booming war industries—washed into Connecticut's cities. By 1970, the black population made up 6.5 percent of the whole population of the state. But in 1959, as the black population began to swell noticeably, 20 percent of Connecticut residents reported that they had never met or talked to an African American. As late as 1959—five years after *Brown v. Board*—5 percent of both blacks and whites in Connecticut opposed integrated schools, and 37 percent of whites opposed integrated residential neighborhoods. And we should remember that as late as 1949 it was not illegal in Connecticut to spend tax money—collected from both black and white taxpayers—to build segregated public housing developments. Indeed, it was another ten years before it was illegal to discriminate in private housing in the Land of Steady Habits.[24]

Notes

1. The low state of public schooling in nineteenth-century Connecticut is thoroughly documented in Christopher Collier, *Connecticut's Public Schools: A History, 1650–2000* (Orange, Connecticut: Clearwater Press, 2009).

2. "Miscellaneous," II:33, Connecticut State Library. Vol. XXX, "John Cotton Smith Papers." Vol. VI. 229, Connecticut Historical Society; Frances Manwaring Caulkins. *A History of Norwich, Connecticut. . . .* (Norwich: The Author, 1866), 556.

3. On the child labor laws, see Collier, op. cit. pf. 191.

4. Henry Barnard, *First Annual Report* of the Board of Commissioners of the Common Schools in Connecticut together with the "First Annual Report" of the Secretary of the Board (Hartford: Case, Tiffany, 1839), 34. Barnard's "Reports" are highly repetitive from year to year and include a lot

of boilerplate. The omission of his comments about truancy laws and black students had to be deliberate.

5. James Mars, "Life of James Mars, a Slave Born and Sold in Connecticut," in *Five Black Lives*, Arna Bontemps, ed. (Middletown, CT: Wesleyan University Press, 1971), 47–48; Carter G. Woodson. *The Education of the Negro Prior to 1861* (New York: G. P. Putnam's, 1915), 239. Barnard, "Report of the Secretary," 1846, 19. The Massachusetts legislature outlawed racially segregated schools in 1855.

6. William W. Ellsworth, *Statement of Facts. . . .* (Brooklyn, CT: Advertiser Press, 1833), 10; J. Hammond Trumbull, *Memorial History of Hartford County, Connecticut, 1633 to 1884*. 2 vols., I (Boston: Edward L. Osgood, 1886.) 633; G. H. Barnes and D. L. Dumond (eds.), *Letters of T. D. Weld, Angelina G. Weld, and Sarah Grimke, 1822–1844*. 2 vols. II (New York: Appleton-Century-Crofts, 1934), 697; Catherine H. Birney, *The Grimke Sisters: Sarah and Angelina Grimke: The First American Women Advocates of Abolition and Women's Rights* (Westport, CT: Greenwood Press, 1969 [1885]), 116n.

7. Leon F. Litwack, *North of Slavery. The Negro in the Free States, 1790–1860* (Chicago: University of Chicago Press, 1961), 23, 226. Ellsworth, *Statement of Facts*, 15.

8. Charles E. Cunningham, *Timothy Dwight, 1752–1817. A Biography* (New York: MacMillan, 1942), 336. Robert Austin Warner, *New Haven Negroes: A Social History* (New Haven: Yale University Press, 1940), pf. 74.

9. Louise G. Wrinn, "The Development of the Public School System in New Haven, 1639–1930: A Problem in Historical Analysis" (dissertation, Yale University, 1933), 63–64, 67, 69, 354. Warner, *New Haven Negroes*, 73–77.

10. Ellsworth Strong Grant and Marion Hepburn Grant. *The City of Hartford, 1784–1984. An Illustrated History* (Hartford: Connecticut Historical Society, 1986), 60–62.

11. Report of the Hartford School Visitors, 1857, p. 10; 1866, 7, 14, 10; 1869, p. 9, Connecticut State Library; Statutes of 1869, 218.

12. Evelen Rosenfeld Harris, "The Transformation of the Bridgeport, Connecticut, Schools: A Study of the Process of Educational Change, 1876–1880," (dissertation, New York University, 1983), 289n17.

13. Middletown Board of Education, *Fourth Annual Report*, 1861, 3; Middletown Board of Education *Annual Report*, 1864; 15; Bridgeport Board of Education, *Fourth Annual Report*; "Historical sketch of the Schools of Bridgeport prior to consolidation," 1880, 15; Richard Michael Jones, "Stonington Borough: A Connecticut Seaport in the Nineteenth Century," (dissertation, City University of New York, 1976), 288.

14. Birdsey N. Northrop, *Report of the Secretary to the Board of Commissioners of Education*, 1874.

15. Herman Edward Thomas, "An Analysis of the Life and Work of James W. C. Pennington, a Black Churchman and Abolitionist" (dissertation, Hartford Seminary Foundation, 1978), 256–65. On the perpetual underfunding of Connecticut's public schools, see Collier, *Public Schools*, especially chapters 3 and 22.

16. Thomas, "Pennington," 258–59; Carter Godson Woodson, *The Mis-Education of the Negro* (New York: SoHo Books, 2012 [1933]) Passim.; David

O. White. "Hartford's African Schools," *Bulletin*, Connecticut Historical Society, 39 (April 1974): 47–53.

17. Warner, *New Haven Negroes*, 78, 74; Frank Andrews Stone, "African American Connecticut: African Origins, New England Roots," typescript (Storrs, CT.: University of Connecticut, 1991), 136; *Wikipedia*, "Ebenezer Bassett."

18. Warner, "Amos Gerry Beman, 1812–1874; a Memoir on a Forgotten Leader," 200–221.

19. Warner, *New Haven Negroes*, 74, 78.

20. *Public Acts*, 1867. Title XI. Ch. II., Section 1. 129. "Report" of the Hartford School Visitors, 1857, 1860, 1866, 7, 14, 10; 1868, Connecticut State Library. The principal object of the statute of 1868 was to do away with tuition and make the common schools open and free to all. The abolition of racial segregation was a secondary purpose. The Act is thoroughly discussed in the "Annual Report" of the Secretary of the Board in the *Annual Report* of the Board of Education for 1879 (New Haven: Tuttle, Morehouse, 1879), 33–36, and in Collier, *Connecticut's Public Schools*, 178–80.

21. As we have seen, in the Prospect Street School in Bridgeport, African-American children were kept in segregated, ungraded classrooms until 1880. On how the common schools "mis-educated" black children, inculcating in them feelings—even convictions—of inferiority, see Woodson, *Mis-Education*, passim.

22. Population statistics are derived from Grace Pierpont Fuller, *An Introduction to the History of Connecticut as a Manufacturing State*, Smith College Studies in History No. 1, "Introduction" and passim.

23. Wrinn, "Development," 299, 315; Mark Jones, "When Hartford Almost Segregated Its Schools," *The Hartford Courant*, November 6, 1994, D1–3; John W. Jeffries, *Testing the Roosevelt Coalition: Connecticut Society and Politics in the Era of World War II* (Knoxville: University of Tennessee Press, 1979), 217, 61, 52; Henry G. Stetler, *Attitudes Toward Racial Integration in Connecticut* (Hartford: Commission on Civil Rights, 1961), 1, 8, 29.

24. "Census Finds Blacks Leaving State," *New York Times*, April 16, 1978; "Race, Ethnic Shifts Shown," *New York Times*, April 19, 1981, Section 11, 14; Stetler, *Attitudes*, 29, 39. Stetler surveyed 556 white and 527 black respondents.

## 21 "Cast Down on Every Side"

### *The Ill-Fated Campaign to Found an "African College" in New Haven*

In 1831, a group of black and white abolitionists from across the eastern seaboard launched a campaign to build the nation's first black college. With Simeon Jocelyn, a young white minister from New Haven, and Peter Williams, the head of New York's St. Phillip's African Episcopal Church, at the helm, the group sought to expand black men's access to higher education. As few white institutions would admit people of color, the group envisioned an "African College" where black men could obtain mechanical and agricultural training and pursue classical studies.

On the first Monday of September 1831, college supporters placed a small advertisement in the *Philadelphia Chronicle* announcing their intentions. They deemed New Haven, Connecticut the most suitable location for the new institution. The seaport's maritime connections with the West Indies, they hoped, would induce island residents to send their sons abroad to the college. They described New Haven's townspeople as "friendly, pious, generous, and humane" and its laws as "salutary and protecting to all, without regard to complexion."[1]

It took white New Haveners just three days to disprove such characterizations. The following Saturday, at the request of New Haven's mayor Dennis Kimberly, more than seven hundred white men packed into town hall. As one attendant observed, "so great was the interest to hear the discussions that notwithstanding the excessive heat and the almost irrespirable atmosphere of the room, the hall was crowded throughout the afternoon."[2] By the day's close, white townspeople had rejected the proposal and agreed to "resist" its establishment "by every lawful means." The vote had passed 700 to 4.[3]

College supporters never expected the path to be easy. They had come of age at a time when African Americans' access to primary learning was expanding largely through the black community's own efforts, but collegiate education remained out of reach. In 1826, for example, E. F. Hughes publicized his school for "colored children" in New York. In Philadelphia the same year, black men and women formed an "Education Society" to "raise funds" to "secure a suitable building . . . for the reception of colored youth."[4] In Hartford, blacks formed the city's first African church in 1827 and opened a small schoolroom in its basement; this was the first such school for black children in city history. Four years later, free blacks in the city constructed a meetinghouse that included a separate Sabbath school.[5]

During the previous decade in New Haven, white townspeople had encouraged free blacks to build their own schools and open Temple Street, a black church. Simeon Jocelyn had found his white neighbors generally supportive of his efforts to expand black education.

In light of such efforts to expand blacks' educational opportunity, college planners did not anticipate a rejection so swift and so bitter. Many later recalled being awed by the ferociousness of the response against them. As college supporter and black Philadelphian James Forten remarked, "the New Haven opposition was . . . quite unlooked for, [it] is one of the most discreditable things for a free state, that I ever heard of."[6]

On the surface, it is not hard to understand why college proponents put so much faith in New Haven. By 1830, New Haven was the largest city in Connecticut, and its population was growing rapidly. Alternating with Hartford as the capital of Connecticut, the town offered both the benefits of a large, cosmopolitan city and those of a small community intimately linked by ties of family and church. The seaport was conveniently located between New York, some 75 miles to the south, and Boston, about 130 miles to the north. Transportation networks to and around the town were improving daily. The turnpike system was largely finished by 1814; a year later, regular steamboat service connected New Haven with Manhattan. Commercial activity bustled around the wharf, Custom House Square, and East Water Street, where an active West India trade fueled the local economy. Still, its population of just more than 10,000 was tiny in comparison to those of the other eastern ports of Boston, Philadelphia, Baltimore, and New York. And while the free black populations in those cities were numerous and expanding, New Haven's black population was small, self-contained, and stagnant, numbering around 600 people. Relations between the white majority and black minority appeared stable and harmonious. "No place in the Union," abolitionist William Lloyd Garrison concluded, is "the situation [of blacks] more comfortable, or the prejudices of a community weaker against them."[7]

New Haven's general enthusiasm for reform also attracted the college planners. Predominantly Protestant, white, and native-born, New Haveners enthusiastically championed the benevolent movements of the age, especially temperance, colonization, and education.

The seaport also had a tradition of embracing educational outsiders. In addition to Yale College, the town hosted three male academies, two female seminaries, and several boarding schools. At least on the surface, college supporters had good reason to believe their institution would complement New Haven's commitment to religion, education, and uplift.

New Haven's swift assault against the college suggests champions of the African college had woefully overestimated white New Haveners' broadmindedness. Underneath the city's progressive veneer, college advocates encountered a white community violently hostile to black improvement, particularly to efforts to develop black men's vocational skills. As Forten observed in the aftermath of the institution's collapse, the African college was "cast down on every side."[8] Opposition crossed class and ethnic boundaries. New Haven's wealthier male residents, those eligible to attend the September meeting by virtue of their status as freeholders, were eager to keep college education the sole preserve of the white elite. For many of these men, themselves Yale alumni, calling a school for black men a "college" (and building it beside their alma mater) was profoundly unsettling. The concerns they voiced centered around the deleterious effects of the college on the social and economic status of their community, on Yale, and, by extension, on themselves.

Expressing their outrage on street corners and in the local press, New Haven's working classes opposed the college with a similar intensity. They rejected the manual labor college because they perceived it jeopardized their social and economic stability. For the preceding half-decade, construction on the Farmington Canal had been attracting scores of unskilled workers (predominantly Irish but also free blacks) to the city. Many white mechanics feared this alternative source of cheaper labor endangered their own socioeconomic security.

While status and economic anxieties contributed to the proposed college's downfall, such tensions alone do not adequately explain why this seemingly progressive community would rise so swiftly against a proposal with reform at its center. How could the college planners have been so wrong in their perception of New Haven?

The planners had failed to take into account two additional factors that brought about the planned college's demise. In short, the timing could hardly have been worse.

First, beneath this small seaport's liberal exterior, the racial fabric that tenuously bound its social and economic order had been quietly unraveling for decades. To white dismay, the excruciating process of gradual emancipation Connecticut initiated in 1784 had been eating away at the legal and occupational strictures that had fixed blacks' physical, social, and economic mobility. Emancipation in Connecticut moved at a slow and uneven pace. The 1784 statute decreed that all "Negro" or "mulatto" children born within the state after March 1 of that year would be free after their 25th birthday. In other words, masters did not have to release a single slave until 1809. By 1790, approximately 2,700 slaves remained. By the turn of the nineteenth century, Connecticut whites still held nearly a thousand blacks in bondage. Whites sold black slaves on New Haven's Center Green into the 1820s. In 1830, papers still carried the occasional notice of a "servant" for sale. In 1831, twenty-three people of color remained enslaved in Connecticut. The state would not formally abolish slavery until 1848.

In response to this protracted emancipation, many whites attempted to fashion systems of control to replace chattel slavery; in the process, free blacks lost many "freedoms" they exercised as bondspeople. For example, while enslaved, people of color were trained in all sorts of occupations, as free men and women they no longer received vocational education and were often excluded from profitable trades.

Diminished opportunities for vocational education paralleled declines in blacks' rights of citizenship. Connecticut's property-owning free blacks could vote in local and national elections throughout the eighteenth century, but in 1814, the state denied all African Americans suffrage. That statute gave Connecticut the dubious distinction of being the only state in New England to disenfranchise its black population.

In New Haven through the first decades of the nineteenth century, a rigid system of socio-occupational and residential segregation emerged to replace the boundary that once demarcated enslaved from free. With few exceptions, New Haven's free blacks lived cloistered in the ramshackle neighborhood dubbed "New Liberia," not far from the Mill River, laboring as seamen, domestics, and unskilled workers. And while the percentage of free blacks in New Haven was tiny and decreasing in the fall of 1831, the perceived threat engendered by their presence was on the increase. Few blacks living in the city were controlled by a master's direct supervision or a formal system of curfew laws and travel restrictions. White New Haveners' opposition to the college stemmed from their desire to halt more black arrivals. As one New Havener complained, "The establishment of a College here . . . would hurry in the blacks, as bees to a hive."[9]

By the fall of 1831, tensions surrounding free people of color in New Haven were reaching their breaking point, exacerbated by calls to extend emancipation nationwide. White abolitionist William Lloyd Garrison's radical publication *The Liberator* hit New Haven streets in January 1831. Just one year earlier black Bostonian David Walker had published his *Appeal*, which sanctioned black-on-white violence to secure social change. Where the process of gradual emancipation in New Haven had been eroding white power to control black physical, occupational, and socio-economic mobility, escalating pressure for national emancipation made the notion of an African college (championed by black and white abolitionists) even more unsettling.

Then, in early September, whites' worst fears about emancipation were confirmed. The same week college supporters published their intentions news reached New Haven of the worst black-on-white violence in the nation's history. When New Haveners opened their local papers on September 13, 1831, they learned simultaneously of the plan to build a college for black men in their back yard and of Nat Turner's rebellion in Southampton, Virginia (during which 55 whites would be killed and, in retaliation, as many as 200 blacks). In some newspapers, articles about the college and the massacre in Virginia appeared side by side. Coverage of the rebellion made no secret of its leader's education. The *Columbian Register*, for example, highlighted Turner's literacy by observing, "Nat is a shrewd fellow" who "reads and writes, [and] preaches."[10] To many New Haveners, the implication that black education fomented black-on-white violence must have been clear. Thus, when white townspeople responded to the college proposal, it was almost impossible for them not to invoke the Turner episode. For a community already uneasy with the free black population that seemingly was increasing in their midst, the shock of Turner's rebellion was too much to withstand. Little could Turner have imagined that among the casualties of his uprising would be the first college for African Americans.

Even after college proponents rescinded their plans, unrest in

New Haven persisted. Less than a month after the meeting, New Haven whites unleashed their anger over the African college by attacking tangible symbols of their frustrations: a black-owned hotel, a black-owned property, and a white abolitionist's summer home. By destroying the New Haven home of abolitionist and college supporter Arthur Tappan, rioters denounced federal interference with local affairs and renounced the prospect of immediate emancipation. The townspeople who attacked Tappan's home were never identified, though Tappan believed they were southern medical students attending Yale. By also razing a black-owned home to its foundations, rioters declared their desire to halt the black economic progress they perceived as occurring at their expense. And by raiding a black-owned hotel also rumored to be a "house of ill repute," white men crushed the figurative and literal "amalgamation" a "college for colored youth" would invariably, in their opinion, propagate. Such attacks quashed any hope that the African college might one day open in New Haven.

The abandonment of the plan for the nation's first African college in New Haven represents a critical turning point in the history of black education. This episode ushered in one of the bleakest periods for black schooling in New England. Within the next five years, four other towns in the region would erupt over efforts to expand black education. In 1833, Canterbury, Connecticut exploded into violence in response to Prudence Crandall's effort to establish a school for black girls. On May 24, 1833, the Connecticut legislature passed its notorious "Black Laws" banning the education of African Americans who were not state residents. In September 1834, an unidentified group assaulted Crandall's house, throwing bricks through the window and attempting to set the residence on fire. The following summer, an irate mob in Canaan, New Hampshire, stormed Noyes Academy, an integrated classical school. On August 10, 1835, a mob attacked again, removing the school from its foundations and depositing it in a nearby swamp.

Connecticut repealed its "Black Laws" in 1838. Still, it would be another two decades before the first institution of higher education for blacks would be established—in Ohio—with the opening of Wilberforce University, owned and operated by African Americans, in 1856. Ultimately, the planned demise the New Haven college exposed a widespread white uneasiness with black aspiration and abolitionist agitation, the twin motives behind the college campaign. In the immediate aftermath of Turner's rebellion, a community uneasy with decades of gradual emancipation and increasing pressure for immediate abolition would not endorse any proposal that might facilitate such racial change. To many white New Haveners, black education and emancipation were intertwined. They refused to sanction such an unholy alliance.

## Notes

This essay originally appeared in the Summer 2007 issue of *Connecticut Explored*. It was adapted from "Education's Inequity: Opposition to Black Higher Education in Antebellum Connecticut," which appeared in vol. 46, no. 1 (Spring 2006), 16–35, in *History of Education Quarterly*.

1. "Education—An Appeal to the Benevolent," *Philadelphia Chronicle*, September 5, 1831; *Minutes and Proceedings of the First Annual Convention of the People of Color* (Philadelphia, 1831).
2. *Connecticut Journal*, September 13, 1831.
3. "Negro College and City Meeting," *Columbian Register*, September 13, 1831.
4. *Freedom's Journal*, May 11, 1827.
5. Ibid., November 23, 1827.
6. James Forten to William Lloyd Garrison, October 20, 1831, Anti-Slavery Collection, Boston Public Library.
7. "Extracts from a Letter from the Editor," *Liberator*, June 18, 1831.
8. James Forten to William Lloyd Garrison, July 28, 1832, in *The Black Abolitionist Papers* (microfilm collection), edited by George E. Carter, C. Peter Ripley, and Jeffrey Rossback, 1:0206.
9. "New Haven," *Connecticut Journal*, October 11, 1831.
10. "Southampton Affair," *Columbian Register*, September 13, 1831.

*Barbara M. Tucker*

# 22 Sarah Harris and the Prudence Crandall School

In the 1830s anti-black sentiment intensified throughout Connecticut. Residents in Hartford, New Haven, Meriden, Torrington, and Danbury demonstrated against abolitionist speakers, attacked black residents, and raided black people's neighborhoods. Much of this anger was directed at those abolitionists and outsiders who wanted to establish schools for the education and training of black people. At the time, the climate was not favorable for such educational experiments. In 1831 the Nat Turner rebellion traumatized a nation. In Virginia a black slave, Nat Turner, led an uprising against local white residents in Southampton County; the rampage left fifty-five white people dead and the local community shocked. Panic spread. In Connecticut white people feared that their life and property would be imperiled if large numbers of blacks were allowed to congregate in their towns. What would prevent black mobs from rioting, setting fire to their property, and killing local residents? So when a coalition of black and white abolitionists selected New Haven as the preferred site for a black men's college, the local population got angry. In September 1831 they voted 700 to 4 to prevent such a college from opening; still, rumors spread that the college would be built, and residents took additional actions: They rioted, stoned the homes of antislavery leaders, broke down doors, and attacked black businesses and their patrons. Few people, including members of the Yale community, supported the college. Those who had organized or financed the black school, including William Lloyd Garrison, Arthur Tappan, and Rev. Simeon Jocelyn, were forced to abandon their plans.[1]

Yet shortly thereafter, another attempt to educate black people was undertaken. This time the small, rural, agricultural community of Canterbury was the location. Rather than establish a college, this experiment would afford "little Misses of color" a high school education. Several of those engaged in the earlier New Haven venture, including Garrison and Tappan, supported and encouraged this school as well. Unlike the New Haven enterprise, the Canterbury Female Boarding School would in fact open and enroll black students.

The principal of the Canterbury school was Prudence Crandall, and one of her first black pupils was Sarah Harris. The Harris family had recently moved to Canterbury from Norwich, a commercial town several miles away. During the early nineteenth century, Norwich was a center of African American culture. Most black people lived in the Jail Hill section of town, a somewhat inhospitable hilltop area that overlooked the harbor. Bypassed by local residents because of the cliffs and the steep sloping terrain, it became the home for many disadvantaged African Americans. Because of the topography, house lots were inexpensive and the houses themselves had to be stair-stepped up steep slopes. Among those who lived there in the antebellum era were people who played a significant role in the anti-slavery movement, including the family of William and Sally Harris.

Born in the West Indies, William Harris married Sally Prentice in April 1810, and together they had twelve children, including Sarah, born in April 1812. While in Norwich, members of the Harris family attended the Second Congregational Church of Norwich. Although the congregation was predominantly white and wealthy, African American parishioners were encouraged to attend services. Indeed, the minister and his congregation actively courted the black community. As early as 1815, a Sabbath school was opened for black students and within two years, forty-one pupils matriculated, including the children of William and Sally Harris. Their association with the Congregational Church continued, and in 1828 Sarah was accepted into the church. By then her minister offered long orations on the evils of slavery and the need for public action to do away with it. Reverend James Dickinson, for example, called upon his congregation to establish an abolitionist society because "we need such a society to correct and embody public sentiment and cause it to bear against this sin."[2] The Harris family embraced the movement, and William and his son Charles even became local agents for the abolitionist newspaper *The Liberator*. Its editor, William Lloyd Garrison, was to have a major part in the upcoming drama in Canterbury.

The Harris family moved to Canterbury. In January 1832 Sally purchased sixty-four acres of land in the Westminster section of town from Samuel Hough. The property conveyed was sizeable for the time and included a dwelling house, barn, and granary. For this she paid $900, money she borrowed from J. G. W. Trumbull of Norwich, a well-known attorney, commercial agent, and community leader. The Harris land bordered the property of some of the town's leading figures: Daniel Frost, Jonathan Adams, Samuel Dyer, and David Butts. The deed was signed by Sally and not jointly with her husband. Six months later William and Sally together acquired additional land on credit. Within four years the loan was repaid from the proceeds of their farm, and they were ready to expand once again. In 1836 they bought almost twelve acres and paid $120 for the land.[3]

All of this occurred while the residents of Canterbury and the Harris family were involved in a struggle over the education of the Harrises' daughter. Some of the same families who objected to Prudence Crandall and her academy were the same household heads who either sold land to the Harris family or whose land bordered their farm. Could this help explain some of the hostility directed at Sarah and the other black students? Did the Harris neighbors use Prudence Crandall's school as a means to limit the influence of the Harris family, acquire the Harris property, or so threaten them that they would leave the area? And why was Sally the only signatory to the land deed conveyed by Samuel Hough? These questions remain unanswered.

Initially the process of settling into their new environs went smoothly for the Harris family. They attended the Westminster Congregational Church, the children went to local schools, and the family appeared to be hardworking and respectable. While in the district public schools, Sarah attended classes with some of the white girls who would later matriculate at the new Female Academy. But this period from January 1832 to early 1833 would prove to be a brief interlude before the town was torn apart by Crandall and her determination to admit a black student to her Female Boarding School.

The story of Prudence Crandall's school has been told many times over. Born in Hopkinton, Rhode Island in 1803, Crandall moved with her family to the Canterbury area in 1813. She graduated from Moses Brown School in 1827 and began her teaching career first in Providence and then in Plainfield, Connecticut. Then the good people of Canterbury invited her to open a school for girls, right in the center of town. Her school opened in November 1831. With a strong curriculum that stressed not only the basics such as reading, writing, arithmetic, and grammar, but also geography, history, philosophy, chemistry, astronomy, music, and French, the school quickly gained a good reputation.

In January 1833 Sarah entered the school, not as a servant but as a day student. Crandall's comments some time later suggest that Sarah or her parents asked if she could attend classes. Crandall later confessed "that at first she shrank from the proposal, with the feeling that of course she could not accede to it. But why not? The girl was well known to be correct in her deportment . . . was pleasing in her personal appearance and manners. Her father was able and willing to pay for her tuition, and she evinced an ardent desire to be instructed."[4] Sarah wanted to become a teacher.

For Crandall, the decision took several months to make, but as she explained to the readers of the *Liberator* in May 1833, prejudice was "the mother of all abominations," and since "wealth was not mine, I saw no other means of benefiting them, than by imparting to those of my own sex that were anxious to learn, all the instruction I might be able to give, however small the amount. This I deemed my duty. . . ." The public disagreed; they reacted with disgust and threatened to remove their daughters from the school. It was at this point that Crandall decided to reopen the school and dedicate it to the education of "young Ladies and little Misses of color." The curriculum would remain the same, and the students would be drawn from Connecticut and beyond.

Local residents now circulated a protest petition against Crandall's "new" students and brought the matter before a town meeting. There, on March 9, 1833, the moderator announced that Prudence Crandall would be opening her school to "misses of color" or "in other words, for the people of color, the obvious tendency of which would be to collect within the town of Canterbury large numbers of persons from other states where character and habits, might be various and unknown to us, thereby rendering insecure the persons, property, and reputation of our own citizens." The meeting concluded that the school should not be allowed to operate and that Crandall be apprised of "the sentiments and objections entertained by this meeting in reference to said School, pointing out to her, the injurious effects, and the incalculable evils resulting from such an establishment, within this town and persuade her if possible to abandon the project."

Lydia Maria Child, author, abolitionist, and a friend of Crandall's, attended the meeting and wanted to speak on her behalf and ascertain whether a compromise could be reached. Crandall had informed her that she would be willing to vacate her current location and move to a more remote one but that she would not relinquish her right to educate black girls. Child was refused a hearing before the town meeting.[5] Then the Reverend Samuel May of Brooklyn, Connecticut, asked to be heard in Crandall's defense and was told the meeting had ended. He spoke briefly before being escorted by six local men to the door.

The school opened in April 1833. The number of pupils at Crandall's school was small and included students from Connecticut and other states. Those from Connecticut included Sarah Harris and her sister Mary, Harriet Lansom, a ward of Reverend Simeon Jocelyn (who had been associated with the New Haven black college), Eliza Glasko of nearby Jewett City, and Mariah Davis. Crandall's school also attracted a number of students from Boston, New York, Philadelphia, and Providence. The presence of out-of-state students was seized upon as an excuse to shut down the Canterbury Female Boarding School.[6]

Distraught, the townspeople turned to Hartford for support. That May the General Assembly passed a "Black Law," which read in part: "no person shall set up or establish in this State any school, academy or literary institution for the instruction or education of colored persons who are not inhabitants of this State" without the consent "of a majority of the civil authority, and also of the Selectmen of the town . . ." Passed on May 24, 1833, the law was applied retroactively to Crandall's school.

One month later, Crandall was arrested and taken to the Brooklyn jail. Her first trial began in August 1833 at the Windham County Courthouse in Brooklyn, Connecticut. While Canterbury Town Clerk Andrew Judson was one of the prosecuting attorneys, Crandall was ably represented by three of Connecticut's leading lawyers: W. W. Ellsworth, Calvin Goddard, and Henry Strong. A trial took place, but the jury was unable to come to a verdict, and a second trial date was set for October 3. The case was transferred from the county court to the state supreme court. At this second trial, however, the verdict was guilty. An appeal was filed, and the case was heard before the Supreme Court of Errors of the State of Connecticut. The questions now posed extended far beyond Prudence Crandall and the fate of her school. The arguments presaged those that would take place decades later: Were black people citizens of their states? What did the Constitution say about race? Crandall's attorneys argued, "coloured persons mentioned in the information are citizens of their respective states." Judson and his colleagues called for a strict interpretation of the Constitution. He asked, referring to the founding fathers, "Did they mean to place persons of colour on the footing of equality with themselves, and did they mean to make them *citizens*." He argued that the answer was no. The judge, however, chose not to rule on the larger issues and merely overturned Crandall's conviction on a technicality.

During this period, the school remained operational and would remain so until September 1834. But throughout these many months, Canterbury was unbearable for Sarah and her fellow students. The girls were under constant duress, and Crandall feared for their lives. Her house and grounds became the target of mob violence; fires were set, the house was damaged, the well was poisoned, and she found it hard to buy food or acquire other supplies. Some of the girls, including Sarah, left. On September 10, 1834 the school officially closed. Some students continued their education elsewhere; Julia Williams went to the Noyes Academy in New Hampshire; others including Elizabeth Smith and Mary Harris were able to find positions as teachers, but most of them, like Sarah, married. Crandall also married and shortly thereafter put her property up for sale. Her husband, Rev. Calvin Philleo, placed an advertisement in the September 1834 issue of the *Unionist*. It read:

[I]t appears that another cowardly attack has been made upon Miss Crandall's (now Mrs. Phileo's) dwelling by some midnight ruffians in Canterbury, and that it has been deemed advisable to abandon the school in that heathenish village, and to let ANDREW T. JUDSON and his associates, with the whole State of Connecticut, have all the infamy and guilt which attach to the violent suppression of so praiseworthy an institution.[7]

In November 1834, her house was sold, and six months later they left for New York.

What happened to Sarah Harris and her family? After the second trial and a few days before Christmas, the *Liberator* announced the marriage of Sarah to George Fayerweather of Kingston, Rhode Island, a blacksmith by trade. The evening ceremony was presided over by the Reverend Asa King at the Westminster Congregational Church, where she had made her profession of faith. She was twenty-one years old, and he was ten years her senior.

Fayerweather was of mixed black and Native American ancestry, as were many residents of Kingston. In southern Rhode Island, many families counted both former slaves and Native Americans in their lineage. George, for example, was one of eight children born to George Fayerweather, Sr., and his wife Nancy, a member of the Narragansett tribe. The Fayerweathers, father and sons, were blacksmiths, a career accorded respect throughout southern New

England. Sarah's husband George practiced this trade first in New London and later back in Kingston.

In the nineteenth century blacksmiths were important members of the community. Their services were much needed: Not only did they shoe horses, they also made and repaired farm implements, pots, latches, locks, and household utensils, among many other products. Residents of fishing villages and port towns depended on their local blacksmiths to forge anchors and ship fittings. So important were these men, that they were praised in the literature of the day. In his poem "The Village Blacksmith," New England poet Henry Wadsworth Longfellow applauded these artisans and their commitment to their communities.

> Toiling,—rejoicing,—sorrowing,
> Onward through life he goes;
> Each morning sees some task begin,
> Each evening sees it close
> Something attempted, something done,
> Has earned a night's repose.

Those who knew George Fayerweather believed he embodied the hardworking, dedicated, family man and community leader Longfellow's poem portrays.

By the 1840s Sarah and George Fayerweather were in New London, where George purchased a blacksmith's shop, formerly owned by B. S. Scoville. Like other members of his trade, George made a comfortable living, and by 1850 he owned real estate valued at $800. By then the couple had four daughters: Prudence, Sarah, Mary, and Isabelle. George was active in the black community and in 1849 represented New London in the Colored Men's Convention held in New Haven, an organization that spotlighted black injustice and supported black suffrage. Convention members demanded that the state "secure the acknowledgment of our rights, and the enactment and administration of impartial laws affecting us. . . . [As it now stands] we have no political existence. We are dead to citizenship— struck down by an unrighteous State Constitution, and our life spark quenched by a cruel and unreasonable prejudice." The men called for the state to change its laws, to acknowledge their citizenship, and to allow black suffrage.[8]

Sarah also figured large in the black community. She supported William L. Garrison and the *Liberator*, attended antislavery rallies, and maintained a correspondence with her former teacher Prudence

Crandall, who was now living in the Midwest. Together the Fayer-weathers worked with the Underground Railroad to assist fugitive slaves in their flight north.

While the couple resided in New London, Sarah's parents chose to remain in Canterbury. The terrible opinions that forced the closing of the school were recorded in the town meeting minutes the following year: "Resolved that the Government of the United States, the Nation with all its Institutions, of right belong to the white men who now possess them, they were purchased by the valor and blood of their Fathers, and must never be surrendered to any other nation or race."

Throughout the remainder of the decade, the Canterbury black community maintained a low profile. They represented a little more than four percent of the local population, with the Harris family among the largest black families in the area. That decade none of the black children in town attended local schools. The following decade only twelve black families remained in Canterbury, though the Harris family continued to live there. By 1850 William Harris was sixty-seven and Sally was fifty-six. He continued to farm and appeared quite successful, with real estate holdings valued at $1,500. His two youngest children, William and Almira, age sixteen and fourteen, respectively, attended the local schools. Still, prejudice persisted; in this rural community local residents refused to acknowledge their black neighbors' obvious occupation as farmers. Rather than address them as such, they called the black farmers "laborers," regardless of how much money they had or how much property they owned, even as white residents with less property were called farmers.[9]

Unlike her parents, Sarah Harris Fayerweather did not remain in Connecticut. In 1855 the couple moved to Kingston, Rhode Island, George's hometown. They purchased a house near his brother, Solomon. Together the brothers worked as blacksmiths, continuing the family's trade. George became a respected member of the Kingston community; he was considered "honest, faithful, and virtuous" by his neighbors and associates. Meanwhile Sarah continued her involvement with the antislavery movement. At home she entertained such dignitaries as William L. Garrison and Frederick Douglass; she attended antislavery rallies and remained a significant presence in the movement. One woman who met her at a rally described her as "very intelligent and lady-like, well informed in every movement relative to the removal of slavery and converses very well."[10] Sarah died a widow on November 16, 1878.

The events surrounding the Prudence Crandall School remained

FIGURE 22-1 Prudence Crandall Museum, Canterbury, Connecticut. *Photo: Kindra Clineff, courtesy of the Connecticut Department of Economic and Community Development*

a vivid memory for many Connecticut residents, and education continued to be a topic of concern. During the 1840s the common school movement spearheaded by Henry Barnard was successful; a common school education was to be free to all residents, at least the white residents, of Connecticut. Local community leaders spearheaded special academies, one of the most significant of which was the Norwich Free Academy. In 1854, the residents of Norwich, Sarah's hometown, undertook a groundbreaking experiment. Businessmen and community leaders such as William Buckingham, the future Republican governor of Connecticut, and John Fox Slater, a manufacturer and philanthropist who endowed the Slater Trust for the education of former slaves, took up a collection to build a new, privately funded secondary school. It would be free and open to local residents: boys and girls, rich and poor, black and white. Black students were among its earliest graduates.

## Notes

1. James Brewer Stewart, "The New Haven Negro College and the Meanings of Race in New England, 1776–1870," *New England Quarterly*, 76 (September 2003): 323–26.

2. James Dickinson, *A Sermon Delivered in the Second Congregational Church, Norwich* (Norwich, 1834).

3. Canterbury, Connecticut, Land Records, 1831–1850, Town Clerk's Office, Canterbury, Connecticut

4. Lydia M. Child, ed., *The Oasis* (Boston: Benjamin C. Bacon, 1834), 181.

5. Ibid., 184–85.

6. Diana Ross McCain, *To All on Equal Terms: The Life and Legacy of Prudence Crandall* (Hartford: Connecticut Commission on Arts, Tourism, Culture, History and Film, 2004).

7. Ibid.

8. *Proceedings of the Connecticut State Convention of Colored Men: held at New Haven, on September 12th and 13th, 1849* (New Haven: William H. Stanley, 1849).

9. U.S. Bureau of the Census, *United States Federal Population Census, Manuscript Schedules*, Seventh Census of the United States (Washington, D.C., 1850), Canterbury, CT, New London, CT; ibid., Eighth Census of the United States (Washington, D.C., 1860), Canterbury, CT., South Kingston, Rhode Island.

10. Carl R. Woodward, "A Profile in Dedication, Sarah Harris and the Fayerweather Family," *The New England Galaxy* 15 (Summer 1973): 10–14.

# 23 "No Taxation without Representation"

The right to vote is an expression of political participation, human dignity, and control of one's destiny. For the majority of people of African descent in Connecticut in the 1700s, emancipation from slavery, the rights of citizenship, and voting rights were linked. Connecticut legislators passed a Gradual Emancipation Act in 1784 that eliminated hereditary enslavement, and finally abolished slavery in 1848.[1] Numbers of African Americans in Connecticut obtained their freedom, purchased property, organized churches and other institutions, and attained education. Despite these achievements, the state of Connecticut limited the full rights of citizenship even for those who fought for the independence of the United States from England. As discussed earlier, throughout the eighteenth century and for much of the nineteenth century African Americans expressed their goal for achieving political empowerment in part by electing "Negro Governors," or "Black Governors." These terms conveyed honor and leadership within the African American community, though the position carried no political authority within the white power structure. A second avenue to political participation was through voting in state and local elections. Some African American men were able to vote before 1812. A September 7, 1803 editorial in the *Connecticut Courant* suggested that "two citizens of colour" in Wallingford who were Democrats (the contemporary Democratic Party) and "free" had voted.[2]

The editorial, more than two hundred years old, read:

Two Plain Questions.

It seems that in the town of Wallingford there are two citizens of colour, both democrats, and both admitted to be free of this state by the democratic Justices and Select-Men of that town.

Question I. In case the aforesaid citizens should at the next election of representatives to the General Assembly, obtain a clear majority of votes to represent said town, whether they would be returned as duly elected?

Question II. If chosen and returned as aforesaid. Would they be admitted to seats in the House of Representatives of this State?

A plain answer by some persons who is acquainted with the laws and the rights of the people of this State would greatly oblige.

[signed] A White Freeman.[3]

The designation "freeman" was a social designation denoting a property owner with voting rights and other rights to participate in political activities. The editorial suggests that African Americans not only voted but held elective office as well. Between 1812 and the passage of the new State Constitution in 1818, Connecticut political authorities enacted laws to restrict the suffrage to white adult men. African Americans protested.

In 1814, the General Assembly denied the franchise to African Americans. Bias Stanley and William Lanson of New Haven asked that they be exempt from paying taxes since they could not vote. Lanson was not exempted from tax obligations. New Haven records contain Lanson's receipts showing proof of payment of his taxes.[4]

More petitions of protest followed Lanson and Stanley's 1814 petition. In 1817 Josiah Cornell, William Laws, William Harris, Deppard [Dedford] Billings, Ira [Tossett] Forset, Olney M. Douglass, Anthony Church, Thomas Hamilton, Joseph Facy, and John Meads—free persons of color from New London and Norwich—presented petitions against paying the poll tax since they could not vote. The General Assembly rejected the petition.[5] The 1818 Connecticut Constitution enacted Article VI, Section 2. It affirmed the right of all white males to vote if they were twenty-one years old and older and possessed property worth at least seven dollars.

The issue of voting-rights restriction emerged again in 1823 when Isaac Glasko in Griswold, a man of African American and Native American descent, presented a petition asking for exemption from taxation because of a lack of voting rights. The General Assembly rejected the petition.[6] The Connecticut State Constitution article prohibiting black voting rights would not be struck down until the passage of the Fifteenth Amendment to the U.S. Constitution in 1870.[7]

Throughout the nineteenth century African Americans sought the right to vote through petitions to the state legislature. African Americans petitioned the General Assembly invoking the language of the Revolutionary War patriots: "no taxation without representation."

The Connecticut State Library Archives contain twenty-six sets of papers from African Americans in Hartford, New Haven, New

London County, Middletown, and Torrington, regarding the right of African Americans to vote. These additional petitions were presented to the General Assembly between 1838 and 1850. In 1845 members of Hartford's African American community, followed in 1850 by members of New Haven's African American community, petitioned the General Assembly to amend the State Constitution by removing the provision that granted the franchise only to white adult men.[8] African American men and women signed the petitions. The General Assembly rejected all the petitions.

To the Honorable, the House of Representatives of the State of Connecticut: The undersigned Free People of Color of the town of Hartford in the County of Hartford respectfully pray your honorable body to pass a resolution proposing such amendment of the second section of the article of the Constitution of this State as shall secure the elective franchise to all men the requisite qualifications, irrespective of color.[9]

This was the opening paragraph of an 1842 petition by African Americans from Hartford. Among those who signed the document were James Mars, James W. C. Pennington, and George Jeffrey, and Leverett Beman from Middletown. George Jeffrey was a barber by trade and a political activist who became a pivotal member of the congregation at Parker Memorial African Methodist Episcopal Zion Church in Meriden during the late nineteenth century. He was a prime mover in the Meriden-area Lincoln League that African Americans organized to advocate for black voting rights during the late nineteenth century. Named in honor of President Abraham Lincoln, Lincoln Leagues were formed around the country to carry on the unfinished work of achieving full citizenship, voting rights, and economic opportunity.

In the 1830s, Amos Gerry Beman moved to New Haven. He joined the interracial abolitionist community and continued to work for African American voting rights. Clarissa Beman carried on her family's involvement in the antislavery struggle as a member of a women's abolition society. African American voting-rights activists linked their advocacy for political inclusion to a wider objective to abolish slavery and fulfill democratic principles enshrined in the nation's Declaration of Independence. The 1839 Middletown petition argued:

[T]he last reason is of much weight—the violation of it was the great moving cause of the revolution—and if to enforce that principle a whole nation took up arms, your petitioners ask whether it should by your Hon. Body be regarded as a . . . chimerical principle or one of practical application? Some of us . . . fought and bled in a glorious struggle to establish that very principle which (as regards application to us) has been denied. Have we not reason to complain?

Although Connecticut's legislators rejected the petitions, African Americans mounted pressures to transform the political system. The 1850 petition from New Haven's black community listed signatures from both men and women.[10] This is important, as it demonstrates that African American men and women joined together in a common effort to obtain the franchise. The petition requested that the legislature "take the necessary measures for amending the Constitution of this State by expunging the word white in the first line of the 2nd Section of the 6th Article of Said Constitution."

In 1870 the states ratified the Fifteenth Amendment, which stated that no one should be denied the right to vote based on race or previous condition of servitude (though women, black or white, would be excluded until 1920). After considerable and often acrimonious debate, the Connecticut General Assembly amended the state constitution to comply with the federal amendment, which empowered most African American men with the right to vote. Still, voter intimidation, poll taxes, the grandfather clause, and other devices disfranchised many eligible African American voters across the United States. In Connecticut these tactics were not as pervasive as in other parts of the country, but even so voting rights remained insecure for African Americans. When the states ratified the Nineteenth Amendment that granted women voting rights in 1919, African American women's access to the franchise was still curtailed due to race.

While African American women in Northern states such as Connecticut had greater legal access to the polls, in Southern states and other states such as Oklahoma, literacy tests, poll taxes, and the grandfather clause were among the many legal restrictions that disfranchised African American women and men. Drawing attention to disfranchisement and the under-representation of black women voters, the NAACP's *Crisis* published two "Votes for Women" issues, one in September 1912 and the other in August 1915.[11] Determined to secure political participation, African American Mary Townsend Seymour, co-founder of the local NAACP in Hartford, was a leading advocate for social justice and voting rights.[12]

Despite late-nineteenth-century court challenges over practices such as those listed above that limited or prevented black voter participation, it was not until the 1960s phase of the civil rights movement that activists were able to secure federal safeguards for the franchise. The African American community's effort to achieve this important right of citizenship was based on coalition building that attracted national attention. Congress passed and President Lyndon B. Johnson signed the Voting Rights Act of 1965. Signed into law in 1993 during the William J. Clinton administration, the National Voter Registration Act reinforced the right of all citizens to participate in the political process. Still, new challenges on the state and national levels continue to restrict the full exercise of political rights. But the inclusion of young people and members of the Latino and Latina communities and other underrepresented groups in the political process has been an important result of the African American struggle for the franchise. For African Americans in Connecticut, these events could be viewed as a fulfillment of their efforts to expand the electorate and the democratic process.

## Notes

1. Lorenzo Greene, *The Negro in Colonial New England 1620–1776* (New York: Columbia University Press, 1942), on slavery and gradual emancipation in Connecticut, 93–99.

2. *Connecticut Courant*, September 7, 1803, cited in Franklin and Higginbotham, *From Slavery To Freedom*, 112.

3. "A White Freeman," *Connecticut Courant*, September 7, 1803.

4. These receipts are located in the Lanson files at the New Haven Museum and Historical Society.

5. Box 4, doc. 5, Connecticut State Library.

6. Box 2, folder 3, Connecticut State Library.

7. The 1818 Connecticut State Constitution.

8. *Office of the Public Records Administrator and State Archives Finding Aid To African Americans and Native Americans 1808–1869*, General Assembly State Archives Record Group No. 2, Connecticut State Library, Hartford, Connecticut, 2001.

9. Hartford Petition (1842 93 a)

10. New Haven Voting Rights Petition, 1850.

11. The poll tax was a monetary fee African Americans were required to pay in order to vote. Some of the literacy tests required the prospective voter to interpret passages of the U.S. Constitution, while other restrictions based eligibility to vote on whether the person's grandfather voted. In January 1964, on behalf of their states, federal congressional officials and senators ratified the Twenty-fourth Amendment, which outlawed the poll tax. The 1965 Voting Rights Act prohibited literacy tests and the grandfather clause. Franklin and Higginbotham, *From Slavery and Freedom*, 267, 262, 269, 353, 375–78, 545.

12. Mark H. Jones, "'To Tell Our Story': Mary Townsend Seymour and the Early Years of Hartford's Branch of the National Association for the Advancement of Colored People, 1917–1920," *Connecticut History*, vol. 44, no. 2 (Fall 2005): 216, 218.

*Barbara Donahue*

# 24  A Walk Along the Underground Railroad

Dozens of Connecticut towns played some part in the mid-nineteenth-century drama of the Underground Railroad, but Farmington claims a starring role, with a wealth of authenticated "Railroad" sites and stories. A walk from south to north on Farmington's Main Street leads you past several of these, evoking the spirits of brave fugitives and the friends who helped them in their flight. Except for the First Church of Christ, Congregational, all sites are private property and are not open to the public. However, each site is marked with a granite post placed by the Farmington Historical Society, and each post bears a metal plaque with symbols of the "Railroad," the North Star, and a lantern.

Number 127 Main Street holds a cluster of sites. On the right is the former home of Austin and Jenette Williams, abolitionists and "stationmasters" on the Railroad. At some personal risk, they publicly welcomed runaways. On the left is a grey carriage house; it was built as a safe home for the survivors of the *Amistad* mutiny. Concealed beneath its floor is a windowless cellar, a possible Railroad hiding place. Though it's no longer standing, a third important building was the modest home of Henry Davis, a farmer and a fugitive from slavery himself.

In his autobiography *Some Reminiscences of a Long Life* (Belknap & Warfield, 1899), John Hooker, abolitionist and brother-in-law of Harriet Beecher Stowe, told Davis's story: Henry Davis, born in Virginia, escaped bondage in South Carolina and eventually reached Farmington, where he found refuge and a job on the Williams place. After he had been in Farmington a few months, another fugitive from South Carolina came through town and reported that Davis's former master had charged his aged mother with aiding in her son's escape and flogged her violently.

Infuriated, Davis dared the long trip back to the South, despite its threat of capture and cruel punishment. He visited his mother and then took revenge on her oppressor by gathering eight other enslaved people and leading them north. They moved slowly because one young woman in the party was heavily pregnant and soon became unable to walk. Her husband and Davis took turns carrying her. Still, "worn out with weariness and anxiety," as Hooker wrote, she collapsed and died. Her friends "buried her in the darkness in a secluded spot, and went on their anxious and perilous way." Davis returned to Farmington, where he lived until his death in 1930; the others went on safely to Canada.

Farther up Main Street, at 116, is the home of Rev. Noah Porter, minister of the Congregational Church. He once invited a "contraband," or fugitive, to lecture in his church. His daughter Sarah Porter, who shared her father's abhorrence of slavery, made sure her entire school turned out to hear the man.

Farther north, at 75 Main Street, is the First Church of Christ, built in 1752 and still home to an active congregation. Rev. James W. C. Pennington, a Hartford minister and former slave, preached here at Noah Porter's request, and Farmington's abolitionists worshipped in this church. The spare, elegant building is open for services and can be visited at other times by request.

Across from the church, at 66 Main Street, is the home of abolitionists Samuel and Catherine Deming. Catherine was among the many Farmington women who raised money and signed petitions to help the abolitionists. Because both she and her husband Samuel were so outspoken, their house has traditionally been considered a stop on the Railroad, though no individual, named fugitive is connected with it.

The last stop on Main Street is number 27, home of Horace and Mary Ann Cowles. Once, while they were housing a fugitive, they had to leave home unexpectedly. They put their young daughter, also named Mary Ann, in charge, with strict instructions to turn away all visitors and let no stranger in the house. They did not tell her why she should be so vigilant. All day the girl guarded the doorstep, until up galloped a harried-looking man with his horse in a lather of exhaustion—clearly a slave-hunter in search of his prey. Mary Ann stood her ground, and the man left empty-handed. When her parents returned, they revealed their secret. Contrary to romantic Underground Railroad lore, the fugitive had not spent the day huddled in a secret compartment somewhere in the house. He rested, instead, in the parlor bedroom, behind shutters, no doubt, but fully visible to anyone entering. Fugitives were often sheltered like this, in plain view.

Other sites scattered through town yield their own stories. But the Main Street sites, easy to reach, offer an immediate, personal look at a time when Farmington was called on to be courageous—and rose to the challenge.

Note

This essay originally appeared in the Fall 2005 issue of *Connecticut Explored*.

# 25 Augustus Washington

## *"Portrait of a Young Man"*

Charles Edwin Bulkeley, a good-looking young man fashionably dressed in mid-nineteenth-century clothes, stares straight at the viewer. He is seated stiffly and a little awkwardly, his right hand resting on the arm of his chair. The brass mat surrounding his portrait is stamped to indicate that it is the work of "A. Washington, 136 Main St. Hartford, Ct."

The African-American daguerreotypist Augustus Washington opened his Hartford studio in 1846, barely seven years after the Frenchman Jacques-Louis Daguerre announced his invention to the world. His process, which used light-sensitive chemicals to capture an image on a silver-coated copper plate, seemed almost miraculous at the time. The silvered surface of the daguerreotype plate was like a little mirror. It was as if the daguerreotype somehow was able to capture the reflection in the mirror and make it permanent. Suddenly daguerreotype studios were everywhere and these exquisitely detailed portraits were readily available.

Washington was born in Trenton, New Jersey, around 1820. He originally learned the daguerreotype process while a student at Dartmouth College, in hopes of earning enough money to continue his studies there. However, his financial troubles continued, and in 1844 he moved to Hartford to teach at the Colored District School operated by the Rev. James W. C. Pennington at 12 Talcott Street. Two years later he set up a "daguerrean gallery" in the Waverly Building; by May 1847 he had moved to the Kellogg Building at 136 Main Street, across the street from the Wadsworth Atheneum. Although he was not Hartford's first daguerreotypist, he was one of the most successful. His prices ranged from fifty cents to ten dollars, and his patrons included some of Hartford's most prominent citizens. Many of the earliest daguerreotype studios lasted no more than a few months, but Washington remained in business until 1853, when he and his family left to join the African American colony in Liberia.

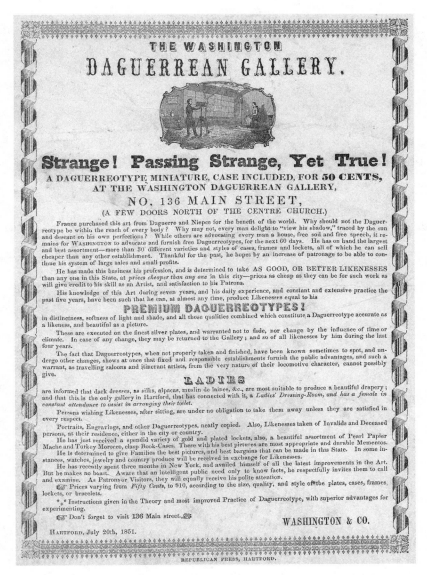

FIGURE 25-1 Broadside for the Washington Daguerrean Gallery, Washington & Co., 1851. *The Connecticut Historical Society, Hartford, Connecticut*

Charles Edwin Bulkeley was the son of Aetna founder Eliphalet Adams Bulkeley and his wife Lydia, and an example of the type of customer Washington attracted. In 1852, when this portrait was made, Charles was sixteen years old and about to enter Yale College. He could have walked from his family's home at 38 Church Street to Washington's studio in just a few minutes. There he would have climbed the stairs to the top floor, where skylights provided the ample light required for the long exposures, usually about twenty seconds. Charles's rather rigid pose and solemn expression are explained by the fact that he had to hold absolutely still for almost half a minute. That is why his hand is supported by the arm of the chair; his head would also have been supported by a head rest. Many people complained about the need to remain motionless for so long, and occasionally a daguerreotype survives in which the sitter is partially blurred because he or she moved.

Washington not only arranged Charles's pose and exposed the plate in a large, rather crude camera, he also developed the daguerreotype, sealed it in an airtight package with a glass cover sheet, and mounted it in a leather-covered case with a brass mat surrounding the portrait. Having Washington's name and address stamped on the mat or embossed on the cover of the case makes his products unusual; most daguerreotypists did not sign their work so prominently. His parents must have liked Charles's portrait, as a year or two later Washington made their portraits also. Their daguerreotypes, in contrast to Charles's, are mounted in silver-bordered cases, the most expensive and elegant type of case. All these early daguerreotype portraits were treated as precious objects. As with painted miniatures, each daguerreotype was unique: There was no negative, and the only way to get a copy was to take another daguerreotype—or later a photograph—of the portrait.

Augustus Washington continued to take daguerreotypes for a short time after emigrating to Liberia in 1853, but agriculture and trading soon proved more lucrative sources of income. He also pursued a political career. He was elected to three terms in the Liberian House of Representatives, where he twice served as speaker of the house, and one term in the Liberian senate. When he died in 1873, he was one of Liberia's most distinguished citizens, and his death was mourned as a "severe loss" to all of Western Africa.

The Connecticut Historical Society collection includes ten daguerreotypes by Augustus Washington; a selection may be viewed in the eMuseum, The Connecticut Historical Society's online museum catalog, emuseum.chs.org:8080/emuseum/.

Note

This essay originally appeared in the Winter 2004/2005 issue of *Connecticut Explored*.

*Charles (Ben) Hawley*

# 26  The Twenty-ninth Regiment Colored Volunteers

For the first two bloody years of the American Civil War the subject of allowing blacks to enlist was heavily debated. Opponents argued that blacks would not make good fighting men and that they lacked the military skills and fortitude to effectively participate in the war. The argument ignored the fact that blacks had fought in and made important contributions to every previous American war, most notably the Revolutionary War.

In January 1863, President Lincoln signed the Emancipation Proclamation, a document that freed slaves in the border states and authorized the enlistment of black soldiers. On May 22, 1863, the United States Department of War issued General Order No. 143 establishing the Bureau of Colored Troops. Connecticut did not move as quickly as other New England states such as Massachusetts and Rhode Island. Nonetheless, on November 13 at a special session of the General Assembly, Col. Dexter R. Wright, seconded by Col. Benjamin S. Pardee, both from New Haven, proposed a bill authorizing Governor William A. Buckingham to organize regiments of "colored" infantry. Connecticut Democrats denounced the bill in unmeasured terms, arguing it would let loose upon the helpless South "a horde of African barbarians." They predicted black cowardice, disgrace, and ruin as the result of the experiment.

Governor Buckingham moved swiftly, though, authorizing the bill on November 23 and calling for volunteers to make up the Twenty-ninth Regiment Colored Volunteers. Despite the fact that many black laborers earned wages that were higher than army pay and enlistment bounties, the response was immediate and enthusiastic. By January 1864 more than 1,200 men flocked to the Twenty-ninth and more than 400 joined an additional colored regiment, the Thirtieth (and, eventually, the Thirty-first) Regiment United States Colored Infantry. Civil War historian William A. Gladstone in *United States Colored Troops 1863–1867* (Thomas Publications, 1990) indicates that 1,764 men of color served Connecticut during the

FIGURE 26-1 Detail
of the 29th Colored
Regiment Monument.
The monument is on
the site where the 29th
mustered in 1864,
Criscuolo Park,
New Haven, 2008.
*Private collection*

Civil War between 1863 and 1867. The level of black participation
in Connecticut regiments was astounding considering that the 1860
census revealed only 8,726 blacks lived in the state; of them only
2,206 were men between the ages of 15 and 50 (the most likely ages
for service). This meant that some 78 percent of eligible black men
enlisted. Just over 15 percent of these men died as a result of the war.

The men were offered an enlistment bounty of $600 and the
same pay and uniforms as white soldiers. The Twenty-ninth and
Thirtieth regiments were encamped near Fair Haven, and by the

end of January, as the regiments' officers—all of them white—were chosen, daily drills and a system of rigid inspections were established. On January 29, 1864, the colored soldiers of the Twenty-ninth and Thirtieth were addressed by the famed black abolitionist Frederick Douglass, who told them (according to William A. Croffut and John M. Morris, in *The Military & Civil History of Connecticut During The War of 1861–65* (Ledyard Bill, 1868)),

You are pioneers of the liberty of your race. With the United States cap on your head, the United States eagle on your belt, the United States musket on your shoulder, not all the powers of darkness can prevent you from becoming American citizens. And not for yourselves alone are you marshaled—you are pioneers—on you depends the destiny of four millions of the colored race in this country. If you rise and flourish, we shall rise and flourish. If you win freedom and citizenship, we shall share your freedom and citizenship.

But these men already understood this. Ministers Alexander Newton in *Out of the Briars, An Autobiography and Sketch of the Twenty-ninth Regiment Connecticut Volunteers* (1910) and Isaac Hill in *A Sketch of the Twenty-ninth Regiment of Connecticut Color Troops* (1867) both reflected on their time in the Twenty-ninth. Newton, who was an abolitionist before the war and active in the Underground Railroad, wrote, "Although free born, I was born under the curse of slavery, surrounded by the thorns and briars of prejudice, hatred, persecution and the suffering incident to this fearful regime." In going to war, he suggested, he was "doing what he could on the battlefield to liberate his race."

On March 8, the regiment was mustered into service and soon thereafter received as its commanders Colonel William B. Wooster of Derby, Lt. Colonel Henry C. Ward of Hartford, and Major David Torrance of Greenville (part of Norwich). On March 19, after receiving a United States flag from a group of black women from New Haven, the regiment assembled on the New Haven Green. As they paraded toward the waterfront for their departure, wellwishers showered them with flowers. The men embarked on the *Warrior* for Annapolis, Maryland.

The Twenty-ninth was ultimately transported to Beaufort, South Carolina, where its members performed guard and picket duty for four months. In August, they were brought to the siege lines of Virginia. The Thirtieth served on guard duty in Virginia during the first half of June, then entered the Petersburg trenches and participated in the famous Crater attack on July 30, when the Union military attempted to dig and explode a tunnel directly under Confederate lines. The Thirtieth suffered 82 casualties in a slaughter by rebel forces. The Twenty-ninth and Thirtieth regiments, along with the rest of the Army of the Potomac, moved around the city, fighting in a host of battles, from Bermuda Hundred to the Battle of Fair Oaks, before achieving success in April 1865, when Petersburg finally surrendered. When the Confederate capitol, Richmond, fell to Union forces in early April 1865, soldiers from Companies C and G of the Twenty-ninth were among the first to enter the city.

When the war ended, the Twenty-ninth was sent to Texas, where the regiment remained on duty until mustered out of service on October 24. The soldiers returned home to Connecticut in November and were greeted by Governor Buckingham, who honored their patriotism and the role they played in the war.

In September 2008 a monument dedicated to the Twenty-ninth Regiment Colored Volunteers was dedicated in Criscuolo Park in New Haven. It is the first monument in the state specifically to honor black soldiers.

Note

This article originally appeared in the Spring 2011 issue of *Connecticut Explored*.

# 27 Fighting for Freedom

## *Joseph O. Cross*

Joseph O. Cross of Griswold served in the Twenty-ninth (Colored) Regiment Connecticut Volunteer Infantry during 1864 and 1865. Recruiting began for the Twenty-ninth in the fall of 1863. Recruits came from throughout the state and from as far away as Hawaii, France, and Spain, according to Diana Ross McCain, writing in the Connecticut Historical Commission's *Connecticut's African-American Soldiers in the Civil War* (2000). The Twenty-ninth was mustered into service on March 8, 1864 and fought in nine major battles, including the Siege of Petersburg. The regiment was discharged in Hartford on November 25, 1865. A second regiment, the Thirtieth, served from June 1864 to December 1865.

This letter from Cross to his wife Abby is in the collection of The American Civil War Center at Historic Tredegar, donated by Connecticut resident John Motley. A number of Cross's letters are also in the collection of the Connecticut Historical Society (see the Connecticut Historical Society Bulletin 60, Summer/Fall 1995).

Nov 3d, 1864 Chapines Farm, in Front of richmond

My Dear Wife,

Your letter found me all well & I hope these few line will find you enjoying the same Blessing in answer to your letter I will say this that I had heard of the death of Henry Simones & John By way of Central village I hear nothing but Bad news all the time except some times I hear Good news about the War the Joneyes [Confederate soldiers] Comes over some once in a while, them does come over are glad to get away We had Been called to go into Battle oct 27 th our hole Brigade we fought 24 houres & then left we drove the rebs Back one mile to their Brest workes & their they stood their ground. We took 3 prisnornes they holard, don't shoot me don't shoot me. We had our gunes cocked & aimed, ready to fire at them they threw down their armes & came in. They are afraid of the Coones Abby I sent you one 10 dollar Check not long ago and you never rote wheather you received it or not Now then if you will inform me about it I shal be

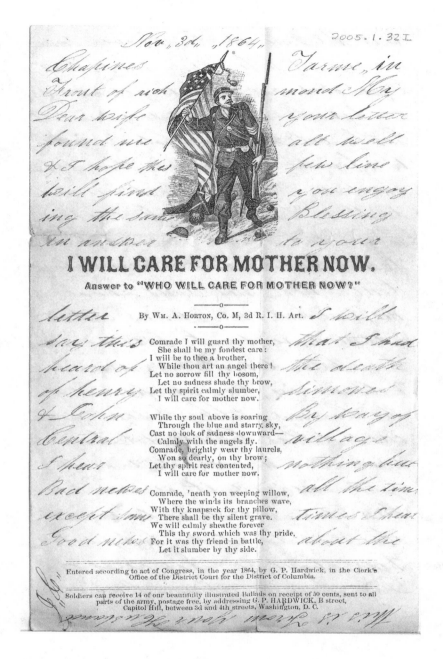

happy to hear about it. Newes of the Day. Sargent Amos Brewster got shot in the Battle the other day in the foot John rogers had his leg Blowen off & Charles hasard shot in the Back & henry Jackson shot dead. he Belong to Co. H. We lost over one hundred killed and wonded we lost more this time than we did Before Abby, I got payed off oct 18th & my pay for three months. 71.25 cts & I Bought 2 checks one I sent home to you & the other

I will send in this Abby I had made up mi mind to let you starve to death on the account of the newes that I heard about you that Came to me I mad up my mi mind if that was trew that you might sherk the best way that you Could you have not ritten to me until now since august 24 & I did not know what it ment nor I don't know now But anyhow I will drop that. I want you to get one half a hog & half barrel flour & then weight until I get Payedd off again Now Abby please to Give my regards to all enquiring Friends & receive a shair you self tell Jane that I have not heard from horace for a long time But if he is as well as he was when I heard from him he will be at home Before long for they are giving furlowes at the hospital to them that are able to go home please to tell me if you got that Cotton that I sent you Charles Pearce is well but ragged & sascy. No more this time O tell aunt that I wold like to have the pleasure to bild up fire for her But as to the Bed I shoutd not know what that ment I am so used to the ground.

   This is From your husband Joseph O Cross

Note

This essay originally appeared in the November/December/January 2004 issue of *Connecticut Explored*.

# PART III

## Post Civil War to World War I

# 28 Connecticut and the Aftermath of the Civil War

When the Union finally decided to organize African American regiments to serve in the Civil War, men from throughout Connecticut answered the call. In 1863 African Americans in Hartford, as in other communities in the state, sent volunteers for service in the Connecticut Twenty-ninth Regiment Colored Volunteers. By January 1864 the Twenty-ninth infantry had a full complement of troops, including thirty-two members of Hartford's Talcott Street Congregational Church.

African Americans fought valiantly in the Civil War. But after the Union finally defeated the Confederacy, African Americans across the nation and in Connecticut experienced moments of celebration, the harsh reality of fleeting freedom, and a struggle ahead to acquire political, economic, and educational equality.

With the Union victory, African American troops returned home to their communities' elated embrace. On August 1, 1866, the African American community in Hartford welcomed the troops with a Grand Union Jubilee. Visitors, friends, and family gladly paid a twenty-five-cent entry fee to be part of the celebration. Addie Brown, an African American resident, remarked: "Been nothing but excitement here today. Colored people for one can say that they have had the city."[1]

The pursuit of education became central to African Americans in both the North and the South during the period of Reconstruction. Northern allies graciously aided Southern African Americans in that effort, and the American Missionary Association provided funds to help bring education to the newly freed people. When the call for teachers reached Connecticut, talented educators such as Rebecca Primus, a member of Hartford's prominent Primus family, left New England to teach among the freedmen in South Carolina. In 1867 Rev. Amos Beman traveled to the South to help found schools for newly freed people. He, like many Northerners, found living conditions among the former enslaved worse than they had ever

FIGURE 28-1 This broadside was published in Philadelphia as much as two years before Connecticut recruited black soldiers. "Rally! Rally! Rally! To Men of Color," c. 1862. Broadside lithograph published by U.S. Steam-Power Book & Job Printing Establishment, Philadel-phia, Pennsylvania. *The Amistad Center for Art & Culture, Inc., Simpson Collection, 1987.1.597*

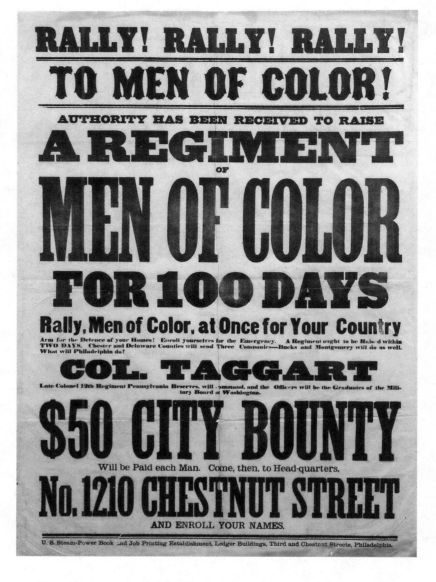

imagined. While many more people are familiar with Beman's name, his less-prominent cousin Nathan Tappan Congdol also helped to organize schools in Mississippi for freed people.[2]

Even as Primus, Beman, and Congdol traveled to the South to educate African Americans, some Connecticut towns maintained segregated school systems, a practice that would be outlawed in the state in the 1870s. This was certainly true of Hartford and New Haven of the 1860s. Still, Hartford's African schools produced outstanding educators such as Selah Africanus, Amos Beman, and Augustus Washington. In the 1850s New Haven operated and supported three segregated schools for youngsters of color. Segregated schools continued through the 1860s in New Haven. Officials finally closed segregated schools in the 1870s.[3]

Other areas such as Glastonbury's Green District included African American students; however, officials wrote the names of African American children in the back of their enrollment list, separate from the names of white students.[4]

Statewide and nationally in the post-Civil War era, the racial climate was less than hospitable for many African Americans. Augustus Washington, a prominent Connecticut resident, decided that true freedom could only come through exodus to Liberia. Washington sold his Hartford daguerreotype studio and migrated to West Africa in 1853. He used the funds from the sale to purchase land to develop a sugar-cane farm and mill. While it took time for Washington to adjust to life in West Africa, he managed to carve out a new beginning for himself and his family.

In the Civil War's immediate aftermath, a group of Southern migrants from Virginia left the South for places such as Hartford. In 1871, for instance, a group of African Americans from Virginia came to Connecticut in hopes of finding better economic opportunity and religious freedom in Connecticut.[5]

No example of the centrality of churches to the African American community is more striking than that of Lucy Roberts. In 1907 blacks in New Haven finished work on St. Luke's Episcopal Church, located on Whalley Avenue. Lucy Roberts, who earned a living as a laundress, gave her life savings of $5,000 to help make the construction possible. The founders of St. Luke's in turn helped to establish St. Monica's Episcopal Church in Hartford.[6]

In 1893, Rev. Adam Clayton Powell moved to New Haven to become the pastor of the Immanuel Baptist Church. Powell established himself as a key Christian advocate and a leader of the community. He also ventured to cities outside the state and brought recognition of his ministry to other parts of the country. In 1908 Powell's wife gave birth to Adam Clayton Powell, Jr., who would eventually become Harlem's first congressional representative.[7]

While ministers had considerable power and influence within the African American community, they held little influence over the hiring practices of major manufacturing firms. Connecticut manufacturing had a long and venerated history. But very few African Americans found a place in this history in the period between 1865 and World War I. In cities such as Hartford, owners and managers of companies objected to placing African Americans alongside white workers. In addition, white workers objected to toiling with African American workers. In New Haven, owners and managers of factories and construction companies clearly favored native and immigrant white employees. When African Americans did find positions in large Connecticut companies before the U.S. entered World War I, those jobs were most often at the levels of janitor, driver, and servant. Colt Manufacturing and Pratt & Whitney had little or no use for African American workers until the war created acute labor shortages.[8]

Still, members of Connecticut's African American community managed to acquire small amounts of property and develop businesses. In 1848 sisters Mary and Eliza Freeman purchased adjoining property in the "Little Liberia" area of Bridgeport. Both earned their livings as domestics. When Mary died in 1883, she owned houses on Main and Gregory streets. The *Bridgeport Standard* reported that the properties were worth between $30,000 and $50,000. Their houses are the only ones that remain of those built in "Little Liberia."[9]

In the latter decades of the nineteenth century, other cities such as Hartford, New Haven, and Middletown saw similar patterns with small enclaves of African American businesses developing. African Americans in Hartford owned and operated restaurants, salons, barbershops, and bars; one operated a tailor shop. New Haven's African Americans operated similar small businesses. In Middletown in 1895 James A. Caples, formerly a chef for Wesleyan University's fraternity Beta Theta Pi, opened a restaurant called Eureka at 54 Rapallo Avenue. Caples, who had served with the Fifty-fifth Massachusetts, also worked as a butcher.[10] Connecticut African Americans were barbers, tailors, mariners, tradesmen, farmers, drivers, domestics, dyers of cloth, and seamstresses.

The prevalence of these occupations and incidence of property ownership, however, did not overshadow the fact that many African Americans lived on the economic fringes of society. Many African American men and women lived simple lives, many, like brothers Ira and Joel Chauncey Peters of Glastonbury, working as laborers. In 1868 when an impoverished Ira Peters died from the ravages of dysentery, the town paid the costs of his burial. Joel Peters lived out his life as a farm laborer. In 1890 Joel, father of twelve children, died. His wife Amelia preceded him in death in 1861.[11]

Throughout cities such as Hartford, New Haven, and Bridgeport, many African Americans worked as servants in the homes of prominent whites. Yale University graduates hired African Americans in service roles.[12] Although many people today consider service roles menial, African American domestic servants saw dignity in their work.

Through local newspapers and grapevine news African Americans in Connecticut learned about the brutal efforts of Southern whites to "redeem" the South. Redemption for southern whites meant, if necessary, using legal and illegal measures to regain control of the South. Southern redemption also saw southern whites using terror and murder to win control over African Americans. Locally, African Americans could do little to halt Southern redemption efforts. But national leaders such as Frederick Douglass waged their ongoing campaign to battle racism throughout the nation, and in 1881 Booker T. Washington began his ascent from a former student at Hampton Institute to the principal and founder of the Tuskegee Institute, a small vocational and industrial school in Alabama. Washington stressed thrift, hard work, devotion to Christ, and developing vocational skills. For many in the African American community, his message seemed extremely positive. Others, though, found it divisive.

African Americans in Connecticut consistently worked to highlight the positive contributions of their community. In 1902 G. Grant Williams ran a successful barbershop that catered to African American and white patrons at 209 Pearl Street in Hartford. He also sold African American publications such as the *Colored American Magazine*, the *Philadelphia Tribune*, and the *New York Age* and stocked the writings of prominent African American leaders and writers Paul Laurence Dunbar, Booker T. Washington, Pauline Hopkins, and Ellen Wetherell.[13] Such newspapers and literature, coupled with grapevine news, provided information that served to bind Connecticut's African American communities to the South. In addition, such papers included news about the horrible crime of lynching that was growing increasingly common in the South. Eventually, newspapers such as the *Age* also served as catalysts to encourage southern migration to the North.

Even so, the majority of white Connecticut residents grew up in the late nineteenth and early twentieth centuries accepting racism, and stereotyping the inferiority of Africans and African Americans. It was not uncommon, for instance, for state theaters to present racist minstrel shows.[14] In the face of all of this, the African American community needed, and sought, uplift.

Booker T. Washington addressed racism with a policy of economic uplift, accommodation, and vocational education for the masses. But Washington had many vocal opponents. Hartford's *Times* newspaper reported on the Boston Riot, a mild disturbance targeting Washington supporters in 1903. Boston's William Monroe Trotter, editor of the *Boston Guardian*, and his supporters hurled verbal barbs during a meeting at which Washington was to speak. Trotter despised Washington and his policies. The *Times* argued that Washington's message failed to resonate with African Americans.[15] In 1913 one of the most virulent Washington critics was New Haven's William H. Ferris, a Yale graduate and devoted supporter of W. E. B. DuBois. Earlier in 1902, Ferris was one of the principal speakers at the conventions of the American Negro Academy in Washington, D.C. He used that opportunity to publicly flay Booker T. Washington with biting criticism.[16]

Although many prominent African Americans in the North disliked Washington, he found vocal supporters in G. Grant Williams and the members of the National Negro Business League. Williams, who strongly condemned the Boston attack on Washington, was leader of the Connecticut contingent of that organization. While Williams worked diligently to bring Washington to Connecticut for speaking engagements, he himself attended and spoke at the national convention. Williams urged African Americans to build businesses and conduct themselves in an upright and positive manner.[17]

Since the days of the Civil War and Reconstruction, New England blacks provided support for the education of African Americans in the South. People in Connecticut were familiar with Virginia's Hampton Institute, which provided vocational and industrial training for African American and Native American students. For Samuel Armstrong and the institute's other white founders, Hampton was meant to civilize the inferior races. Booker T. Washington was Hampton's most prominent graduate and proof of the school's success. The educational system developed in the period of Reconstruction eventually trained tens of thousands of African American teachers and educated millions of young black people.

Connecticut African Americans who managed to acquire access to a college education in Connecticut before the Civil War had few options. As Hilary Moss notes in essay 21, leading residents of New Haven vehemently argued against an attempt by Simeon Jocelyn and supporters to build a college for African Americans in 1831. Although private, liberal arts schools such as Wesleyan University admitted black students in the period immediately after the war, the climate on campus proved less than collegial for African American students. Some white students at Wesleyan boldly declared their disdain for African American students on campus. Although African Americans attended and graduated from the university before 1918, they did so in extremely small numbers.

During the last years of the nineteenth century and first two decades of the twentieth, African Americans had a rocky relationship with the Republican Party, historically the party of Lincoln. In 1896, the Supreme Court dealt African Americans a major human rights and political blow with the *Plessy v. Ferguson* decision, which drew a color line across the South. Regionally, the Court, which argued for "separate but equal" facilities for blacks and whites, legalized segregation and allowed a reign of terror to envelop the South. In need of political allies, African Americans across the nation turned to the Republican Party for support. But the Republican Party, led by William McKinley, did little to alleviate growing African American fears in the South or North.

In Connecticut, African Americans focused on acquiring power and maintaining a visible presence in the Republican Party. A small contingent in Hartford supported Dr. Patrick Henry Clay Arms, a physician of Afro-Cuban ancestry, in his efforts to represent the city's third ward in municipal elections for the city council in 1900. Arms, a little known physician and Independent Republican, decided to use his campaign to raise awareness that African American votes were being taken for granted in the African American community. As a result, some members of the predominantly African American third ward broke away from the Republican Party. Arms said, "The colored voters of the city should show their independence." African American voters, however, failed to support Arms in significant numbers. He received 26 votes among 200 registered African Americans in the third ward and only 90 votes throughout the city.[18] Meanwhile, in New Haven, Adam Clayton Powell urged the members of the Colored Republican State Convention to cast their votes for the Republican Party in the presidential election because Democrat William Jennings Bryan was no friend of African Americans and the Democrats were the party of Southern redemption.

National and state elections from 1904 to 1916 saw the Republican Party of Connecticut continue to hold sway over African American voters. Major politicians and African American supporters lauded the party of Theodore Roosevelt, William Howard Taft, and Charles Evans Hughes. Given the policies and beliefs of Woodrow Wilson, in 1912 and 1916 the majority of African American voters in Connecticut found their views a closer match with Taft and Hughes. With a Republican Party splitting its loyalty between Taft and Roosevelt, in 1912 Wilson won the White House and quickly gave his stamp of approval to the policy of segregation in the city of Washington, D.C. In 1916 Wilson used the slogan, "He Kept Us Out of the War," to rally supporters. Although Wilson was clearly pro-Southern, the ascent of Jim Crow occurred during both Republican and Democratic administrations.

In Connecticut, African American voters lacked the numbers to significantly influence political decisions. As a result, African Americans in Connecticut remained limited in terms of their economic, political, and social standings. Nevertheless, small communities of professional and prominent African Americans began to develop in Hartford and elsewhere in the state. Hartford resident B. Rollin Bowser served as consul general to Sierra Leone in West Africa, a position he gained through support from Senator Joseph B. Hawley. During his time in office (1881–1905), Hawley received most of the African American vote. Other African Americans who achieved a certain prominence included William Rue, an employee of General Electric, who built one of the first automobiles in Hartford, and Raymond Augustus Lawson, who first moved to the South End of Hartford in 1901 and operated a music studio in the Brown Thompson Building.[19] On October 24, 1915, the *Hartford Courant* viewed the African American population in that city as a "peaceful and orderly contingent, creating very little trouble in the way of laws . . . generally the people of this race are industrious, happy, and a credit to the city."[20]

New Haven also had a growing professional African American population. George Crawford developed a distinguished legal career primarily through working with esteemed clients in the white community. In 1908 Henry G. Tolliver received his law degree from Yale. Like George Crawford, he and other professionals lived an upper-middle-class life. In 1902 Dr. Richard Fleming, a black dentist from St. Kitts, moved to New Haven after graduating from dental school in New York. Fleming married an African American woman from Brooklyn and set up his practice on the edge of New Haven's African American community, a short distance from Yale. His son followed him into a practice with a mostly white clientele, and his daughter became a social worker. Dr. Fleming's family worshipped at St. Luke's Episcopal Church each Sunday.[21]

Although these small pockets of prominent citizens had little economic impact on the plight of the majority of African American residents in Connecticut, the potential for greater changes came with new emerging organizations such as the National Association for the Advancement of Colored People. In 1909 white and African American leaders organized to form the NAACP. The leaders of the organization established an office in 1910 in New York. The most prominent—and only—African American on the board was W. E. B. DuBois, a native of Great Barrington, Massachusetts whose paternal grandfather had deep roots in New Haven. His grandfather, Alexander, was a founding member of St. Luke's and a businessman, operating a local grocery store. In later years, the younger DuBois helped found local chapters of the NAACP in New Haven and Hartford.

In 1915 the death of legendary African American leader Booker T. Washington opened the door for the greater ascent of the NAACP and its leaders; his death severed his paternalistic ties to prominent white leaders. In addition, Florida native James Weldon Johnson, took the organization's message into the South directly to African Americans of that region. Their call for an integrated fight for freedom would be met with rage and anger through the South, and even parts of the North. African Americans in Connecticut began to embrace a steady and vigilant campaign to slay the dragon of *Plessy v. Ferguson*'s separate but equal doctrine. The struggle was not to be waged only in the South. Southern African American allies soon made their way northward to swell the ranks of those supporting freedom and equality in Connecticut. Technically, "separate but equal" had been outlawed in Connecticut in the 1870s, but in reality it remained in place, and African Americans in the state were well aware of the continued practice.

As World War I got underway, African American southern migrants streamed into Connecticut hoping for a better life, employment, better housing, and safety from violence. Initially, the call of the Connecticut tobacco fields seemed to signal the beginning of quality life in the "Promised Land." African Americans increased the populations of cities such as Hartford, New Haven, Bridgeport, and Waterbury, creating a visible southern African American contingent. According to the 1910 census numbers, 15,174 blacks resided in Connecticut; 10,673 were listed as urban dwellers. By 1920 the black population increased to 21,046, with 16,655 people listed as urban dwellers. By 1930 the statewide black population increased to 29,354 people. The majority, 24,531 people, resided in urban communities, while 4,823 lived in rural areas.[22] These thousands of new arrivals could not easily be ignored nor quietly controlled. They often initially had to deal with tension, including among the African Americans born in Connecticut. Over time, Southern-born and

Connecticut-born African Americans began to break down cultural walls and build lasting bonds in a campaign to challenge racism and discrimination in the state.

## Notes

1. Letter from Addie Brown to Rebecca Primus, 1866, in *Beloved Sisters and Loving Friends: Letters of Rebecca Primus of Royal Oak, Maryland to Addie Brown of Hartford, Connecticut, 1854–1868*, ed. Farah Jasmine Griffin (New York: Alfred A. Knopf, 1999), 90–91. See also "Addie Brown's Hartford," 57–64.

2. Vicki S. Welch, *And They Were Related, Too* (Self published, Xlibris Corporation, 2006), 174.

3. Constance Baker Motley, *Equal Justice Under Law* (New York: Farrar, Straus, Giroux, 1998), 21.

4. Patricia Trapp, "Silent Voices and Forgotten Footsteps: A Chronicle of the Early Black Culture of Glastonbury, 1693–1860," (MA. thesis, Wesleyan University, 1996), 40.

5. Donald Spivey, "Point of Contention: The Historical Perspective of the African American Presence in Hartford," in *The State of Black Hartford*, ed. Stanley Battle, 50–54 (Hartford: Greater Hartford Urban League, 1994).

6. Motley, 21.

7. Charles V. Hamilton, *Adam Clayton Powell, Jr.* (New York: MacMillan Publishing, 1991), 21–22 and 42–43. See also Vicki S. Welch, *And They Were Related, Too*, 175.

8. Charles S. Johnson, "The Negro Population of Hartford, Ct. 1921" (New York: National Urban League, 1921), 25–26. Motley, *Equal Justice Under Law*, 21, 30. See also Mary White Ovington, *Half A Man* (New York: Hill and Wang, 1969), 1–120 for information on immigrants and migrants.

9. http://www.nps.gov/nr/feature/wom/1999/freeman.htm

10. Welch, *And They Were Related, Too*, 276.

11. Trapp, 80, 84.

12. Motley, *Equal Justice Under Law*, 21.

13. Advertisement for G. Grant Williams General Agent for High Class Negro Literature, 209 Pearl St., Geer's City Directory, 1902. For information about Pauline Hopkins, see http://paulinehopkinssociety.org/. For information on Ellen Wetherell, see http://www.archive.org/stream/infreeamericaooweth#page/n7/mode/2up. Ellen F. Wetherell, *In Free America or Tales from North and South* (Boston: Colored Co-Operative Publishing Company, 1901), 141–48.

14. Advertisement for Palace Theater, "Go Get 'Em Rogers," *Hartford Courant*, January 18, 1917; "New Dickinson Play On Its Way Here," *Hartford Courant*, January 20, 1917; "Black Face Boys Star at Poli's," *Hartford Courant*, April 13, 1917.

15. Louis Harlan, *Booker T. Washington: The Wizard of Tuskegee, 1901–1915* (Oxford: Oxford University Press, 1983), 47.

16. Ryan Hurst, "William H. Ferris," www.blackpast.org/?q=aah/ferris -william-henry-1874-1941. See also David Levering Lewis, *W.E.B. DuBois, 1868–1919* (New York: Holt, 1994), 170, 466, 513.

17. Advertisement for G. Grant Williams General Agent for High Class Negro Literature, 209 Pearl St., Geer's City Directory, 1902. See also "G. Grant Williams: Speaks on 'Barbering as a Profession,' His Address Before the National Negro Business League," *Hartford Courant*, August 28, 1902. Booker T. Washington was the founder of the league that urged African Americans to seek uplift through vocational training, self-help, and economics.

18. Don Noel, Jr., "The Negro in Hartford: The Politician," *Hartford Times*, November 26, 1963; Constance Neyer, "John B. Stewart Sr. Dies: A Forceful Voice for Blacks," *Hartford Courant*, April 1, 1996.

19. Robert E. Pawlowski, *How the Other Half Lived: An Ethnic History of the Old East Side and South End of Hartford* (West Hartford, Connecticut, 1973.), 20–29; and "The Colored People Who Live in Hartford," *Hartford Courant* [part three], October 24, 1915.

20. "The Colored People Who Live in Hartford," *Hartford Courant*, [part three] October 24, 1915, Hartford Collection: Hartford Public Library.

21. Motley, *Equal Justice Under Law*, 34–35.

22. See Fourteenth Census of the United States, and Fifteenth Census of the United States.

# 29 Rebecca Primus and Addie Brown

I'm glad there is so much sympathy manifested in behalf of the Col[ore]d man's Rights, and I hope the subject will continue to be agitated throughout the country by our smart & intelligent col[ore]d men, as well as white, until these rights which are so unjustly withheld from us now, have been obtained.
—REBECCA PRIMUS

Rebecca, I have been working for nothing comparatively speaking and I have come to a decision stand that people shall pay me for my work I don't care *colored* or White. —ADDIE BROWN[1]

Two voices, two lives. Two African American women, writing in the 1860s, offer unique insights into the world they lived in as they revealed their different but connected lives. Rebecca Primus wrote weekly letters to her family in Hartford, Connecticut, from Royal Oak, Maryland, where she had opened a school for newly freed African Americans in 1865. Addie Brown, a young working-class woman in Hartford, wrote to her absent friend in Maryland as often as twice a week.[2]

Detailing their days, the two women recount experiences involving race—as we might expect—and class—which we might not. Their letters also emphasize the importance to both of the local networks to which they were linked. As a result the letters present an inside view of Hartford's black community at the height of its nineteenth-century economic and social gains. These gains, along with the Union victory in the Civil War and the end of slavery, fed the hope that race prejudice would in time be eradicated. While the writers express confidence and optimism, they clearly rely on their ties to the Primus family—Rebecca as daughter, Addie as friend.

Rebecca's father, Holdridge Primus (1815–1884), worked as a porter in a white-owned Main Street grocery store, an unskilled occupation. Her mother, Mehitabel Jacobs Primus (1817–1899), worked at home as a skilled dressmaker. Their children were Rebecca (1836–

1932), Henrietta (1837–1920), Nelson (1842–1916), and Isabella (or Bell) (1843–1920). By 1860, the Primuses owned a two-story frame house not far from the new Bushnell Park and within blocks of the store where Holdridge worked. They furnished their home with mirrors, books, paintings, silver spoons, and the badge of middle-class achievement, a piano. Both parents were prominent members of the Talcott Street Church, an all-black Congregational house of worship, and both established connections with Hartford's white elite. The Primuses were stalwarts of Hartford's black leadership, a group that emerged from the antebellum struggle to counteract race prejudice through education and self-improvement, a process known as racial uplift.

In her role as teacher, Rebecca had clearly set out to further these goals, and her mission in the mid-South extended her reach beyond the local arena. Addie Brown, less educated than her friend, and lacking a close-knit family of her own, struggled to make a living, even as she sought middle class status. She hoped to replicate in her own life the security, unity, and support she saw in the Primus family.

## Rebecca Primus

The precision of her grammar, her insistence on propriety, and her interest in public affairs, show that Rebecca had set out to create in herself the model of an educated black woman.

You wish to know whether those who attend school exhibit the same interest in it. I wish you could see for yourselves. [It] is the topic at home and abroad, among the children as well as adults.[3]

She had become a teacher for the high purpose of uplifting her race. Unmarried at twenty-eight and living at home, she was chosen just after the end of the Civil War by Hartford's all-white Freedmen's Aid Society to join the army of teachers, black and white, who founded schools in the South for newly freed slaves. The chance to teach those to whom reading had been forbidden placed her in the front lines of the struggle for racial equality.

While Rebecca's preparation for teaching remains unknown, the 1860 census lists her occupation as "teacher," and she and Addie both mention in their letters a school she conducted, probably in the Primus parlor. Obviously her credentials met the requirements of the sponsoring agencies, and in December of 1865 she opened the first school for blacks in Royal Oak, a village on the Eastern Shore of Maryland. She taught day and night classes for children and adults, and conducted a Sunday school for "between 50 & 60 members who seem to take great delight in attending it."[4]

Like present-day teachers, Rebecca dealt with a many-headed bureaucracy, beginning with the Royal Oak School Committee. She also reported monthly to the United States Bureau of Refugees, Freedmen, and Abandoned Lands (the Freedmen's Bureau), the Baltimore Society for the Moral and Educational Improvement of the Colored People, and the Hartford Freedmen's Aid Society. That she found time to write regularly to family and friends shows the importance she placed on ties to her Hartford base.

In "Home Weeklies," as she called her letters, Rebecca shared with a sympathetic audience not only the progress of her school, but also a number of unsettling discoveries regarding race and class that she encountered in her new surroundings. As to the first, she found that racial discrimination in the mid-South showed a different face than she had seen in Hartford:

It seems a very respectable colored man . . . was on his way to church and en-route he was shot by a white rascal so that he fell a dead man immediately. . . . There are some very lawless fellows in these towns and there is nothing to [sic] bad for them to do to a colored person. I trust something like justice will be given to the black man one of these days, for some are persecuted almost as badly now as in the days of slavery.[5]

She wrote of attacks on other Freedmen's Bureau teachers, one of whom was "stoned by white children and repeatedly subjected to insults from white men."[6]

While she bristled at instances of racial oppression in Maryland, the discovery that surprised her most was the difference between her own ways and those of Royal Oak blacks. Their background in bondage had produced a way of life that warred with Rebecca's ideal of an educated, respectable black citizenry. Faced with this culture gap, she responded with humor, embarrassment, and sometimes shock. She was amused when school attendance fell off during what she called "the great hog sacrifice"—hog-killing week.[7] She was discomfited when the women of Royal Oak came to church "wearing new spring hats, bonnets & dresses some in the last styles I judge, & oh! Such looks as some presented! Some of these people do make themselves appear so much more ridiculous than they really are." She added, "I don't know what they think of my always dressing so plainly."[8] Certainly she meant for her own plain style to be noticed, for the teachers of the Freedmen's Bureau schools, white and black, intended "to remake the culture blacks had inherited from slavery."[9] Firmly entrenched in her middle class convictions, Rebecca could not help reacting to Royal Oak ways:

The children, having taken advantage of the warm days by taking off their coats, shoes &c during play hours many of them now have bad colds. It's useless to advise to the contrary, for the adults are no better themselves, like black snakes, as soon as the sun shines & it begins to get warm they come out. . . .[10]

Still, she confined her dismay to her letters, for her conviction of the importance of her mission overrode class bias. Indeed her over-all purpose, racial equality, remained foremost in her mind:

Whites are mostly secesh [secessionist] here they give colored men employment; the greatest difficulty is they do not pay sufficient wages & if the people will not accept their terms they send off and get "contrabands" as they are here denominated, to work for them so that it takes the labor right out of these people's hands & they are obliged to submit. I hope there will be justice, impartial justice, given to the colored people one of these days.[11]

By the end of her first year in Royal Oak Rebecca had begun an energetic campaign to build a dedicated schoolhouse in accordance with Freedmen's Bureau policy. Having enlisted support in Washington, D.C., New York, Baltimore, and Hartford, by the fall of 1867 she could announce that the building, "a little larger than the white schoolhouse here," was completed.[12] "Our schoolhouse is looking finely," she declared. "I only wish you all could just take a peep into it . . . it will soon be entirely paid for. It is surrounded with a neat fence which has been whitewashed."[13] The black community of Royal Oak honored the teacher's dedication by naming her school the Primus Institute.

Rebecca served in Royal Oak for five years and left her post only when the Freedmen's Bureau re-directed its funding.

I began with 10 day and 26 night scholars. The number soon increased to 75, including persons of all ages. . . . But few, very few could read, others only knew the letters or a part of them. . . . In a remarkably short time many learned them, . . . Now they're using "Hilliards Third Reader," can spell well, study Geog. and arith. & are learning to write.[14]

Writing home to her family Rebecca could share her misgivings about the culture of the mid-South and her anger at the blatant oppression she observed and encountered, but the dominant theme of her letters was dedication to the task she had undertaken. The years in Royal Oak widened her horizons as they afforded her a sense of participating in the vital work of spreading literacy—the basic need of the formerly enslaved facing life as freed people, and indeed the cornerstone of racial uplift.

### Addie Brown

Without her letters we would have no inkling of the intense cross-class friendship between Addie Brown and Rebecca Primus:

Dearest friend & only Sister, I will never doubt your love for me again you say you put my picture under your pillow I wish I had the pleasure laying along side of you.[15]

In fact, we would have no inkling that Addie Brown ever existed. We find no birth certificate, church membership, marriage license, obituary, or census listing recording the life of this feisty young woman, but in a torrent of letters to her absent friend she firmly establishes her presence.[16]

Through her friendship with Rebecca, Addie gained indirect or what is called fictive kinship with the Primus family, and thus access to the middle-class society to which she aspired. Based in Hartford during most of the 1860s, she presents in her letters an inside look at the city's black community, particularly the Primus circle of friends and associates.

Addie Brown appeared in Hartford in her mid-teens in the 1850s with no known family connections, although she mentions relatives in New York City and Philadelphia. Lacking particular skills, she led a hand-to-mouth working-class existence. Typically she traded long workdays for board, room and minimal pay:

Dear Sister, I have just come from up stairs I have put the children to bed I believe I am done for the night. Do you know that I have five pairs of stairs to go up 20 times and sometime more[.] yesterday . . . I went up and down before breakfast six time you can judge for yourself there is a hundred and seven steps when it time for me to go to bed my limbs ache like the tooth ache I think I shall leave the second week April."[17]

Searching always for a better position, Addie changed jobs fairly often. Worn out by domestic work, she tried sewing, which proved even less satisfactory, and finally found a place as assistant cook at Miss Porter's School for Young Ladies in Farmington. Sarah Porter, daughter of a local minister, founded her school in 1843 to prepare the daughters of the well-to-do for their future roles in family and community. Raphael Sands, head cook at the school, was married to one of Mehitabel Primus's sisters, so we might suppose that Addie secured the job through the Primus family network. At first she was pleased: Sarah Porter paid higher wages than Addie had earned previously, allowed her to use the school library, and summoned a doctor when Addie was sick. Still, work in the kitchen entailed hard physical labor. "Some of the cooking utensils," she marveled, "are as large as I am."[18] When Porter offered a more responsible position, Addie wrote that she "would not stay under no consideration."[19] By then she was planning to marry and move to Philadelphia, where she believed the family of her husband-to-be would replicate the supportive relationship she enjoyed with Rebecca and the Primus family.

While Addie's letters record her work life in great detail, her chief subject in the early years was her affection for Rebecca. Whenever they were separated, Addie grieved: "you are the only [*sic*] that I love or ever try to love nobody will come between us."[20] She expressed her longing for intimacy, wishing in one letter "that we could sleep together this winter," and elsewhere "that I could exchange pen and paper for a seat by your side and my head reclining on your soft bosom."[21]

We learn from Addie's letters that her friendship with Rebecca drew varying responses in the black community. She recounts a scene in the Primus home in which Bell (Isabella) and Mehitabel Primus were showing her a letter they had received from Rebecca, when Henry Jones, visiting from Boston, came into the room.

Mr. Jones came up and wanted to [know] if it was a gentleman letter . . . [Mrs. Primus] said I thought as much of you if you was a gentleman she also said if either one of us was a gent we would marry. I was quite surprise at the remark . . . Mr. Jones . . . says when I found some one to love I will throw you over my shoulder. . . . I told him never.[22]

Henry Jones dismissed the idea of love between women; Addie defended it; Mehitabel Primus accepted it. The three opinions open up new questions, for example, was Jones's response based on class or gender? Unquestionably Addie's account of her deep friendship with Rebecca has added a new dimension to our understanding of the lives of black women in the nineteenth century.[23]

Since none of Rebecca's letters to Addie have been found, we see only one side of the relationship, although the quote that opens this section shows that it was indeed mutual. At the same time Addie understood that in order to achieve the security she sought, she must eventually marry one of her several suitors. "Dear Sister," she wrote in a moment of clarity, "I am very much delighted to hear you say that you like Mr. Tines if I should marry him I hope to have some pleas[ure] and comfort for he likes you very much.[24]

The love between Addie and Rebecca closely resembles findings on same-sex relationships between young white women in the nineteenth century.[25] Such friendships, which did not exclude relationships with men, featured strong attachment, intimacy, and dread of separation, all of which appear in Addie's early letters. Over time she wrote less about missing Rebecca and more on the course of her own life. Her social schedule, surprisingly busy, revolved around the extended Primus family and their friends. Her candid style is evident in this description of a holiday celebration:

I understand they had a ball Thanksgiving night. Lydia Jackson and her husband was there and both inebriated. Jim Nott . . . fell down three pairs of stairs . . . he laid so quite that they suppose he was dead. Some of them afraid to go down to him. He ask for his umbrella and that his mother gave it to him and did not wish to [lose] it . . . it really strang[e] that he don't kill himself.[26]

On one occasion she refused an invitation to attend a show at a Hartford theater: "I did not go for they has the minstrels."[27] Addie objected to whites in blackface portraying African Americans as buffoons.

Her pithy vignettes bring to life many of the individuals that Rebecca mentions in her letters, and together the two correspondents bring into focus an active, diverse community of individuals united in resistance to the racial oppression that surrounded them.

Beginning in the 1820s, activists in that community organized and maintained separate institutions and organizations in the quest for recognition and equality. For a time, they enjoyed a measure of success. The gains reached a high point around 1860, with a peak number of black homeowners, a ninety-eight-percent literacy rate, and a rising number of black households, the result of fewer blacks isolated in the homes or businesses of whites.[28] There followed a brief period during which "respectable" black men and women were invited to join the boards of white civic organizations. Thus as they wrote their letters, Rebecca and Addie were in a sense riding the crest of a season of hope.

Of course that hope was ill founded. By 1870 the upward arc of data on Hartford blacks had reversed, while on the national stage Jim Crow laws in the South and increasing bigotry in the North mocked earlier expectations. The Primus correspondents were not spared. Rebecca came home from Royal Oak in 1869 for the last time to find that Connecticut schools had been integrated for students, not for teachers. Unable to pursue her chosen career, she taught Sunday school and made her living alongside her mother, sewing. Later she lived with the family of her younger sister, Isabella. Addie Brown married and moved to Philadelphia, but died at age twenty-eight, as we learn only from a hand-written note among the Primus Papers.

What persisted from the early hopeful years was a way of life. The middle-class model that Rebecca inhabited and Addie sought, failed to bring about racial uplift, but proved of value in itself—an orderly existence, an expression of self-worth, a hold on dignity. Photographs show Rebecca late in life at a reunion of Primus descendants, and again in a gathering of the Talcott Street Church congregation: graphic evidence of family and community celebrating perseverance and survival. The black middle class, like the institution of the family itself, has changed over time, but it endures and indeed prospers as agent and evidence of change, however slow.

## Notes

1. Rebecca Primus, Royal Oak, to family, Hartford, April 7, 1866, and Addie Brown, Hartford, to Rebecca Primus, Royal Oak, February 25, 1866, in *Primus Family Papers*, 1853–1924, Connecticut Historical Society Library, Hartford, CT. See also Griffin, *Beloved Sisters and Loving Friends*.

2. The letters, part of the Primus Papers collection, provided a base for the following works: David White, "Addie Brown's Hartford," *Connecticut Historical Society Bulletin* 41 (April 1976): 57–64; Karen V. Hansen, "'No Kisses Is Like Youres': An Erotic Friendship Between Two African-American Women During the Mid-Nineteenth Century," *Gender and History*, 7 (July 1995): 153–182; and Griffin, *Beloved Sisters and Loving Friends*.

3. Rebecca Primus, Royal Oak, to family, Hartford, February 16, 1867.

4. Ibid., February 16, 1867.

5. Ibid., June 2, 1866.

6. Ibid., April 8, 1866 and June 2, 1866.

7. Ibid., December 14, 1866.

8. Ibid., Hartford, May 18, 1867.

9. See Eric Foner, *Reconstruction: America's Unfinished Revolution: 1863–1877* (New York: Harper and Row, 1989), 146; see also Sandra E. Small, "The Yankee Schoolmarm in Freedmen's Schools: An Analysis of Attitudes," *Journal of Southern History* 45 (August 1979): 381–402, 393.

10. Rebecca Primus, Royal Oak, to family, Hartford, April 13, 1867.

11. "Contrabands" were displaced former slaves. Rebecca Primus, Royal Oak, to family, Hartford, April 7, 1866.

12. Rebecca Primus, Royal Oak, to family, Hartford, March 2, 1867.

13. Ibid., September 30, 1867.

14. Statement by Rebecca Primus on the progress of her school, September 1, 1867. Filed with Rebecca's letters, Primus Family Papers, Connecticut Historical Society, Hartford.

15. Addie Brown, Hartford to Rebecca Primus, Royal Oak, January 16, 1866.

16. The letters of Addie Brown preserved in the Primus Papers number 120; of Rebecca, 51.

17. Addie Brown, Hartford to Rebecca Primus, Royal Oak, March 25, 1866.

18. Ibid., Farmington to Rebecca Primus, Royal Oak, May 5, 1867.

19. Ibid., January 19, 1868.

20. Ibid., Hartford to Rebecca, Hartford, August 31, 1861.

21. Ibid., May 20, 1866.

22. Ibid., January 21, 1866. Mr. Jones was a former Hartford resident who had moved to Boston.

23. See Hansen, "'No Kisses Is Like Youres,'" 153–54.

24. Addie Brown, Hartford to Rebecca Primus, Royal Oak, January 16, 1866.

25. See Carroll Smith-Rosenberg, "The Female World of Love and Ritual: Relations Between Women in Nineteenth-Century America," in *Disorderly Conduct: Visions of Gender in Victorian America* (New York: Oxford University Press, 1985), 53–76. For a more specific examination of the friendship between Addie and Rebecca see Hansen, "'No Kisses is Like Youres,'" 153.

26. Addie Brown, Hartford, to Rebecca Primus, Royal Oak, dated "November" 3, 1866, but probably December 3, 1866.

27. Addie Brown, Hartford, to Rebecca Primus, Royal Oak, January 21, 1866.

28. Data derived from U.S. Census returns 1850 to 1880. See Barbara J. Beeching, "Great Expectations: Family and Community in Nineteenth Century Black Hartford" (Ph.D. dissertation, University of Connecticut, 2010).

*Wm. Frank Mitchell*

# 30  The Fisk Jubilee Singers
Tour the North

We understand that every seat in Music Hall [in New Haven] was sold for the Jubilee concert last night and when the doors were opened only standing room could be had. . . . The [Fisk University Jubilee] singers sang well and were warmly encored. . . . During the evening Rev. Henry Ward Beecher was prevailed upon to make a statement. . . . He made a good begging speech [and] about $600 were pledged on the condition that $1000 should be raised for the Fisk University. . . . The singers were not met with ovations when they began their tour. Until they reached New York their expenses exceeded [their fundraising] but the success that now attends their efforts, makes up for past losses. They will probably return and sing here again.
—NEW HAVEN REGISTER, February 15, 1872

On October 6, 1871—six years after the Civil War's end—a small group of African-American youth, some recently freed and others born into freedom, began a musical journey from Nashville. The Fisk Jubilee Singers went on tour to raise funds to help settle the school's debts. Fisk University's Jubilee Hall is evidence of the tour's ultimate financial success. While on that tour, the Singers introduced Negro spirituals to a curious American public fascinated by the recently freed black Americans and their culture. The young singers personified a broader effort to safeguard and raise awareness of the culture free and enslaved blacks had created while in America. They found support and allies in Connecticut and New England. Their efforts, along with those of other black performers of the period, helped to focus a movement to resurrect the black image in late nineteenth-century America.

Enslaved blacks created regionally specific cultures adapted to their lives. In places as disparate as Louisiana, South Carolina, Pennsylvania, and Connecticut, black communities found ways to worship, communicate, cook, and celebrate that were familiar and comforting. While those cultural forms might have been understood and even shared by blacks and whites in a given region, the Civil War

ORIGINAL JUBILEE SINGERS,
NASHVILLE, TENN.
SANG BEFORE THE CROWNED
HEADS AND EUROPES' SMART
SET, BUILDERS OF JUBILEE HALL.

*Maggie Porter. Thos. Rutling.
Isaac Dickerson, Jennie Jackson, Ella Sheppard, Benj. M. Holme.*

FIGURE 30-1 Original
Jubilee Singers, 1872. *The
Amistad Center for Art
& Culture, Inc., Simpson
Collection, 1987.1.3451*

brought broader exposure of the cultures and of slavery and other
circumstances in those regions. That exposure also opened opportunities to exploit political ideology, music, dance, worship style,
and even the clothing blacks favored to both the benefit and the
detriment of the enslaved and the free. As Democrats and Republicans, Northerners and Southerners, abolitionists and slaveholders,
and citizens and immigrants had argued the issues that would lead
to war, public images of black life and culture had become increasingly politicized—and ultimately reduced to sentimental or mean-
spirited stereotypes.

The spirituals the Jubilee Singers sang were solid cultural forms of
African America. The combined musical influences of different con-
tinents produced music that entertained crowds of working people
at minstrel shows and eventually the elite in concert halls. Arrangements of those songs influenced the African American composers
Charles Albert Tindley, Harry T. Burleigh, and William Grant Still.
But before their work reached the concert hall, elements of the music appeared on the minstrel stage in humiliating performances that
mocked black people's speech, intellect, movement, and even style
of dress.

The Jubilee Singers and their handlers set off for their first tour in an uncertain environment. Early audiences in Ohio and a few other Northern states received the singers with indifference or even hostility. Some expected they would perform comic and degrading minstrel songs. The singers made very little money from donations, faced discrimination in their accommodations—when housing could be secured—and struggled to gain support for the tour from a reluctant American Missionary Association.

Their fortunes changed once the Rev. Henry Ward Beecher agreed to support the tour. The Connecticut native was the nation's preeminent celebrity preacher; by inviting the singers for a December performance at the prestigious Plymouth Church of Brooklyn, Beecher ensured the tour's success. After the triumph at Plymouth, the singers received offers from other churches and larger halls, and the American Missionary Association finally agreed to back the tour.

Connecticut dates followed, and the Jubilee Singers enjoyed a warm welcome, favorable press coverage, and solidly respectable donations from audiences. They sang in Westport, Farmington, Plainville, Bristol, New Britain, Norwich, and Waterbury. Mark Twain attended one of the Hartford performances and began a long and favorable association with the singers. Their New York and Connecticut dates proved a welcome respite from the difficult early tour dates, but they still faced complications. The singers stayed at the homes of some of New Haven's leading citizens after several hotels appeared wary of renting them rooms.

The Connecticut appearances, made profitable by Beecher's patronage, helped sustain the tour—and the singers. Connecticut press reviews show evidence of an appreciation of the music and the singers' experience in a way that acknowledged their humanity. In particular, these reviews evaluated the music and performers in comparison to other concert music, not to popular minstrel music. Twain endorsed the Jubilee Singers as a more realistic musical experience—based on his knowledge of the South—than the popular Negro minstrel performances. The tour had many objectives, among which raising money was paramount, but through their music, the Jubilee Singers began to broaden the spectrum of what could be expected of African Americans in the years after the Civil War. Their national tour meant that in many newspapers there was at least one favorable story about black life and culture while the singers were in town.

Other African-American public intellectuals, performers, and activists would follow the Jubilee Singers' effort to reclaim and resuscitate representations of black life and culture in the late nineteenth century and into the twentieth century, though black artists often struggled to control their creative endeavors and determine the venues in which they would perform. Through success and failure, the Jubilee Singers' experience blessed all of these performers by insisting that critics and audiences begin to consider the creative achievements of the then recently freed people. They endured a long struggle, but African-American performers' efforts helped maintain the integrity of a potent cultural form and inspired its use as a tool in later political efforts.

Note

This essay appeared in the Spring 2011 issue of *Connecticut Explored*.

*Carolyn B. Ivanoff,*
*with Mary J. Mycek and*
*Marian K. O'Keefe*

# 31 Ebenezer Bassett's Historic Journey

On June 5, 1869, on a hot day in New York City, thirty-six-year-old Connecticut native Ebenezer D. Bassett (1833–1908) and his family boarded the steamship *The City of Port-au-Prince*. Bassett was surrounded by a crowd of dignitaries and on-lookers who wished him well as he embarked on a historic journey to the world's only independent black republic, Haiti (or, as it was spelled in the nineteenth century, Hayti). He had been appointed by the Grant administration as minister resident, our nation's first black ambassador.

The United States was in the midst of Reconstruction after a devastating Civil War. As Bassett boarded the ship, he was aware that he was breaking historic ground as the first black American appointed to a top diplomatic post. He acknowledged the risk of failure and the difficult diplomatic challenges that lay ahead. A few days earlier he had addressed a large audience in New York City, pledging to President Grant and the nation that he would bring to his work "An honest heart, a generous purpose, and unflagging industry, and an elevated patriotism."

Bassett's great-grandfather Pero had endured the Middle Passage to the New World as an enslaved African. Pero had married Hagar, another enslaved African, who was owned by Reverend Richard Mansfield of Derby, Connecticut. One of Pero and Hagar's sons, Tobiah (Bassett's grandfather), was sold to John Wooster of Oxford, Connecticut; Tobiah won his freedom through his service in the American Revolution. Tobiah had a reputation for honor and intelligence in both the white and black communities and was elected a Black Governor by the black community of Derby in 1815. Tobiah's son, Eben Tobias, was Bassett's father. Eben Tobias was elected and served as a Black Governor from 1840 to 1845. He married Susan Gregory Bassett, and used the Bassett surname. Bassetts, white

FIGURE 31-1 Ebenezer
D. Bassett, 1853. *Special
Collections Department,
Elihu Burritt Library,
Central Connecticut State
University, New Britain*

and black, populated the lower Naugatuck Valley, and the family
may have chosen the Bassett name for reasons of kinship. Around
1830 or 1831 the couple moved to the Litchfield area, presumably for
economic opportunity. They had three children: Charlotte in 1832,
Ebenezer Don Carlos on October 16, 1833, and Napoleon in 1836.
Sometime before the 1850s the family returned to the lower Naugatuck Valley and farmed land belonging to Dr. Martin Bull Bassett
of Derby on Great Hill along the banks of the Housatonic River.

In the late 1840s Ebenezer's formal education began at the Birmingham Academy established in 1838 and located near the Derby
green. Unlike other towns in the state, Derby did not exclude Bassett from an education because of his race. Reflecting on this period,
Bassett later said, "My success in life I owe greatly to that American
sense of fairness which was tendered me in old Derby, and which ex-

acts that every man whether white or black, shall have a fair chance to run his race in life and make the most of himself."

While attending school at the Birmingham Academy, Bassett was working in the office and running errands for the most prominent citizen in town, Dr. Ambrose Beardsley, who recognized the young man's academic talent. It may have been through Beardsley's recommendation that Bassett attended the Wesleyan Academy in Wilbraham, Massachusetts (now Wilbraham & Monson Academy). Wesleyan Academy was a stop on the Underground Railroad, and undoubtedly it was here Bassett came into contact with the injustices of antebellum America. Bassett next attended the State Normal School in New Britain, now Central Connecticut State University. He graduated in 1853, the first and only black in his class.

After graduation, Bassett began his career as a teacher at the Whiting School, (for children of color) in New Haven at a salary of $300 a year. After his first year the school board's report noted that Bassett had "transformed 40 or 50 thoughtless, reckless, tardy and reluctant youngsters into intelligent ambitious, well-disciplined and well-behaved students." Hungry to continue his education, he attended classes at Yale in mathematics and classics. In 1855 he married Eliza Park in New Haven. While in New Haven he also met Frederick Douglass for the first time. Their lives would intersect many times in subsequent years, and their friendship would last until Douglass's death.

In 1855 Bassett became principal of the Institute for Colored Youth in Philadelphia (now Cheyney University). This prestigious appointment doubled his salary. ICY was then a national flagship institution for black education, and the Bassets became members of the black elite in Philadelphia. Basset became active in abolitionist efforts and was in constant touch with Frederick Douglass.

During the Civil War, Bassett actively recruited black soldiers, often standing beside Douglass on the podium. During and after the war, Bassett, who did not serve in the military, was involved in civil rights, was nationally recognized as a pioneer black educator, and was active in Republican politics. His experience made him a perfect fit for the post of minister resident (the term "ambassador" didn't come into use until 1893) to the newly recognized black republic of Haiti, which the Grant administration was determined to fill with a "worthy" black man.

Haiti was a Caribbean nation on the western side of the island of Hispaniola (the eastern two-thirds of which were occupied by the Dominican Republic) that had been claimed by Columbus on behalf of Spain in 1492 and by the French in the 1660s. By 1790 Haiti had overshadowed the eastern part of the island to become the "Pearl of the Antilles," the richest French colony in the New World, producing sugar, coffee, and indigo under the intense brutality of the French plantation system. Under the French system, it was cheaper to work a slave to death and purchase a new one than to care for existing workers. French plantation owners imported 30,000 to 100,000 slaves annually during more than a century of domination from 1697 to 1804.

Haiti's enslaved people struggled with revolt, civil war, and foreign invasion. Inspired by the American and French revolutions and led by Toussaint L'Ouverture, a formerly enslaved coachman and genius of guerrilla warfare, Haiti was brought under black control. Napoleon invaded in 1802 in hopes of using Haiti as a platform to create a French empire in the new world. The Haitian army fought fanatically under L'Ouverture until L'Ouverture's betrayal by his chief lieutenant, General Jean-Jacques Dessalines, and his death in a French dungeon in 1802. Despite that loss, the French invaders were decimated and finally driven out by the slave armies, yellow fever, and the jungle. Nearly 80,000 Haitians perished in the conflict, but the Haitian forces had defeated one of Europe's finest armies in the first successful slave revolt in world history. On January 1, 1804, Haiti proclaimed independence, becoming the second independent republic in the western hemisphere and the first free black republic in the world.

As a free republic, Haiti provided the U.S. with a valuable trade. For racial reasons the U.S. refused to recognize the country diplomatically until 1862, under the Lincoln administration. When President Grant sought a U.S. ambassador to Haiti in 1869, Bassett was endorsed by prominent Republicans for the post and submitted his name for consideration. His credentials as an educator, linguist, and activist made him a perfect fit for the post, and the Senate confirmed his appointment unanimously.

By the time Bassett accepted his diplomatic post in 1869, Haiti, the former Pearl of the Antilles, had fallen into a pattern of disaster after disaster, facing revolution, revolt, and civil war followed by famine, disease, earthquake, and hurricanes. When Bassett landed on the island after a tempestuous sea voyage, Haiti was in the midst of yet another one of its violent civil wars. He found himself the most powerful American on the island, yet his proper French did not equip him to communicate in the Creole that was the language of the island, and he lacked diplomatic experience. One of the first things he did was to lease a fireproof building for his records to protect them from the violence of the on-going civil war.

Bassett served as minister resident for almost nine years of Haitian turmoil and trial. His diplomatic efforts were made extremely delicate due to the desire of the U.S. to annex the Dominican Republic. Bassett had to repeatedly allay Haitian suspicions of an American takeover to protect American merchants and interests on the island. In the midst of all this, he carried on with his personal life; three of his eight children were born on the island, and two died there. Haiti, despite its travails, could be a deceptively lovely, tropical paradise, and Bassett came to love the island's beauty.

During his tenure, Bassett proved a pioneer in providing political asylum and protecting human rights, often angering his superior, Secretary of State Hamilton Fish, and creating tension with Washington. Bassett regularly granted asylum to refugees at the American compound at a time when political asylum and human rights were not of widespread concern; nor was this practice common among other diplomats. Fish believed that Bassett had no legal basis for accepting refugees into the American compound. Bassett often risked his own safety and that of his family in doing so. But Bassett saved many lives through this controversial practice, including that of General Boisrond Canal, who later became president of Haiti, twice. One of the elements that played in Bassett's favor was the slowness of communications. Dispatches had to be sent by ship and took weeks. Bassett often found it expedient to do what he felt was right and ask for forgiveness after the fact. Canal and other future leaders Bassett saved would later hold him, and the U.S., in high esteem.

As was customary, at the end of the Grant administration Bassett turned in his resignation, though he hoped the new administration would reinstate him. The Rutherford B. Hayes administration appointed another black man, John M. Langston, who had been born a slave in Virginia, earned his freedom, and was serving as dean of Howard Law School. Langston was rewarded with the diplomatic post for his work on behalf of the Republican Party and the new president and fellow Ohioan, Hayes.

Bassett, at forty-four, found himself unemployed. On December 1, 1877, he and his family boarded the steamship *Atlas* for the two-week trip from Haiti to New York City. Back in New Haven, Bassett became reengaged in public speaking and in political and civil rights issues. Bassett would never receive another U.S. diplomatic appointment, but he was not forgotten in Haiti. In 1879, Haitian President Lysius Solomon, who brought some stability to that country, appointed Bassett Haitian consul in New York City. Bassett held that position until 1889, when he resigned in protest because American merchant ships were illegally running arms to Haitian rebels.

In 1888, with Benjamin Harrison's election as president, Bassett felt the time was ripe to again seek his former post. But Frederick Douglass was offered the job. Bassett heartily supported the appointment and signed on as Douglass's secretary. By this time, Douglass was elderly, he had no diplomatic experience, and he could not speak French. His tenure was not entirely successful, and he resigned in 1891, leaving Bassett again unemployed. Returning to Connecticut, he went back to his old avocation of speaking about civil rights and Republican politics. Benjamin Harrison lost to Democrat Grover Cleveland in 1892; the nation fell further into the grip of Jim Crow, and Bassett fell ever deeper in debt. Eliza, Bassett's beloved wife of forty years, died in August 1895. Douglass also died in 1895, ending an era for the nation and a life-long friendship for Bassett.

In 1898, with the outbreak of the Spanish-American War, Haiti again feared annexation by the U.S. Bassett was appointed vice consul general by the Haitian government and held the position until his death.

Bassett passed quietly from life and the public eye in 1908 at his home in Brooklyn, New York. He and Eliza and all of his children, of whom several had followed him into the field of education, lie together in the family plot in Grove Street Cemetery in New Haven. Largely forgotten today, Ebenezer D. Bassett triumphed over the obstacles of race and inequality in the nineteenth century to live an exemplary life devoted to educating and serving others as a pioneer black educator, the first black diplomat of the United States, and a quiet American hero.

Note

This essay appeared in the Winter 2011/2012 issue of *Connecticut Explored*.

# 32 Charles Ethan Porter

In October 1869, Charles Ethan Porter, a young man from Rockville, Connecticut, enrolled at the National Academy of Design in New York City, where aspiring artists longed to study and where many of the leading American artists had done so. Admission to this art school represented a major achievement for anyone and an extraordinary one for an African American so soon after the Civil War. Porter was the first of his race to be admitted.[1] The epithet "color'd" after his name in the register remains offensive, but it also serves as a reminder that African American fine-arts practitioners were once extremely rare.

No place for beginners, the National Academy required proof of exceptional ability. The school did not charge tuition, but New York City was expensive and hostile to people of color. Many public places barred African Americans; blacks had few housing choices and paid dearly for those they could get. That Porter, a poor man without patronage, was able to study at the Academy for four years says much about him.

Porter was born in Hartford about 1847.[2] His family later moved to the mill town of Rockville, fourteen miles east. He attended high school there, an opportunity he would not have had in Hartford. He said that his talent for picture making made him popular at school.

The Porters were for some time the only African Americans in town. Both parents had been born free, had mixed black, white, and Indian ancestry and were devout Methodists. Charles's father, a Massachusetts native, was a laborer who could not work at times because of illness or injury. He bought a plot of land in Rockville in 1857 and built a family home. Census reports describe Charles's mother, originally from Ellington, as "keeping house," but she often hired out as a laundress or house cleaner.

Destitute for years, the family suffered emotional and financial hardships. Six children died in childhood, and two adult sons perished, one from illness and the other, a Union soldier serving in the

Twenty-ninth Regiment Infantry, from a musket ball on a Virginia battlefield in 1864. Another Union army son barely survived the malaria he contracted while on duty with the Fourteenth Rhode Island Heavy Artillery (Colored) near New Orleans in 1864. Nonetheless, his family encouraged Porter's ambition to be an artist, despite badly needing the income he might otherwise have provided. His younger brothers worked in a local textile mill at ages thirteen and ten, but Charles was sent to high school. He also had a course of drawing lessons.

After high school, Porter worked on farms and in mills for three years until he saved enough money to enroll in 1868 at Wesleyan Academy in Wilbraham, Massachusetts (now Wilbraham & Monson Academy), where he studied drawing and painting. His drawing teacher urged him to apply to the National Academy of Design.[3] In New York, he earned a little money by working the six-to-eleven night shift at the residential YMCA (segregated) at 23rd Street and 4th, across from the Academy, where he studied drawing during the day.[4]

Porter moved rapidly from the required drawing courses to advanced classes in painting. Back home for the summer of 1872, he exhibited at the Tolland County Agricultural Fair. An editorial in the *Tolland County Journal* spoke glowingly of Porter's entries, history, and talents, then sharply rebuked the jurors for taking no notice of his pictures: "They should have occupied a most conspicuous place . . . in this way a true appreciation is shown of talent, which is real genius."[5] Porter would always have admirers, in his hometown and elsewhere, but he would meet prejudice, often veiled, at every turn.

Porter completed his studies at the National Academy of Design in 1873 and planned to spend every fall, winter, and spring in New York City. Artists fled to the country or seaside in the summer, but Porter went home to Rockville, where his mother's garden was bountiful with the flowers and fruits he liked to paint. He was back in New York by the fall of 1873, but the following year he was still in Rockville in November. Caring townspeople, realizing that he was out of money, organized a benefit entertainment. Porter contributed a painting for a raffle at the event.[6]

In New York in the 1870s, Porter showed paintings at the American Society of Watercolor Painters and the National Academy of Design. A recently discovered newspaper article, based on an interview with Porter, reveals why he left New York for Hartford in the late 1870s. "Strains on his nerves and lack of necessary comforts of life" led to a paralytic stroke that sent him home to Rockville in 1876 or 1877 for more than a year. When he finally felt well enough to return to New York, his family and friends persuaded him to open a studio in Hartford, where he would be near his family if he had another attack.[7] By March 1878 Porter was working in the tower studio of Hartford's elegant new Cheney Building (designed by noted architect Henry Hobson Richardson and later renamed for him).

Hartford, which prospered during the Civil War, had long seen itself as a center for the arts. When Porter arrived, a dozen or so artists had studios on or near Main Street. Conservative and respectful of tradition, this group stood in sharp contrast to young artists in New York, who were so excited about recent advances in Europe that they vilified the National Academy as stuffy and old-fashioned. Collectors wanted European art, too, and all art was selling better in the city's new commercial galleries than in artists' studios. Landscapes were becoming more popular than portraits, and Porter's chosen genre of still life, never highly regarded in the European and American art worlds of the nineteenth century, was dismissed as appropriate only for women and amateurs.

Hartford, however, hailed Porter's fruit and flower paintings as marvels of realism, painted in unbelievably close detail and drenched with rich, deep color. His butterflies, according to a December 18, 1877, review in the *Hartford Courant*, showed "the individual feathers of the wing . . . and these he painted without *microscopic* aid!" The *Hartford Daily Times* (September 11, 1879), saw in Porter "an artist whose paintings, in minute accuracy of detail, and particularly in fidelity to nature in some of the most difficult points of color, are hardly surpassed by any painter in America." Frederic Edwin Church, the world-famous landscapist, dropped into Porter's studio one day, bought a painting, and declared him to be the best colorist in America.[8] He urged him to paint landscapes, and afterward Porter often did. But people preferred, and continue to prefer, his still life paintings.

Buoyed by his warm reception in Connecticut, Porter held an auction of his work in 1881. He wanted to study in France and was ready to part with every painting in his studio, even at the low prices that made auctions a boon for buyers rather than artists. Although the sale of nearly a hundred paintings netted him little more than $1,000, Porter crossed the Atlantic at the end of the year, carrying letters of introduction from Mark Twain, ex-Governors Marshall Jewell and Gen. Joseph Hawley, and other distinguished Hartford citizens.[9] Porter wanted to stay in France for three years but came back after two, his money gone. (The persistent story that Mark Twain financed Porter's studies in France is untrue.) He was disappointed, especially about his failure to have a picture accepted at the prestigious Paris Salon, but he had much to be pleased about.

He had studied at two fine schools in Paris: the French National Academy for Decorative Arts, familiarly known as the Petit Ecole, and the Academie Julian, where one of his instructors, the famous Jules Lefebvre, had praised his originality. In the art museums and galleries, he absorbed the work of two very different French artists. From the contemporary flower painter Henri Fantin Latour he learned that realism could be achieved with looser brushwork and less detail than he had been using, and that flowers look more natural when painted in lighter, softer colors. The superb kitchen still lifes of the great eighteenth-century artist Jean-Baptiste-Siméon Chardin taught him about texture and highlights, and how subtle and evocative backgrounds can refine and embrace objects and unify pictures.

Porter also spent months at a time in the French countryside, painting landscapes outdoors in the village of Fleury, near Barbizon, where artists were still emulating Millet, Corot, and the other 1830s rebels who abandoned academic traditions in favor of atmospheric tone poems that stir emotions. A friend and fellow painter there was Charles H. Davis, the ex-patriate landscapist from Boston who later became dean of the artists who gathered at Mystic, Connecticut.[10]

Racial prejudice was uncommon in France. Still, it's unclear whether Porter enjoyed the fabled camaraderie and bohemian lifestyle of Parisian art students. He was older than most and a devout Methodist. In America, prejudice against African Americans was rapidly increasing in the mid-1880s. Porter encountered many obstacles before coming to Hartford; he was about to confront many more. The remainder of his long career spanned what is generally called America's Progressive Era. For African-Americans, it became known as the Nadir.

Porter was back from France in time to address Meriden's February 1884 Lincoln Club meeting on "The Courage of the Abolitionists." The club's two founders, one of whom was his brother-in-law, were related to the Bemans, a historic Connecticut family that fought tirelessly for abolition, suffrage, and temperance. Other Porter brothers and brothers-in-law were also deeply involved in this club and in other civil rights and religious groups. Porter shared their strong beliefs but usually devoted himself to his art. They understood and did what they could to help him, exhibiting his paintings in the Meriden barber shops two of them owned and providing him with a studio in Rockville (in the remains of a felled observation tower) just yards from his family home.

In the spring of 1884, Porter reestablished a Hartford studio in the tower of the Cheney Building and invited the public to assess his new work. Critics agreed it was even better now that it incorporated the broader, freer style and harmonious tones of contemporary French art—faint praise, perhaps, since conservatively aesthetic Hartford generally perceived France as a breeding ground for radical art. Still, the city's three newspapers all endorsed Porter's recent paintings, especially the florals: "Gorgeous in design and surpassing rich in color."[11] Porter still painted the same subjects as before—flowers and fruits—but he now achieved beautiful effects in more interesting and subtle ways by melding the technical sophistication he had developed in France with the enchanting, primitive-like lucidity of his pre-Paris art. He indulged more, too, in what he had previously only hinted at: a touch of quirkiness that tweaks the established conventions of still life. His art now had a look of its own.

Porter needed money, however, even more than approval. In December 1884, he rented a hall and mounted an auction of some one hundred pictures painted in France or afterward. Scheduled for two days, the sale dragged on for an unprecedented nine. On December 15, the *Courant* bluntly announced that, "Mr. Porter wants money—that's the plain English of it." A similar statement appeared four days later: "Absolute necessity compels us to sell." Finally word came that Porter would sell even the apple painting he considered his masterpiece.

Porter moved to New York City soon after the auction. Despite praise for his new art, Hartford seemingly missed the meticulous detail and finish of his pre-Paris work. Yet the paintings from 1884 to about 1900 remain the most accomplished of his career (see plate 1). More than his noteworthy early efforts, these works qualify him to be called a master of still life. At the end of 1886, after two years in New York, Porter returned to Hartford. He participated in two auctions sponsored by art dealer A. D. Vorce, in which he was partnered with Daniel F. Wentworth, a white landscape painter. Vorce, who had been exhibiting Porter's work since 1878, energetically marketed this sale to a middle-class audience. Important Hartford people owned Porter paintings, including Mrs. Samuel Colt, Francis Goodwin, Mark Twain, and silk manufacturers Ira Dimmock and the Cheney brothers.[12] But rising artists such as Porter and Wentworth needed a broader client base, and Vorce wanted to get it for them. The local newspapers probably followed his lead when they urged people to go to these auctions and buy paintings because "every nice house has them." Auctions such as this, declared the *Hartford Times* at the time of the first Wentworth-Porter sale in 1887, are "for people that are not rich, that cannot order their pictures or buy them at high prices."[13] Still life, still seen as an inconsequential genre, went for bargain prices. Wentworth's pastoral landscapes sold for prices two and three times higher than Porter's lovely still lifes.

By summer 1889, Porter recognized that he could not accomplish his artistic goals in Hartford, and he left the city for good, returning briefly only to sell new work or teach a few students. Until 1896, when he moved to Rockville permanently, he spent winters in New York and the rest of the year in Rockville. In New York in the winter of 1892, he was one of several artists collaborating on an enormous panoramic view of Niagara Falls.[14] For four or five years in the late 1890s he had small annual exhibitions at Horace Rude's art store in Springfield, Massachusetts. His last solo exhibition in Hartford was in 1898 at the YMCA. He exhibited work regularly in Rockville and made summer painting forays into eastern Connecticut.

In the early 1890s, Porter had grown close to two young white Connecticut artists: Samuel Morley Comstock of Essex and Gustav Hoffman of Rockville. Comstock and Porter toured galleries and had dinner together in New York, visited one another in Rockville and Essex, and spent a couple of summers painting in Essex. They exhibited jointly in the Rude exhibitions in Springfield and at the Hartford YMCA until Comstock died of tuberculosis in 1900 at age twenty-nine. Hoffman visited Porter often in Rockville and sometimes painted with him there and elsewhere.

The downhill slide of Porter's life had begun, however, and would continue until his death in 1923. First came personal losses. Horace Rude died the same year as Comstock, closing one of the last outlets Porter had to exhibit his work. Five years later Porter's parents died within months of one another. Bereft, Porter felt the need soon after to leave the Methodist church, where he had been a tenor soloist. He became a Christian Scientist.

Porter continued painting and remained self-supporting. Finally he was reduced to peddling his paintings door-to-door in Rockville, asking to do chores if no one would buy. Some women, it is rumored, used their maids as go-betweens in order to avoid meeting him face to face.

Porter's ability to paint gradually declined, possibly from a physical or emotional disorder. Hartford, which had once hailed him as a genius, forgot him. In 1892, the Hartford Society of American Artists was formed to include every artist who had ever worked in the city but did not invite Porter. In 1904, the *Hartford Courant* ran a long article about the city's art spirit, listing numbers of historic artists, including Daniel Wentworth—but not Charles Ethan Porter.[15] Until about the 1980s, even African American art historians and art dealers usually overlooked him, possibly because his work didn't address the African American experience, the focus of African American art since the twentieth century.

The Porter family, along with many others of their race after the Civil War, had believed in the promise that African Americans would at long last be accepted as full citizens of the United States. On the strength of that promise, Charles Porter thought he could become a professional artist if he worked hard enough, even though he was poor and without patronage.

In his time, Porter had no choice but to conform to mainstream American art. He needed to accommodate himself to a hostile white world, for his clients would be mostly white. People of his race, generally confined to menial jobs, could seldom afford art. Mindful and proud of his African American heritage, he counted on his close-knit family to keep him grounded, and ample evidence suggests that they did. Amazingly, Porter met the challenge of living in one world and working in another so successfully that he supported himself through his art for some forty years.

Porter mastered the still-life genre. He is known to have painted portraits, but white people rarely commissioned them from a black artist. He painted *plein air* landscapes, but that required going to picturesque country or seaside places, which he could seldom afford to do. Ultimately, however, his depictions of commonplace fruits and flowers captured an African American experience after all—one that is universal to all humankind—the profound beauty in humble bits of nature, such as daisies, pansies, apples, onions, a butterfly, or, as in one of his loveliest little paintings, a perfectly fried egg, sunny side up, in a small cast-iron pan.[16]

Notes

1. "Charles Ethan Porter: Short Sketch of a Bright and Versatile Artist—Promising and Rising Painter," *Plain Dealer* (Detroit, MI), Mar. 17, 1893.

2. Porter listed his birthdate variously. His death certificate reads 1847; his gravestone is inscribed 1849. For the *Plain Dealer* article noted above, Porter said he was born in 1850.

3. "Porter: Short Sketch," Mar. 17, 1893.

4. Ibid.

5. No headline, *Tolland County Journal*, Nov. 8, 1872.

6. "Local Notes," *Tolland County Journal*, Nov. 20, 1874.

7. "Porter: Short Sketch," Mar. 17, 1893.

8. "An Artist Who Deserves Fame," *Hartford Daily Times*, Sept. 11, 1879.

9. "Porter: Short Sketch," March 17, 1893.

10. Ibid.

11. "Two Charming Pictures," *Hartford Daily Times*, Sept. 9, 1884.

12. "Porter: Short Sketch," Mar. 17, 1893.

13. "A Fine Chance Tomorrow Afternoon—Good Paintings," *Hartford Daily Times*, Apr. 25, 1887.

14. "Porter: Short Sketch," Mar. 17, 1893.

15. "Art Spirit in Hartford," *Hartford Daily Courant*, Nov. 1, 1904.

16. At present, the most complete source about Charles Ethan Porter and his work is Hildegard Cummings, *Charles Ethan Porter: African-American Master of Still Life* (New Britain: New Britain Museum of American Art, 2007), published in conjunction with the exhibition of the same name.

# PART IV

## Photo Essay

*Wm. Frank Mitchell*

# 33 A Veil Lifted

*Double Consciousness and Images from*
*The Amistad Center for Art & Culture*

*The Sweet Flypaper of Life*, Roy DeCarava and Langston Hughes's 1955 photo album and essay, captivated young Deborah Willis when her father brought it home. Willis grew up to become a photographer and won a MacArthur fellowship in 2000. She treasured the photographs her father, police officer Thomas Willis, took of friends and family from her Philadelphia neighborhood. *The Sweet Flypaper of Life*, though, gave her a context for her father's pictures. Willis remembers,

I always looked forward to my father coming home with the past week's prints and negatives. I enjoyed placing the photographs in the photographic album and trying to structure the album the way Hughes and DeCarava had set the photographs in *Sweetflypaper*. *Sweetflypaper* spoke of pride in the African American family, good times and hard times, with an emphasis on work and unemployment. *Sweetflypaper* said to me that there was a place for black people's stories. Their ordinary stories were alive and important and to be cherished . . . For me a veil was lifted. I made it a point from that day in 1955 on to continue to look for books that were about black people and to look at photographs that told or reflected our stories.[1]

In her images and books, Willis creates and interprets so that her viewers will see and appreciate themselves as subjects, just as *Sweet Flypaper* helped her to see beyond the veil: a veil that separated but also shielded, making it possible to recognize and share the good and the hard times.

A half a century before Willis pledged herself to photography another African American genius used the metaphor of a veil to describe what separates blacks from full citizenship. W. E. B. DuBois begins *The Souls of Black Folk* with his now-famous description of the veil:

After the Egyptian and Indian, the Greek and Roman, the Teuton and Mongolian, the Negro is a sort of seventh son, born with a veil and gifted with a sort of second sight in this American world, a world which yields him no true self-consciousness, but only lets him see himself through the revelation of the other world. It is a peculiar sensation, this double-consciousness, this sense of always looking at oneself through the eyes of others, of measuring one's soul by the tape of a world that looks on in amused contempt and pity. One ever feels his two-ness,—an American, a Negro; two souls, two thoughts, two unreconciled strivings.[2]

Looking at African Americans in historical photographs and documents can seem like an exercise of peering through the veil. Many of those photographs, while confirming that blacks existed in this nation, were not meant to be affirmations of African American humanity. "Wanted" posters for the enslaved posted by those who took their freedom; bills, receipts, ledgers, and wills that reveal the fate of enslaved blacks or their daily living conditions; even the cherished early photographs of black people; all of these documents require the conscientious viewer to acknowledge that this material is the record of conquest, domination, and oppression, and its subject is a reluctant participant in these records.

Early daguerreotype photographs of white children and their enslaved black caregivers, for example, challenge viewers to use their "second sight" to find the enduring humanity and compassion within an image that is a record of the "other world's amused contempt and pity," as DuBois termed it. Second sight might be understood as a survivor's semiotics. A set of clues to interpret the subject's life circumstances transforms these images into opportunities for reflection and celebration, though they belong to the perfidious records of slavery. From the safe and compensatory distance of these many decades, there is now space for reflection and enough objectivity to find inspiration in the evidence of a momentous struggle that has been spiritual, political, cultural, sexual, intellectual, financial, and environmental, though it is most often defined as racial.

A century of change in this country and the scholarship and theory it has generated reveals new dimensions in these pictures. The images now have a gravitas that transcends their origins. It grants them the depth, beauty, and truth we hope to find in art. With a survivor's semiotics and the gift of double consciousness, our interpretation of images from the archives is manageable. Photographs and objects from The Amistad Center's Simpson Collection follow an African American narrative of possibility. They document the journey of blacks from the position of object as enslaved, non-citizen to the position of person with rights. African Americans now control their images, and powerful contemporary photography is inspired by historic images. The work of Fred Wilson, Carrie Mae Weems, Whitfield Lovell, Glenn Ligon, and other artists remind viewers of the possibilities locked in archives and photography collections. Everyone benefits from this material's potential to teach and inspire, and our collective ability to understand, appreciate, and debate the African American historical experience is enriched by repeated viewings. Time, experience, nuanced theory, and increasingly better tools pull back the veiled layers, allowing new understandings of these images.

Plate 2, taken by the African American photographer Augustus Washington, presents the viewer with the ultimate exercise in seeing beyond the veil. His Hartford clients were primarily prosperous whites with limited opportunities to engage someone with Washington's political, educational, and artistic background. He opened his Hartford studio in 1846, seven years after the French inventor Louis Daguerre introduced his process for capturing a "likeness." Washington hoped to earn more with photography than he had earned teaching in the North African School at Hartford's Talcott Street Church. He needed the money to continue his studies at Dartmouth College, but his success as a photographer may have kept him from returning to school. By 1850 he had established a reputation through his portraits of Hartford poet Lydia Sigourney, the Torrington-born abolitionist John Brown, and other Connecticut notables. Washington, troubled by personal frustrations and the hazards of the 1850 Fugitive Slave Law, left America for Liberia in 1853. Liberia, he believed, was "the last refuge of the oppressed colored man."

Washington prospered in Liberia. His land investments, business dealings, and choices as a public official were profitable. The author of his 1875 obituary acknowledged, "Mr. Washington was favorably known in the New England States, where he was prominently identified with various schemes for the elevation of his race. He acquired a high reputation as a skillful daguerreotypist at Hartford, Conn, from which city he removed to Liberia in 1853. Nothing could induce him to return to this country, having acquired a handsome property and freedom and a home in his ancestral land."

In broadside ads for his Hartford studio, Washington quoted Shakespeare's Othello's "Strange! Passing Strange" to describe his art and the intimate interracial experience of creating it. He didn't shrink from photographing difficult subjects including the deceased. His advertisements counseled women on the kind of fabrics that would photograph nicely, and he outfitted his studio with a dressing room and attendant. Washington's portrait subjects, often posed seated with a book or some other small prop, project formality and uncertainty. Undoubtedly, the length of time and the pose required for a daguerreotype could make a subject uncomfortable but the photographer's personality and politics might have the same effect.

In this image the young girl's pose, her formal dark dress, her non-descript facial expression, and the tilt of her head reveal the degree of commitment the process exacted. Washington is out of the frame and but always present. From his spot behind the camera, Washington created the desired reality for white clients in Hartford and later for his Liberian compatriots. He belonged to a mid-nineteenth-century black entrepreneurial class that laid the foundation for black accumulation and middle class formation. Their efforts were often unseen or unnoticed by their employers, but the results they achieved were essential for the continuing civil rights struggle. Washington understood double consciousness at its most fundamental level; it structured his life, and the photographs he left behind testify to that reality.[3]

Forty years after Washington successfully photographed Hartford's bold-faced names, black faces regularly appeared in photographs, postcards, and other media. Many of these images were not in the spirit of the racially uplifting agenda that culminated in the birth of the National Urban League (1910) and the National Association for the Advancement of Colored People (1909). Racist depictions of blacks and black life proliferated in the late nineteenth and early twentieth century and could regularly be found in ads and postcards. These racist graphics ran rampant in American popular culture. People mailed racism to their friends and family across the nation by sending outrageous postcards depicting black children as alligator bait, grease paint-faced grotesques in absurd domestic scenes, or demeaning musical caricatures.

Plate 3—a postcard advertising piece for the *New Haven Register* newspaper—by contrast, is practically a celebration of African Americans, with its intriguing focus on sensitively drawn children who appear to be winning a downhill contest at a toboggan party. This is indeed a progressive depiction, though it adheres to the graphics rule of the era by placing African American figures in unlikely or presumably exotic situations. But the children in this card, despite being dressed in pajamas, are totally competent and commanding as they fly to the bottom of the hill to the cheers of enthusiastic spectators. Unlike those black subjects who find themselves flustered and harried when placed in middle-class American milieu, these naïfs triumph.

This genre of card is reminiscent of the concerns that plagued Connecticut's white citizens in the 1820s and 1830s as enslaved blacks gradually became free to move around the state and make their own choices. Some whites worried that their free black neighbors—who could not vote even if they were free—would not easily adapt to freedom or the obligation to care for themselves and their families. In conversation, sermons, and commissioned studies, Connecticut's citizens debated the possibilities as if the enslaved blacks who had managed the lives and fortunes of their enslavers in addition to their own might suddenly prove incapable once relieved of their double burden. When freed, many thrived, and some did not. But the anxiety expressed in these genre postcards proves that the odds for free blacks' success or failure were not fair or equal. This *Register* advertiser's decision to offer this card is evidence of a black community large enough to be interesting to the rest of New Haven but not big enough to pose a threat.

Plate 4, a postcard of a boisterous, integrated group of children meeting at and drinking from the Bennett Memorial Fountain on the New Haven Green appeared a few years after the *New Haven Register* card. The scene suggests speedy progress for the city and for its black residents. The fountain, a symbol of New Haven's City Beautiful efforts, replaced a hundred-year-old town well and brought water from a nearby reservoir. Danziger and Berman released other postcards to recognize the milestone, but those were restrained depictions of the city's leading citizens admiring the new monument. Though there are girls in this scene, the group is primarily boys; boys with a purpose. They appear to be carrying tools of the street trades and may be members of the junior "union" that protected children who sold newspapers and shined shoes in New Haven. Though it was not technically a union, The Friends of Boys helped to organize and defend young workers, both black and white, at a time when there were few opportunities for racially integrated activity.

Plate 5, the New Haven Letter Carriers portrait, is the formal, adult version of the playful postcard. This integrated group of the city's workers—evidenced by a couple of men of African descent—had a real union to organize them, protect them, and build their morale. The ill-at-ease letter carriers stand in stark contrast to the interactive vitality in the image of the children at the fountain.

These portraits belong to a genre of photographs that detail the continued exodus of black residents from Connecticut's towns in the late nineteenth and early twentieth centuries. The few black faces visible in these group portraits personify the shifting residential patterns in some towns as people lost or left land that had belonged to their families. The Bennett Memorial Fountain postcard is unique because it encourages the viewer to imagine the spontaneity of this exchange. As adults, these young people would ultimately find themselves posed awkwardly with their peers for portraits that revealed *de facto* diversity. And they might wonder about the subtle instruction that taught them to recognize and respect a racial hierarchy that pushed children who found ways to share common space to become adults who couldn't.

Migration in the early twentieth century fortified Connecticut's cities and made the prospect of an African-American Connecticut a reality. These cities never rivaled Pittsburgh, Cleveland, or Detroit as destinations, but migrants who came to the state in the first half of the twentieth century found opportunity in Greenwich, Branford, and Norwalk as well as Waterbury, Bridgeport, Hartford, and New London. Ingenious grassroots marketing encouraged idealized visions of New York City, Chicago, and other migration magnets as exotic, fast-paced centers of sophistication and opportunity that were in sharp contrast to the slower-paced familiarity of the agrarian South. Some adjusted easily, but the obstacles could be formidable.

Residents in Connecticut's already crowded black neighborhoods struggled to accommodate new neighbors. Their presence transformed churches, social clubs, community organizations, and political networks as they introduced some new ways and adjusted to the old. Hartford, Waterbury, New Haven, and New London, among other cities supported a thriving network of live music venues for local and nationally known performers traveling between Boston and New York. There were neighborhood theater groups, community centers, garden clubs, and black college alumni groups. The relative comfort and security of these neighborhoods gave newcomers the freedom to adjust and redefine themselves to life in the urban North. Curtained off in their own neighborhoods, black residents created common ground where possible while maintaining the distinct traditions that seemed essential. This helped foster new churches, new social and benevolent organizations, new long and short-term living situations, and a growing service sector.[4]

Black neighborhoods in cities offered spaces for work, worship, and new kinds of creativity, but bucolic spots outside the city still held an appeal. Some people kept the land and ways of living that they and their families had known for generations. And there were many new residents who longed for the small towns they left.

Plates 6 and 7, portraits of people appreciating the environment, link the pre- and post-migration experience through the reality of leisure. The expectation of steady, reasonably well-compensated work meant that fishing and gardening—tasks that once were a subsistence necessity—could be enjoyed as leisure pursuits. With a secure income and a safe neighborhood, many found they had also gained the freedom to create or find new joy in old skills. For those who had come to Connecticut's cities from the coastal Carolinas or Virginia a trip to the shoreline could be familiar and restorative. Fishing or church picnics balanced the more exotic experiences of shoreline summer camp, Savin Rock amusement park, and Greenwich's Lee Haven Beach Club.

Edward Brooke (see plate 8), Republican senator from Massachusetts (1967–1979), was the first African American to serve as a senator in the twentieth century. Brooke graduated from Washington D.C.'s famed Dunbar High School and followed his father by attending Howard University. He joined the army as a second lieutenant in 1941 and was stationed with the all-black 366th infantry regiment on a segregated base in Massachusetts. The discrimination he and the other black soldiers experienced on the base led him to law school after his military service in Italy. From his law practice in Roxbury, Massachusetts, Brooke launched a campaign for Congress that would ultimately make him that state's attorney general and a U.S. senator.

Brooke, like Augustus Washington several generations earlier, lived his early life in a context structured by race but managed by African Americans. Dunbar High School and Howard University were black environments where educators drilled on DuBois's Talented Tenth ideology prepared their students for the challenges ahead and protected them from adversity for as long as they could. Both men's epiphanies resulted from the racial policies of the federal government: The 1850 fugitive slave law motivated Washington, and military segregation inspired Brooke. Each decided public service combined with community capitalism was the solution. Washington chose a progressive, all black, self-determination in Liberia, and Brooke chose to fight his way into the U.S. Senate. As a neighborhood lawyer in Roxbury, Massachusetts with Republican ties and a

Howard University pedigree, Brooke was an economic and political symbol with a sentimental association to the early black voters from Lincoln's Republican Party and prosperous black Washington, D.C. Younger generations found Brooke credible because he endorsed some traditionally liberal issues. In period photographs he appears as a hopeful sign of the rapid change that redefined New England in the late 1960s and 1970s. Brooke's achievements beckoned to parents of students at Project Concern, A Better Chance, and similar programs promoting student diversity at independent schools. Those students and their college-aged peers who integrated elite Northeastern colleges and universities were beneficiaries of the legacy Brooke embodied. His presence in the senate was vindication of Dr. King's vision of integration when critics farther to the left and on the right challenged the goal and tactics. As a high-profile Republican in an era of venerated black political figures whose approaches ranged from liberal to radical, Brooke was unique both within the party and black America. He pushed for the unexpected as Lowell Weicker would later do in Connecticut.[5]

Edward Brooke is symbolic of a transition from a tradition familiar to Augustus Washington, W. E. B. DuBois, and other generative cultural figures who accepted the veil's potential to shield and protect even as it segregated or limited. At times their eagerness to protect their community led to a stumble. Other times a little more of their defensive caution would have helped. Brooke embodied that legacy, and he pushed past it to bring another perspective to the civil rights debate. He expanded the vocabulary for images of Northeastern activist lawyers who were also moderate Republicans just as early Affirmative Action anti-discrimination policies began redefining expectations and images of African America.

Augustus Washington would recognize the America of Deborah Willis's youth, but Barack Obama's presiding over the United States would require explanation. The careless proliferation of images that saturate daily life would be unbelievable to a photographer whose medium was the daguerreotype. Successive generations have benefited from technology and access: Everyone is now his own muse, photographer, and curator. In a world where images are omni-present and reveal micro-details, the value of veils and the discipline of parsing the visual through various perspectives seems an essential skill for appreciating the archive and evaluating the images we find stuck to the flypaper of daily life.

# Notes

1. Deborah Willis, ed., *Picturing Us: African American Identity in Photography* (New York: New Press, 1994), 4.

2. W. E. B. Dubois, *The Souls of Black Folk* (1903), with Introduction by Dr. Nathan Hare and Alvin F. Poussaint, MD (New York: Signet Classic, 1969), 45.

3. Deborah Willis, *Reflections in Black: A History of Black Photographers 1840 to the Present* (New York: W.W. Norton & Co., 2000). "A Durable Memento: Portraits by Augustus Washington," National Portrait Gallery online exhibition, www.npg.si.edu/exh/awash/.

4. Henry Louis Gates, Jr., and Gene Andrew Jarrett, *The New Negro: Readings on Race, Representation, and African American Culture, 1892–1938* (Princeton: Princeton University Press, 2007). Jonathan Gill, *Harlem: The Four Hundred Year History from Dutch Village to Capital of Black America* (New York, NY: Grove Press, 2011). Farah Jasmine Griffin, *Who Set You Flowin'? The African–American Migration Narrative* (New York: Oxford University Press, 1995). Adam Green, *Selling the Race: Culture, Community, and Black Chicago, 1940–1955* (Chicago: University of Chicago Press, 2007). Joe W. Trotter, and Earl Lewis, eds. *African Americans in the Industrial Age: A Documentary History, 1915–1945* (Boston: Northeastern University Press, 1996.)

5. Edward W. Brooke, *Bridging The Divide: My Life* (New Brunswick: Rutgers University Press, 2007).

PLATE 1 Charles Ethan Porter, *Hollyhocks*, 1885. *The Dorothy Clark Archibald and Thomas L. Archibald Fund, The Ella Gallup Sumner and Mary Catlin Sumner Collection Fund, and Partial Gift of Thomas Colville, 2004.11.1, Wadsworth Atheneum Museum of Art*

PLATE 2 Augustus Washington, "Unidentified Young Girl," 1851. *The Amistad Center for Art & Culture, Inc., Simpson Collection, 1987.1.842*

PLATE 3 "The New Haven Register is the Acknowledged Progressive Paper of the City," JH Bufford's Sons Lithography, 1887. *The Amistad Center for Art & Culture, Inc., Simpson Collection, 1987.1.3888*

The Bennett Memorial Foun'ain,
New Haven Conn.

24-23

PLATE 4 "Bennett Memorial Fountain,"
Danziger & Berman Lithographers, 1909.
*The Amistad Center for Art & Culture,
Inc., Simpson Collection, 1987.1.1.3428*

PLATE 5 "Letter Carriers New Haven," 1910.
*The Amistad Center for Art & Culture, Inc.,*
*Simpson Collection, 1987.1.650*

PLATE 6 "Portrait of Mrs. Sara Warner," Branford, Connecticut, 1915. *The Amistad Center for Art & Culture, Inc., Simpson Collection, 1987.1.1486*

PLATE 7 "Man with Pipe Fishing," c. 1930.
*The Amistad Center for Art & Culture, Inc.,*
*Simpson Collection, 1987.1.1524*

PLATE 8 "U.S. Senator Edward Brooke and U.S. Senator Lowell Weicker
meeting with Republican leaders in Hartford, Connecticut," 1975. Brooke,
Republican senator from Massachusetts, is *center right*; Connecticut Senator
Weicker is *far right*. *The Amistad Center for Art & Culture, Inc., Simpson
Collection, 1987.1.1615*

PLATE 9 Ellis Walter Ruley, *Grapefruit Picking Time*, c. 1930. *The Amistad Center for Art & Culture, Inc., Simpson Collection, 1987.1.53*

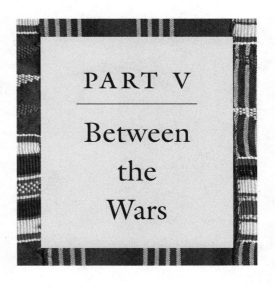

PART V

Between
the
Wars

# 34 Black Southern Migration and the Transformation of Connecticut, 1917–1941

Although when people think of the beginning of the "Great Migration" during the period of World I, Chicago often comes to mind, Emmett Scott, Booker T. Washington's former secretary, thought that the "New England Migration" served as the first instance of the "Great Migration."[1] This movement of thousands of African Americans, beginning around the time of World War I, transformed the demographic make-up of Connecticut. Thousands of blacks, including African American Southerners, black immigrants from the Caribbean, and Cape Verdeans, moved to major urban areas of the state. In turn, these migrants carved out communities within communities.

When thousands of Polish, Lithuanian, and Czech workers left Connecticut to return to Europe to fight in World War I, New England tobacco growers urgently tried to locate a replacement labor force. In their frantic search for an alternative workforce, their initial desperation led them to New York. In 1915 Connecticut Leaf Tobacco Association owners and managers recruited 200 eager New York women to work tobacco in a rash move that proved an utter failure for the association, particularly socially.[2]

The association decided to turn to the National Urban League, one of the nation's major human rights organizations, for help.[3] Seeing opportunity to aid the educational pursuits of young people, Urban League officials sent inquiries about work opportunities to the presidents and leaders of historically black colleges in the South. One of the first people they contacted was President John Hope of Morehouse College. An astute academician and politician, Hope was among the first to recognize that blacks were migrating away from Southern states. While traveling in New England in 1916, Hope saw firsthand Southern African Americans working as "section men with pick and shovel" for Northern railroads. The New

York, New Haven, and Hartford railroad lines all had a visible African American presence in their workforce.

While Hope would have preferred to have working-class African Americans remain in the South, he muted his criticism of the migrants themselves. Instead, he tossed the blame for the exodus into the political lap of Southern white leaders. He knew that most leading Southern white politicians remained silent on vigilante violence directed at innocent African Americans. In addition, landowners had no qualms about using guns to maintain sharecropping, the economic system that dominated the lives of most African Americans. Although people worked for a share of the crop to be used to offset yearly expenses, most sharecroppers found themselves sinking deep into debt, never receiving enough in compensation to rise to land ownership.

However, Hope's immediate focus was on his students. He carefully oversaw the hiring of twenty-five young men for tobacco work. While these students labored in Connecticut tobacco fields other Morehouse men toiled in summer jobs in the Midwest, other parts of New England, and Pennsylvania.[4] Fellow college presidents from African American colleges and universities followed suit. In pursuit of jobs, poor and working class African Americans soon followed the wave of college students.

But migrants' survival depended on their building relationships with people who were already knowledgeable about life in Connecticut. Similarly, New Haven minister Rev. Edward Goin, concerned about the plight of new arrivals, organized to meet their needs by building a social center in a boxcar and enlisting African American students at Yale to provide support. Migrants adopting New Haven as their new home now had advocates from New Haven as part of their network.[5]

Given the terror many dealt with daily in the South, Connecticut seemed like an oasis for those willing to leave. In Southwest Georgia, for instance, an area from which large numbers of African Americans made the exodus to Connecticut, brutal lynchings were common. On October 4, 1916, white marauders murdered an African American woman from Calhoun County, Georgia for her supposed role in the murder of a local white person.[6] Lynchings took place in other counties in areas such as Randolph County, Lee County, and Early County in 1915–1916.[7] Some labor recruiters capitalized on this fear to lure workers northward.[8]

Once migrants decided to make the trek, Southern injustices made their northbound travel difficult. Some African American travelers paid equal fares to whites, while others sometimes paid more expensive fares than whites for similar travel. Clerks at ticket counters in the South frequently ridiculed and yelled at African American passengers. Railroad companies sometimes placed the white workers' lavatory in the railcar designated for African Americans. Every African American traveler knew to pack a lunch because venues where trains stopped often refused dignified service to African Americans.[9] Some police officials in small Southern towns detained travelers without provocation.[10]

White Southerners soon began to feel the impact of the out-migration of valuable laborers. Dwindling labor numbers in some Southern counties forced landowners to double monthly wages, while other landowners found themselves toiling in the hot sun when they couldn't find workers to hire.[11] The need to ease the labor shortage even moved white Southern landowners to contact white Connecticut employers in hopes of locating black workers who might be convinced to return.[12] Although people migrated to Connecticut from more than twenty states, no state felt the brunt of the exodus quite as profoundly as did Georgia.[13]

Not all the blacks who moved to Connecticut were from the South. Black immigrants, primarily from the Caribbean islands, also came to urban areas such as New Haven and Hartford areas to work. The 1920 census listed the birthplaces of such immigrants as Jamaica, Bahamas, and the Virgin Islands. For other Caribbean immigrants, the census listed the immigrants simply as "West Indian." The census also documents the presence of a small group of Puerto Ricans, some of whom may have been of African ancestry. Cape Verdeans further helped to increase Connecticut's black population. Most of these immigrants found steady, though low-paying, working-class positions, with occupations that in many cases were similar to those of African Americans from the South.[14]

The family of Constance Baker Motley, the legendary civil rights attorney from New Haven, came from the island of Nevis. Her father immigrated to that city in 1906—a decade before the Great Migration. Motley's mother followed a year later. Her mother managed to pay the tidy sum of $25 for travel via a ship's steerage-class fare. While her family resided in a mixed neighborhood of Caribbean people, Greeks, German Jews, and Italians, most African Americans in New Haven called the Dixwell Avenue area home.[15]

Although World War I opened employment opportunities in some areas, African Americans from the South soon discovered what many local African Americans already knew. Many white Connecticut residents held disdain and contempt for people with African roots. Unskilled and skilled white immigrants found work at Winchester Repeating Arms Company, New Haven Clock Company, and New Haven Box Company, places that remained off limits to African American workers. Samuel Gompers and the American Federation of Labor loudly supported the rights of white skilled laborers, but not those of African Americans working in any capacity. In Connecticut's larger towns it was well known that law enforcement jobs "belonged" to Irish people and sanitation jobs to Italians. Sanitation, gardening, and housekeeping fell to African Americans throughout the South, but not in Connecticut.[16]

While Southern migrants clearly welcomed the job opportunities that tobacco growers and other companies offered, they eagerly searched for higher-paying work, often only making inroads in certain service occupations. But higher-paying jobs generally were available only to those with union connections—and unions often denied membership to African Americans.[17] That denial ultimately benefited tobacco growers and companies that used non-union labor.

While World War I mobilization led to economic growth for the state as a whole, the 1920s saw economic growth for the nation. African Americans, however, saw limited economic opportunities in the period after World War I. According to Charles S. Johnson, a leading sociologist of the period, African Americans found few opportunities in either skilled or unskilled work. His survey of Hartford, started in 1921, revealed that the majority of Hartford industries (sixty percent of those in his survey) did not employ substantial numbers of African Americans.[18] One heavy-industry company, Pratt and Cady, had 100 African American workers at the peak of the war; by 1923 that number had dwindled to 25, while white workers remained at the plant. When African Americans did find work, their duties tended to be extremely demanding physically and often seasonal. Hod carrier duties, coal yard work, and lumber work are examples.[19]

Such hardships notwithstanding, though, when companies offered steady work, savings plans, and benefits, African Americans jumped at such opportunities.[20] But such opportunities remained severely limited. Colt's Patent Firearms Manufacturing Company, Hartford Machine Screw Company, Pratt & Whitney, Royal Typewriter Company, and Underwood Typewriter Company preferred to hire African Americans only to perform unskilled duties such as custodial work. The apprenticeship program at Pratt & Whitney included no African Americans during the war years.[21] Some companies that sent workers to make repairs in other cities feared that prejudice against African American workers might lead to a loss of business revenue.[22] The huge insurance giants surveyed by Charles S. Johnson were no better than heavy industry.[23]

Inadequate housing was a perpetual problem for African Americans in urban areas. In the state's major urban areas white landlords routinely gouged African American tenants. While many landlords lived among whites, the influx of thousands of African Americans desperate to find housing gave slumlords ample opportunity to overcharge new arrivals from the South. As Charles Johnson's survey documents, slumlords overlooked poor plumbing, and city policies allowed large numbers of people to be packed into already overcrowded areas. New Haven's Dixwell neighborhood and Hartford's North End quickly became densely populated. And as in larger urban areas, discriminatory local policies played a major role in creating and maintaining substandard housing.

Although most African Americans in the cities lived in inadequate housing, small numbers became substantial property owners or found quality housing. For example, in 1915 a master mechanic at the Hartford Machine Screw Works owned both a house for his family and tenement houses in Hartford.[24]

The mass migration of Southern African Americans occurred around the same time that leadership among national African American leaders reached a turning point. W. E. B. Du Bois and other members of the Niagara Movement forged an integrated alliance with whites that became the National Association for the Advancement of Colored People (NAACP). In 1917 Connecticut cities launched efforts to build NAACP chapters. New Haven citizens were the first in the state to organize and receive an NAACP charter. Hartford's local NAACP initially drew its membership from among distinguished members of the African American and white communities, with twenty people meeting to organize at Mary T. Seymour's New Britain Avenue home in 1917. On December 10, 1917, the national organization granted the Hartford branch's charter.[25] Nationally, Connecticut's branches became part of a nationwide organized and integrated movement to combat racism and discrimination against people of color. Although key national figures such as W. E. B. DuBois, James Weldon Johnson, and Mary White Ovington visited and spoke to state branch members, local people carried out the organization's daily business. Local members carried out a campaign to eradicate continued discrimination, inadequate housing, racism, and Southern lynching. Statewide membership came from an alliance of native-born African Americans, Southern migrants, and local white supporters. One of the major efforts of the war period was a campaign by Connecticut NAACP members to push the state assembly to pass a civil rights act.

While the NAACP's actions produced some benefits, the World War I migration of thousands of African Americans to Hartford during the 1910s and 1920s caused class conflict and tension between Connecticut-born African Americans and African American migrants from the South.[26] Alabama native and author Rev. W. B. Reed, pastor of Shiloh Baptist Church, a well-established congregation on Albany Avenue, criticized Southern-born migrants for organizing independent churches, separate from those attended by African Americans born in Connecticut. Reverend Goode Clark, an ordained pastor from Americus, Georgia, followed his members to Hartford. Clark drew Reed's ire by organizing Mount Olive Baptist Church in 1917.[27]

Along with Bethel A.M.E., Ebenezer Baptist Church, Friendship Baptist Church, and Primitive Baptist Church, Mount Olive offered services patterned after those offered in the South. Whooping and shouting became routine occurrences in area churches.[28] The Baptist denomination's membership surpassed that of other denominations in Connecticut towns. In New London, Shiloh Baptist Church's congregation grew in size to exceed that of any other African American religious organization in the city.

African American churches accorded dignity and respect to people whom mainstream society often dismissed. Domestics, gardeners, tobacco plantation laborers, hod carriers, and others received respect as sisters or brothers. Other members received with blessings the honorific titles of deacon, pastor, elder, bishop, or missionary. Members understood that the church was the one place in which all were equal in the eyes of their God. Pastors and leaders dutifully chastised members for inappropriate behavior and "backsliding."[29]

While religious and spiritual freedom in African American churches provided solace throughout the week, Connecticut lacked true social freedom. White theater owners, for instance, regularly segregated African Americans in the galleries.[30] When African Americans decided to seek legal redress to end discrimination by the State Theater, they turned to attorney Thomas J. Spellacy to take the case. Owners of Hartford's *Observer*, a local African American paper, led the charge against the theater.[31] Eventually, the theater opened all seating to African Americans.

When it came to the nation's military, blacks' distinguished service during the Civil War and Spanish American War failed to change perceptions of African American inferiority and ability. The Selective Service Act of 1917 allowed the military to draft millions of men, including some 370,000 African Americans. As for military officers, NAACP leaders and its supporters had to first convince the military that a sizeable pool of qualified African Americans existed. They used the pool of young men on the campuses of what we now refer to as Historically Black Colleges and Universities as proof that qualified candidates existed.[32] These soldiers, like white counterparts, aided in the allied victory.

With the war over, some African American working-class families, even those who needed at least two breadwinners, managed to find small pockets of opportunities. Among typical examples of working-class families documented in the 1920 census, the father in one family of eight worked in the coal yards, while a daughter toiled in a local store. An elevator operator went off to work daily at an insurance firm, while his spouse worked for a tobacco firm. While her husband spent his days in a machine shop, one woman worked in a Connecticut garment factory.[33] In other cases, families survived primarily through the efforts one chief wage earner. One Connecticut railroad worker earned enough to support his family of four. A Connecticut butler received wages large enough to supply the needs of his family of seven. A coal yard trucker's salary also was enough to take care of his family.[34]

In order to make rent and life more manageable, Connecticut residents often defrayed expenses by offering rooms for rent. One minister, who had a large family of seven, rented space to boarders.[35] Some African American residents simply announced and advertised that they ran boarding houses. These boarding houses offered space to as many as seven or eight people. While their spouses were at work, African American women carried out much of the daily work in the boarding houses. They not only cleaned rooms but also provided meals for patrons.[36]

In the 1920s, the urbanization and clustering of African Americans in Connecticut allowed for the growth and development of African American businesses and political power. Grocers, barbers, painting companies, dress making shops, beauty salons, restaurants, saloons, and pool halls dotted the Connecticut landscape. African American physicians and attorneys conducted business in most major Connecticut cities. In the countryside near Lyme, one man, listed as a mulatto, operated a blacksmith shop for years.[37]

The roar of the 1920s ushered in the age of jazz. The music roared into Connecticut's African American community as it did elsewhere. One of the most prominent local jazz artists in Hartford was Bessye Fleming Profitt.

The Atlanta native was a contemporary of Count Basie, Lionel Hampton, and Sophie Tucker. Profitt's first move to New England was not to Hartford, but to Willimantic, where she married a local man. In 1921 she moved to Hartford and gained a solid local following.[38]

For African Americans, the roaring twenties was also a time of leadership battles. The Universal Negro Improvement Association, first formed in 1914 in Jamaica, eventually became arguably the largest mass cultural movement nationwide to date among people of African ancestry. Founder Marcus Garvey brought a message of hope and redemption to millions of African Americans and people of African ancestry worldwide. After reading Booker T. Washington's *Up from Slavery*, Garvey dreamed of building a school system in his homeland of Jamaica along the lines of Washington's Tuskegee Institute. Washington's death in 1915 prevented a meeting, and Garvey was initially rebuffed by R. R. Moton, Washington's successor. When it came to W. E. B. Du Bois, the nation's other most prominent African American leader, and the NAACP, Garvey thought Du Bois's notion of integration was detrimental to African Americans and that white racism would never change. Garvey, through the Universal Negro Improvement Association (UNIA) that he founded, demanded respect and urged black people to build their own government and large-scale businesses. His message of uplift caught the attention of millions of black people across the world.

Black Connecticut was not immune to Garvey's message. By 1922 Connecticut had several UNIA divisions with large memberships, including one in Hartford. Hartford's division met regularly for more than a decade at halls on Chapel Street and Windsor Street. Local leaders, primarily Southern-born African Americans and Caribbean immigrants, attended national and international conventions for years. The division offered an alternative to the integrationist stance of the NAACP.[39] Other areas of Connecticut had visible and active divisions of the UNIA, including New Haven, New Britain, Portland, East Granby, and Rockville.

One of the great highlights of the Hartford UNIA was the 1924 visit of Marcus Garvey to Hartford. While his movement began to decline significantly after his arrest for mail fraud, conviction, and incarceration (1925 to 1927), his ideas remained ingrained in the memories of Connecticut members. (In 1927 the U.S. government decided to release an ailing Garvey and deport him back to Jamaica.)

One follower, Edward Countryman, adhered to the message until 1936. When he decided to embrace new teachings, he chose to be a follower of Noble Drew Ali, founder of the Moorish Science Temple. When the ravages of the depression came, the Moors had enough resources to provide for their members and people requesting aid. According to Constance Baker Motley, Mr. James, one of her father's friends, decided to forsake his friends' advice and move to Liberia, the West African nation where Garvey dreamed of establishing a foothold.[40]

Hartford's John E. Rogers, who went on to become one of the foremost leaders in educating the state on African American history, cast his hopes and dreams on employment with the U.S. Postal Service. In 1928, Rogers scored high enough on a U.S. Postal Service entrance exam to qualify for a position as a clerk. Hartford hadn't hired an African American as a clerk since 1906. Postal officials, however, suggested that African Americans that passed the exam should be letter carriers, a lower-ranking (and lower-paying) position than clerk. Rogers and his fellow African American applicant Edward Swett, who had also scored well on the exam, decided to fight for the clerkships they believed they had earned. Members of Congress who learned of their plight ordered the Hartford postmaster to act. Rogers was required to take a physical exam and passed; however, he received notice from the Postal Service that he had failed the physical because of poor vision. Seeking justice, Rogers sought a second opinion from a leading Connecticut optometrist, who refuted the Postal Service's findings. A second federal doctor then pronounced Rogers fit to work.[41]

The 1929 stock market crash was followed by a decade-long economic depression that battered poor and working-class people throughout the state. For African Americans, surviving the "Old Hoover Days" often meant living in fear, going on relief, receiving church aid, being uplifted by ministers' sacrifices, and embracing New Deal programs. The election of Democrat Franklin Roosevelt brought fear and dread to the hearts of many African Americans in Connecticut. The Democratic Party's ties to Reconstruction and the Jim Crow South caused many to view it as supportive of terror policies and discrimination against African Americans.

African American churches opened soup kitchens and cooperatives to aid the community. Hartford's Rev. Robert Moody and

Shiloh Baptist Church provided food, clothing, and firewood for the needy. Rev. John Jackson, pastor of Hartford's Union Baptist Church and a native of South Carolina, simply decided not to take a salary during the height of the Great Depression, even after the 1938 hurricane devastated Connecticut.[42]

Another positive force in the lives of Connecticut's African Americans, particularly the young ones, the Works Progress Administration provided jobs in which youngsters could shine. One of the actors in the WPA program, Gwen Reed, went on to portray Aunt Jemima (see essay 45).[43]

Although times were difficult, the turbulent 1930s failed to totally derail small African-American-owned businesses. Business owners usually located themselves in the heart of the African American community. Aware of cultural needs and wants, African American grocers sold staples of the African American diet—many for Southern recipes—such as black-eyed peas, "side meat," chicken, Argo starch, and vegetables. In addition, African American women operated salons where they pressed hair and provided nail care. In Hartford, the owners of Richardson's Beauty Shop, Martha's Poro Shoppe, and Powder Puff Beauty Salon were African American, and they provided important social, psychological, and economic benefits to their African American clients. For African American women, who were often ridiculed for their looks and features, a salon visit both affirmed their sense of their own beauty and strengthened their social network. In salons, women vividly and openly discussed community news, just as African American men did in barbershops throughout Connecticut. Because the owners owed their livelihood to African American customers and patrons, not the white establishment, those customers felt free to express their political views. In addition to these black-owned hair-care facilities, cities such as New Haven, Hartford, and Bridgeport had a small and respected contingent of dentists and physicians of African descent. Throughout Connecticut, African American undertakers conducted solid business enterprises in embalming and burials.[44] In hair care, medicine, and undertaking, African Americans typically chose to deliberately patronize African American merchants.

Connecticut's African American population of this period believed in keeping itself economically and politically aware. In 1938 African Americans from throughout the state attended the Connecticut Negro and Occupational Conference. John E. Rogers set the tone by articulating the beliefs of African American attendees, arguing that although whites had long held paternalistic attitudes toward African Americans, increased education would empower African Americans to look after their own affairs.

That same year the Supreme Court decided the *Missouri ex el Gaines v. Canada* case, ending the practice by which Southern state governments provided financial scholarships for qualified African American students to seek professional degrees in the North simply to keep them from attending college with whites in the South. Excited about the decision, African Americans and other blacks in New Haven gathered at the Dixwell Avenue Community House to hear remarks by local African American attorney George W. Crawford on the case. Crawford delivered the disappointing opinion that explained that the decision would have only minimal impact on the racially segregated South.[45]

As the 1930s drew to a close, Connecticut's African American community huddled primarily in the state's largest cities, clustering together for strength and survival. Rev. John Jackson of Hartford's Union Baptist Church met with Governor Raymond Baldwin to highlight the lack of economic opportunity for Connecticut's African American workers. Rev. Jackson demanded that the governor provide better treatment of African Americans in the state. As a result, African Americans received appointments working at state tollbooths and in clerical positions. Greater changes would come in the 1940s, and in the process, Jackson would feel the brunt of Southern injustice and bring the crusade home to Hartford.

## Notes

1. Emmett J. Scott, and David Kinley, eds., *Negro Migration During the War* (New York: Arno Press, 1969), 56.

2. Charles S. Johnson, "The Negro Population of Hartford, Ct. 1921," (New York: National Urban League, 1921), 25–26. Connecticut State Library, Hartford, Connecticut.

3. Ibid.

4. Ibid. See also Leroy Davis, *A Clashing of the Soul: John Hope and the Dilemma of African American Leadership and Black Higher Education in the Early Twentieth Century* (Athens: University of Georgia Press, 1998), 223.

5. Milton Sernett, *Bound for the Promised Land* (Durham: Duke University Press, 1997), 67, 124. Charles Johnson, 141. See also Don Noel, Jr., "The Negro in Hartford: Americus, Ga.—Segregated 'Sister City,'" *Hartford Times*, November 26, 1963; Don Noel, Jr., "The Negro in Hartford: First War Brought Southern Influx," *Hartford Times*, November 26, 1963; and Emmett J. Scott, David Kinley, eds. *Negro Migration During the War* (New York: Arno Press, 1969), 40, argued that African Americans believed that God was

punishing the South through pestilence, floods, and other calamities for its sins against God's people.

6. For brief information on the lynching of Connell, see a list of African Americans who died in racial violence in the United States, 1865–1965 at www .autopsis.org/foot/lynchdates2.html.

7. W. Fitzhugh Brundage, *Lynching in the New South: Georgia and Virginia, 1880–1930* (Urbana: University of Illinois Press, 1993), 276–79.

8. Scott, 166–67.

9. W. E. B. Du Bois, *The Autobiography of W.E.B. Du Bois* (New York: International Publishers, 1997), 234–35.

10. Scott, 74–75.

11. Ibid., 60–61.

12. "Want Negroes to Return to the South," *Hartford Courant*, February 22, 1918.

13. Johnson, 20–22.

14. The 1920 Census provides information on the country of origin of immigrants and race. In addition, the census takes note of whether individuals were naturalized.

15. Motley, 14–15.

16. Mary White Ovington, *Half A Man* (New York: Hill and Wang, 1969), 1–120.

17. Ibid., 103–4.

18. Johnson, 40–42, 89, 110–14, 119.

19. Ibid., 110–19.

20. Ibid., 114–19.

21. Ibid., 106–8.

22. Ibid., 120–21.

23. Ibid., 118–21.

24. "The Colored People Who Live In Hartford," *Hartford Courant*, October 24, 1915.

25. Frank Simpson, "They Seek Equality for All People," *Hartford Courant Magazine*, September 14, 1952, 6. See also NAACP, Minutes of the Meeting of the Board of Directors, December 10, 1917, Papers of the NAACP, Part 1, Meetings of the Board of Directors, Records of Annual Conferences, Main Speeches, and Special Reports, Reel, University Publications of America, held by Southern Connecticut State University, New Haven; "Would Fight Plan to Establish Jim Crow School Here," *Hartford Courant*, November 27, 1917; and NAACP, Minutes of the Meeting of the Board of Directors, November 12, 1917, Papers of the NAACP, Part 1, Meetings of the Board of Directors, Records of Annual Conferences, Main Speeches, and Special Reports, Reel, University Publications of America, held by Southern Connecticut State University, New Haven. The board report mentions that the acting secretary visited Hartford and organized a branch. This may have been the first 1917 meeting.

26. Johnson, 40.

27. "Comments on the Reed Pastorate," *Hartford Courant*, August 25, 1919.

28. Orlando Patterson, *The Ordeal of Integration: Progress and Resentment in America's Racial Crises* (New York: Basic Civitas, 1998), 106.

29. For general discussion of the African American church's move from the rural South to the North, see C. Eric Lincoln and Lawrence Mamiya, *The Black Church and the African American Experience* (Durham: Duke University Press, 1990), 95–163.

30. Johnson, 36–37.

31. "Spellacy in Fiery Talk to Negroes," *Hartford Courant*, March 29, 1927.

32. Franklin and Moss, *From Slavery to Freedom*, 360–63.

33. Stacey K. Close, "Black Southern Migration, Black Immigrants, Garveyism, and Transformation of Black Hartford, 1917–1922," *The Griot* 23, no.1 (Spring 2004): 61–62. The census of 1920 contains valuable information about the racial, ethnic, and gender make-up of Hartford. The occupations and employments status of blacks is quite evident from a study of the census. Most black people lived in the third district. There were still black families in the city's first district in the South End of the city.

34. Census, 1920.

35. Ibid., Gilbert Osofsky indicated that African Americans in New York often bought apartments larger than necessary out of necessity. They then used money from renters they housed to pay their rent to white landlords. See Gilbert Osofsky, *Harlem: The Making of a Ghetto* (Chicago: Ivan R. Dee, 1996), 138. See also Close, 62.

36. See the Census of 1920. African American residents knew the business at 1235 Main Street, Hartford, as the Parrish Hotel.

37. Census, 1920.

38. Diana Ross McCain, *Black Women of Connecticut: Achievement Against the Odds* (Hartford: Connecticut Historical Society, 1984), 38.

39. "Colored People Await Report of NY Convention," *Hartford Courant*, August 5, 1922. Marcus Garvey, *Philosophy and Opinions of Marcus Garvey*, ed. Amy Jacques Garvey, 380–84 (New York: Athenaeum, 1969). The 1920 Census entry for Frederick Smart indicates that he lived at the home of Daniel Parrish and worked as a newspaper reporter. List of UNIA chapters 1921–33, in *The Marcus Garvey and UNIA Papers*, vol. 7, ed. Robert Hill, 987–88 (Berkeley: University of California Press, 1989). Earl Shepherd, *Ancestor Book: The Wards, Countryman, Pertillar, Shepherd, Williams, Sherman, Swans, Richardson, Moore, Boone, Stewart* (unpublished, Hartford, Connecticut, August 2000), 140–41. The 1920 Census entry for Edward Countryman, former UNIA president, lists the Georgia native as working at a tire shop. John (Jack) Woods, a railroad worker, resided with his family on Sanford Street. Garvey, *Philosophy and Opinions of Marcus Garvey*, 380–84.

40. "Appeal Is Made by Marcus Garvey," *Hartford Courant*, February 28, 1924. "Display Ad, Edward Countryman-bey," *Hartford Courant*, June 2, 1980. Motley, *Equal Justice Under Law*, 29. Karlynn Carrington, "Building on a Lost Heritage," *Hartford Courant*, October 18, 1982.

41. City work permit of Thomas Jones, 1926, and union membership book in the personal possession of Gladys Fisher. Don Noel, Jr., "John Rogers: You were a good boy if you came from an old family," *Hartford Times*, November 26, 1963.

42. Gerald Renner, "City Honors a Pastor of Legend," *Hartford Courant*, June 21, 1986.

43. "Equality Is Seen Ahead for Negro," *Hartford Courant*, January 3, 1933.

44. See *Geer's Hartford City Directory*, 1936 and 1938, for African American business owners; and *Business Directory Listing*, 1938, for Negro Achievement Week, February 13–19, 1938. List titled "Making Acquaintance with Hartford's Negro Groups" of African American businesses compiled by the Hartford Negro Interest Group in the 1930s, Hartford: Hartford Collection, Hartford Public Library. See also Motley, *Equal Justice Under the Law*, 34–35.

45. Motley, 34.

# 35  Anna Louise James

Down Old Saybrook's main street, just past the bustling section of shops and restaurants, as the street begins to return to a quieter residential neighborhood, stands the James Gallery & Soda Fountain. Once the location of the James Pharmacy, owned by Anna Louise James, the first African American female pharmacist in the state of Connecticut, the site has been listed on the National Register of Historic Places since 1994. Though this former pharmacy and soda fountain has changed hands many times, many of the original historic dark wood shelving and apothecary drawers of the turn-of-the-twentieth-century pharmacy remained in 2007.

The soda fountain is small and intimate with its original long marble counter. An original James Pharmacy sign hangs low on the wall just inside the front entrance, while a glass case in the back of the shop is full of artifacts. It contains old medicine bottles, glass ice-cream goblets, photographs, articles about the pharmacy, and books written by James's niece, the noted author Ann Petry. Taking a close look at the mementos allows you a peek into the time when fifty cents could buy you medicine and a life lesson from the town pharmacist.

Anna Louise James's father, Willis Samuel James, was enslaved on a Virginia plantation and escaped to Connecticut at age sixteen. Anna was born in Hartford in January 1886, but her family moved to Old Saybrook when she was a child. She became the first licensed African-American female pharmacist in Connecticut in 1908, after becoming the first African-American woman to graduate from the Brooklyn College of Pharmacy. In 1911, she joined her brother-in-law Peter Lane's pharmacy in Old Saybrook. Six years later, she took over the business, changing its name from Lane Pharmacy to James Pharmacy.

Though it would seem likely that an African American woman might, in the early twentieth century, have difficulty gaining acceptance as a professional in a mostly white community, James appar-

ently had no such trouble. Harriet Naughton, who lived near the pharmacy, was quoted in a 1996 *Hartford Courant* article about the pharmacist that "Miss James had the highest possible reputation. She was someone you could trust with your life, which you did, since she was a pharmacist . . . She was a civic personality, so to speak, and she had a role in town as Miss James the pharmacist."

James was described by her niece and others in the *Courant* article as a reserved, hard-working woman who wore her hair pulled back into a tight bun. She hired local teenagers and held them to high standards, which required her to be strict at times. Despite her intensity and strong work ethic, though, James also had a soft side. She loved chatting with her customers, giving advice, and interacting with the children who came in for ice cream. It is said that she often gave medicine to those who could not afford it. Known as "Miss James" to everyone in Old Saybrook, she grew to become a well-known and beloved member of the community. She retired and closed the drugstore in 1967 at the age of eighty-one but lived in the building until her death ten years later. The pharmacy was reopened in 1984 but closed again in 1994. Since then, the building has traded hands several times.

The James Gallery & Soda Fountain is now owned by the Deacon Timothy Pratt Bed & Breakfast, located next door to the former pharmacy. Though many things have changed, the soda fountain is still a place where families and friends can enjoy a variety of delectable treats. It was bustling the day I stopped in, in 2007, and I knew that in order to capture the full experience of visiting the James Pharmacy, trying something from the large list of milkshakes and floats was essential. I ordered a delicious vanilla sundae topped with whipped cream and hot fudge, dubbed the "Miss James' Dusty Rhodes Sundae" in honor of this local legend.

## Note

This essay appeared in the Spring 2007 issue of *Connecticut Explored*.

*Mark H. Jones*

# 36 World War I Homefront

## *A Short Photo Essay*

During World War I, African Americans and whites were segregated in their activities both at war and on the home front. The first photograph, which was published in the *Hartford Courant*, shows African American draftees leaving for Maryland's Camp Meade. African American soldiers traveled to boot camps in "colored only" trains, and while some saw combat, most worked behind the lines and at major Allied ports in menial jobs that were very similar to those they held before the war, serving as stevedores, messengers, and chauffeurs. About their sendoff, the *Courant* commented: "the contingent bid farewell to Hartford amid a demonstration of loyalty seldom shown by friends of anyone." Women experienced similarly segregated activities in their support of the war effort. The second photo shows members of the Colored Liberty Loan Committee. Liberty Loan parades and promotions were an important way for the U.S. government to raise funds to pay for World War I. Hartford's African American community rendered valuable service toward winning the war.

### Note

This essay appeared in the November/December/January 2004 issue of *Connecticut Explored*.

FIGURE 36-1 The first contingent of African American draftees from the state poses
on the corner of Trumbull and Pearl streets, *The Hartford Courant*, April 30, 1918.
*Photo: Edward M. Crocker. RG 012 Connecticut State Library, War Records Department,*
*World War I Photographs from Hartford by the Hartford Courant, Box 270*

FIGURE 36-2 Mrs. James
A. Morris, committee
chair (*left*), and uniden-
tified women of the
Colored Liberty Loan
Committee. *The Hartford*
*Courant*, October 9, 1918.
*Photo: Edward M. Crocker.*
*RG 012 Connecticut State*
*Library, War Records*
*Department, World War I*
*Photographs from Hart-*
*ford by the Hartford*
*Courant, Box 270*

*Mark H. Jones*

# 37 Mary Townsend Seymour

In early twentieth-century Hartford, Mary Townsend Seymour fought battles and formed daring alliances to promote the cause of local African Americans. She was a charter member of the Hartford chapter of the National Association for the Advancement of Colored People (NAACP) and, during World War I, served in various war relief groups. Her public life extended into the arenas of union organizing and politics; she was the first African American woman to run for state office. Seymour was particularly active in public advocacy from 1917 to 1920, but she remained influential in Hartford's African American community for decades afterward. Hers is the remarkable story of the rise of an African American woman into a position of community leadership during the early decades of the twentieth century.[1]

Mary Seymour's origins were humble. She was born in Hartford May 10, 1873, the youngest of seven children of Jacob Townsend and Emma Smith, who had come to Hartford from Flushing and Brooklyn, New York, respectively. By 1880 Jacob Townsend had disappeared from the city directories, and his fate is unknown. The Lloyd G. Seymour family had taken Mary in before August 1888, when Emma Townsend died, leaving her fifteen-year-old daughter's future uncertain. On June 3, 1888, Mary visited the city's old Halls of Record at Trumbull and Pearl streets to see her birth record. Since her first name was not listed, she asked the clerk to write in "Mary Emma" in the appropriate column. The clerk also wrote in the margin that on this date the young woman had given her name as "Mary Emma Townsend Seymour." This was an emphatic declaration of selfhood. Perhaps it was her difficult childhood, tempered by her relationship with her adoptive family, that led to Mary Seymour's fierce independence and her empathy for impoverished mothers and children.

While living with the Seymour family, she began a friendship with Lloyd G. Seymour's son Frederick Seymour. In 1891 he landed a position with the U.S. Postal Service, one of the better jobs African

American males could obtain at that time. Their relationship blossomed, and they married on December 16, 1891. Mary was eighteen years old, but the marriage register listed her as 22. In 1892 the couple had a boy they named Richard, but he died within the year and was buried in Old North Cemetery next to Mary's mother. Though Frederick and Mary were childless for the rest of their marriage, their tragedy freed her to work on social causes.

## Hartford's African American Community

African Americans had lived in Hartford since colonial times and over the years had achieved a tenuous peaceful coexistence in a largely white city. African American men found jobs as messengers, porters, cooks, and chauffeurs, while African American women worked as domestics and laundresses. On October 24, 1915, the *Hartford Courant* ran an article with the headline, "The Colored People Who Live in Hartford." A sub-headline declared, "They Have Their Own Churches, Fraternities and Other Organizations and Have Been and Are a Peaceful and Orderly Contingent, Industrious and a Credit to the City in Which They Live."

Yet this seeming harmony was a matter of perspective. Hartford's African Americans resided in poor housing, paid exorbitant rents, and were not hired for well-paying jobs. When investigating serious crimes, police cordoned off African American residential areas and checked every person coming in or going out.

Within a year of the *Courant*'s upbeat assessment, the world of these Yankee blacks would change dramatically, and that change prompted Seymour's awakening to political and social activism. Across the industrial North, a great migration of thousands of African Americans from Dixie transformed the cities. In 1916 and 1917, hundreds of African Americans from the South moved to Hartford for better jobs and education for their children—and to flee lynchings. At first, students from southern African American colleges came to work in the local tobacco fields, but letters and word-of-mouth descriptions about opportunities soon attracted families and entire church congregations. By 1917 the city's African American population more than doubled, rising from 1,600 to, according to the highest estimate, 4,000. Overnight the African American Yankees in Hartford were outnumbered by Southerners who dressed differently, worshipped in a more exuberant style, and spoke with a noticeable dialect.

Whites noticed this influx and worried about its effects. For example, 700 to 800 African American students had entered Hartford schools in 1917–1918. In order to protect these students, many of whom attended evening classes, from harassment by whites, Superintendent of Schools Thomas Weaver announced that he would introduce a proposal for consideration by the board of education to segregate evening school classes by race. The African American Ministerial Alliance vigorously condemned such segregation, and Weaver dropped the idea. Instead, in one district there was a separate room for students of color, following a practice that educators referred to as "specialization."

### Co-founded NAACP Chapter in Hartford

It was during this time that Mary Seymour emerged as a leader in her community; she led twenty whites and African Americans in forming a chapter of the NAACP in Hartford. In January 1917, after attending an NAACP fundraiser against lynching, she and other attendees had discussed forming a local chapter. During the school controversy, they put their plan into action.

The NAACP was a fledgling national organization formed in 1909 by whites and African Americans. By 1917, local chapters had multiplied, and the organization had gained a reputation as an active opponent of discrimination and lynching. Its field secretary was James Weldon Johnson, a former teacher, novelist, poet, musical lyricist, and diplomat. Mary White Ovington, a white Socialist and settlement worker, was a vice president of the organization who worked out of the New York City headquarters. Another leading force behind the NAACP's founding was Dr. W. E. B. Du Bois, a pioneering African American sociologist and eloquent advocate for equal rights for African Americans. He edited the *Crisis*, a magazine associated with the organization.

On October 9, 1917 these three officials came to Hartford and spent an evening in the living room of Frederick and Mary Seymour at 420 New Britain Avenue. Others present included Reverend R. R. Ball of the A.M.E. Zion Church, Dr. Rockwell H. Potter, dean of the Hartford Theological Seminary and a leading white reformer, and three white female reformers and suffragists: Mary Bulkeley, Josephine Bennett, and Katherine Beach Day. They agreed to form an NAACP chapter and elected an African American, William Service Bell, as president. On November 26, Johnson, Du Bois, and Ovington returned to Hartford to attend the chapter's first open meeting, which was held at Center Church.

Like other African American female members of local NAACP chapters across the country, Seymour carried out the day-to-day administrative work of the chapter. In the early days of the chapter she also served as its spokesperson in the absence of Bell, who was fighting overseas. In the 1920s this dual work would become a burden for her.

During the war years, women in African American Hartford formed clubs to address the problems of caring for soldiers and their families and helping newcomers from the South assimilate into the urban North. But Seymour went further than that. She joined the home service section of the Red Cross and observed the wretched conditions of African American soldiers' families. In the spring of 1918, she was instrumental in forming a local chapter of the Circle for Negro War Relief, Inc. to care for soldiers abroad and stateside and for their families. Seymour and two allies from the NAACP, Rev. R. R. Ball and William S. Bell, served on the executive committee. Around this time, Seymour joined the newly formed Colored Women's League of Hartford, which intended to teach the newcomers basic "domestic sciences" and bought a house on North Main Street with donations from the city's whites and blacks for meetings and classes.

In May 1918 Seymour corresponded with Caroline Ruutz-Rees, a suffragist, scholar, and educator, who was chairperson of the Woman's Committee of the Connecticut State Council of Defense. Seymour informed Ruutz-Rees about the Hartford chapter of the Circle for Negro War Relief and wrote a report on its activities. She also detailed the discriminatory practices that African American men and women faced from the army, the navy, and the Red Cross. Seymour referred to the lynching of a pregnant African American woman in Georgia that had occurred a few days earlier while the victim's brother was serving the cause of "freedom" abroad. "If we are to win this war," she exhorted Ruutz-Rees, "this thing of color prejudice has got to be reckoned with by those friends of your race who have the courage of their convictions to talk about it."

### Involvement with Labor Issues

Seymour's war relief work led her to become interested in labor issues, especially those involving African American women working on tobacco warehouse assembly lines; she had visited such women in her capacity as a Red Cross home service worker. Seymour and Josephine Bennett interviewed female African American tobacco workers and learned that white warehouse foremen, some from the South, were cheating them out of an honest wage. The workers were never told what the piecework rate was each day, and they never knew whether those who weighed each worker's tobacco leaves were ensuring an honest total. In a long letter to the NAACP that was later published in the June 1920 issue of the *Crisis*, Seymour described her own experience on a tobacco warehouse assembly line: She appeared at a warehouse in working clothes and spent time stripping and stemming tobacco leaves. Her account verified the women's complaints.

Seymour and Bennett urged female African American tobacco workers to organize their own union to fight for their rights. This was a daring notion because, as Seymour noted, the idea of forming a union was not supported by the local African American clergy, who railed against unions from their pulpits. Bennett and Seymour were able to secure signed union cards from sixty courageous African American women; Seymour served as the local's secretary. However, the local organization remained stagnant and its members became discouraged; within a year it fell apart. In Hartford, as in other cities in the North, white unions viewed the migration of southern blacks as a threat. Certainly racism was one reason for this viewpoint—the bosses and the white unions believed that African Americans did not have skills or aptitude to work on the assembly-line machines—but there were also economic reasons. For instance, industrialists had used the African American migrants as "scab" labor to break strikes.

Bennett and Seymour, on the other hand, believed in a different vision. They foresaw a day when African American and white workers would form an alliance to advocate their shared rights and defend their common interests. As an officer of the local, Seymour sat on the Central Labor Union, an assembly of representatives from the city's locals. During meetings, she discussed the racial attitudes of white workers and the common stake the two races shared. Seymour read articles from the *Crisis* to attendees, including one that pointed out how white bosses divided black and white workers.

### African American Women and the Vote

Seymour also worked to enfranchise African American women, particularly after World War I ended. For her generation of white and African American female reformers, the suffrage movement should have been a unifying cause. But unlike their white counterparts, African American women had to fight gender and class battles, as well as overcome racial barriers. After the Armistice, as women revived the fight for the Nineteenth Amendment, many white suffragists such as Alice Paul, head of the National Women's Party, declared that they were interested only in removing the gender requirement for the vote. How states chose to qualify voters was of no interest to her organization. The National Women's Party announced this position in order to retain the support of Southern white women and to reassure Southern senators and congressmen that extending the suffrage to women would not enfranchise African American women. It was a stance that African American suffragists such as Seymour naturally opposed.

On February 18, 1919, *The World* quoted Alice Paul's remarks regarding the intention of "Negro women" in Carolina to vote if the Nineteenth Amendment were passed. Paul reaffirmed that, if passed, the amendment would not enfranchise these women. "We are organizing the White women in South Carolina but have heard of no activity or anxiety among the negresses." The article inflamed Mary Seymour so much that she wrote to Paul demanding an explanation; she also called the NAACP headquarters. As a result NAACP national leaders did ask Alice Paul and the National Woman's Suffrage Association to clarify where they stood regarding African American women's voting rights. But their responses were evasive and unsatisfactory.

In April 1919 Seymour wrote NAACP national headquarters assessing the commitment of Hartford's prominent white suffragists to extending the voting rights to all women. She noted that Josephine Bennett, a member of the Hartford NAACP and the Women's Party who knew Alice Paul, did not engage in "expediency" in order to get the Nineteenth Amendment passed. On the other hand, Seymour noted, Katharine Houghton Hepburn (mother of the actress), who served on the executive board of the Woman's Party, was "very democratic in some things—but not to be trusted too far on the Negro question. She is a politician," Seymour cautioned, "in every sense of the word."

### More to Seymour's Story

There is much more to Mary Seymour's story. Seymour knew that she must address the issues of education and literacy among the newly arriving southern blacks. Having learned how to work the system, Seymour formed one of her more audacious alliances when she convinced Hartford's Americanization Committee (entrusted with teaching English and reading to immigrants and instilling in them patriotic values) to sponsor literacy classes for the African American newcomers. In 1920, she ran for state representative on the Farmer-Labor Party ticket. Though the party did poorly in the election, Seymour had the distinction of being the first African American woman to run for the Connecticut General Assembly. She remained active in the local chapter of the NAACP in the 1920s and continued to exert influence behind the scenes long after she had resigned as chairperson of the chapter's executive board in November 1926. Her word was trusted, and for years she recommended African Americans for jobs in the white community, a duty usually reserved for the male African American Ministerial Alliance. Upon her death at age 84 on January 12, 1957 newspapers eulogized her. In 1998, My Sister's Place in Hartford dedicated a new apartment building, named the Mary Seymour Place, on North Main Street as a shelter for women. Seymour would have approved.

## Notes

This essay appeared in the Summer 2003 issue of *Connecticut Explored*.

1. See Darlene Clark Hine, Elsa Barkley Brown, and Rosalyn Tearborg-Pen, eds., *Black Women in America* (Bloomington, Indiana: Indiana University Press, 1994). Darlene Clark Hine and Kathleen Thompson, *A Shining Thread of Hope: The History of Black Women in America* (New York: Broadway Books, 1998). Charles S. Johnson, "The Negro Population of Hartford, Connecticut," Internal report of the National Urban League, 1921. David Levering Lewis, *W.E.B. Du Bois: Biography of A Race, 1868–1919* (New York: Henry Holt & Co., 1993). The following were indispensable primary sources: *Hartford Courant, Hartford Times*, and *Hartford Evening Post*; Hartford Vital Records, 1873, Microfilm; City Directories of Hartford. Seymour's correspondence with NAACP headquarters in New York is found in the Records of the NAACP (copies of which are in the Hartford Studies Project, Trinity College, Hartford, CT), Library of Congress, Branch Files, "Hartford, Connecticut"; Administrative Subject Files, "Labor Party 1920," "Suffrage-Women." For correspondence between Seymour and Caroline Ruutz-Rees, see Record Group 30, Connecticut State Council of Defense, Box 170, Americanization Department, "H. H. Wheaton," Connecticut State Library, State Archives.

# 38 Laboring in the Shade

At the height of shade tobacco's popularity in the first half of the twentieth century, more than sixteen thousand acres of this premium cigar wrapper tobacco were under cultivation in Connecticut. The introduction of such a labor-intensive crop to Connecticut's economy drew black migrant labor from the South and the Caribbean.

The search for a reliable labor source led to an ongoing relationship of more than fifty years between growers and a special group of Southern workers: students. For these young people, a summer away from their Southern homes was an opportunity to earn money for their education, enjoy freedom from parents, and get some relief from their segregated existence. Among the thousands of black Southern students who seasonally came north was a young Martin Luther King, Jr.

According to probate records, Connecticut farmers grew broadleaf tobacco (shade tobacco would come later) as far back as the 1600s. Originally brewed as a beverage or smoked in pipes, by the late eighteenth century tobacco was being hand rolled into cigars in family workshops. After the Civil War, as farmers faced competition from foreign-grown tobacco, increasing tariffs did little to protect them. When a thinner and superior cigar wrapper was imported from Indonesia, the challenge to the domestic cigar tobacco market could not be ignored.

In an attempt to help farmers grow a more competitive product, the U.S. Department of Agriculture began experimenting in Florida with tropical tobacco varieties. By 1899, W. C. Sturgis, a botanist in Connecticut, was successful in growing Sumatra tobacco from seed and reproducing the thinner leaf. Marcus Floyd, the USDA's leading tobacco expert at the time and a Florida native, came to Connecticut to oversee the first crop of this experimental tobacco known as shade tobacco. The product proved equal to the imported leaf.

Fifty acres was put into the production of shade tobacco in 1901. Following the first flush of success, several wet growing seasons dashed the hopes and finances of many small farmers, who ended up selling out to larger growers. Still, by 1910 shade tobacco was well established in Connecticut, with hundreds of farmers cultivating it.

Connecticut farmers were used to the simple cultivation process and single harvest of broadleaf tobacco that was most commonly used as filler in cigars. Shade tobacco is more complicated. The growing season begins in May with weeding and transplanting seedlings in long rows. As the plants grow they are fastened to guide wires, and then cloth tents are spread over them to increase humidity, protect the tender plants from direct sunlight, and maximize the short New England growing season.

The remainder of cultivation takes place by hand. Field workers spend weeks in high humidity and extreme heat moving among the rows, pulling off shoots and tobacco worms. Multiple harvests of leaves are brought to sheds, where workers—most of them female—sew the leaves together to string on wooden lath. The laths are then hung up in the rafters of the slat-sided tobacco barns or sheds to cure. After curing, the tobacco is moved to sorting sheds and warehouses, where processing continues throughout the rest of the year.

Until the advent of World War I, Hartford-area whites, both residents and immigrants, filled the need for seasonal labor. When war broke out in Europe, these workers took jobs at munitions plants, which promised higher wages, and many immigrants returned home to serve in their own military. New immigration was hampered by the restrictive immigration laws of the era.

In an attempt to find labor, the Connecticut Tobacco Company placed an ad in the *New York World* in December 1915 for 500 girls to work as sorters, offering free transportation. This led to a public relations disaster. Emmett J. Scott included the incident in *Negro Migration During the War* (Oxford University Press, 1920). "The planters . . . promiscuously gathered up 200 girls of the worst type, who straightaway proceeded to demoralize Hartford. The blunder was speedily detected and the employers came back to New York seeking some agency which might assist them in the solution of their problem."

The National Urban League, already serving as a clearinghouse for Northern migrants, helped growers recruit workers using black newspapers such as the *Chicago Defender* that also circulated in the South. A trickle of Southern blacks responded to advertisements and moved north with their families. By 1920 seven black families from Georgia and Alabama were renting tobacco company housing in Granby alongside Polish and Lithuanian immigrants. These sources did not provide sufficient labor.

Marcus Floyd, by 1911 president of the Connecticut Tobacco Company, "offered a solution for this difficult problem through the further importation of negro labor," Scott notes. "The response to this suggestion was not immediate, because New England had never had large experience with negro labor . . . Because of the seasonal character of the work, an effort was made to get students from the southern schools by advancing transportation." According to Charles Spurgeon Johnson in *The Negro Population of Hartford, Connecticut* (The League, 1921), "The material for this first experiment was sought in the schools of Virginia, North Carolina, Florida and Georgia. More than 1,400 students were transported to the State of Connecticut."

The National Urban League introduced Floyd to Dr. John Hope, the first black president of Morehouse College in Atlanta, Georgia. Students from historically black colleges such as Morehouse were already accompanying their professors north to work seasonal service jobs at New England resorts. The transition to working shade tobacco provided more students with jobs that helped them pay their tuition and removed them, for a time, from the escalating racial tensions at home. College students provided Connecticut growers with an English-speaking, educated work force. These students also appealed to employers because, accustomed as they were to the way blacks were treated in the South, they were not as likely as Northerners or immigrants to agitate for better working conditions. Also, as temporary seasonal workers they would theoretically not have much impact on the communities in which they worked.

Floyd first recruited Morehouse students for the 1916 season at Connecticut Tobacco's Hazelwood plantation on the Windsor/East Granby border. According to the *Hartford Daily Courant* (August 13, 1916) students were paid $2 per day, and they in turn paid $4.50 per week for their room and board. Working from June 1 to September 1, students could clear as much as $100 (about $2,000 in 2011 dollars) after expenses. The same article reported, "The Connecticut Leaf Tobacco Association considers the importation of Southern help to have passed the experimental stage."

Recruiters sought student workers from other schools too. Students from Florida A&M, Morris Brown College (Atlanta, Georgia), Howard University (Washington, D.C.), Livingstone College (Salisbury, North Carolina), and Talladega College (Talladega, Alabama) also worked tobacco in Connecticut throughout the 1920s and 1930s.

Corporate growers were able to minimize their labor problems by creating residential camps on their tobacco plantations. A Morehouse dormitory was built on the Simsbury/Granby border in 1936; Martin Luther King, Jr. spent the summers of 1944 and 1947 there. By building dorms or using abandoned Depression-era Civilian Conservation Corps camps, growers made their labor supply wholly dependent upon them.

Providing housing also enabled recruitment of Southern black high school students. One legendary recruiter was black school principal Henry Lawrence Summerrall, who modeled his rural youth program in central Virginia on the one Morehouse College (which he briefly attended) established in 1916. From 1941 to 1976, more than 12,000 high school students ages thirteen and up made the trip north to work for the Hartman Tobacco Company at Camp Buckland for boys in Manchester and (after 1949) Camp Stewart for girls in Windsor.

While work in the fields was long and hard, efforts were made to provide residential students with religious and social opportunities. As a bonus, these also often served as good public relations for the tobacco companies. A rally in 1929 arranged by the Hartford Y.M.C.A. at the A.M.E. Zion Church brought students from plantations in Tariffville, East Windsor Hill, Simsbury, Poquonock, and Windsor to meet Hartford residents.

William S. Spencer, then 15, from Lynchburg, Virginia, recalled in 1952: "We were taken into Hartford on a company bus (looked like a school bus) and we parked down in what is now known as the Front Street section . . . my brother and I spent our time going to the movies." Other students remembered being taken to a shopping center. Camp managers also planned end-of-season trips to Riverside Park in Agawam, Massachusetts to send students off on a positive note, in hopes that that might benefit the next year's recruitment effort.

High school guidance departments also steered students toward work in Connecticut. For black students unable to secure summer jobs in the retail or service industries, tobacco was "really the only job opportunity," according to a group of female students from Plainville. These students, including Anita Baldwin, Taffie Bentley, Norene Robinson, and Gail Williams, responded to flyers distributed at their school in the mid-1950s and were hired to sew in the sheds. The work left them at the end of the day covered in tobacco juice and tar. Their recollections showed that tobacco was not a summer job of choice: "And it was most embarrassing, so when you

FIGURE 38-1 Student Workers at Hartman Tobacco's Camp Buckland, 1950. *Collection of Dawn Byron Hutchins*

got off the bus . . . we used to run all the way home because we didn't want anybody to see us . . . once we got home at 5, it was still an hour to get clean before you could feel comfortable to sit at the kitchen table and eat your dinner."

But for students with few economic choices, summer tobacco work provided both opportunity and motivation. "The work was hard and unbelievable at times but my learning experience away from home taught me such values as endurance, cooperation, getting along with others, and being responsible," wrote Spencer in his unpublished memoir. Anita Baldwin of Plainville had similar sentiments: "It was hard labor, you got paid almost nothing. But I almost felt like—as an African American person I didn't have the opportunity of my classmates, who got summer jobs working at some of the retail stores or working at some of the factories . . . I knew that I had to get an education and have something that I could offer an employer to have a decent job, because just competing with my [white] classmates, I wasn't getting anywhere."

Seasonal hiring of students was always supplemented with other labor. Growers during World War II looked to Jamaica and the West Indies for help. After the war, Puerto Ricans came to the Hartford area. These groups agitated more strenuously for reform and fair labor practices than the students ever would. Child labor (employing children as young as eight), which became an increasing problem in the 1940s, was not addressed until Connecticut legislation finally passed in 1947 set fourteen as the minimum age for farm labor.

We now know that many of the students who came north for the summer went on to become prominent and successful individuals, Dr. Martin Luther King, Jr. being the most noted example. The Luddy-Taylor Tobacco Museum in Windsor, Connecticut holds hundreds of Morehouse employment cards from the Cullman Brothers in the 1930s. A brief search yields a cross-section of future teachers, doctors, lawyers, religious leaders, and other professionals, some of whom even returned north to establish their families.

While not everyone cares to remember their time working tobacco, many people are now beginning to share their experiences. Since 2000, several reunions have been held in Amherst and Nelson counties in Virginia, where more than two thousand former black high school recruits reconnected. In conversations, these former students have been quick to identify others, better known than they, who also came north to work in Connecticut. The young Arthur Ashe, Mahalia Jackson, Thurgood Marshall, and Hattie McDaniel were named among the thousands of students who, virtually unnoticed at the time, labored in the shade.

## Note

This essay appeared in the Summer 2011 issue of *Connecticut Explored*.

# PART VI

## World War II
## to
## Civil Rights

# 39 World War II and the Civil Rights Years

On December 7, 1941, Japan's attack at Pearl Harbor led the United States government to declare war to protect American people and allies from being overrun by the brutal regimes in Japan, Germany, and Italy. While the New Deal programs of Franklin Roosevelt provided some minor opportunities for African Americans in Connecticut, the nation's entrance into World War II and massive economic mobilization pulled the United States out of the malaise of the "Old Hoover Days." Connecticut African Americans joined the nation's battle for freedom abroad and freedom at home; they also used the period during and after World War II to propel a movement for civil rights.

Although the United States maintained a segregated military during World War II, African American service men and women served in every theater of the war and in factories at home. Hartford's Lemuel Custiss was among the first group of Tuskegee Airmen, the nation's first elite corps of African American pilots in the U.S. Army Air Corps. Boce Barlow, a son of Georgia migrants, was a soldier in the Pacific theater. Susan Freeman of Stratford became a nurse and officer in the army. On the home front, African American men and women found work in leading factories in the state that produced items for the war. The numbers of African American workers in major factories such as Pratt & Whitney increased dramatically. Their labor helped transform the war and Connecticut. In fact, the war and service became springboards for greater change.

Although many scholars of the modern civil rights era consider 1954 the beginning of the nation's civil rights years, Connecticut's modern statewide struggle began with a case of audacious Southern injustice against one of the state's best-known citizens. While aboard a train in the South in 1942, Rev. Dr. John Jackson, pastor of Hartford's Union Baptist Church and a native of South Carolina, decided to walk through a railcar to meet friends. The car was for whites only. Two white men, who took offense at Jackson's presence in the railcar, pummeled the silver-haired minister savagely. Although the incident was widely publicized throughout the country, the guilty men went unpunished. Although it took place in Alabama, this brutal attack on a Connecticut man drove home to African Americans, Governor Raymond Baldwin, and supporters of civil rights the recognition that something needed to be done about the plight of African Americans in Hartford as in the rest of the country.[1]

In 1943 small and large cities such as Beaumont, Texas, Detroit, Mobile, and New York experienced periods of rioting and rebellion. With the nation in the midst of war, governors feared war in the streets and war abroad simultaneously. The impact on the nation, if such a situation materialized, could be potentially devastating. As a result, concerned governors from across the country, eager to avert upheaval in their states, organized "inter-racial commissions." Connecticut's Governor Baldwin was among them. Morris Silverman, a leading rabbi who would later serve on the commission, noted that he accepted his appointment to help curtail "racial conflicts" in the state.[2] The state's Inter-Racial Commission (IRC), in addition to working to eliminate discrimination, focused on equality in employment. The governor received two annual reports from the commission, which had only three African American members (including the Rev. Dr. John Jackson); nevertheless, the Colored Republican State Organization hoped the governor's oversight would achieve results. Frank Simpson, an African American from Florence, Alabama, served as the organization's first full-time staff member.[3]

Given the work of the IRC and other organizations, many national leaders considered Connecticut's race policies enlightened; however, they had plenty of work to do. Pratt & Whitney of East Hartford, for example, was one of the nation's worst offenders in equal employment policy. The company's violations were so blatant that Connecticut's Department of Labor and Factory Inspection complained to Governor Robert A. Hurley (who was governor from 1941 to 1942, between Raymond Baldwin's two stints as governor in 1939 to 1941 and 1943 to 1946). In 1941 and 1942 the company allowed its handful of African American employees to work only in heavy manual labor and cafeteria duties.[4]

Pratt & Whitney officials excused the discrimination on the basis a number of false beliefs. They felt that African Americans were "not mechanically inclined and therefore do not render satisfactory service when assigned machine work," according to Leonard J. Maloney, director of the state Department of Labor and Inspection. Officials at Pratt & Whitney and other defense companies also argued that discrimination occurred because white employees did not want to work alongside African Americans;[5] however, Maloney found that excuse "over-worked." Some state businesses feared that the breaking of racial barriers might lead to an influx of African Americans to Connecticut.[6]

Connecticut of the 1940s had a hand in shaping the ideas of a young Martin Luther King, Jr., who became one of the world's greatest human rights ambassadors and breakers of racial barriers. King helped to continue the tradition by which Morehouse College students worked in Connecticut's tobacco fields.[7] During the summer of 1944, King experienced life in a non-segregated society for the first time.

Statewide, positive changes were afoot. Connecticut followed other states of this period with the creation of a state Fair Employment Practices Commission (FEPC). The establishment of the commission clearly placed Connecticut ahead of a number of states, though African American activism in the state was by no means militant or radical. Local NAACP branches and the IRC chose to meet quietly with business leaders to solve perceived employment inequities. When it came to the passage of legislation authorizing a national FEPC, local branches contacted Connecticut's U.S. senators and urged their support for the measure. In 1949 state leaders also began working to integrate the state guard. (Harry Truman had officially integrated the United States military in 1948.)[8]

In 1948, Willimantic State Teachers College, now Eastern Connecticut State University, hired the state's first African American professor, Dr. Juliette Phifer Bursterman. Bursterman, a native of North Carolina, was a graduate of Winston Salem State Normal School, Columbia Teachers College, where she received her M.A., and New York University, where she received an Ed.D. Her appointment at the Teachers College in Willimantic involved teaching college students, working in the laboratory school, and serving as a hall director. When she received her appointment, very few African Americans attended college in the state, and only two attended her school. The only other African American employee there was a custodian. Bursterman carved out a distinguished career that included study and work in the Caribbean and with historically black colleges and universities.[9]

In 1940 African American businessmen in Hartford launched the *Hartford Chronicle*. The newspaper, available throughout Hartford, offered a powerful critique of race relations in the state. In addition, the paper provided a flow of news about life below the Mason-

Dixon Line. Business managers hired young residents and future leaders such as Gladys Fisher to sell the paper. Reporters surveyed residents on issues of race, employment, and discrimination. The paper changed its name (becoming the *Connecticut Chronicle* and the *Connecticut Bulletin*) several times over the nine years it remained in business, maintaining a strong African American voice. When a Connecticut high school decided to allow an integrated group of seniors to visit Washington, D.C., and provided Jim Crow accommodations for African American students, the paper's editor and reporters objected. The paper helped to set a foundation for today's African American print media in Connecticut. The newspapers of the 1940s laid the foundation for the *Inquirer*, a well-known African American paper that currently circulates throughout Connecticut's African American community.[10]

By the 1950s, African American residents continued to be concerned for family and friends in the Jim Crow South. Connecticut NAACP branches operated throughout the state. The state organization sought and made organizational alliances with branches across New England. They rallied in support of *Brown v. Board of Education*, Emmett Till, and African American bus boycotters in Montgomery. A generation of young people came of age with the memory of Emmett Till etched in their souls. In 1955, Till, an African American from Chicago, reportedly wolf-whistled at a local white woman while on a visit to Mississippi. The woman's husband and brother in-law later took him, under threat, from his uncle's home. He was never seen alive again. Although the state held a trial, it saw the quick acquittal of the two men, and a generation of African Americans remembered the photo of Till's mutilated body shown in *Jet* magazine. Statewide, NAACP membership numbers grew into the thousands. Branch members marched on rent gougers, demanded better employment, and built alliances with the Connecticut Civil Rights Commission, formerly the IRC.[11]

During the Cold War, a harsh spotlight shone on new Connecticut resident Paul Robeson and a concert he gave in Hartford in 1952. In 1941 Robeson, a former Phi Beta Kappa at Rutgers University and talented actor and singer, moved to Enfield, Connecticut, with his family. Robeson was known for his fiery criticism of American racism. More troubling to the federal government were his purported ties to the Soviet Union and communism. Not only did Robeson visit and perform in the Soviet Union, he also considered their treatment of the race question to be enlightened. He even decided to educate his son in the Soviet high school system. In November 1952 Hartford's school board voted six to three to allow Robeson to perform at Weaver High School.[12] Immense citywide pressure forced a new vote. Robert Moody, the only African American board member, decided not to change his vote; he cast his vote for Robeson's right to sing.[13] The new vote was still six to three in favor of the concert's proceeding. Robeson's concert also became a forum for his personal right to choose his political friends in America, even if the majority of people opposed their political views.

African American voters in Connecticut refused to cast their lot with the communist party, but they continued a slow and steady move out of the wings of the Republican Party and into the folds of other parties. New Haven's African American community had already celebrated the ascent of Republican Harry G. Tolliver to the post of alderman, but in order to get an African American elected in Hartford, that city's young leaders joined the Concerned Citizens Committee (CCC) to support the candidacy of prominent businessman John Clark in 1951.[14] Democratic leaders in Hartford, particularly John Bailey, wanted African Americans to wait for the right time to run a candidate. A small group of leaders including Ella Cromwell decided not to wait. In order to support Clark and the CCC though, African American supporters of Clark had to sever ties with the legendary Mary Parkman Watson. A stalwart in the

Democratic Party and head of the North End Democratic Party State Central Committee, Watson had been a power player in shaping the party's role among African American voters since the 1930s. In addition, she was a successful independent businesswoman. Her success as beautician, tea-room owner, and bail bondsmen was known throughout Hartford. The ensuing campaign was bruising and vicious for the CCC and powerful Democrats, with each side angrily accusing the other of voter fraud and irregularities such as destroying the ballots of the opposition.[15]

In New Haven African American voters played a huge role in the election of Richard Lee, a white Democrat. Lee failed to win office in 1951 by only two votes; however, in 1953 African Americans propelled Lee to a victory by a margin of more than 3,000 votes.

Even while exerting political influence, African Americans throughout the state found themselves continuing to be limited and hampered by policies in cities. According to historian Yohuru Williams, meaningful efforts to affect change fell to groups such as the Hill Parents Association. Williams considered the HPA to be one of the leading grass-roots organizations among African Americans in New Haven.[16]

Inadequate housing and jobs continued to plague the African American community throughout the 1950s and 1960s. New Haven decided to raze sub-standard housing occupied by 5,000 families but to rebuild only 1,500 homes. The units razed were all in an area with a large number of African American families. The city divided the new housing units among middle class and elderly households, displacing thousands of poor families. The city also agreed that more than 700 of the new units would be "luxury housing." In 1963, Ella Anderson, president of the local Bridgeport-Stratford NAACP, joined more than 200 people to condemn the presence of slum housing in Bridgeport after two children died in a fire inside one of the homes. More than a year earlier, an official from U.S. Commission on Civil Rights actually had urged the city to demolish hazardous housing on the city's East Side.[17] In 1967, Hartford's NAACP leader Wilber Smith railed against the building of parking garage in one of the areas being redeveloped in that city. For years, Smith had argued for affordable housing to be built.[18]

On the jobs front, in 1964, the Bridgeport-Stratford NAACP picketed a local employment agency for "exploitation" of domestic workers hired from the South. The organization also worked to encourage voter registration and provide transportation to the polls. NAACP members managed to find appointments for African

Americans as sales staff, clerks, stenographers, cashiers, truck drivers, and trainees.[19]

The protest movement and tactics resonating throughout the Southern civil rights movement would soon come to Connecticut. In 1960, Rev. Richard Battles accepted the pastorate of Hartford's Mount Olive Baptist Church. Known for his charismatic preaching, Battles organized and worked with the Southern Christian Leadership Conference (SCLC) affiliate and a chapter of the Congress of Racial Equality (CORE). His time with the SCLC nurtured his friendship with Rev. Dr. Martin Luther King, Jr., the nation's most prominent civil rights leader. Whenever King visited and spoke in Hartford over the years, Battles was at his side. He was among the more than 5,000 Connecticut residents who took part in the March on Washington in 1963. Battles also met and worked with members of North End Community Action Program (NECAP), which had ties to the Northern Student Movement. In 1964 the integrated NECAP's kneel-ins, picketing, and boycotts rocked Hartford.[20]

In 1962 Connecticut protesters solidified their bond with protesters in the South by joining activists in Albany, Georgia, on the frontline of the movement to integrate the city. The NAACP, Student Non-violent Coordinating Committee (SNCC), and SCLC all had a major presence in the campaign. Albany, Georgia, was a segregated city that forced African Americans to pay the same price for city buses, but then ride in the back of the bus. In addition, all citizens paid taxes; however, African Americans were allowed to enter the courthouse only at the rear. Protesters in Albany and elsewhere received quality legal aid and support from people such as New Haven native and NAACP lawyer Constance Baker Motley. Motley went to Albany to ensure the safety of the young people marching there.[21] Three years later, SCLC embarked on the Selma, Alabama, campaign for voter rights. Many Connecticut people who wished to support the Selma campaign were unable to make the long trip to Alabama, so they organized a protest of their own in Hartford on March 24, 1965. The March with Selma for Freedom Committee led 1,200 marchers from throughout the state from the Old State House to the State Capitol. Such protests, although applauded by those involved, troubled some people.[22]

No one in the African American community voiced their troubles quite as Malcolm X did. A member and minister in the Nation of Islam (NOI), Malcolm echoed his leader and teacher Elijah Muhammad when he called for separation between the races, not integration. In 1954 Malcolm met in Hartford with people interested in the NOI message. By the 1960s, everyone in the North End knew that the NOI held regular meetings on the second floor of 38 Albany Avenue.[23] There, Malcolm delivered a message of the disenchanted that resonated with urban dwellers who saw little hope in an integrationist and non-violent message. He and his driver traveled often from meetings in Hartford to Bridgeport.[24] His silencing by Elijah Muhammad in 1963 subsequent to his comments after the death of John Kennedy eventually led him to leave the NOI. The NOI remained a visible part of Connecticut's urban world, but Malcolm's attempt to build membership in his Muslim Mosque, Inc., and Organization of Afro-American Unity never had a major impact in the state.

On March 18, 1965, Whitney Young of the National Urban League spoke at a meeting at Connecticut General Life Insurance Company in Bloomfield, Connecticut. The Urban League played prominent roles in the lives of urban dwellers throughout the state. The organization focused considerable effort on building working relationships with businesses, creating adult education programs, increasing employment, and improving governmental ties. These were efforts that Connecticut local Urban League pioneers and leaders such as William Brown wrestled with daily.[25]

Even so, young people, some within the world of civil rights and some outside of that world, began to grow restless. In August 1963 more than 250,000 people marched on Washington; in September 1963 came the bombing at the 16th Street Baptist Church in Birmingham, Alabama by Robert Chambliss. Rev. A. A. Garvin of New London's Shiloh Baptist Church, New London NAACP members, and Rotary Club members joined forces to raise funds to send Mrs. Charlie Mae Jones, a sister of Cynthia Wesley, one of the young people murdered in that bombing, to Birmingham for the funeral. Jones, who worked in New London, was unable to afford the cost of plane fare to attend her sister's services.[26]

In 1964 the federal Civil Rights Act passed. On the heels of its passage, Mississippi Klansmen murdered Michael Schwerner, James Chaney, and Andrew Goodman. The three young men had been working as Freedom Summer volunteers, helping African Americans register to vote, and in addition, providing education and social uplift. Young people connected with the Student Nonviolent Coordinating Committee witnessed the national Democrat party's horrendous treatment of Fannie Lou Hamer and members of the Mississippi Freedom Democratic Party in Atlantic City. Vicious murders carried out by Southern vigilantes and Klansmen during the Selma Campaign disillusioned young people. Finally, the war in Vietnam began to weigh heavily on the minds of young people and leaders.

The repercussions of all of this violence were felt in Connecticut. Young people throughout the country and state were weary and frustrated. In 1966 SCLC, SNCC, and CORE joined with protesters in Mississippi for the last major united non-violent protest march in Mississippi. The Greenwood March saw Dr. King still urging people to continue to embrace the weapon of non-violence. However, SNCC's Kwame Ture, then Stokely Carmichael, boldly uttered the words: "Black Power." Many powerful white leaders and older African American leaders believed that he simply wanted separation and violence. Ture argued that he meant that African Americans should control the destiny of their communities. He saw nothing wrong with self-defense, self-love, and respect for Africa.[27] The late 1960s saw Black Power movements emerge in most urban areas.

When rebellions erupted throughout the country, President Lyndon Johnson and other major leaders seemed sure that militant black power leaders were responsible for such rebellions. In July 1967 Hartford experienced the smashing of windows with rocks and throwing of firebombs after the arrest of William "Billy" Toules. Police had arrested Toules after an altercation in a luncheonette owned by Rev. Richard Battles' brother Adam Battles. John Barber, a former NAACP leader in New Haven, became one of the key faces of Black Power in Hartford. Barber helped to organize the Black Caucus to serve as the voice of the powerless in the North End ghetto. In September 1967 this organization shocked local sensibilities when members decided to march from the city's North End to the South End to highlight discrimination. Police, after witnessing conduct deemed disorderly, decided to halt the march. Police arrested Barber and a number of other young protesters for things such as breach of peace and inciting to riot.[28]

That summer of 1967, New Haven, which the federal government considered a "model city" of inclusion and opportunity, also experienced upheaval that saw property damage—and also death. Mayor Richard C. Lee of New Haven responded by providing funding for summer jobs. The rebellion, in the eyes of the students, highlighted the cities' and the state's failure to address problems in urban communities. This new breed of rebels frightened white and African American leaders throughout the state. Groups such as the Black Caucus and Hill Parents Association received heavy surveillance and policing.[29] The state experienced additional violent protests in the following years up to 1970.

In 1969 the Black Panther Party for Self-Defense entered the state. The party first made inroads in Bridgeport; however, it acquired greater visibility and impact in New Haven. Organized in Oakland, California in 1966, the party focused attention on social and health programs. In addition to its social programs, the group believed in the right of armed self-defense. Panther founders Huey Newton and Bobby Seale saw an opportunity to organize young disadvantaged and disillusioned young people that other leaders ignored. The Panthers knew that the gulf between rich and poor was on the increase in New Haven. When they made a call for "land, bread, housing, education, clothing, justice, and peace," poor people listened.[30]

The Black Panthers also organized in cities such as Hartford. Wherever Panthers existed, FBI chief J. Edgar Hoover saw a threat to national security. The FBI held in great distain the fact that the organization embraced communism and revolutionary philosophy. Hoover, with the help of some local authorities, worked to disrupt party activity. The world of New Haven's Panthers would be forever changed in May 1969 after the murder of Panther Alex Rackley, which set off the famous trial of nine Black Panther party members in New Haven. Panther party members and supporters waged a tireless and eventually effective campaign for the rights and freedom of those arrested at the time. While the ensuing arrests and trial focused the nation's attention on New Haven, Panthers members brought important leaders and funds to the city. Their efforts were effective in the eyes of many of the poor.[31]

The movement for civil rights in the state that focused heavily on housing, discrimination, employment, and education managed to pay some dividends; however, education remained a huge concern. Efforts to desegregate schools met with strong white resistance and flight from urban areas. Although programs such as Project Concern attempted to achieve integration, out-migration quickly left urban schools in Connecticut more segregated than in some areas of the South.[32]

Often forgotten in the state's struggle for civil rights was the plight of African American women working to gain access to education and positions as professionals, such as lawyers. When Boce Barlow, Jr. received his appointment as a judge in the municipal courts in 1957, there were still no African American female graduates of the state's largest public law school. Twelve years later, the University of Connecticut's law school admitted Constance Belton Green. In 1972 Green, a native of Portsmouth, Virginia, and daughter of a public school administrator and teacher, became the first female African American to graduate from the law school. In her second year, in 1970, Green was joined by Bessye Anita Warren Bennett, a first-year law student at the university. Bennett, a native of Prairie View, Texas, and daughter of a college professor and elementary school principal, earned her undergraduate degree from Radcliffe College. By the time of her admission to the law school, the mother of three had found time to teach in the Hartford public school system and earn an M.A. from Trinity College. In 1973 Bennett received her degree from the law school, and in 1974 she became the first African American woman admitted to the bar in the state (Green was admitted the following year). Over the years, Bennett had a private practice and worked in a number of other capacities, such as chairman of the Victim Services Commission, executive director of the Children First Initiative, and president of the Crawford Law Society. In 1974 Patricia Lilly Harleston earned her law degree from the University of Connecticut. Harleston, a Washington, D.C., native, opened her private practice in 1975. A former assistant attorney general, in 1996 Harleston received an appointment to the Connecticut Superior Court System.[33]

The movement for civil rights opened eyes and doors for a number of African Americans in major Connecticut industries, companies, and government positions. In the 1970s and 1980s insurance firms actively recruited in the South and historically black colleges and universities for talent, finding workers from areas in Virginia and North Carolina. Some major companies could eventually boast that key executives were African Americans. In the late 1980s and early 1990s Hartford eventually elected two African American mayors, Thirman L. Milner and Carrie Saxon Perry. Denise Nappier's continued tenure as Connecticut Secretary of State remains a point of pride.

For the families that initiated the famous *Sheff v. O'Neill* case, the battle for the education of their children was part of the great struggle for education and freedom that has been a part of the African American struggle for freedom since the colonial period. While the period of World War II began to see barriers against discrimination falling across several fronts, most African American leaders understand that significant work remains, particularly in the vital areas of education and employment.

# Notes

1. Curtis S. Johnson, *Raymond E. Baldwin: Connecticut Statesman* (Chester: Pequot Press, 1972), 83–84. The "1943–1968 25th Anniversary of the Connecticut Commission on Human Rights and Opportunities," Gov. John Dempsey Papers, RG-5, Box-A 236, Civil Rights Folder 3, Connecticut State Library Archives.

2. Letter from Morris Silverman to Gov. Raymond Baldwin, August 2, 1943, Gov. Baldwin Papers, Rg-5, Box 463, IRC Folder, CSL Archives. See also letter from John H. Johnson (*Negro Digest*) to Baldwin, August 10, 1943; letter from Florida Club (Hartford) to Baldwin, January 14, 1943; and letter from James P. Gifford (Columbia University Law Professor) to Baldwin, February 10, 1943, Gov. Raymond Baldwin Papers, RG-5, Box 463, IRC Folder, CSL Archives.

3. "1943–1968 25th Anniversary of the Connecticut Commission on Human Rights and Opportunities." See also letter from John H. Johnson to Baldwin, August 10, 1943; letter from Florida Club (Hartford) to Baldwin, January 14, 1943; and letter from James P. Gifford to Baldwin, February 10, 1943. Letter from Colored Republicans State Organization to Baldwin, November 3, 1943; and letter to Rev. Robert Moody from Governor Executive Assistant, August 9, 1943, Gov. Baldwin Papers, Hartford: CSL Archives, RG-5, Box 463, IRC Folder. See also Stacey Close, "Fire in the Bones: Hartford's NAACP, Civil Rights, and Militancy, 1943–1969," *Journal of Negro History*, vol. 86, no. 3 (Summer 2001): 229; and letter from Walter H. Gray (Sufragan Bishop) to Baldwin, January 3, 1944, Governor Raymond Baldwin Papers, RG-5, Box 463, IRC, Hartford: CSL Archives.

4. Letter from Gray to Baldwin, January 3, 1944. See also Stacey Close, "Fire in the Bones," 229.

5. Letter from Gray to Baldwin, January 3, 1944. See also Stacey Close, "Fire in the Bones."

6. William Cockerham, "World War II Set Stage for Blacks to Activate Civil Rights Efforts," *Hartford Courant*, September 28, 1992. For other significant changes, see also "Report of Connecticut Inter-Racial Commission to His Excellency Raymond Baldwin, Governor of Connecticut," September 8, 1944 (12, 18, 21), Governor Raymond Baldwin Papers, RG-5, Box 463, IRC Folder, Hartford: CSL Archives.

7. Frank T. Simpson, "They Seek Equality for All People," *Hartford Courant Magazine*, September 14, 1952.

8. Memorandum to Miss (Ella) Baker from Madison S. Jones, May 8, 1946, Papers of the NAACP, Selected Branches File, 1940–55, gen. eds. John Bracey, Sharon Harley, and August Meier, reel 2, Group II, Box c-24, Hartford, CT Branch, microfilm, University Publications, 2000; letter from Percy Christian to Senator Raymond Baldwin, January 27, 1948, Papers of the NAACP, Selected Branches File, 1940–55, gen. eds. John Bracey, Sharon Harley, and August Meier, reel 2, Group II, Box c-24, Hartford, CT Branch, microfilm, University Publications, 2000. See also Keith Schoonrock, "Bowles Would End Guard Segregation," *Hartford Courant*, January 8, 1949.

9. Dr. Juliette Bursterman Papers, Box 18, "Letter from State Board of Education," October 7, 1948, file folder, ECSU, J. Eugene Smith Library,

Archives and Special Collections. See also Dr. Juliette Bursterman Papers, Box 18, "Letter from Erwin H. Sasman, August 28, 1948," file folder, ECSU, J. Eugene Smith Library, Archives and Special Collections.

10. "Citizens Council Re-Organize," *Hartford Chronicle*, November 2, 1946; "NECC Makes Annual Report," *Hartford Chronicle*, January 5, 1947; "FePC Considered Unimportant," *Hartford Chronicle*, January 25, 1947; and "State FEPC Presents Bill," *Hartford Chronicle*, February 1, 1947. For other information on the newspapers see Stacey K. Close, "Black Hartford's Print Protest: *Hartford Chronicle, Connecticut Chronicle*, and *New England Bulletin*," *The Griot*, 22, no. 1 (Spring 2004): 47–60.

11. Monique Jarvis, "Conscience of the Community: Art Johnson," *Hartford Inquirer*, September 8, 1999, and Stan Simpson, "Art Johnson's Past Shaped An Activist's Rich Life," *Hartford Courant*, September 8, 1999. See also "Commission on Human Relations Set Up to Promote Racial Harmony," *Hartford Courant*, November 30, 1963. Specific functions in decrying discrimination were: to foster mutual understanding and respect among all racial, religious, and ethnic groups in the city; to encourage equality of treatment of any racial, religious, or ethnic group or its members; to cooperate with governmental and non-governmental agencies and organizations having similar power; and to make such studies in the field of human relations as in the commission's judgment will aid in effectuating its general purpose.

12. Herbert Janick, *A Diverse People* (Chester: Pequot Press, 1975), 79. Also see Mary Goodwin, "Education Board Sticks to Stand on Robeson; Concert Will Be Held," *Hartford Courant*, November 14, 1952. Helen O'Neill, "A Life That Sang of 'Pure Courage': Career Never Colored Convictions for Paul Robeson," *Hartford Courant*, February 11, 1996. See also Stacey K. Close, "Historical Impact of Brown II on Black Hartford 1954–71," *Illinois Schools Journal*, vol. 84, no. 2 (Spring 2005): 37–39.

13. Mary Goodwin, "Education Board Sticks To Stand On Robeson; Concert Will Be Held." Helen O'Neill, "A Life That Sang of 'Pure Courage': Career Never Colored Convictions for Paul Robeson." See also Don Stacom, "Renaissance Man Revival in Enfield," *Hartford Courant*, December 1, 1997; Janick, 79; Martin Baum Duberman, *Paul Robeson* (New York: Alfred A. Knopf, 1988), 414. See Roger Catlin, "Hartford Activist Honored," *Hartford Courant*, November 16, 1986; "City School Board Will Act Today on Robeson Concert," *Hartford Courant*, November 13, 1952. See also Stacey K. Close, "Historical Impact of Brown II on Black Hartford 1954–71," *Illinois Schools Journal*, vol. 84, no. 2 (Spring 2005): 37–39.

14. Jack Zaiman, "Cronin Elected City's Mayor; CCC Barely Controls Council" *Hartford Courant*, November 7, 1951; "Independents Win on School Board," *Hartford Courant*, November 7, 1951; interview with local leaders at home of Mr. and Mrs. Gladys Fisher, April 7, 2000. See also Arthur Johnson, "Progressive Politics in Hartford," in *State of Black Hartford*, ed. Stanley Battle (Hartford: Greater Hartford Urban League, 1993), 70; and Jose Cruz, *Identity and Power: Puerto Rican Politics and the Challenge of Ethnicity* (Philadelphia: Temple University Press, 1998), 23.

15. Jack Zaiman, "First Negro in History on Council," *Hartford Courant*, November 9, 1955. See also Business Directory Listing, 1938 for Negro Achievement Week, February 13–19, 1938; The Hartford Negro Interest

Group, "Making Acquaintance with Hartford's Negro Groups," Hartford: Hartford Collection, Hartford Public Library.

16. Yohuru Williams, "No Haven: From Civil Rights to Black Power in Connecticut," *The Black Scholar*, vol. 31, no. 3-4 (Fall/Winter 2001): 55–56.

17. Sam Negri, "Slum Landlords Blasted at Walter Court Rally," *Bridgeport Telegram*, January 14, 1963.

18. Williams, 55; "NAACP Leader Against Proposed Parking Garage," *Hartford Courant*, November 1, 1967.

19. Bridgeport-Stratford, Annual Report of Branch Activities, 1964, Papers of the NAACP, Branch Files, Part 25, Series B, Regional Files and Special Report, 1956–65, Wesleyan University, Middletown, CT, Olin Library (microfilm reel 10).

20. "King Stirred State Audiences," *Hartford Courant*, April 5, 1968. Michael Kenney, "Boycott Urged to Win Visible Jobs for Negroes," *Hartford Courant*, July 14, 1963, "NECAP Commended by National Movement," *Hartford Courant*, July 19, 1963, "NECAP Shuns Warning Its Picketing Is Illegal," *Hartford Courant*, July 21, 1963, "NECAP Warned Not to Break Law, " *Hartford Courant*, July 20, 1963, and "NECAP to File Charges Against Windsor Police," *Hartford Courant*, July 14, 1963.

21. Interview on 7/29/98 with Mayor Thirman Milner. See also Motley, *Equal Justice Under the Law*, 158; "Spurred by Albany, GA: Rallies, Voter Drive Set for City Negroes," *Hartford Courant*, September 2, 1962.

22. "1,200 Call for Freedom in City Rights March," *Hartford Courant*, March 25, 1965.

23. "Black Muslim Minister Sees U.S. a Sinking Ship," *Hartford Courant*, July 24, 1962.

24. Malcolm X's 1960s visits to Hartford were major media events. The *Times* and *Courant* both made sure that reporters covered his lectures. "Malcolm X at U of H: Muslim Leader Warns of Racial Bloodshed," *Hartford Courant*, October 30, 1963; "Malcolm X Visited City 3 Times in Recent Years," *Hartford Courant*, February 22, 1965. See also Les Payne, *The New Crisis: The Magazine of Opportunities and Ideas* (January/February 2001): 22–25; and "Malcolm X States Creed Of Muslims at Bushnell," *Hartford Courant*, June 5, 1963.

25. Malcolm Johnson, "Urban League Shuns Demonstrations to Stress Education, Director Says," *Hartford Courant*, March 19, 1965.

26. "Strangers Pay Woman's Way to Sister's Funeral," *Hartford Courant*, September 18, 1963.

27. Kwame Ture and Charles V. Hamilton, *Black Power: The Politics of Liberation* (New York: Vintage Books, 1992), 44–45; Chuck Stone, *Black Political Power* (Indianapolis: Bobbs-Merrill Company, 1968), 16–25; "Urban League Criticizes 'Black Power,'" *Hartford Courant*, July 14, 1966; David Holmberg, "Peaceful Path Upheld to SNCC by Local Man," *Hartford Courant*, July 3, 1966.

28. Thomas D. Williams, "City Stores Hit by Bricks, Fire," *Hartford Courant*, July 13, 1967. Jon Briggs and Thomas D. Williams, "Arrest Triggered First Bombs," *Hartford Courant*, July 14, 1967. "'Can't Happen Here' Resident Thought," *Hartford Times*. See also "North Side Regains Calm," *Hartford Times*, July 15, 1967; "Not Guilty, Says Black Caucus—Violence

Was Already There," *Hartford Courant*, September 21, 1967; and Theodore Driscoll, "Negroes Split on Riots," *Hartford Courant*, July 17, 1967.

29. Yohuru Williams, "No Haven: From Civil Rights to Black Power in Connecticut," *The Black Scholar*, vol. 31, no. 3-4 (fall/winter 2001): 55–59. William Borders, "Hartford is Calm As Patrols Go On," *New York Times*, July 15, 1967; Theodore Driscoll, "Negroes Split On Riot Cause," *Hartford Courant*, July 17, 1967; "Negro March Ends in Vandalism," *Hartford Courant*, September 19, 1967.

30. Williams, 59–64.

31. Ibid., 55–64.

32. Manning Marable, *Black Liberation In Conservative America* (Boston: South End Press, 1997), 87. See also "Education Association Board Supports 'Project Concern,'" *Hartford Courant*, September 27, 1967; and "A Racial Isolation in the Public Schools," A Report of the United States Commission on Civil Rights 1967.

33. Constance Belton Green, "Three Black Women Lawyers in Connecticut: Reflections," unpublished manuscript.

## 40 "I Wanted to Fly"

*Connie Nappier, Jr.*

Connie Nappier vividly recalls the moment around 1927 when, as a small boy walking with his father on Wooster Street in Hartford, Connecticut, he saw his first airplane. He decided "right then I wanted to fly. Little did I know that a war would come along that would give me the opportunity to fly."[1]

As a teenager attending Weaver High School, Nappier closely followed the news regarding the struggle of African Americans to enlist in the Army Air Corps. Although African Americans had served in the military since the American Revolution, the belief that African Americans were not capable, either physically or mentally, of serving in the military persisted, fueled by several biased studies conducted after World War I.

With the approach of World War II, however, the black community relentlessly lobbied the War Department through black newspapers, labor organizations, and the National Association for the Advancement of Colored People (NAACP). A January 1941 lawsuit against the War Department brought by Yancey Williams, a Howard University graduate who had been rejected by the Army Air Corps and backed by the NAACP, was the final straw that forced the Air Corps to open to African Americans. On January 16, 1941, the 99th Pursuit Squadron (later re-designated the 99th Fighter Squadron) was activated, and in July 1941 the "Tuskegee Experiment," later renamed the Tuskegee Experience, was inaugurated. The Tuskegee Institute in Alabama was selected as the site for the men to receive their primary instruction to become pilots.

Nappier, though still in high school, jumped at the opportunity to enlist in the Air Corps. He walked to the recruiting center at 555 Asylum Street in Hartford to take the written exam. He was confident that he had aced the test but two weeks later received notification that he had failed. "I was determined to get a fair hearing," he said, so he returned and convinced the recruiter to give him another test, which he again passed with flying colors. This time, he was allowed to enlist.

The next hurdle surfaced at Westover Air Base, where Nappier reported for his physical. The star athlete again was not worried because he was in peak physical condition. But, he says, the doctor examining him measured the distance between the pupils of his eyes and declared the young man a "freak" because they were farther apart than average. Nappier challenged the doctor, saying, "If my pupils are further apart than the norm, it means that my peripheral vision is greater and that makes me better suited as a flyer." The physician replied with a chuckle, "I think you're going to make it." The Air Corps accepted Nappier after he graduated from high school.

In June 1943, the new high school graduate was accepted into the Tuskegee program and reported to Keesler Field in Biloxi, Mississippi for basic training. He was placed in a segregated unit, as he would be for every stage of his military service, and soon encountered deep racism. Nappier described an incident in which one of the cadets went into town alone and did not return. "They found him the next day on the road with his head bashed in," Nappier recalled. With their hearts set on getting to Tuskegee, the pre-aviation cadets endured racism, discrimination, and mistreatment both from civilians and the military.

When Nappier arrived at the Tuskegee Institute at the end of 1943, he immediately sensed a different atmosphere. He soon realized the caliber of the men with whom he was training, recalling, "I felt like I was walking amongst giants." One of the men his own age had already earned his master's degree from the Massachusetts Institute of Technology. Nappier enrolled in an accelerated college course at the College Training Detachment and completed his primary flight training at Moton Field. Unfortunately, Nappier's class (class 44–45B) was reassigned and would become the first class of bombardiers and navigators. Nappier's lifelong dream of becoming a pilot was put on hold. He was reassigned to Midland, Texas, where he qualified as a bombardier and navigator, receiving his wings on December 1, 1944.

After a short stint at Godman Field in Kentucky, Nappier and more than a hundred African-American officers were sent to Freedman Field in Indiana. Racial tensions there flared almost immediately over the airmen's access to the two officers' clubs, resulting in the house arrest of 101 African-American officers, including many, Nappier included, who had not been to the officers' clubs. Facing possible court martial, not one of the 101 detained airmen agreed to sign a directive designating one club as whites only. Nappier recalls, "Well, we knew that, but the fellas said, 'Well, if we can go overseas and die, we might as well die here for what we know is right.'"

FIGURE 40-1 Connie
Nappier, Jr., c. 1944–
1945. *Courtesy of Connie
Nappier and The Veterans
Oral History Project at
Central Connecticut
State University*

Rather than prosecute, Colonel Robert Selway, the unit's interim commander, placed a formal reprimand in each man's service record. While in custody, the men learned of the death of President Theodore Roosevelt; Harry Truman was now president. To the surprise of Nappier and others, a rumor circulated alleging that when Truman, a Southern white man, was apprised of the situation, he said, "Turn my boys a loose and let them do what they were trained to do." The airmen were freed and swallowed the insult of having been called boys, but the reprimands remained in their files.

That undeserved reprimand later caused problems for Nappier when he requested a transfer back to Tuskegee for pilot training. Selway denied the request, but it nonetheless made it up the chain of command, and Nappier received orders to report in July 1945 for pilot training. Nappier joined Class 46D and became a skilled pilot in both the PT-13D and the AT-6D. Nappier still recalls the feeling when he first flew solo: "When I got up there and I looked down, it was really a high point in my life at that point. Everything looked so clean, and the sun was shining. I forgot about the war. I really, really truly felt that the Maker has got to be somewhere close around here. Many things ran through my head. One was, 'Well, Connie, you made it.'"

Nappier was not to savor the triumph for long. The war officially ended in September, before Connie had an opportunity to graduate, and the Air Corps immediately closed the Tuskegee program. Class 46C, the class just ahead of Nappier's, became the last official class of the Tuskegee Experience.

Perhaps equally as important as their military service was the Tuskegee Airmen's role in paving the way for the desegregation of the military. The high caliber of hundreds of young airmen produced by the Tuskegee Experience and their unparalleled record of air superiority certainly dispelled any myths about the ability or the patriotism of African Americans. It was men such as Connie Nappier, Jr., who influenced President Truman to sign Executive Order 9981 in 1948 to integrate America's military, years before Rosa Parks made her famous stand, or Martin Luther King, Jr. became the voice for civil rights. Nappier is proud of the part he played in improving the country for all African Americans. After the war, Connie went on to become a prominent architect.

In 1995 General R. Fogelman, chief of staff of the United States Air Force, officially pardoned the 101 officers, and twelve years later, the government finally recognized the Tuskegee Airmen for their contributions to World War II. President George W. Bush presented

the airmen with the Congressional Gold Medal, the most prestigious medal Congress can bestow. Nappier was one of the airmen in
attendance for the long overdue honor.


Notes

This essay appeared in the Fall 2011 issue of *Connecticut Explored*.

1. Connie Nappier, Jr., interviewed by Eileen Hurst, Veterans History
Project, Central Connecticut State University, March 15, 2006 and February
26, 2010.

# 41 Susan Elizabeth Freeman, World War II Officer and Nurse

As a young child, Susan Elizabeth Freeman often provided medical care and aid for family members, the family dog, and dolls. Freeman's mother referred to her daughter as her "little nurse." When the former "little nurse" became a teenager, she dealt with tragedy in November 1918: Early on a Tuesday morning, she joined her father and siblings at the bedside of her dying mother. With his wife, Susie Louise Freeman, in the last moments of her life, William Joseph Freeman, young Susan's father, requested that family members fall to their knees to offer prayer. As he prayed, his wife quietly passed away.[1]

William spent part of his life working as a laborer in Stratford for a wealthy attorney and publisher Frederick Converse and the family of Alfred Beach, for whom he performed such tasks as milking the cow and serving as driver for the family. William fulfilled some of his spiritual yearnings by working with and building up—literally—the church where he worshipped, the First Baptist Church. He and his wife instilled a strong work ethic and Christian beliefs in their children.[2] The strong work ethic and Christian beliefs sustained their daughter throughout her career as a nurse and soldier in World War II.

In 1921 Susan, a talented student and athlete at Stratford High School, received her diploma. She had been ill for much of the year, suffering through a horrible case of diphtheria. In 1923 her desire to work in health care propelled her into nursing school at Freedmen's Hospital Training School for Nurses in Washington, D.C., Freeman also engaged in graduate studies at Howard and Catholic universities and advanced studies at Columbia University.[3] With her education under her belt, she joined a distinguished lineage of African American nurses in Connecticut, proving to be a caring and understanding nurse. Martha Franklin, a registered nurse, organized the National Association of Colored Graduate Nurses in 1908. Franklin worked professionally in both Bridgeport (1901–1903) and New Haven (1900, 1906–1911).[4]

As the nation geared up for World War II, the National Association of Colored Graduate Nurses recommended that its members join the efforts of the American Red Cross to provide a pool of nurses. The Red Cross served as a clearinghouse for the Army Nurses Corps. Initially, the army rejected African American applicants. When they finally accepted black women, Surgeon General James C. Magee informed the nurses that they could serve only in segregated hospitals and health-care units.[5]

The Army Nurses Corps required that its officers be registered nurses and members of the Red Cross. Mary McLeod Bethune, who founded Bethune Cookman College, Mabel K. Staupers, president of the Negro Graduate Nurses Association, and Eleanor Roosevelt helped to organize a campaign to recruit African American women into the corps. Stratford's Susan Freeman became part of this early wave of African American female recruits. The military assigned her to Camp Livingston in Louisiana.[6]

Even for officers, life for African Americans in the military often meant enduring the humiliation of segregation in travel and camp facilities. Army regulations required officers to travel long distances via Pullman berths. It was during such travel that Susan Freeman encountered her first experience with the Jim Crow South. A train conductor in St. Louis told Freeman that the Pullman was off limits to "Negroes" who traveled through the South. Instead, she had to ride "Lower 13," an area designated for African Americans. Estelle Massey Osborne, a friend of Freeman who, as a native of Texas, had experienced and understood the rules of life aboard segregated trains, overheard Freeman speaking with the conductor about the confusion. Osborne, who often rode Lower 13, did not grasp that Freeman, a native of Connecticut, had not experienced such indignities in public travel. (Osborne was the first African American woman to receive a master's degree in nursing; she went on to lead the National Association of Graduate Nurses, the premier organization at the time for African American nurses.) The conductor led Freeman to a private room, where she completed the "Jim Crow" trip to Louisiana with accommodations superior to those afforded most African American travelers.

Although the camp initially placed all white and black nurses in the same area, camp officials quickly organized efforts to construct segregated housing. In addition, African American doctors and nurses provided care only for African American soldiers.[7]

The Army sent Freeman to Fort Huachuca in Arizona in 1942 to become chief nurse. The military gave her limited time, just ten days, to prepare, and she and other nurses received notice that they had to travel in the day coach. Freeman objected strenuously, which forced a meeting with the colonel. When she informed the colonel about the wretched encounters and conditions that African Americans endured on trains in the South, the nurses were accommodated in Pullman berths and placed under the protection of two federal officials. When the train made a stop at El Paso, Texas, the conductor told the nurses that they could purchase food at the back of the station stop. Refusing to submit to Jim Crow service, they chose not to eat at all. After the trip resumed, a white woman inquired if the seat beside Freeman was open. The Stratford native's response—that she didn't know whether the seat were taken or not—did not please the inquirer, who asked the question again. Finally, she asked if Freeman was the "porterette." Freeman fired back quickly, reminding the woman that the nation was at war and pointing out that she should have been able to recognize the military uniform of a nurse.[8]

Once at Fort Huachuca, Freeman and eleven other nurses found themselves working in a hospital unit lacking any organizational structure. They set about creating wards for 700 patients, increasing the number of patients they could house to 1,000. Freeman's staff increased to 110 nurses.[9]

With the nation fully engrossed in war, the country's military needs called for her to serve overseas in 1943. Aboard the *USS James Parker*, Freeman and a unit of African American nurses sailed to Africa. Wind, rain, and rough seas battered the ship and the people within for more than four days. The horrible weather forced most service personnel to avoid dinner, but not Lt. Freeman. In the midst of the storm, the ship's surgeon needed her help with an emergency appendectomy. With aid of another nurse, the team successfully completed the surgery. Her voyage also included a harrowing alarm call to abandon ship into the cold waters of the Atlantic Ocean; however, the final order never came for the terrified passengers to disembark.[10]

The ship docked in North Africa, and Freeman's unit made its way to Liberia for service. Because their housing lacked window screens, the nurses had to sleep under mosquito nets. Even so, mosquitos caring malaria infected nineteen of the thirty nurses. Freeman's nurses went out into the countryside to care for military personnel in distress. She even encountered a man from Bridgeport, a former member of Marcus Garvey's UNIA (Universal Negro Improvement Association) living in Liberia, who knew her family. On

November 8, 1943, the Office of the Commanding General honored Freeman and eight of her nurses for their dedicated efforts.[11]

From 1943 to 1945 Freeman's work received other honors. Her return to Camp Livingston saw her promotion to the rank of captain and full integration of the camp. In 1945 she also received the Mary Mahoney Award from the National Association of Colored Graduate Nurses for her Red Cross work in aiding people who suffered through the ravages of the 1937 Ohio-Mississippi Flood. On July 31, 1945, she quietly received her honorable discharge and went home to Stratford.[12]

After the war, she put much of her energy into church and civic activities. She helped establish a nursing sorority, Chi Eta Phi. Freeman continued to work until her retirement. In 1979 the pioneering veteran passed away at the Veterans Administration Hospital in West Haven. Susan Freeman's legacy and importance to African American women and military personnel has always been clear. She honorably served her country, community, and state. Her passion for saving lives extended from her earliest days in Stratford to the war zones of North Africa.[13] While fellow Connecticut residents such as Lemuel Custiss and Connie Nappier shattered negative stereotypes about African American military pilots, Stratford's Susan Freeman and other nurses shattered negative beliefs about the intelligence of African American service women and their capabilities.

Notes

1. "Susan Elizabeth Freeman," in *The Negro Heritage Library* (Yonkers, N.Y.: Educating Heritage, Inc. 1966), 108.

2. Letter from Lewis G. Knapp to Cora Murray (Historic Sites Researcher, Connecticut Historical Commission), December 10, 1990, from collection of Lewis G. Knapp (Town Historian, 1987–2004).

3. "Freeman," *The Negro Heritage Library*, 110.

4. See "Martha Franklin," Connecticut Women's Hall of Fame, http://cwhf.org/inductees/science-health/martha-minerva-franklin/.

5. See "Army Nurses at Huachua," 3, http://www.huachuca.army.mil/sites/history/PDFS/anc.pdf.

6. "Freeman," *The Negro Heritage Library*, 110.

7. Ibid., 110–11.

8. Ibid., 111.

9. Ibid.

10. Ibid.

11. Ibid. The Chi Eta Phi Sorority Web site indicates that she received the award in 1945, while the Huachua Museum cites 1944. See www.huachuca

.army.mil/sites/history/PDFS/anc.pdf; www.members.chietaphi.net/
regions/Bio_freeman.html.

    12. "Freeman," 111.

    13. Ibid.; www.members.chietaphi.net/regions/Bio_freeman.html.

# 42 Ellis Ruley

Ellis Ruley (1882–1959) lived all his life in Norwich, Connecticut. His day job for decades was that of common laborer, but his primary occupation was with the paintings that long after his death would bring him national recognition as an African American folk artist. Nearly all of his paintings were done with cheap house oils on Masonite or poster board. The fact that Ruley once used the back room of a local restaurant as a gallery to sell his paintings suggests he wanted an audience for his work and conceived of himself as an artist (see plate 9).

According to his entry in the Encyclopedia of American Folk Art (2004 edition), only sixty-four of Ruley's paintings survived to make their way into private or museum collections. Among the museums that own his work is Norwich's Slater Memorial Museum, whose long-time director, then an art teacher, arranged the only solo exhibition Ruley had in his lifetime. It was held in December 1952 at the art school connected to the museum. Others collections that hold his work are the Wadsworth Atheneum Museum of Art in Hartford and the American Folk Art Museum in New York City, both stops on the touring retrospective that introduced him nationally beginning in 1996.

In his paintings, Ruley depicted cowboys on horseback, bathing beauties in lush landscapes, bountiful farmsteads, and a back-to-nature Englishman known as Chief Grey Owl, who was a major celebrity between the two world wars. The common denominator in this odd array is a world shared, rather than dominated, by human beings.

It was "Adam and Eve" that opened the way to Ruley's posthumous renown. Considered Ruley's masterpiece, the painting is of a Garden of Eden inhabited by a chalky-white Adam and Eve. In September 1990, Glenn Robert Smith, an art collector from California, bought it at the famed Brimfield, Massachusetts, flea market. Though the painting was unsigned, Smith paid $3,000 on the hunch that it was an important piece. Inquiries took Smith to the Slater Museum's Joseph Gualtieri, who remembered seeing the painting at Ruley's house around the time of his first Norwich exhibition.

Smith then began the crusade and the search for more Ruley paintings that culminated in the 1993 publication *Discovering Ellis Ruley: The Story of an American Outsider Artist*,[1] and the 1996 retrospective exhibition that began at the San Diego Museum of Art and later traveled to the Wadsworth Atheneum and venues in six other cities. Besides reproducing nearly all the known paintings, *Discovering Ellis Ruley* includes a critical essay by the American Folk Art Museum's curator Stacy Hollander and senior research fellow Lee Kogan. The book also includes a biographical essay by Smith that was part murder mystery.

In his essay, Smith reveals the strongly held suspicions of some family members that Ruley died the victim of foul play. His partially frozen body was found the morning of January 16, 1959, about 200 feet from the front door of his isolated farmhouse. The cab driver who had picked Ruley up at a tavern early the evening before remembered dropping him within 25 feet his house. Based on injuries to his head and a long trail of blood, police speculated that a drunken Ruley had fallen, become disoriented, and stumbled off in the wrong direction.

But his family's suspicions were compounded by an earlier death that had occurred under even more inexplicable circumstances. In 1948, the body of Ruley's only son-in-law, a man about forty named Douglas Harris, was found upside down in a well on Ruley's property. Police had deemed that death accidental also. On top of all that, the family also wondered how Ruley's vacant house could have burned within months of his death, but not before his paintings were removed.

Ellis Ruley was only one generation removed from slavery. His father Joshua, born about 1847, is believed to have run away as a young man from his owner in Delaware. He wound up in Rhode Island and married Eudora Robinson, whose mother may also have been enslaved. According to a family memoir, *A Promise to My Mother: The Saga of the Ellis Walter Ruley Family*, published by two of Ellis's great granddaughters, DeLois C. Lindsey and Sheila L. Traynum, Joshua bore scars on his back from beatings and had screaming nightmares about being chased by dogs and men on horseback.[2]

*A Promise to My Mother* puts the year Joshua and Eudora were married as 1877 and says they relocated to Norwich before Ellis was born. At the time, Norwich, founded in 1659, was one of the wealthiest small cities in New England, made rich by textile mills processing Southern cotton. Norwich also benefited from being an important stop on the rail line connecting Boston and New York. It would not be by-passed until 1889 when a rail bridge opened across the Thames River at New London.

Ellis's own life would coincide with the city's slow decline. He was the oldest of twelve children, four of whom died very young. The extent of his schooling is uncertain. The report of his death in 1959 in the *Norwich Bulletin* describes him as being educated in city schools.[3] It also states that he worked for most of his life as a mason's tender and had been retired for only ten years.

Lindsey and Traynum, in *A Promise To My Mother*, add that his first employment, before masonry, was shoveling coal on barges that came up the Thames River from New London. Neither *A Promise to My Mother* nor the Smith biographical essay give the date of his first marriage to a black woman named Ida Bee. But Lindsey and Traynum report that Bee suffered at least eight miscarriages or still-born children before their only child, daughter Marion, was born on August 31, 1912. It also says Bee did not live to see her daughter's fourth birthday.

The 1920s was a turning point for Ruley and for Norwich. According to Lindsey and Traynum and the *Bulletin*'s death notice, Ruley married for a second time in 1924 to a white woman named Wilhelmina Fox. She previously had been married to one of Ruley's brothers, and she had also had a son from an earlier relationship with a man whom Lindsey and Traynum describe as overtly racist.

On October 6, 1927, Ruley's unwed teenage daughter Marion gave birth to his first grandchild. A girl named Gladys, she would remain with Ruley and Wilhelmina when Marion moved to Hartford, and it would be her recollections that form the basis of *A Promise to My Mother*. Perhaps an even more transformative event in Ruley's life occurred just two years later.

On September 19, 1929, according to Smith, Ruley and a co-worker were seriously injured in a truck accident soon after leaving a construction site. His injuries were severe enough to warrant a $25,000 insurance settlement. Soon after, he would purchase several acres on a hilltop overlooking the city. The farmhouse on the property was run down, and without electricity or running water, but the selling price was cheap. The insurance money gave Ruley the wherewithal to devote more time to his painting, to turn his hilltop acres into a kind of mini-estate (he added stone walls and a duck pond and planted gardens and fruit trees), and to buy a green Chevrolet convertible.

According to Norwich historian Arthur Lathrop, hundreds of textile jobs had gone south over the course of the 1920s, though they still accounted for more than half the city's roughly 8,000-person workforce. The erosion of the textile industry occurred at the same time that Eastern European immigrants flooded the city, with the single largest group coming from Poland. Their particular ethnicity did not matter as much as their foreignness and non-Protestant religion.[4]

One response to the immigrant influx was that Norwich became a center of Ku Klux Klan activity in Connecticut. The first cross burnings occurred in early 1924, and the Klan claimed more than 1,000 members in Norwich alone, though Lathrop claims that number was almost certainly exaggerated. A national Klan leader who visited the area later in 1924 attracted a crowd of 600 who heard him preach about the need to preserve the values of the nation's Anglo-Saxon, Protestant founders. In the 1920s, Klan membership was at its peak, and its supremacist beliefs almost mainstream.

In his biographical essay, Smith makes much of the presence of the Klan and its possible threat to Ruley. Lindsey and Traynum, on the other hand, mainly portray his hilltop homestead as a kind of sanctuary. Much of the book is devoted to tracking the comings and goings and shifting relationships there. Gladys, the granddaughter Ruley helped raise, eventually came back home to live with four daughters she had from a relationship with a man from Boston. His daughter Marion returned there to live after her marriage in 1937 to Douglas Harris. They later had a son who was a toddler when Harris was found dead in the well.

Wilhelmina remained a central figure in the household as domineering stepmother and step-grandmother. A source of tension, according to Lindsey and Traynum, was Ruley's decision to deed his property to Marion while he was still alive. But Wilhelmina stayed with Ruley until almost the end, moving out only months before his death. Three decades later, when Smith began his research, family members told him they suspected Ruley's possessions and white wife may have aroused resentment among his white neighbors and provided a motive for violence or murder. Their suspicions carried enough weight that in 1996, with Ruley's reputation as an important artist now established, the New London County state's attorney's office agreed to review the case file. Their finding was that the evidence did not justify the family's request to have his body exhumed.

The whereabouts of Ruley's paintings posed a second mystery for those more interested in Ruley's art. During his life Ruley is believed to have produced hundreds of paintings. The results of his artistic urges were so prolific that they even included painted scenes on the window screens in his house. Lindsey and Traynum note that Ruley stored paintings by the bunch in two rooms of his farmhouse. The Slater Museum's Gualtieri, in *Discovering Ellis Ruley*, recalled that when he visited Ruley around the time of the 1952 exhibition, he found paintings stacked so thick that that bugs ran when he moved them.

Given the spectacular view of Norwich that Ruley had from his hilltop sanctuary, Gualtieri was struck by an omission in Ruley's subject matter for his paintings. Gualtieri was quoted as wondering why nothing of Norwich was recognizable in any of the paintings. "I concluded that this type of subject matter didn't interest him," Gualtieri told Smith. The consensus of scholars and critics searching for the wellspring of Ruley's art, however, is that his hometown is indeed present, that it had seeped into his paintings, giving them the tension that lifts them from ordinary to great. Reviewing the retrospective during its stop at the American Folk Art Museum, *New York Times* critic Holland Cotter, noting the location of Ruley's property, wrote that his "Eden is less a place than a state of mind, dappled with sunshine but troubled by distant thunder."[5]

The obvious source of that thunder was the racial friction cited by Hollander and Kogan in their critical essay. "Ellis Ruley was an African-American man living in the often hostile environment of the white community of Norwich. . . . He owned his own home, property and car, allowing him an independence that seems to have at once amused and goaded his neighbors," they write.

Hollander and Kogan trace many of the subjects of Ruley's work to photographs he would have seen in mass magazines such as *Life* and *National Geographic* and in newspapers. That explains how he might have become fascinated with movie-star cowboys or the famous Chief Grey Owl, whose real name was Archibald Belaney. His paintings may look pretty at first glance, but they soon can turn disturbing. Many have hunting themes, some in which the predators are other animals and some in which the predators are human. Only one painting, "Stag Hunt," shows a figure who is recognizably black. He stands with a rifle on a rocky outcropping watching a deer defend itself from a pack of dogs.

His "Adam and Eve" contains no threatening elements, but the two figures look somber. Scholars speculate the bearded Adam may be a near self-portrait, but at least one great-grandchild scoffed at that possibility. In a *Hartford Courant* interview DeLois Lindsey gave at the time the Atheneum hosted the Ruley retrospective, she said her mother told her his models for Adam and Eve came from a Bible. Lindsey also said she couldn't believe Ruley would portray himself as white. She guessed he populated his paintings with white people mainly to make them more marketable.[6]

Gualtieri was also interviewed in conjunction with the Atheneum exhibition. He thought Ruley was less influenced by racism than the essays in *Discovering Ellis Ruley* suggest. Gualtieri said Ruley struck him as an almost joyous man whose main struggle was with his art. He said some saw a religious quality in his paintings. Holland Cotter in his *New York Times* review judged Ruley to be a "moralist at heart" like many other "paradise seekers." His search for his particular Eden was conducted through his paintings.

In his brief foreword to *Discovering Ellis Ruley*, Yale art professor Robert Farris Thompson depicts Ruley as being spiritually akin to two people whose lives were widely separated by time and space. The first was Boston Trow Trow, who died in 1772 and is now remembered as a Black Governor in Norwich. As a leader of Norwich's "African tribe," Trow Trow organized parades and other festivities with an aesthetic that predicted the coming of Ruley and his art, Thompson writes.

Ruley's other "spiritual brother," Thompson suggests, was the Bahamian artist Amos Ferguson, another paradise seeker. Thompson wrote that Ferguson once told him that he painted from nature because he was following the advice God gave Adam and Eve in the Garden of Eden. "The Lord said: I give you the prettiest space goin': water and flowers and birds flyin' round. Find happiness in the flowers and the birds."

So too, Thompson concludes, Ruley sought in his paintings the same source of happiness.

Notes

This essay was adapted from one written for connecticuthistory.org.

1. Glenn Robert Smith and Robert Kenner, *Discovering Ellis Ruley: The Story of an American Outsider Artist* (New York: Crown Publishers, 1993).
2. DeLois C. Lindsey and Sheila L. Traynum, *A Promise to My Mother: The Saga of the Ellis Walter Ruley Family* (San Diego: Black Forest Press, 2003).

3. Ellis Ruley obituary, *Norwich Bulletin*, January 17, 1959.

4. Arthur Lathrop, *Twentieth-Century Norwich, Connecticut* (Salem: Higginson Book Co., 2007).

5. Holland Carter, "Ellis Ruley," *New York Times*, April 5, 1996.

6. Joel Lang, "Discovering Ellis Ruley," *Northeast Magazine/The Hartford Courant*, September 8, 1996.

## 43 "Just Like Georgia Except for the Climate"

*Black Life at Mid-Century in Ann Petry's* The Narrows

Award-winning writer Ann Petry explored many facets of the black experience in her fiction. Born in Saybrook (now Old Saybrook), Connecticut, just after the turn of the twentieth century, she brought to her work the sensibility of someone who grew up as part of a tiny minority and who saw the horrors of ghetto living during the nine years she spent in New York City. Her novel *The Narrows* (1953) offers a commentary on the racial, class, and economic conflicts that lie beneath the surface in mid-century New England. It is the story of a doomed love affair between a handsome, brilliant young black man and a rich, white, married woman. Drawing on an incident that occurred in Hawaii in the 1930s, Petry set her novel in a port city in Connecticut just after World War II. Petry has "Cesar the writing man" scrawl the novel's theme in chalk on the sidewalk: "Is there anything whereof it may be said, See, this is new? It hath been already of old time, which was before us."[1]

Early in the story, Camilla (Camilo) Treadway Sheffield, the heiress to a gun-manufacturing fortune, wanders down to the dock in the black section of Monmouth. She becomes frightened and runs into the arms of a man she cannot see clearly in the dark and fog. Lincoln Williams (Link) has returned to the city of his birth from a four-year stint in the navy. Despite his Dartmouth education, the only job he can find is behind the bar at the Last Chance, a dive run by the local black crime kingpin. Link and Camilo fall in love, but when her mother and husband learn of the affair, they exact their revenge.

Much of the story unfolds in the ghetto called The Narrows where the orphan Link has grown up in the household of a couple he calls Aunt Abbie and Uncle Theodore. The place and the people, including Abbie Crunch, the kingpin Bill Hod, and Abbie's tenant Malcolm Powther, butler to Camilo's mother, embody the range of black experience. Link can easily navigate black and white worlds. Abbie wants to be white. Hod is a black-power advocate. Powther stands on propriety as he sees it.

With its cramped living quarters and undesirable spaces, The Narrows becomes a character in the novel. It goes by a variety of names, among them The Bottom, Little Harlem, Dark Town, and Niggertown, common terms for ghettoes throughout the country. Petry fashioned The Narrows after the black sections of Hartford and New London. Monmouth resembles Hartford, which thrived on gun manufacture and attracted successive waves of immigrants, and was "half-city, half-suburban," with "residences brick, many of them frame, almost all with some kind of backyard, even if only a scrap, streets fairly wide." New London with its waterfront catering to sailors was by the 1940s "a curious place—retrograde—I think—going backward not forward—subject to certain kinds of forces" because of the long decline of the whaling industry.[2]

The effect *The Narrows* has on people can be corrosive. The people are "bobtail, ragtail, flotsam and jetsam," Petry writes.[3] It is a place of inferior goods, of defeated expectations, of many dreams deferred. Abbie's friend the funeral director Frances Jackson, who aspired to practice medicine, has learned to live with the humiliation of being called "[t]hat nigger woman undertaker" by the Irish casket maker.[4]

A stranger to Monmouth asks if they have just buried his brother in a colored cemetery. Assistant funeral director Howard Thomas (who wanted to be a lawyer), replies, "No . . . but in another ten years or so we'll have that, too. We've got two practically colored schools and we've got a separate place for the colored to live, and separate places for them to go to church, and it won't be long before we'll work up to a separate place for the colored to lie in after they're dead. . . . Then you'll feel right at home here in Monmouth. It'll be just like Georgia except for the climate."[5]

Not everyone shares that view. Petry shows the attitudes of some Northern blacks hold toward the South when Frances Jackson discusses her trip to South Carolina to retrieve the body of the mother of the local numbers baron. She tells Abbie, "They don't want her buried there. They say they won't even leave their dead in the South, nothing of theirs will they leave there. . . ."[6] They find Northern discrimination preferable to the beatings and lynchings they have escaped.

Each character encounters a different facet of the color line, reflecting Petry's own experiences growing up and living in Connecticut.

As Petry did, Link suffers because of a racist teacher. Miss Dwight has Link play Sambo in a minstrel show. Petry's sixth-grade teacher made her read the part of Jupiter, the former slave and "elderly negro" in Edgar Allan Poe's "The Gold Bug." Poe rendered Jupiter's words in the broadest dialect, "dey" for "they" and "goole" for "gold." Petry felt mortified as her classmates laughed at her.[7]

Another teacher restored her self-esteem, and she gives Link that uplift as well. Petry's teacher was Harold White, the basis for the character Robert Watson White. Harold White noticed that she seemed to duck and frown whenever the issue of slavery arose. He had her read widely and encouraged her to talk about the subject. He convinced her that "slavery was not my shame."[8] The fictional Mr. White gives Link a passion for history that contributes to his downfall. He reflects that he knows too much about "the various hells" that began when the first blacks arrived on a Dutch slaver in 1619.

The irony was that in 1964, Petry stopped Harold White's wife from putting blackface on my white schoolmates for a high school production of Carson McCullers's *The Member of the Wedding*.[9] My mother was so protective that I knew nothing of this incident until I read her journal. She always shielded me from the soul-destroying racism that she encountered.

While Petry used her own experience in writing about Link's early life, her models for the adult Link were her husband, George Petry, and a friend Carl Offord.[10] My father, like Link, had stunning good looks, played football, attended an Ivy League school, and was intellectually overqualified for the available jobs. Offord was a newspaper publisher and writer whose 1943 novel *The White Face* concerned a black man driven by hatred to violence against whites. Both men served in World War II and grew up without their mothers.

Link suffers the sting of racism but does not automatically assume that white people mean danger. Unsure whether Camilo is white or "high yaller," he watches the waiter Bug Eyes, who grew up in the South. As he sees Camilo from a distance, Bug Eyes is smiling, friendly. He looks again, and his face becomes hostile, "complex and dangerous." When he realizes she is white, his defenses go up against the expected attack. Link draws his own conclusion based on a different cue. Camilo lets him drive her Cadillac and comments, "Oh, you've driven one of these before." Link thinks, "Oh, you've held a tennis racket before, oh, you've worn shoes before. . . . That surprised condescension in the voice is an unmistakable characteristic of the Caucasian, a special characteristic of the female Caucasian."[11] Petry has Link recognize the tone that no black woman, however pale, would use in addressing another of her own race.

Petry draws Abbie as someone who wants to be white. Though struggling financially, she is ever the patrician: "[S]hort, plump, . . . expressive-eyed. . . . She had New England aristocrat written all over her, in the straight back, . . . in the Yankee twang of her speech."[12] That description also fit Petry's mother, Bertha James Lane. The similarities do not end there. Both the character and the woman became the first black president of the local Women's Christian Temperance Union. This position gives Abbie a degree of superiority over the white members of the organization. Her attitude carries over into her dealings with the shopkeepers. She calls the grocer "Davioli" and the tailor "Quagliamatti," without honorifics. Here Petry raises the possibility that even an impoverished colored woman can raise herself above the average run of white people.

Among the burdens Abbie imposes on Link is the necessity to uphold The Race, to be superior to white people: "cleaner, smarter, thriftier, more ambitious"; also polite, punctual, and conservatively dressed so that white people will like him. Abbie refuses to buy watermelons and porgies because whites associate them with colored people. She never fries fish or chicken because the house will smell. Link's reaction to these admonitions is two-fold. "[I]t made him feel as though he were carrying The Race around with him all the time."[13] And it made him recognize that Abbie feels superior to most blacks. When she says she thinks colored people are all stomach and no mind, "He was temped to say, 'But Miss Abbie, that's not possible. Aren't you colored, too?' and never did."[14] Abbie's attitude reflects the feelings of Petry's mother, who had benefited from the help of powerful white women in Hartford. In a letter to her younger sister, Lane wrote, "is there anything that can beat white?"[15]

Even more proper and class-conscious than Abbie is Powther, the Treadway butler and Abbie's tenant. Petry modeled Powther on Hartford resident Barksdale Hicks in that they both worked as butler for a private family. Powther appears to Abbie with elegant manners and skin "just a shade darker than her own," with "creased trousers, highly polished shoes."[16] He appreciates his employer's riches—Gainsborough paintings, Bateman tea set, Versailles flatware, Imari bowls. He is also racist, as he refers to the chauffeur as "Al the Nazi," who dislikes Powther but changes his mind after Powther saves his life "just like a white man."[17] Powther establishes his superiority to the white servants by making it clear that he has worked for wealthier and more established people than the Treadways.

Powther believes himself to be superior to most blacks (and many whites) but comes to realize that even Mrs. Treadway can't distinguish him from Link. All black men look alike to her. Weak Knees, the cook at the Last Chance, escalates the complaint, saying that "whafolks" believe all black people think alike. They ask what he thinks of actor, singer, lawyer, and activist Paul Robeson (who lived in Enfield, Connecticut from 1941 to 1953) because one black man can speak for them all. Petry reflects the feelings of many blacks when she has Weak Knees respond that Robeson ought to return to the Soviet Union because "'[O]ver there if he went around talkin' about the changes he wanted made, why he'd get hisself shot full of holes, but nobody over there would be goin' around about to piss in their pants because he was a black man talkin' the wrong kind of politics. . . . And if his boy went and married hisself a little white chickadee over there in Russia, the whafolks wouldn't waste their time runnin' to all the colored folks they see askin' 'em what they thought about it.'"[18]

Abbie reflects on the differences between Powther and her deceased husband, Major Theodore Crunch. He has been dead for eighteen years when the novel opens but looms over the action. The Major was based in part on Petry's paternal grandfather, "Major" Theodore Lane, who moved his family from "Jersey" to Hartford in the 1870s. Abbie wants to attend a white church, but Major Crunch says he can't rise to a position of authority there. Both the fictional and real Majors became deacons. Major Lane served at Talcott Street (now Faith) Congregational Church. Petry also borrowed from the life of her maternal grandfather, Willis Samuel James. Major Crunch works as a chauffeur for a governor as did Sam James, who received a letter of recommendation from Connecticut Governor Marshall Jewel.[19] Petry's grandfathers had overcome, respectively, a hardscrabble farming life and slavery to become successful men, and she embodied their successes in Major Crunch.

The Crunch family adds another dimension. Stand-ins for the Lanes, they are "an ungodly crew." The Major calls them "swamp niggers": Uncle Zeke can levitate; a great-grandfather bites off the ear of an Irishman; the witch doctor Aunt Hal, forbidden to attend a funeral, appears riding atop the hearse and thumbing her nose at the rest of the family who try to kill her. Petry uses the "emotional, primitive" Crunches to show that not all black people want the trappings of whiteness and that hostility can run both ways.

In the same lawless category is Bill Hod, who rescues young Link after Abbie neglects him after her husband's death. Hod owns the bar, the local house of prostitution—and the local (white) police chief. He intervenes on Link's behalf after the Sambo incident. A word from Hod, and the teacher no longer singles out Link and is instead carefully polite to him.

Petry's defender was her father, Peter C. Lane. He wrote to *The Crisis* in about 1920 complaining that a woman refused to teach his daughters and niece. The teacher "told them before the whole class that they could 'go to Glory to get a lesson.'" She also told them at the beginning of the term that they would not be promoted. Not only were they promoted, they all graduated. Petry's sister, Helen, went to Pembroke College, and the niece, Helen Chisholm, to Russell Sage College. Petry went on to receive a degree from the Connecticut College of Pharmacy.

Link's re-education begins with Hod's story of the 1919 Chicago riots in which white people attacked innocent blacks. When a mob arrived at Ma Winters's rooming house, she "stood at the top of the stairs with a loaded shotgun in her hand, not shouting, not talking loud, just saying, conversationally, 'I'm goin' to shoot the first white bastard who puts his foot on that bottom step.' And did. And laughed. And aimed again. 'Come on,' she said, 'some of the rest of you sons of bitches put your white feet on my stairs.' And they backed out of the door, . . . left a white man, a dead white man, there in the hall, lying on his back, a bloody mess where his face had been."[20] Hod and Weak Knees also imprint on Link the beautiful side of blackness, praising the beauty of black birds, the strength of ebony, and the rarity of black jewels.

Petry drew many of the details of Hod's life from her most outrageously colorful maternal uncle, Willis Howard James, from whom she learned the Ma Winters story. Uncle Bill admitted shooting a white man, spent time on a chain gang in Georgia, and was nearly lynched. He hopped freight trains all over the East Coast and worked the eastern seaboard and midwest as a waiter, a barber, a circus roustabout, and apparently as a smuggler. Someone in *The Narrows* asks what a "Chinaman's chance" means. Frances Jackson says it refers to Chinese immigrants who were tied up in burlap and weighted with stones. "I have heard it said that Bill Hod used to bring them in over the Canadian border. Years ago. At a thousand dollars a head. If the border patrol stopped him, challenged the great god Hod, why he dumped the Chinese overboard."[21] Petry gleaned this bit of information from Uncle Bill. Through him, she makes the point that even those with comparatively little power can maintain control in their own limited spheres.

While blacks in *The Narrows* live in isolation from whites, Petry also explores their common ground. Link and Camilo both realize that adults treat children as though they lack feelings and that children can be equally cruel. A teenaged Camilo was teased by her schoolmates because she was fat. Link can still hear the kids telling him the pigeons were saying, "Lookitthecoon."[22]

Meals in *The Narrows* resemble those eaten all over New England. Abbie serves baked beans, brown bread sliced with a string, homemade pickles, coleslaw, gingerbread, and applesauce. Other residents balance the fried chicken, kale with ham, and red rice of the Great Migration as well. Powther's wife cooks roast beef, potatoes, and fresh vegetables. Weak Knees creates world cuisine, making his shrimp salad with avocado and garlic.

These shared experiences do not mean that the white residents of Monmouth are becoming more accepting, but the novel does conclude with two small rays of hope. As the local newspaper is sensationalizing crimes by black people, an escaped convict startles a woman in her kitchen. He stuffs a gag in her mouth, grabs some food, and runs. The woman tells a reporter, "'I hollered because I didn't know he was there in the kitchen. . . . I'da hollered the same way if he'd a been a big white man showing up so sudden and unexpected. . . .'"[23] She insists that he never "bothered" her and instructs the reporter not to say he did.

Abbie Crunch offers greater expectations. When she realizes that Bill Hod is planning to kill Camilo, she heads for the police station to try to stop him. Here is a black woman reaching out to a white woman she has previously spurned.

Despite its dark message, *The Narrows* teaches that reactions born of ignorance or fear can be changed. Perhaps Monmouth is not becoming like Georgia. Rather than breeding the expected contempt, familiarity may breed understanding and acceptance. Maybe there is something new under the sun.

Notes

1. Ann Petry, *The Narrows* (New York: Kensington Publishing Corporation, 2008), 91.

2. Ann Petry's journal, January 20, 1949, and other undated notes. No page numbers. For more information on the place and the people, see

Elisabeth Petry, ed., *Can Anything Beat White? A Black Family's Letters* (Jackson, Mississippi: University Press of Mississippi, 2005); and Elisabeth Petry, *At Home Inside: A Daughter's Tribute to Ann Petry* (Jackson, Mississippi: University Press of Mississippi, 2008).

3. *The Narrows*, 418.

4. Ibid., 235.

5. Ibid., 229.

6. Ibid., 218–19.

7. Ann Petry's journal, May 6, 1990.

8. Notes for a lecture delivered May 12, 1990, at Wesleyan University; Ann Petry's journal, May 10, 1990.

9. Ann Petry's journal, November 13, 1964.

10. "And if I give Link the characteristics of G and say Carl Offord ought to be able to produce a believable male," in Ann Petry's journal, January 14, 1949.

11. *The Narrows*, 72.

12. Ibid., 171.

13. Ibid., 138.

14. Ibid., 124.

15. Letter from Bertha Lane to Anna Louise James, October 28, 1906. The original is at the Beinecke Rare Book and Manuscript Library at Yale University.

16. *The Narrows*, 7.

17. Ibid., 162.

18. Ibid., 265–66.

19. The original is at the Beinecke Library, Yale University.

20. *The Narrows*, 144.

21. Ibid., 423.

22. Ibid., 134.

23. Ibid., 377.

# 44 Marian Anderson's Studio

Connecticut's African-American Freedom Trail includes a stop at the Marian Anderson studio in Danbury. Marian Anderson was one of the most celebrated opera singers of the twentieth century and the first African American to perform in New York City's Metropolitan Opera, in 1955. Anderson and her husband, architect Orpheus Fisher, established a home base in Danbury on Joe's Hill Road in 1940, naming it Marianna Farm. The twenty-four-foot by twenty-foot practice studio was saved by the Connecticut Trust for Historic Preservation from destruction by developers who proposed a privately owned subdivision on the land in 1999. The studio was relocated to the Main Street site of the Danbury Historical Society.

Born in Philadelphia on February 27, 1897, Marian Anderson earned the nickname "Baby Contralto" by the age of six. She became renowned worldwide for her "rich in timbre" and "smooth as satin" voice, as a 1930 review in the *New York Telegram* noted, yet in her home country Anderson struggled for success. In a now famous 1939 incident, she was denied use of Constitution Hall in Washington D.C., by the Daughters of the American Revolution, the proprietor of the building that had, in 1932, inserted a "white artists only" clause into its rental contract. First Lady Eleanor Roosevelt resigned from the D.A.R., explaining she was "in complete disagreement with the attitude" the organization showed in banning Anderson from Constitution Hall.

What followed was the concert for which Marian Anderson is best remembered. On April 9, 1939, Anderson sang from the steps of the Lincoln Memorial, directly south of Constitution Hall, giving a free outdoor concert to an estimated audience of 75,000. The statue of Abraham Lincoln stood steadfast behind her. Alan Keiler, in *Marian Anderson: A Singer's Journey* (2002), reported that years later Anderson simply explained that after the concert was initially canceled, "Mrs. Roosevelt then invited her to sing at the Lincoln Memorial." (The D.A.R. later did away with the whites-only restric-

FIGURE 44-1 Marian
Anderson, D'Arlene
Studios, 1936.
*The Amistad Center
for Art & Culture, Inc.,
Simpson Collection,
1987.1.1561*

tion, and Anderson sang at Constitution Hall several times in the
1940s, 1950s, and 1960s.)

Seeking a retreat away from the public eye, Anderson and Fisher
bought a three-story Victorian farmhouse on 100 acres of land in
Danbury in 1940. Keiler reports that they chose the site because it
was the only property whose seller was not aware of who Fisher's
wife was. (Fisher, while African American, was light skinned enough
to not attract scrutiny.) At Marianna Farm, Anderson could regroup
after months of touring and rehearse undisturbed in the studio,
which was built with a cove ceiling that allowed for favorable acous-
tics. A kitchen and washroom were added in anticipation of long
hours spent at the piano by Anderson and her accompanist, Franz
Rupp.

Over the more than four decades they lived in Danbury, Anderson and Fisher became valued citizens. Anderson joined the Danbury Music Centre board of directors, ensuring that she stayed musically connected to her local community. Fisher designed Danbury's New Hope Baptist Church, where they were active members and where Anderson held a memorial for her husband after he died in 1986. Anderson also helped to open, in 1966, the Danbury Museum's Huntington Hall, the modern exhibit building at the Danbury Historical Society. She is remembered as being friendly to all she crossed paths with. Anderson lived on Marianna Farm until 1992, a year before she died at age 96. For fifty years she traveled the world, but there is no doubt Danbury was where Marian Anderson felt most at home.

Today, the blue clapboard studio contains relics of a bygone era—compositions from which the famed contralto practiced, black-and-white photos of life on the farm, and four vintage gowns Anderson wore while performing on stage. It is now used as an exhibition space and for small concerts, and it is available for weddings. The Danbury Historical Society offers educational programs about Marian Anderson every February.

Note

This essay appeared in the Fall 2008 issue of *Connecticut Explored*.

# 45 From Fields to Footlights

## *Gwen Reed*

The start of Gwen Reed's acting career is like something out of a Hollywood movie. Raised in Connecticut's tobacco fields, she was working as a secretary with a small theater troupe when she stepped out from behind the scenes to take a bit part. Noticed by critics and audiences, she continued acting for more than three decades. Though fame and fortune were not part of Reed's story, she was a familiar face on Hartford area stages and afternoon television, playing many roles, from the imposing Maria in *Porgy and Bess* to the mysterious Assunta in *The Rose Tattoo* to the wise and loving Bernice in *The Member of the Wedding*. None of these roles had as long a run, however, nor brought as much attention, as her seventeen-year stint as an employee of the Quaker Oats Company. At grocery store openings, Jaycee breakfasts, and school assemblies, dressed in the familiar apron and red-and-white bandana, Reed was one of many women employed by the company to play Aunt Jemima, serving up freshly cooked pancakes and sometimes a song or two. Quaker Oats maintained the illusion that, like department store Santas or theme-park characters, Aunt Jemima herself, not a performer in costume, had stopped by for the festivities. From 1946 to 1964, Gwen Reed worked more or less anonymously as the famous pancake-box cook. "Honey, it doesn't make any difference who I am," Reed told the *Portland Evening Press* (Maine) when asked to reveal her identity, "I'm happy to be here."

Portraying Aunt Jemima provided steady employment for Reed, a coveted situation for a performer. Though Reed now is most often associated with the character, the actress was also involved in two historical theatrical ventures in Hartford—the ambitious Depression-era Federal Theater Project, with which Reed made her debut, and the regional theater movement of the 1960s, experienced in Hartford via a brash new theater called the Hartford Stage Company, where Reed performed in its early seasons.

Her theatrical career and other aspects of her life are recorded in newspaper clippings, theater programs, scrapbooks, and other personal documents, which are now part of the Hartford Collection of the Hartford Public Library. These papers give an incomplete glimpse of a fascinating woman who came to the city as a migrant farm worker and stayed to become a beloved stage and television personality and teacher.

Gwen Reed was born Gwendolyn Clarke in 1912 in Harlem to Georgianna and George Nathanial Clarke. After Gwendolyn's birth, Georgianna fled both husband and Harlem, taking her daughter with her. The two drifted for many years as Georgianna worked as an itinerant field hand in Maine, Florida, California, and elsewhere.

The tobacco fields of Connecticut lured Georgianna and Gwendolyn to Hartford again and again. As a young child, Gwen earned money picking up fallen tobacco leaves in the sheds for ten cents an hour. The two permanently settled in Hartford in 1921, where Gwen graduated from Arsenal Elementary and Hartford Public High School. Her greatest education may have come, however, at her mother's knee, where she acquired a love of literature and storytelling. In the migrant camps, after writing or reading letters for illiterate workers, Georgianna would read Tennyson and Shakespeare. "She taught me the twenty-third Psalm," Gwen once told a reporter, "while she knelt weeding cucumbers and radishes." After high school, Gwen continued to work in the tobacco fields. Though she attended Hartford Federal College hoping to become a lawyer, illness forced her to drop out. In 1935 she married John T. Reed. The marriage license lists his occupation as "truck driver," hers as "tobacco worker." After four years the couple separated and in 1948 divorced.

Reed eventually took a job as a secretary in a small black theater group, the Charles Gilpin Players. Named after the great African American actor who created the leading role in Eugene O'Neill's *The Emperor Jones*, the troupe was formed (as were many other Gilpin Players around the country) shortly after President Warren G. Harding honored Charles Gilpin at the White House in 1921. In the fall of 1936, in the midst of the Depression, the financially strapped Gilpin Players turned to the federal government for financial and artistic help, which was provided through the Federal Theater Project.

The Federal Arts Program was inaugurated in 1935 as a program of the Works Progress Administration (WPA) to put writers, painters, musicians, and theater practitioners to work. Though the idea provoked controversy, WPA head Henry Hopkins answered his critics with the line, "Hell, they've got to eat just like other people."

FIGURE 45-1 Gwen Reed, c. 1950s. *Hartford History Collection, Hartford History Center, Hartford Public Library*

The Federal Theater Project was the theatrical arm of the WPA. It funded companies throughout the nation and sent professionals to groups that needed them. Project Director Mollie Flanagan insisted on the highest artistic standards, though WPA rules often hindered planning and created tension between amateurs and professionals. Within the WPA, the Federal Theater Project was seen as an unwelcome stepchild, often ignored by the very officials who were administering the program. Nevertheless, the Federal Theater Project forged ahead, with notable successes by Orson Welles and John Houseman. Its Connecticut arm began in New Haven with a production of *Men Must Fight*. It then moved to Hartford, where it provided work for a young Ed Begley and premiered the stage adaptation of Sinclair Lewis's novel *It Can't Happen Here* simultaneously with troupes in twenty other cities.

## "The Charles S. Gilpen Dramatic Club of Hartford formed in 1922"

The Charles S. Gilpin Dramatic Club of Hartford was formed in 1922 by a few Blacks who were interested in the theater. Among them were Benjamin and Lillian Tillinsen, in whose home they met; W. Earle Smith, Bertha Washington, Fannie Carroll, Ethel Goode, Harriett Brown. J. Carl Canty, Katie Hartnett, Sidney Lopez, Ella Miller, Carl Ball, Norman Ball, Mr. and Mrs. Eugene Shaw, Mr. and Mrs. Joseph Callaway, Mary Blade and Ed Sweat.

They soon moved to a rented rehearsal hall on Chappell St. when other people joined the group including Katrina Flagg, Miriam White, Marietta Canty, who went on to nine years in summer stock and Broadway and 11 years in Hollywood, Mrs. Sydney Johnson, Ada Jacklyn, Cicero Wiggins, Elizabeth Lane, Daisey Pounds, Theodore Howard, Ted Lane, Roland Irving, Ethel Hicks, Marie Walker, Harriet Johnston and others.

They were directed by Hallie Galbert Reynolds who was a member of the Church of the Redeemer, on whose stage most of their plays were given. When the Federal Theater came to Hartford in the early 1930's the Gilpin Club became the nucleus of their group.

To be continued.

Lois Tillman

BR — Russell Moore, Marietta Canty, J.D. Marshall, Albert James, Donald Wheeldin, Dave Majors, Sidney Lopez, Katie Hartnett, William Taylor, Harriet Brown.
FR — Bertha Washington, Fannie Carroll, Ethel Goode, W. Earle Smith, Miriam White, Mary Blade, Lillian Tillman, Katrina Flagg. Photo taken on stage of the Church of the Redeemer about 1923  *Source: NORTHEND AGENT'S FEB. 8, 1978 P.5*

FIGURE 45-2 Marietta Canty (*back row, second from left*) also had a successful acting career after appearing in the Gilpin Players. This February 8, 1978 *Northend (Hartford) Agent* article reprinted a c. 1923 photo. *Hartford History Collection, Hartford History Center, Hartford Public Library*

The Charles Gilpin Players applied to the program for a professional director and in 1936 was organized as one of the Federal Theater Project's Negro Units. These specialized companies for African American performers had less support than the white troupes and were usually run by white directors. They were suspected, both in and out of the WPA, of being social programs rather than artistic initiatives. But the Negro Units remain an important chapter in American theatre history, having nurtured the careers of important black artists and funded notable productions such as *Swing Mikado*, *Turpentine*, *Big White Fog*, and the "voodoo" *Macbeth* directed by Orson Welles. Negro Units were also formed in New York, Chicago, Seattle, Philadelphia, Boston, San Francisco, Atlanta, Oklahoma City, Tulsa, Durham, Raleigh, New Orleans, Detroit, Cleveland, Portland, Los Angeles, Greensboro, and Birmingham.

In Hartford the Negro Unit was under the direction of Michael Adrian (born Victor Ecchevaria in Puerto Rico), who also worked with Hartford's white unit as a director and designer. His 1936 production of *The Sabine Women* at the Palace Theatre on Main Street excited both public and critics. "There is no limit to what might be accomplished by Hartford's Negro Unit," the *Hartford Times* wrote, "which is now under the guiding genius of Michael Adrian, as remarkable a director as ever put on a show in Connecticut." Aside from Adrian and some technicians, the Charles Gilpin Players only had a staff of four, including Reed, relying on some one hundred volunteers. The success of *The Sabine Women* led the WPA to establish the group as a fully paid operation. For all intents and purposes The Gilpin Players were no more, having been completely transformed into Connecticut's Negro Unit. Most of the subsequent productions were staged in the Wadsworth Atheneum's theater in the Avery Memorial, though some toured to other locations.

On June 18, 1937, the Negro Unit presented *Trilogy in Black*, commissioned by the troupe from playwright Ward Courtney. Gwendolyn Reed played the small role of "1st Lady." Though she had often made up her own plays as a young girl and had performed in some church presentations this was truly her debut as an actress. No longer the company's secretary, Reed then appeared in the chorus of *The Emperor Jones* and in *Jericho*; the press singled her out in reviews of both performances. Subsequent roles in *The World We Live In*, *Mississippi Rainbow*, and *In the Valley* established Reed as a Federal Theater Project favorite. As May in Paul Green's *The Field God* in February 1938, one reviewer lauded the actress as "by far the best player." The next month she played Marie in Dorothy and Du-Bose Heyward's *Porgy*, the *Hartford Times* calling her "voluble and convincing . . . with a heart as big as all outdoors."

In October 1938, the Negro and white companies in Hartford combined forces to present William DuBois's *Haiti*, in which Reed played a small role. She was part of the ensemble when they merged again in January 1939 to present the agit-prop play about the housing crisis, *One Third of A Nation*, at the Avery and Bushnell memorials. In preparation for that massive project, intensive classes in speech and movement were held for members of both companies. Later that year the entire Federal Theater Project ended, torpedoed by congressional opponents of the New Deal who painted the enterprise as a platform for Communist propagandists. The Hartford Negro Unit disbanded. Reed went back to the tobacco fields to earn a living. Her acting career, however, was not over.

In 1946, Reed began impersonating Aunt Jemima. Mostly in New England, Reed appeared at fairs, parades, picnics, hotels, and department stores and went into schools with a musical program. She was not, of course, the only one to perform as Aunt Jemima. Quaker Oats employed performers across the country to portray the fictional cook. From 1893, when Nancy Green first impersonated Aunt Jemima at the World's Columbia Exposition in Chicago, though the 1960s, actresses flipped pancakes while repeating the company's invented legend about being the Higgim Plantation's culinary genius.

In newspaper clippings and announcements of her appearances, Gwen Reed's name is never mentioned. A *Manchester* (Connecticut) *Herald* photo caption of 1955 is typical: "Aunt Jemima arrived in town today, brilliant in her red and white check outfit, and Mayor Harold A. Turkington, together with Elk dignitaries, welcomed her." When she went into the schools with her music program, however, the teachers knew the actress's real name, as letters of thanks and praise attest. As Reed became a veteran spokesperson, Quaker Oats accommodated her family obligations; when Reed's mother grew increasingly ill, her territory was adjusted so she would never be far from home. In her sixteenth year, she was "inducted" into the company's Aunt Jemima Hall of Fame.

Playing Aunt Jemima did not keep Reed from playing other roles. An active participant in community theaters, she appeared with the Mark Twain Masquers, Cue and Curtain, Glastonbury Players, Center Playhouse, Image Playhouse, Triangle Players, and The Oval, winning rave reviews for her performances in *Stage Door*, *Rain*, *Finian's Rainbow*, *Purlie Victorious*, *Raisin in the Sun*, *The Little Foxes*, *The Member of the Wedding*, and *Showboat*. She was also a director of the Hartford Community Players, a black troupe dedicated to promoting theater in the African American community, in the 1940s and 1950s.

Reed's work in those theaters brought her attention, but no pay. One theatrical venture with which Reed was involved, however, not only paid, but grew to become a major cultural institution. On April 1, 1964, in a converted grocery store warehouse on Kinsley Street, the Hartford Stage Company opened its doors with a production of *Othello*. Its mission was to bring serious professional theater to the area, in contrast to the educational, community, or touring commercial shows that were available at the time. Though founder Jacques Cartier focused his attention on Hartford, the company's creation was part of a movement across the country. In Minneapolis, New Haven, Louisville, Los Angeles, and elsewhere, theaters dedicated to classical works, innovative new plays, and high standards of professionalism sprang up. Hartford Stage Company proved a fertile ground for major talents of the next four decades. Reed played Sookie in Cartier's production of Tennessee Williams's *Cat on a Hot Tin Roof* in 1965 and was an understudy for Max Frisch's *The Firebugs* in 1968. That same year she appeared in Williams's *The Rose Tattoo* as the medicine woman, Assunta. In 1970, she joined the theater's board of directors for a four-year term.

By the time of *The Rose Tattoo*, Reed had been active in educational and community work for many years. She worked in schools, with the Jobs Corp, and with early childhood initiatives. She developed the preschool project Story Time for Tots and taught in the nascent Head Start and Reading Is Fundamental programs. Reed's educational and theatrical pursuits combined in her 1960s television show "Story Time with Gwen Reed" that had Hartford-area children tuning in every Friday afternoon to Channel 3.

Gwen Reed's career was not a lucrative one. When she died in 1974, she left behind few material possessions in the Bellevue Housing Project where she lived. But those who knew her, knew her life was rich, as the many awards, citations, and letters in her collection attest. When Reed could not appear one Friday for her Story Time program, children wrote in telling her how much they missed her. A local group organized a tribute to her in 1968 to honor her theatrical, educational, and community work. Surprisingly, for a woman who portrayed a renowned pancake-maker for so many years, she claimed she could not "cook a morsel" and that she relied on her many friends for her meals. After her death a few friends acquired her personal papers for the Hartford Public Library, enabling later generations to learn of her work. On May 2, 1981, Hartford Mayor George A. Athanson dedicated the Gwen Reed Room at the Ropkins branch of the Harford Public Library to be used, appropriately, for storytelling.

Many remember Reed from her Friday afternoon television show, some as a teacher, others as Aunt Jemima. But the whole of Reed's life and career is worth remembering, for it reveals the life of the artist, struggling to work for one's art and to work to pay one's bills at a time when neither was easy for an African American woman. From tobacco fields to television, from Hartford Stage to Head Start, from WPA projects to publicity appearances for a national consumer products company, Reed's life and career intersected important historical moments and social movements. We celebrate her today as a pioneer who stepped out of the tobacco fields and onto center stage to pursue her dreams.

Note

This essay appeared in the May/June/July 2004 issue of *Connecticut Explored*.

# 46 Baseball Legend Jackie Robinson's Sacrifices Off the Diamond

On April 11, 1947, the *Hartford Courant* announced in one of its sports stories that the Brooklyn Dodgers purchased the contract of Jack Roosevelt Robinson of the Montreal Royals.[1] Few people in Connecticut could have ever imagined that within seven years of breaking the color line in the Major Leagues Jackie Robinson would become a resident of Connecticut. While a resident of the state for nearly two decades at the end of his life, Robinson boldly continued his efforts to break the color line outside of baseball and confront discrimination nationally and in Connecticut.

His road to a home in Connecticut began in humble beginnings in the South and West. Although Robinson's place of birth on January 31, 1919, was near the small town of Cairo, Georgia, he spent his youth in Pasadena, California. Refusing to accept the harshness of the Jim Crow South, his mother, Mallie Robinson, decided to seek a better life for her children in the West when Robinson was very young. She also made the move to escape her marriage to Jerry Robinson, which failed because of his infidelity. Once the family settled in Pasadena, Mallie, like many poor mothers of the period, found steady work as a domestic and raised her five children with a focus on their acquiring a solid education. It soon became evident, however, that athletic talent was a part of their gifts. After completing his public school education, Robinson attended Pasadena Junior College (1937–1939) and UCLA (1939–41). He quickly emerged as a star athlete at both schools. His talents in baseball, football, and track were glowingly evident.[2] He followed in the footsteps of older brother, Mack Robinson who won a silver medal in the sprints at the 1936 Olympics.[3]

Although few people know it today, Robinson served as a Lieutenant in the U.S. Army during World War II. His stint in the military was not without controversy. Although he suffered through a humiliating court-martial for standing up for his rights aboard an army post bus, he survived the ordeal without punishment because of the work of a skillful young attorney, vigorous support of fellow African American officers, and watchful reporters from African American newspapers. In 1944, Robinson received an honorable discharge.[4]

His exit from the military set him on a course that would forever change Robinson and the nation. Looking for work, he found it playing professional baseball for the legendary Kansas City Monarchs of the Negro Leagues. Because the Major Leagues barred baseball players of African descent, the best black players toiled in the Negro Leagues.[5] They played an exciting brand of baseball in regular league games, plus players often went on barnstorming trips throughout of the United States. Other Negro League stars took their talents to leagues in the Caribbean, Mexico, and South America.

While Robinson did not know it at the time, he was soon, with the aid of legendary baseball executive Branch Rickey, to become one of nation's greatest trailblazers in sports and human rights. By 1945 Branch Rickey, president of the Brooklyn Dodgers, began to skillfully maneuver to integrate the Major Leagues. While Rickey talked about developing a team called the Brooklyn Brown Dodgers, his true focus was the integration of baseball. He received aid and support in the process from well-known African American newspapers such as the Pittsburgh's *Courier* and Baltimore's *Afro-American*. The discussion of building the Brown Dodgers allowed his elite scouts to scour the Negro Leagues for the best available talent. The names and talents of Leroy "Satchel" Paige and Josh Gibson were known widely among Negro League fans and barnstorming audiences in the country. However, Rickey wanted a special player, younger than thirty with little baggage. Both Paige and Gibson, entrenched stars, were past their prime. Dodger scouts reported to Rickey that Jackie Robinson seemed to have the promise and gifts needed to survive and excel in the majors. The scouts were clearly accurate.[6] Robinson's courage to integrate baseball forever changed the game and the nation. He went on to a Hall of Fame career and opened the door in the National League for future and lesser-known young stars, while Larry Doby, another future African American Hall of Famer, did the same in the American League.

With incredible dignity, Robinson spent ten years battling horrible racism and prejudice inside the baseball world. The move with his wife, Rachel, and three children to Stamford, Connecticut, came near the end of his remarkable professional baseball career. His family's move to Connecticut revealed the blatant discrimination in housing faced by all African Americans, celebrities and the general working class alike.

As early as 1952 or 1953, Rachel and Jackie Robinson decided to move from Long Island where they had bought a home in 1950. They were concerned about the deteriorating schools in their Long Island neighborhood, and wanted particularly to offer Jackie Jr., their eldest son, an opportunity for a quality integrated public education. Rachel took the lead in trying to find the right community where they hoped to build or purchase a new home. When they found appealing property in Purchase, New York, and tried to place a down payment, the owners removed the property from the market.[7]

Around this same time, the *Herald* of Bridgeport, Connecticut, began a series of stories on housing discrimination. The newspaper contacted and interviewed Rachel about the covert and overt difficulties of locating housing. In Robinson's autobiography, he said the *Herald* inaccurately argued that residents of North Stamford, Connecticut, worked tirelessly to keep their neighborhoods white only. Robinson believed that the article failed to capture Rachel's positive views on North Stamford. The article helped, however, to open an avenue of conversation among local ministers who wanted to make sure that outsiders viewed their community as anything but racist. North Stamford organized a committee to combat housing discrimination. Andrea Simon, wife of one of the founders of publishers Simon and Schuster, served as one of the stalwarts of the committee. When Rachel met with the committee, she squashed notions that she and Jackie simply wanted to stir up trouble. Simon asked a local real estate agent to join the meeting and afterwards, the real estate agent took Simon and Rachel to view several properties in the area. The agent showed them a large undeveloped piece of property on Cascade Road with a private lake. Rachel considered the property all she ever desired. In 1954 the couple placed a down payment for the Stamford property; they moved into their new home after construction was completed the following year.[8]

The Robinson family, Jackie, Rachel, Jackie Jr., Sharon, and David, became fixtures in the Stamford community. As history would have it, the family made the transition to Connecticut as the modern civil rights movement geared up for a new phase of activity. In 1954 the United States Supreme Court issued the famous *Brown v. Board of Education* decision that overturned *Plessy v. Ferguson* (the case that had legalized segregation in 1896.) By 1955 African Americans in Montgomery, Alabama, organized and carried out the successful boycott of the segregated bus system.

Always concerned about the plight of African Americans in the country, Jackie Robinson immersed himself in the struggle for community improvement and civil rights. After years of working to build a community center for its young people, in 1953 African Americans in the North End of Hartford turned to Robinson for help. Ella Brown, a local resident and police officer, was a major driving force in the efforts to build the community center. Speaking before a large audience at Weaver High School, the baseball star stressed that community centers often served as major support centers for the development of young people. He knew that he was an example of the impact that organized programs have on youngsters. Thanks to Robinson's public plea, the leaders of the efforts to build the center hoped to raise $500,000 for the project.[9]

Robinson retired from baseball in 1957, and Bill Black of New York–based Chock Full of Nuts's offer to work for the company as a well-paid vice president and director of personnel provided an excellent income and a boss who was sympathetic to the struggle of African Americans for civil rights.[10] Robinson, like many leading African American athletes of the period, fully immersed himself in the civil rights struggle.

When Chester Bowles, former governor of the state of Connecticut, decided to seek the Democratic Party's nomination for the U.S. Senate from Connecticut in 1958, he contacted Robinson for support. In his letter to Robinson, the liberal politician highlighted an article he planned to write for *Saturday Evening Post* about Gandhi's time as an attorney in South Africa and the needs of Americans in the South. Bowles also planned to include information on the movement for non-violent social change in Montgomery led by the Rev. Dr. Martin Luther King, Jr. In a May 1, 1958, reply, Robinson, a life-long member of the Republican Party, indicated that he admired and respected Bowles for his work and stances but decided not to get involved in politics for the moment.[11]

When the NAACP, the nation's oldest civil rights group, asked for his support for a Hartford event, Robinson eagerly agreed to do so. After serving as the national chairman for NAACP Freedom Fund Drive, in 1958 he accepted the offer to serve as master of ceremonies at a State Theatre show in Hartford, Connecticut, to aid the NAACP in its fight to combat racism and discrimination.[12]

Concerned about continued housing discrimination, in 1959

Robinson wrote to the *Hartford Courant* to urge the newspaper to support efforts to strengthen the Connecticut State Civil Rights Commission's "power to prevent discrimination in housing." The state legislature had recently begun deliberations on a bill that supporters believed might improve efforts for adequate housing for minorities. Robinson considered Governor Abraham Ribicoff and the majority of the state's residents "thinking and understanding people."[13]

Robinson was active in other areas of discrimination as well. Most African American men who loved golf played in black-only tournaments around the country, but Jackie's celebrity and name recognition sometimes provided access to play whenever he wanted. However, his celebrity did not totally insulate him from racism in the world of golf. According to Robinson, in 1958 a minority of the membership of a local Connecticut country club refused to accept him because their wives "objected" to his membership.

In 1962, he joined with a group of 969 people who criticized the building of a new high school in Stamford. Robinson, NAACP members, and other critics believed that district lines left few opportunities for African Americans to attend Rippowam, the new high school. Jackie was among the speakers who urged the city to increase the number of African American youngsters attending the new school. The speakers, Jackie included, also wanted to increase the number of wealthy white students at Stamford High School.[14]

Where he once shied away from politics, Robinson's support of Richard Nixon went back to 1960 when he decided to support Nixon's candidacy for the White House. Although Robinson had met and talked with John F. Kennedy, the eventual victor in the 1960 election, he disliked Kennedy's record on civil rights. This dated from Kennedy's conversations in 1959 with Governor John Patterson of Alabama, which outraged Robinson. Alabama was a bastion of racial hatred and discrimination at this time. Robinson felt that Nixon appeared more progressive on civil rights than Kennedy; consequently, the baseball star agreed to campaign for him.[15]

When Georgia officials jailed the Rev. Dr. Martin Luther King, Jr., leader of the Southern Christian Leadership Conference (SCLC) and nation's leading proponent of non-violent protest, for driving with an invalid license and sent the civil rights leader to the Reidsville State Prison in 1960, Robinson urged Nixon to take a stand against the act. Nixon refused to do so. However, the Kennedy brothers intervened. John Kennedy telephoned Coretta Scott King, wife of the civil rights leader, while Robert Kennedy worked political and judicial contacts to free King. John Kennedy would win the election and eventually start efforts to move for the passage of a civil rights act. For the moment, the Nixon move did not sever the candidate's ties to Robinson. In 1962, Jackie campaigned vigorously for Nixon's campaign for the governorship of California. Nixon lost, but later returned to national prominence.[16]

Six years later, Robinson's views on Nixon reached a low point. In 1968 Robinson decided to publicly denounce the Nixon ticket as being influenced by staunch southern conservatives like Senator Strom Thurmond. He believed that Nixon bowed to southerners when he placed Spiro T. Agnew, conservative governor of Maryland, on the ticket. Robinson felt that the Republican convention that nominated Nixon clearly revealed that the party wanted nothing to do with African Americans. In 1968 he would support Hubert Humphrey and the Democratic Party.[17]

Although Robinson continued to maintain close ties to the NAACP, he also decided to offer his full support to the Southern Christian Leadership Conference and movement campaigns in the South. By 1962 King's SCLC was fully involved in the movement for non-violent social change in Albany, Georgia. After civil rights protest began in southwest Georgia in 1962, a group of southern whites, enraged by the integration efforts, burned four churches in rural areas nearby. Robinson traveled to Georgia and then traveled with Dr. W. G. Anderson, leader of the local Albany Movement, and Rev. Wyatt Tee Walker, an aide for King, to see the ruins of two of the burned churches. Civil rights leaders and protesters in the South welcomed his visit, and they also celebrated his efforts to raise funds to rebuild the churches. He was part of a coalition that helped to raise $45,000 for rebuilding, while Atlanta's *Constitution*, Georgia Council of Churches, Albany supporters, and United Church of Christ raised $21,000. On February 3, 1963, Rev. Dr. Martin Luther King, Jr., led ceremonial services for the rebuilding effort. A knee operation at a Mount Vernon, New York, hospital prevented Robinson from attending.[18]

Never one to shy away from an opportunity to support the freedom of African Americans, Robinson accepted the challenge to lead at one of the most pivotal moments in American history. On August 28, 1963, the world watched as more than 250,000 people converged on Washington, D.C., as part of the March on Washington. Robinson served as the leader of the Connecticut contingent, which numbered some three thousand strong. The Connecticut protesters received a welcome from Robinson, Connecticut's U.S.

Senators Thomas Dodd and Abraham Ribicoff, and other congressional leaders.[19]

Robinson and his family's support of the SCLC did not end at the march. In fact, they began to use their home in Stamford as a rally and fund raising destination. In September 1963, Rev. Richard Battles, legendary minister of Hartford's Mount Olive Baptist Church and a state civil rights leader, announced that Jackie and Rachel Robinson would host a benefit for the SCLC and NAACP. Dr. King and Roy Wilkins, executive director of NAACP, both agreed to attend the event, which included performances by artists such as Benny Goodman, Brook Benton, and Ray Charles.[20]

By 1964 and 1965, civil rights leaders could rejoice at the passage of the Civil Rights Act and Voting Rights Act, while still remembering the painful racially motivated murders of martyrs such as Medger Evers, NAACP leader in Mississippi, and the four little girls who died in the Sixteenth Street Church bombing in Birmingham. The mid- to late-1960s, however, also saw nonviolent protest being questioned by young activists.

Although now weakened by the complications of diabetes, Robinson refused to shy away from trying to confront and talk with young militants. In 1967, as a special assistant to New York Governor Nelson Rockefeller, he visited Buffalo to help mollify tensions in that city after three nights of upheaval. According to press reports, more than 1,000 African American youngsters took to the streets, damaging businesses. Robinson's focus would be on speaking to youngsters on the lower Eastside of the city.[21]

In 1969 Robinson gave a talk to the Stamford Catholic High School Honor Society about a recent protest at Cornell University during which armed students occupied a university building. He declared that he saw nothing wrong with young people being proud of being of African descent, however, he argued, the occupation of a university building and the carrying of weapons "confused" him. Although he could not "condone" the actions, Robinson took the time to listen and understand issues from the views of frustrated young people.

While civil rights remained of major concern to the baseball icon, the conflict in Vietnam crashed directly into his family's life after the return of his son, Jackie Jr., from service. At the age of 17, Robinson's eldest son, a student at Rippowam High School in Stamford, decided to forgo college and enlist in the Army. He received shrapnel wounds while serving in Vietnam and came home with an addiction to drugs. After a run-in with police and arrest, the young veteran received treatment for his addiction. By 1971, Jackie Jr., at twenty-four years old, had been drug-free for three years. He embarked on a career that allowed him to work at Daytop, a drug rehabilitation center in Seymour, Connecticut. Tragically, a car crash on the Merritt Parkway ended his life in June 1971. At the time of his death, Jackie Jr. had been organizing a jazz event to raise funds for Daytop. His efforts paid dividends when on June 28, 1971, 2,000 people attended the jazz concert at his parent's home. The concert eventually became a regular cherished event and part of young Jackie Jr.'s legacy.[22]

By 1972 Jackie Robinson began to physically slow down, however, his work continued. A partnership in both the Jackie Robinson Construction Corporation and Freedom National Bank clearly revealed his belief in economic freedom for African Americans. African Americans seeking bank loans often found opportunities limited. Robinson recalled a statement by George W. Goodman, a Harlem leader of the 1960s and newspaper editor for Hartford's *Chronicle* in the 1940s, on the views of a white Connecticut banker on lending money to African Americans. According to Goodman, the banker argued that he felt that biggest loan an African American could repay was $300. In 1964 Freedom National Bank, an interracial bank Robinson helped to found in Harlem, would serve as proof that an African American could afford a larger loan, plus grant loans. Robinson served as chairman of the bank until his death.[23]

In 1972 the number and quality of African American athletes in baseball was apparent to anyone watching on television or visiting ballparks. When major league baseball offered an opportunity to honor his entrance into baseball and the work of Daytop at a World Series game in Cincinnati, Robinson eagerly accepted the offer. Robinson urged baseball to move toward considering an African American to manage a major league team.[24] Although he would never get the chance to see African Americans such as Hall of Famer Frank Robinson or Cito Gaston serve as managers of teams in the big leagues, his time in baseball set the stage for their opportunities.

On October 24, 1972, the devoted father, Christian gentleman, and warrior passed away at the age of 53. His legacy continued through the work of family members, particularly his wife Rachel. She was a caring mother and career woman, who sacrificed and shared the indignities of early days of her husband in baseball. Rachel, the former UCLA student and nurse, became a professor at Yale University and also carried out management duties with the Robinson's construction firm and eventually the Jackie Robinson

Foundation.[25] While he could have quietly gone into business and forgotten about the African American freedom struggle, politics, and economics, Jackie Robinson willingly sacrificed for the betterment of African Americans and the nation.

## Notes

1. "Jackie Robinson Joins Brooklyn Team Today," *Hartford Courant*, April 11, 1947.

2. Arnold Rampersad, *Jackie Robinson: A Biography* (New York: Alfred A. Knopf, 1997), 55–71.

3. Ibid., 31.

4. Jackie Robinson (as told to Alfred Duckett), *I Never Had It Made* (New York: Harper Collins, 1995, originally published by Putnam, 1972), 18–22.

5. Ibid., 22–24.

6. Lee Lowenfish, *Branch Rickey: Baseball's Ferocious Gentleman* (Lincoln and London: University of Nebraska Press, 2009), 350, 371–75.

7. Robinson, 105–8. See also "Robinson Buys Home in Stamford," *Hartford Courant*, December 13, 1953.

8. Ibid.

9. "Jackie Robinson to Speak Friday at Weaver Rally," *Hartford Courant*, January 29, 1953; and "Jackie Robinson Pleads for North End Project," *Hartford Courant*, January 31, 1953.

10. Rampersad, 303–4.

11. Chester Bowles to Jackie Robinson, February 10, 1958, in Michael G. Long, ed., *First Class Citizen: The Civil Rights Letters of Jackie Robinson* (New York: Times Books, 2007), 50–51, and 55–56.

12. "Jackie Robinson to Take Part in NAACP Benefit," *Hartford Courant*, May 14, 1958.

13. The People's Forum, "The Housing Bill Should Be Supported," *Hartford Courant*, February 6, 1959.

14. "Golf Club Rejects Him, Jackie Robinson Claims," *Hartford Courant*, May 11, 1958; and "Hearing Is Continued on Stamford Bias Plan," *Hartford Courant*, February 3, 1962.

15. Robinson to Chester Bowles, August 26, 1959 in *First Class Citizen: The Civil Rights Letters of Jackie Robinson*, ed. Michael G. Long, 70–71 (New York: Times Books, 2007).

16. "Nixon Ticket Rapped by Jackie Robinson," *Hartford Courant*, August 12, 1968. Robinson to Chester Bowles, August 26, 1959, *First Class Citizen*, 70–71.

17. "Nixon Ticket Rapped by Jackie Robinson," *Hartford Courant*.

18. "Break Ground Today: 3 Georgia Churches Rise Again from Ashes," *Hartford Courant*, February 3, 1963; and "Two Church Burnings in Georgia," *Hartford Courant*, September 10, 1962.

19. "3,000 Leave State to Join Washington Rights March," *Hartford Courant*, August 28, 1963.

20. "Stars to Perform for Rights Units," *Hartford Courant*, September 8, 1963.

21. "Jackie Robinson Shuns Militants," *Hartford Courant*, May 1, 1969; and "Jackie Robinson Gets Task of Calming Buffalo Youth," *Hartford Courant*, July 1, 1967.

22. "Robinson's Son Is Arraigned," *Hartford Courant*, August 27, 1968; "Jackie Robinson Jr. Dies In Car Crash," *Hartford Courant*, June 18, 1971.

23. Robinson, 184; "George Goodman Blasts Critics," *Hartford Chronicle*, March 11, 1946; and Rampersad, 458, 462–63. See also *Jet Magazine*, November 26, 1990.

24. Rampersad, 458, 462–63.

25. Robinson, 184, and Rampersad, 458, 462–63.

# 47 Rev. Dr. Martin Luther King, Jr., Connecticut, and Non-Violent Protest

## *A Transforming Alliance*

As a teenager in 1944 Martin Luther King, Jr. became part of a long tradition of southern students venturing to Connecticut to spend the summer working in the state's tobacco fields. The teenager joined a group of students from Atlanta, Georgia's, Morehouse College at work on a Simsbury, Connecticut, farm. In *My Life with Martin Luther King, Jr.*, Coretta Scott King recalled that her eventual husband experienced an incredible sense of "freedom" while in Connecticut.[1] Unlike in the South, King and other southern youth ate in restaurants and visited local theaters without having to deal with the horror of legalized segregation.[2] Coretta Scott King argued that the opportunity to lead devotional services with other students that summer started Martin on the road to becoming a minister.[3] This visit to Connecticut had a major impact on the teenage King, but his relationship with Connecticut did not stop there. Later efforts by Connecticans would make important contributions to the non-violent civil rights movement he led in the South. People from Connecticut would frequently travel south to bolster the civil rights movement, and Dr. King's visits to Connecticut would helped to support and transform African American communities in urban areas here.

Eleven years after King's first summer in Connecticut, he found himself leading the Montgomery Bus Boycott. In 1955 the heroic refusal by Rosa Parks to get out of her seat on a segregated bus sparked the early boycott efforts, which Jo Ann Robinson and Mary Fair Burks of the Women's Political Council urged city residents to undertake. African American leadership in Montgomery, Alabama created the Montgomery Improvement Association (MIA) to lead and organize the larger boycott of the bus company by African Americans. The Rev. Dr. Martin Luther King, Jr. assumed the presidency of the MIA, which led the boycott for over a year.

The protest efforts in Alabama did not go unnoticed in Connecticut cities. In New Britain and Hartford, ministers supported the national call for a day of prayer for Montgomery, while the New Haven County Bar Association railed against legal action that targeted African American leaders. On March 25, 1956, Rev. Jacob C. Ruffin, pastor of Union AME Zion Church in New Britain, and other ministers in that city organized an evening service that raised funds to help aid the bus boycott in Montgomery. On the nationwide prayer day on March 28, 1956, Ruffin and other clergy leaders opened their churches for prayer and services at noon. They also urged workers in factories to pray quietly at work, however, the ministers indicated that they did not want work to cease. The New Britain ministers welcomed the solidarity of labor, city, and state leaders in the protest.

In Hartford, Rev. Robert Moody, pastor of Shiloh Baptist Church and chairman of the social action committee of the Inter-Denominational Ministerial Alliance (IMA), made a similar call. Hartford's Metropolitan AME Zion served as the host church for services. On March 28, Moody and other ministers urged churches to ring their bells in support of the people protesting in Montgomery. Moody and IMA members also attempted to get Catholic and Jewish organizations to join the struggle. Like their counterparts in New Britain, Hartford ministers decided to raise an offering for the bus boycotters. When white Montgomery officials attempted to crush the boycott by arresting twenty-eight key leaders in 1956, the New Haven County Bar Association considered their actions "an attack on the constitutional provisions insuring life, liberty, and the pursuit of happiness."[4] Eventually, the court system declared segregation aboard buses illegal. The bus boycott victory made Rev. Dr. Martin Luther King, Jr., a household name and sought after speaker.

College campuses in Connecticut eagerly reached out to the young minister for speaking engagements. In 1959 the University of Hartford invited King to be part of the Keller Lectures at Bushnell Memorial Hall. Shortly before the Hartford lecture, he received the opportunity to spend time in India with Prime Minister Nehru, give lectures, and learn about Indian culture. Two years later, King gave the tenth annual Frank Jacoby Lecture before 2,700 people at the University of Bridgeport. Speaking on his recent travels in Asia and Africa, King argued that the nation could not be a world leader of the highest order with "second class citizens" in the country. He also praised President Kennedy's recent executive order that ended discrimination in federal employment.[5]

While the lectures at the University of Hartford and University of Bridgeport established his important place as a lecturer and speaker in the state, his ties at Wesleyan University had a profound impact. Professor David E. Swift remembered Dr. King's lectures and speeches at Wesleyan in the 1960s, but the professor first met King while participating in a freedom ride that protested southern segregation in 1961. The Wesleyan professor found King "genuine" and prophetic. During that protest in 1961, Alabama authorities arrested both Swift and Dr. John McGuire, a native of Montgomery, Alabama, and professor at Wesleyan University, for violating segregation bus laws in Alabama.[6]

Professor Stephen Crites of Wesleyan University, who hosted King in his home in Connecticut for a January 1962 lecture at the University, found that King had a "low-key wit about him." In the lecture before 2,000 people, King spoke candidly about the humiliation that potential African American voters faced. In Mississippi, pollsters, Dr. King stated, had the audacity to ask African American voters "How many bubbles do you find in a bar of soap?" He urged President John Kennedy to issue a "second emancipation proclamation." Marion Wright, an African American Yale law student from South Carolina and freedom rider, was also a speaker that day. She explained the differences and similarities between southern and northern discrimination and the day-to-day difficulties of navigating the world of segregation for African Americans from finding a place to eat to using restroom facilities. She described northern racism as "more subtle and more stinging, but just as real." Wright argued that in New Haven's Dixwell Avenue neighborhood rats infested the area, and homes resembled those in Mississippi. She ended her remarks by saying that people in the North were "real hypocrites."[7]

When King returned to the Middletown campus in October 1963 and June 1964, he focused a portion of his discussion on the murders of four little girls at the Sixteenth Street Baptist Church in Birmingham on September 15, 1963, on discrimination in Connecticut, and on poverty. King believed that the statements uttered by George Wallace, governor of Alabama, caused the deaths of youngsters and vicious brutality. But Dr. King also addressed local issues, and boldly proclaimed that Connecticut discriminated against African Americans in housing and employment. These forms of discrimination, he argued, lead to de facto segregation in Connecticut schools. During a 1964 baccalaureate address at Wesleyan, King confronted the audience about the issue of poverty in America. Poverty was not new, King said. In his view, the security of the wealth of the most affluent depended on making sure that the least "are what they ought to be."[8]

While the need to deal with the problems discussed by Dr. King found the ear of Connecticut, Rev. Richard Battles, pastor of Mount Olive Baptist Church in Hartford, fully immersed himself in the nationwide and state fight to eradicate discrimination against African Americans. In 1960 Battles moved to Hartford. A native son of Arkansas, Battles knew the struggles of the South well. Although Connecticut's NAACP civil rights struggles dated back to 1917, the Southern Christian Leadership Conference (SCLC), established in 1957 by Dr. King and a group of ministers, eclipsed the NAACP in national appeal. Battles proved a driving force in organizing the SCLC presence in Connecticut. Known for his incredible charisma, Battles built a thriving church membership and strong working relationship with King. Battles' leadership increased membership from 360 in 1960 to 1,200 by 1967.[9] Whenever the SCLC needed the support from the Hartford community, Rev. Battles and Connecticut sympathizers helped to forge local efforts to address calls for support throughout the heart of the 1960s movement.

After the SCLC decided to become part of the campaign to end segregation in Albany, Georgia, Battles personally became part of the non-violent campaign to dismantle segregation and discrimination in the southwest Georgia city. When the SCLC initiated a request that a July 1962 prayer vigil be conducted in support of their efforts in Albany, twenty-three communities responded, including Hartford. Rev. Battles organized an integrated group of forty people in prayer on the lawn at the State Capitol. With heads bowed, they listened as Rev. David Benedict of Bloomfield United Methodist Church offered words of prayer. After Secretary of State Ella Grasso warmly greeted those in attendance, Battles announced that they decided to send telegrams supporting protest efforts to President John Kennedy and Governor S. Ernest Vandiver of Georgia.[10]

One month later, Battles, freedom riders, and clergymen engaged in more militant efforts. Fifteen freedom riders traveled by bus to Albany, Georgia in August 1962 to attend the trial of Dr. King, who local Albany officials arrested for his role in leading protests against segregation. The bus riders received a glowing welcome in Georgia at Shiloh Baptist Church and from King. Rev. Battles, who traveled by plane to Georgia, informed those at the Connecticut welcome that he and other supporters of King had no qualms about a return to Albany. Although the fifteen planned to be jailed if necessary, Albany officials simply decided to release King. On August 12, 1962, members of Mount Olive Baptist Church and movement supporters offered a hearty welcome home to the fifteen freedom riders.

In late August, Rabbis Jordan Osfeyer, Sanford Shapiro, Richard Israel, and Robert Boldburg joined with Rev. Robert Forsberg to form a Connecticut contingent that was part of prayer demonstration in Albany. Local officials arrested the clergymen at the Albany City Hall. Osfeyer, Israel, and Forsberg served worshippers in New Haven, while the temples for Shapiro and Boldburg were in Bridgeport and Hamden. All five men received a bond of $200.[11]

Usually religious leaders had the available funds to pay bonds; however, many young high school and college age protesters who participated in non-violent campaigns did not have the money. Consequently, fundraising throughout the 1960s was a major need of the SCLC. Their leaders depended on a network of churches and church leaders to aid the movement monetarily and emotionally. In 1961 Rev. Battles organized a rally to bring King to speak at Bushnell Memorial Hall. An integrated group of freedom riders were also part of the rally. Battles happily reported that the rally raised $4,047.[12] In October 1962, Dr. King's views on the importance of Hartford to the movement resounded loud and clear in points he made about the residents. King considered the people of Hartford to be some of the best supporters for the freedom struggle financially and spiritually. Throughout the year he joined forces with legendary gospel artist Mahalia Jackson at benefit concerts. While the Bushnell served as stop on the concert circuit, concert attendees could also buy tickets at Mount Olive Baptist Church. In 1964 Stamford residents collected $2,580 for the movement, which they requested that Rev. Battles present on their behalf at a Harlem fundraiser that included the SCLC and King.[13]

Although fundraising and support for SCLC remained constant issues for Rev. Battles, he also leveled biting criticism at the inaction of national officials in Mississippi and allied himself with militant protest in Hartford. In a 1962 interview, Battles publicly scolded FBI Director J. Edgar Hoover for his "silence" on the crimes against African Americans in Mississippi, while the director spoke out about the threat of communism. Battles argued that Hoover needed to inform the nation that the current civil rights struggle provided fodder for the believers in communism.[14] When Peter Morrill, once a freedom rider and Trinity College student, and other Hartford young people formed the North End Action Project (NECAP), the organization brought the non-violent skills of the North Student Movement to the Connecticut capitol city.

In an August 1963 mass meeting at Mount Olive Baptist Church, NECAP entered "negotiations" with a local bank to hire more African Americans. The bank had one African American worker, a janitor. Before an audience of 150, Battles announced that he planned to be more engaged in NECAP ventures. Members of NECAP used a variety of non-violent tactics including "kneel-ins" to shake the soul of the city.[15]

On August 28, 1963, thousands of people from Connecticut converged on Washington, D.C., seeking justice. Although they heard from a cross-section of leaders from civil rights to labor, Dr. King's "I Have Dream" speech has remained the most endearing speech of the day. Connecticut residents helped form a rally of more than 250,000 people from the United States focused on transforming the country. The call for justice by this peaceful mass helped to move the nation forward.[16] Even so, the great rally did not end the need to keep pushing for greater equality.

One of the areas in the fight for equality that needed shaking was housing. Mount Olive Baptist Church initiated a project to build moderately priced housing that included one, two, and three bedroom units. The proposed rent was from $89 to $115 per month, which included parking. The Federal Housing Authority accepted the church's application to build housing and granted an allotment of $860,000 to build on Martin and Nelson Streets in Hartford. The church set the groundbreaking for March 11, 1964. When King traveled to Hartford for the dedication, he and Battles had the privilege of digging the first shovels of earth. The day's event also included a dinner at the Statler Hilton, where King spoke to an audience of five hundred people. The other main speaker scheduled for the event, comedian Dick Gregory, failed to attend because he was under arrest in San Francisco for engaging in civil rights protest.

Although King drew frequent accolades from the crowd that gathered, he focused considerable attention on the debates in the U.S. Senate surrounding the civil rights bill. King feared that some senators might attempt to "emasculate" the legislation. During his speech, he paused to thank Governor John Dempsey of Connecticut for his continued support of civil rights; in addition, he applauded Battles and members of Mount Olive in their efforts to address a major problem of northern civil rights—decent housing. Seemingly always on the move and in demand, Dr. King, on this same night, rode by car to another speaking engagement in Bridgeport.[17]

While the time demands for civil rights work were immense, in 1964 King took a pause from movement activity to accept the Nobel

Peace Prize in Oslo, Norway. Rev. Battles was part of the SCLC delegation that joined Dr. King in Oslo. Undoubtedly seeing King receive the prize proved riveting for his closest associates, and Battles spoke candidly to a local Hartford reporter about a dinner that King held just for his U.S. delegation. King told his closest supporters how much he appreciated their individual sacrifices for the movement. These same supporters also spoke about King's importance to them. The night included freedom songs and a quartet, which included Dr. King, Rev. Wyatt Tee Walker, Battles, and Rev. Ralph Abernathy. Battles also received the opportunity to belt out "I Left My Heart in San Francisco," a song that King loved.[18]

In 1965 the nation's attention, in terms of civil rights, turned to the small town of Selma, Alabama. When Dr. King urged "sympathizers" from throughout the nation to join the campaign, Connecticut answered the call. The heart of the Selma campaign was an effort to get the government to initiate voting rights legislation. Throughout huge swaths of the South, local white registrars still routinely denied African Americans the right to vote. In March 1965 at least ninety people from Connecticut ventured to Selma for the campaign. Once in Selma at Brown Chapel, the local movement headquarters, Rev. A. D. King, brother of the Rev. Dr. Martin Luther King, Jr., greeted the Connecticut contingent. The new arrivals attended training on "how to protect themselves from electric cattle prods, from beatings and clubbing, and from passing cars with men who often hurl missiles at demonstrators."

Dr. King wanted ordinary citizens to be a part of the campaign, but he also strongly urged religious leaders to be part of an ecumenical movement to change the nation. Rev. Battles traveled to Selma with Rev. Wilbert Woods of Hartford's Welcome Baptist Church. Rev. James D. Peters, Rabbi Sanford Shapiro, Rev. William O. Johnson, and Rev. Ruben Wiggins, all from Bridgeport, also made the trek to Selma. Peters served as the pastor of East End Baptist Church from 1960 to 1973, and in 1957 had attended the founding meeting of the SCLC. Rev. Robert C. Johnson, Dean of Yale Divinity School, three other faculty members, and a group of Yale students also joined the marchers.[19] They hoped to walk from Selma to Montgomery for a mass rally at the Alabama State Capitol. The protest, together with support for the voting rights bill from President Lyndon Johnson and key members of Congress, led to its eventual passage.

On July 29, 1965, Rev. Battles decided to spend an entire month at work with Dr. King and the SCLC in the South. He planned to focus on voter registration and to travel to Chicago for the annual SCLC convention but not to the crisis in Bogalusa, Louisiana. In August, Battles would be engaged in voter registration campaigns in Little Rock, Arkansas, and Birmingham, Alabama. Battles also hoped to be part of the efforts to arrange the annual SCLC convention, which leaders believed some 5,000 delegates would attend. When the SCLC headed to Chicago, Battles intended to be involved in the talks or protests. The Chicago trip focused in part on "de facto segregation in Chicago public schools." Bogalusa, particularly the presence of the Deacons for Defense and Justice in the town, drew considerable press because the deacons carried weapons to protect African American residents from white marauders. Dr. King criticized the tactics of the deacons, but Battles did not object to people protecting themselves, especially when authorities denied them security.[20]

A year later, four Connecticut leaders joined 2,400 delegates for a civil rights conference at the White House. Rev. Battles, regional director, and Rev. James D. Peters, assistant regional director, represented the SCLC in Connecticut, while Dr. Fred Adams, president of the Danbury NAACP, and Mrs. Ella Anderson, president of the Bridgeport NAACP, attended. The only major civil rights group that decided not to be involved was SNCC (Student Non-Violent Coordinating Committee), which now had key leaders embracing the slogan of "Black Power." The White House settled on Vice President Hubert Humphrey and Solicitor General Thurgood Marshall to give the major addresses. The conference also called for those in attendance to hear a recent report by the council initiated by the White House. The report discussed the need for such things as improved employment, integration of low-income housing, and improved relationships between minorities and police.[21]

When Dr. King returned to Connecticut to provide the keynote address at a dinner in honor of Rev. Battles in 1967, his message, though still addressing civil rights, included a heavy concentration on economics, Vietnam, and riots, particularly those in 1965 in Watts, a neighborhood of Los Angeles, California. King criticized the nation for failing to employ scores of citizens, and allowing others to reside in deplorable poverty stricken slums. For change to truly happen, King argued, the government needed to establish new large-scale programs for poor African Americans. When it came to the conflict in Vietnam, which saw daily loss of lives, King considered it "unjust and ill-conceived." He suggested that the nation could agree to extend a "few billion" dollars to help African Americans, particularly given the fact that the nation paid a bill of "35 billion" dollars for the war in Vietnam. Although he did not agree with riots, King understood that young people who took to the streets in Watts wanted to be heard.[22] By the summer of 1967, riots and disturbances errupted in the streets of other urban areas, including Connecticut's capitol city. Whether it was the riots of Detroit or disturbances in Hartford, authorities at state and national level often blamed the violence on Black Power leaders.

On April 4, 1968, an assassin's bullet ended the life of Rev. Dr. Martin Luther King, Jr., who at the time had joined with Rev. Jim Lawson to lead a protest march of striking sanitation workers in Memphis, Tennessee. The reactions of people in the state to King's assassination varied from joy to anger. A state member of the white racist Minutemen drew delight from the murder of Dr. King. In Middletown, 3,000 grief-stricken people marched quietly to St. John's Church. On April 8, 1968, Rev. James Peters spoke to more than 1,500 people in Bridgeport at the Klein Memorial Auditorium, while hundreds heard his remarks over a loudspeaker at St. John's Episcopal Church. One of King's strongest allies in support of civil rights and condemning the war was William Sloane Coffin of Yale University. After Coffin learned of King's assassination, he said: "I am absolutely crushed." As in many cities nationwide, pockets of young people raged in the streets in the North End of Hartford, breaking windows and damaging stores.[23] In the end, the majority of people chose the path of non-violence and peace after the assassination.

The Connecticut that had a hand in shaping Dr. King's life as a youngster also overwhelmingly decided to embrace and support his message of love, peace, and non-violence. Rev. Ralph Abernathy, his successor as president of the SCLC, did not forget the importance of King's work to people in the North. Before his assassination, King and SCLC embarked on a campaign to organize a Poor People's Campaign that would take the issue of poverty to the doorsteps of the leaders in Washington, D.C. Fellow SCLC leaders did not abandon the cause, and neither did King's friends and supporters in Connecticut. Not only did they take the issue of poverty to Washington over the summer, in September 1968 Rev. Ralph Abernathy confronted poverty in a rally at Rippowam High School in Stamford, Connecticut.[24] The campaign, though not as successful as those in King's prime, brought honor to King's stature as a leader in 1968. In 1977 Connecticut honored King's memory and message with the passage of the Martin Luther King, Jr. state holiday.[25]

# Notes

1. Coretta Scott King, *My Life with Martin Luther King, Jr.* (New York: Holt, Rinehart, and Winston, 1969), 85.

2. King, and Stan Simpson, "Work camp in Simsbury was a haven to student tobacco workers," *Hartford Courant*, January 21, 1991.

3. King.

4. "Prayer Day to Be Asked by Negroes," *Hartford Courant*, March 13, 1956, "Negro Ministers Set Day of Prayer Here March 28," *Hartford Courant*, March 7, 1956; and "New Haven County Bar Hits Alabama Arrests," *Hartford Courant*, February 2, 1956.

5. "Negro Leader to Give Third Keller Lecture," *Hartford Courant*, May 3, 1959; and "Dr. King Says U.S. Prestige at Lowest Ebb," *Hartford Courant*, March 14, 1961.

6. Jean Griffith, "King's Ties to Wesleyan Leave a Mark," *Hartford Courant*, January 16, 1984; Donald Pfarrer, "Segregation a 'Cancer,' Says Rev. Mr. King," *Hartford Courant*, January 15, 1962; John Craig, "Dr. King Blames Wallace for Violent Atmosphere," *Hartford Courant*, October 21, 1963; "Three State Freedom Riders to Appear at Rally Here," *Hartford Courant*, July 4, 1961; and John Craig, "Wesleyan Baccalaureate Is Delivered by Dr. King," *Hartford Courant*, June 8, 1964.

7. Jean Griffith, "King's Ties to Wesleyan Leave a Mark"; Donald Pfarrer, "Segregation a 'Cancer,' Says Rev. Mr. King"; John Craig, "Dr. King Blames Wallace for Violent Atmosphere: "Three State Freedom Riders to Appear at Rally Here," *Hartford Courant*; and John Craig, "Wesleyan Baccalaureate Is Delivered by Dr. King."

8. John Craig, "Dr. King Blames Wallace for Violent Atmosphere; and John Craig, "Wesleyan Baccalaureate Is Delivered by Dr. King."

9. "Rev. R. A. Battles Dies; Rights Activist," *Hartford Courant*, June 23, 1980; and "Martin Luther King Coming Here Sunday," *Hartford Courant*, March 10, 1967.

10. "Group Prayers at Capitol for Integration Leaders," *Hartford Courant*, July 31, 1962.

11. "Five State Clergymen Jailed in Prayer Vigil," *Hartford Courant*, August 29, 1962; William Miles, "'Freedom' Bus Welcomed Back from Albany, Ga.," *Hartford Courant*, August 13, 1962; "Local Group Leaves for Albany, Ga. . . ," *Hartford Courant*, August 9, 1962; and "Busload of Sympathizers Due Back This Evening," *Hartford Courant*, August 12, 1962.

12. Richard Battles, letter to editor, "That Made the Rally Possible," *Hartford Courant*, July 31, 1962; "Negro Leader Speaks at Bushnell Tonight," *Hartford Courant*, July 14, 1961; "Three State Freedom Riders to Appear at Rally Here," *Hartford Courant*, July 4, 1961; and "Negro Rights Crusader to Speak at Bushnell," June 29, 1961.

13. "Gospel Singer, Dr. King Boost Cause of Equality," *Hartford Courant*, October 29, 1962; "Mahalia Jackson, Dr. King to Be Seen at Bushnell," *Hartford Courant*, October 20, 1962; and Jean Tucker, "Dr. King Shared Peace Prize Credit with Aides, Rev. Battles Reports," *Hartford Courant*, December 15, 1964.

14. "Minister Say Events at Ole Miss Aid Reds," *Hartford Courant*, October 6, 1962.

15. "NECAP to Seek Hiring Negotiations with 'Well-Known' Hartford Bank," *Hartford Courant*, August 8, 1963; and Stacey Close, "Fire in the Bones: Hartford's NAACP, Civil Rights, and Militancy, 1943–1969," *Journal of Negro History*, vol. 86, no. 3 (Summer 2001): 236–37.

16. Jean Tucker, "Restraint, Expectations Gave March Its Power," *Hartford Courant*, August 30, 1963.

17. "Rev. Dr. King to Appear at Mt. Olive Ceremony," *Hartford Courant*, January 23, 1964; and Jean Tucker, "Weakening of Rights Bill Is Feared by Dr. King," *Hartford Courant*, March 12, 1964.

18. Jean Tucker, "Dr. King Shared Peace Prize Credit with Aides, Rev. Battles Reports."

19. "King's Brother Greets Sympathizers from State," *Hartford Courant*, March 19, 1965; "On Way to Selma from State," *Hartford Courant*, March 9, 1965; "Yale Dean Takes Part in March," *Hartford Courant*, March 10, 1965; and blog.ct.news.com/connecticutpostings/category/news/page/2/.

20. "Hartford Minister Plans Month Working in South," *Hartford Courant*, July 21, 1965.

21. David Holmberg, "Mount Olive Pastor to Attend Conference," *Hartford Courant*, May 29, 1966.

22. Nedda Young, "Dr. King Tells of '2 Americas' at Dinner Honoring Minister," *Hartford Courant*, March 13, 1967; and "Martin Luther King Coming Here Sunday," *Hartford Courant*, March 10, 1967.

23. "King's Death Pleases Leader of Minutemen," *Hartford Courant*, April 5, 1968; "More Than 3,000 March Down Main Street to Pay Tribute to Dr. Martin Luther King," *Hartford Courant*, April 8, 1968; Jeffrey B. Cohen, "Angry After King's Death Left Lasting Mark on Hartford's North End," hartfordinfo.org/issues/documents/history/htfd_courant_040608.asp; John Burgesson, "Hundreds Turn Out for MLK Celebration," www.ctpost.com/local/article/Hundreds-turn-out-for-MLK-celebration; and "Dr. King Mourned in the Northeast," *Hartford Courant*, April 5, 1968.

24. "Abernathy to Address Rally for Poor in Stamford Friday," *Hartford Courant*, September 26, 1968.

25. Elissa Papirno, "State's Newest Holiday Is Marked by Confusion," *Hartford Courant*, January 15, 1977.

# 48  Black Panthers

## *Interview with Butch Lewis*

Butch Lewis co-founded the Hartford chapter of the Black Panther Party and was an activist in the late 1960s. He first came to Hartford from Fredericksburg, Virginia, in 1956 at age twelve to live with his grandmother. Drafted into the army in January 1965, he served in Vietnam until December 1967. At the time of his release, he was in Oakland, California, birthplace of the Black Panther Party for Self-Defense. (The name was later shortened to the Black Panther Party.) Although he had no contact with the Panthers in California, he read and was inspired by news of their activities. Upon his return to Connecticut in 1968, he helped organize the Hartford chapter and became its leader. The Hartford group was involved in organizing and demonstrating for improvements in housing, education, and jobs for African Americans in Hartford.

As leader of the Black Panther Party, Lewis was contacted by filmmakers from the Film Board of Canada and UCLA who were working on a documentary exploring Hartford as a model city during that era's "War on Poverty." When funding ran out, the filmmakers left all of the Hartford footage and equipment with Lewis. Renewed interest in the historic footage spawned a project, coordinated by Professor Susan Pennybacker at Hartford's Trinity College, to complete the documentary. At the time of the interview, Lewis served as a sexton for the South Congregational Church of Hartford.

I asked Butch to reflect on his experiences working to improve housing, education, and job opportunities for the African American community in the late 1960s.

*Jacobs*: Take us back to 1968, and the early days of the Black Panther Party in Hartford. What drew people to the Party?

*Lewis*: The Party was an organization that people wanted to join because we talked about politics and politicians, we demonstrated, and we helped people in the community. For example, we knew kids were going to school hungry so we started the breakfast-before-school program. That involved getting a place—Father Lenny Tartaglia let us run it from St. Michael's—and getting people to donate food. We never terrorized anybody; people came and gave us stuff. When the kids wanted to walk out at Weaver High School, we went up to help organize it, and we made sure no one got hurt. I think we became a big brother to a lot of people.

Every time we went and did something, we got another member. It wasn't that hard to get people to come into the Party then because we were more together as a community than we are now. We had meetings in the streets and in an apartment we had on Westland Street. Party membership wasn't kept on paper. That way no one could raid us and say, "Well, this cat did this, and this person did that." A lot of people were associated with the Party but didn't do demonstrations and such. There were a lot of black professionals who helped us out but who didn't want it known that they did because they were scared about losing their jobs.

*Jacobs*: How was the Party regarded by outsiders?

*Lewis*: I think a lot of people were scared of it. We didn't back down from confrontation; we faced confrontation. Some ministers worried about us . . . pointed us out to the cops during the riots, told them where we lived.

*Jacobs*: What were the Panthers doing during the riots [Hartford, like cities across the U.S., erupted in violent protest in the summers of 1968 and 1969]?

*Lewis*: We were the ones who met with the fire department and made sure they could come into the neighborhood to put out the fires. People were cutting hoses, throwing rocks, taking axes off the trucks. We were the only ones allowed on the street at night without getting arrested

*Jacobs*: Did you work with other groups in the community?

*Lewis*: Yeah. You knew everybody, you knew all the different organizations, you worked with the different organizations, you demonstrated with the organizations, you did community work. If somebody was running for office and you felt that this was good for the community, you put your people out and did work for them, but still you were going by the rules of the Black Panther Party.

*Jacobs*: What other significant organizations were in existence at the same time?

*Lewis*: The Urban League, The Community Renewal Team,

the Student Nonviolence Coordinating Committee . . . a lot of the groups coming up from the civil rights movement had offices here. A lot of students from Trinity and the Hartford Seminary, white students, were hooked up with the SNCC and Students for a Democratic Society, left-wing organizations. They were hooked up into the Young Communist Party.

*Jacobs*: What needed to change in Hartford?

*Lewis*: Living conditions, the same things as today, the same identical things, it hasn't moved. Housing, jobs, education.

*Jacobs*: Did access to housing improve as a result of the civil rights laws or community organizing?

*Lewis*: I think it was a result of the riots. White people were moving out, ten families a week. That made us get better housing. I mean I shouldn't say it like that but we did advance on the deal, you know what I mean? We migrated. That migration came from The Bottom. The old Bottom was Windsor Street, Pequot Street, Front Street—not the Front Street where the Italians all lived, the other end. All those streets were where black people lived before the riots. It's where the Traveler's Data Center was later built.

*Jacobs*: Did access to professional jobs for blacks improve?

*Lewis*: They started opening up more because there were demonstrations at stores downtown, and no one wanted a demonstration in front of their store. The demonstrations were organized by the Student Nonviolent Coordinating Committee, the Panthers, everybody. Then they started opening up managerial jobs: That created incentive for us to go to college in the sixties. With a college education, you could get a manager's job instead of sweeping floors.

Black people in the sixties didn't have state jobs. You knew how many black people had state jobs and city jobs, too. You remembered when the first black man was hired to drive a garbage truck in Hartford. These jobs I'm talking about weren't Travelers jobs and insurance executives, no vice presidents or any of that, very few black people had those jobs. They were salesmen, they were elevator operators, they were door people, they were people doing all kinds of work. Those jobs opened up. There were more jobs.

*Jacobs*: When Anne Michaels, a filmmaker with the Canadian Film Board, approached you in 1969 about working with her team on a documentary about Hartford, what did you think?

*Lewis*: We saw something positive. To live in the sixties, and you look back now, things were moving fast and to have something on film, to be able to just know maybe you could help somebody, that was good. But then no one really knew what it was, and a lot of us thought it was a hoax. But hey, guys got little jobs; they learned stuff. The film crew was here when the shit broke out again [rioting in the summer of 1969]. They were here about six or seven months and then all of a sudden they said, "Hey we have no more money to finish this program." They left all this equipment. Matter of fact we knew how to run all this stuff because they had taught us. That was one of the agreements; we knew how to run every damn thing there.

*Jacobs*: What are your thoughts about this moment in history, now that the film footage has been resurrected and the documentary you began more than thirty years ago may be completed?

*Lewis*: It brings back memories and sadness that a lot of those people have died and everything they fought for still hasn't materialized and now their children and maybe their grandchildren will have to fight to maybe get it or maybe not get it. That's the sad part about it. The good part about it is that this could maybe help open our eyes so we don't go back to where we were because we're already half way back and don't realize it.

Note

This essay appeared in the August/September/October 2004 issue of *Connecticut Explored*.

*Cynthia Reik*

# 49 "What Would Dr. King Want You to Do?"

On Thursday evening, April 4, 1968, Dr. Martin Luther King, Jr. was assassinated at the Lorraine Motel in Memphis, Tennessee. In response, riots erupted in Hartford's North End. People were angry about the lack of progress on King's dream: integrated education, housing, a fair judicial system, and jobs. Republican Mayor Ann Uccello,[1] the first woman elected mayor of a Connecticut municipality and the first woman in the U.S. elected mayor of a capital city, went into the rioting area in a police cruiser on Thursday evening against the advice of most of her administration, carrying but not wearing a riot helmet. *The Hartford Times* reported that she toured the public housing complexes, "mingling with the people, trying to let them know the city cared."[2]

The police cordoned off the North End and used massive doses of tear gas to quiet the rioters. Residents in the city's West End reported that the tear gas was so heavy that it drifted to Elizabeth Park. Showing the extent to which the city was divided, one Fox Scholar graduate of Hartford Public High School, Tom Smith, then attending college nearby, drove to join his family in the North End to share their sorrow but was turned away by police.

Friday morning, after extensive rioting, when Hartford Public High School (where I was a teacher) opened at 7:30 a.m., John Gale (Hartford Public High School class of 1969) recalled that many students remained outdoors, uncertain as to whether it was appropriate to enter the school.[3] The student body was then about 50 percent African American, 15 percent Latino, and the rest white. The principal of Hartford Public High, Dr. Duncan Yetman, came outside to address the reluctant students, asking the question, "What would Dr. King want you to do?" Most students came inside and went to their homerooms for attendance. Over the P.A. system, Dr. Yetman gave students the option of remaining for a regular day or coming down to the office to phone home for parental permission to leave

school. For two hours students tied up the office phones, making arrangements to leave.[4]

Instead of going directly home, however, four hundred or more students walked down Farmington Avenue to St. Joseph Cathedral and asked the rector, Monsignor Father John S. Kennedy, to hold a memorial service for Dr. King. Msgr. Kennedy agreed. During this impromptu service, *The Hartford Courant*'s David Rhinelander reported, Kennedy said, "the Rev. Dr. King was a great black man. He was 'perhaps the greatest man of his generation.'"[5]

Afterward some of the students continued down Farmington Avenue singing civil-rights freedom songs, arriving at noon at city hall. Donna Nappier and her sister Denise (both HPHS class of 1969) reported that some, fearing parental disapproval, went home on the bus at this point as downtown was filled with rioters.[6] Others stayed, voiced their concerns, and asked to see Mayor Uccello. The mayor, who had had just three hours sleep, greeted the students on the steps of city hall. Ivan Robinson of the *Hartford Times* reported the students "complained about lack of jobs and being given courses that, they suddenly discovered, didn't prepare them for college. The mayor responded, 'When you were in ninth grade, did you want to go to college or were you just dying to get out of school?' The students admitted they didn't think of college until their senior year."[7]

Other students complained that the only time a black person was recognized was if he was good at sports or was elected to a class office. Three girls, unidentified in the *Hartford Times* report, then accompanied the mayor in a police cruiser to a service for Dr. King at the Church of the Good Shepherd.

The rioting continued for most of the weekend. When high school resumed on Monday, Dr. Yetman conducted an all-school assembly honoring Dr. King, assisted by Msgr. Charles Daly, himself a Hartford High graduate. Constance Price, the choral director at the high school, led the choir in music.[8]

After so many years, it is unclear how many students may not have gone to school that day or might have joined the proactive group that marched to the cathedral and city hall. What is clear is that the students might have made different choices if it weren't for the way the adult leaders responded to the needs of distraught young people.

## Notes

This essay appeared in the Fall 2011 issue of *Connecticut Explored*.

1. Uccello was also the first Republican mayor elected in Hartford in twenty years. She was a Weaver High School graduate and became one of the highest-ranking women in the Nixon administration.

2. *Hartford Times*, April 5, 1968.

3. Interview with John Gale, 2011.

4. Personal recollection; letter from Dr. C. Duncan Yetman to Cynthia Reik, 2011; interview with Ann Uccello, 2011.

5. Phone interview with David Rhinelander, 2011.

6. Interviews with Denise Nappier and Donna Nappier, 2011.

7. Ivan Robinson, *Hartford Times*.

8. Interview with Constance Price, 2011.

*Yohuru Williams*

## 50 The New Haven Black Panther Trials

In the summer of 1970, the people of New Haven, Connecticut, braced for the start of what local journalists billed as the trial of the century, the legal proceedings against members of the New Haven chapter of the Black Panther Party for the murder of a twenty-four-year-old New York Panther named Alex Rackley.[1] The murder and trial shifted attention away from efforts by the Panthers and a host of other local civil rights and Black Power organizations to address issues of economic and political equality in the city of New Haven.

Founded in Oakland, California, in 1966, by Huey Newton and Bobby Seale, the Black Panther Party for Self-Defense soon emerged as a national organization. The founders drafted a ten-point program that laid out the basic aims of the Party ready-made for export beyond Oakland. Consistent with point number five, which called for an end to police brutality, the Panthers also began armed patrols monitoring police.

After several high profile confrontations with police, including the incarceration of Party co-founder Huey Newton for the shooting of an Oakland police officer in 1967, in 1968 the Party dropped self-defense from its name and embarked on a series of "Serve the People" initiatives designed to soften its image and highlight its community service programs. The change in focus did little to deflect law enforcement's interest in the party, most notably the Federal Bureau of Investigation. The Director of the FBI would later refer to the Panthers as "the single greatest threat to the internal security" of the United States.

Fear and paranoia within the Panther organization led to efforts to ferret out suspected police informants, often with tragic consequences. In New York, national Panther "Field Marshal" George Sams, Jr., recruited local party member and 24-year-old Florida native Alex Rackley to accompany him on an inspection visit to New Haven. In New Haven, Sams accused Rackley of providing information to New York City police on New York Panthers accused in a bombing plot against the city and ordered him bound and gagged for interrogation. Over the next three days, the New Haven Panthers tortured Rackley in the hopes of extracting a confession. Sams ordered the titular head of the New Haven Party, Ericka Huggins, to tape the interrogation for National headquarters.

Formed in the winter of 1969, the New Haven Panther Party was born in the shadow of violence. Huggins relocated to the Elm City following the murder of her husband and fellow Panther, New Haven native Jon Huggins, on the campus of UCLA in December of 1968 by members of the US organization, a rival Black Power group, seeking to control the future of the Black Studies Program at the university. Prior to Huggins' arrival, attempts at establishing a chapter of the BPP in Bridgeport drew some interest. In January of 1969, the *Bridgeport Post Telegram* reported that an Oakland Panther named Jose Gonzalez had organized a chapter of the Party in that city. With Huggins' arrival, a majority of the would-be Panthers in Bridgeport merged with similarly interested recruits in New Haven and went to work implementing the BPP's programs in earnest. Selling the party newspaper coupled with community service work and political education classes occupied the majority of their time. Although the national offices would later claim that Huggins was the only acknowledged Panther in New Haven, the Party made strong inroads recruiting a small cadre of activists amplified by dozens of volunteers who helped to staff the Panthers programs and who also regularly attended political education classes.

The Panthers community work continued the focus of earlier Black Power organizations in the city such as the Hill Parents Association (HPA), which had also focused on community service initiatives as the key to improving the condition of blacks and Latinos within the city. After a riot took place in the city in the summer of 1967, the Hill Parents Association was virtually driven out of existence by a campaign of police harassment, leaving a void that the BPP would later help to fill.

Like the HPA, the New Haven BPP would also be the subject of intense scrutiny by local, state, and Federal law enforcement. In fact, the Rackley murder resulted in part from efforts of the BPP to root out persons whom BPP co-founder Huey Newton described as "Jackanapes," a network of spies and informers whom the BPP blamed for fomenting dissension within the Party's ranks and engaging in activities that compromised the image of the Party in the eyes of the community. The Panthers concerns were not without merit. In areas where the BPP was active, the FBI, along with various state and local law enforcement agencies, had been closely monitoring the activities of the party and had been recruiting informants to infiltrate its ranks. The Bureau seized upon these efforts as part of its Cointelpro or Counter Intelligence Program that targeted groups like the Panthers whom FBI Director J. Edgar Hoover labeled as "Black Nationalists and Hate type organizations." Unfortunately, for all parties in New Haven, the result of these efforts would have tragic results.

Among those arrested for the Rackley murder were New Haven Panther recruits Warren Kimbro and Lonnie McLucas. New Haven Prosecutor Arnold Markle also sought to implicate Ericka Huggins, as well as national party chairperson Bobby Seale, claiming that the Panthers executed Rackley on Seale's orders. Kimbro, who had been one of the local party's dedicated organizers, turned state's evidence, and agreed to testify against the Panthers. He joined Sams, who claimed he had orchestrated the torture of Rackley at Seale's behest, as one of the prosecution's star witnesses. The state elected to try McLucas first. Jury selection began in May 1970 against the backdrop of growing national interest in the case.

Capitalizing on this interest, and in an effort to help pay for the defense of those accused, the BPP disclosed plans for a three day fund raising campaign on the New Haven Green set to commence on May Day. In an effort to drum up support, the BPP invited a slate of nationally recognized speakers to appear including Youth International Party leader Abbie Hoffman and anti-war activist Dr. Benjamin Spock. Panther supporters planned to descend on the Elm City on May Day weekend to protest the impending trial. Fearing the potential for violence and stoked to a certain extent by the rhetoric of activists like Hoffman, who claimed the protesters' intent would be to "Free Bobby" and "burn Yale," and Panther Chief of Staff David Hilliard, who made similar statements, state and local authorities teamed with Federal law enforcement to prepare for battle.

In advance of reports that anticipated anywhere from 50,000 to 500,000 demonstrators, Connecticut Governor John Dempsey mobilized the Connecticut National Guard, while U.S Attorney General John Mitchell asked the Pentagon to deploy 4,000 marines and paratroopers to military instillations in close proximity to the city. Yale University President Kingman Brewster publicly expressed reservations that a Black revolutionary could receive a fair trial in the United States. While encouraging faculty to cancel classes, he also kept the University open as a resource to house and feed protesters.

Aside from a few minor skirmishes, however, the protests remained peaceful with radical students, antiwar protesters, and a variety of other activists swelling the ranks of the Panthers supporters.

During the McLucas trial that began in July, Kimbro and Sams emerged as the state's star witnesses. Neither proved especially convincing on the stand. Kimbro acknowledged that he fired the fatal shot that killed Rackley after Sams handed him a gun telling him that orders had come down from national to "ice" Rackley. While both testified that McLucas fired a safety shot into Rackley's chest to finish the job, neither could establish McLucas' culpability for the murder. After the trial closed in early August, the jury took several days to acquit McLucas on all charges except conspiracy to kill which earned him a twelve-year sentence.

When the second Rackley murder trial—with Ericka Huggins and Bobby Seale as co-defendants—commenced in October 1970 the tide had turned in the Panthers favor. The prosecution's lackluster performance in the first trial greatly diminished the bluster exhibited by state officials in the aftermath of the initial arrests and pointed to a similar outcome in the Seale and Huggins proceedings. Huggins and Seale were also favored with a strong legal team. Catherine Roraback, a Connecticut civil rights attorney best known for arguing the 1965 Supreme Court case that legalized the use of birth control in Connecticut, represented Huggins. Charles Garry, Huey Newton's attorney from his 1967 trial for murder in connection with slaying an Oakland, California, policeman, represented Seale. The seasoned barristers were accustomed to taking on radical causes and were able to mount a successful defense based on the state's weak evidence. Prosecutor Markle in the meantime struggled to produce witnesses other than Sams who would testify that Seale gave the order to kill Rackley.

Given the immense publicity generated by the legal proceedings and the May Day protests, efforts at seating an impartial jury took four months shattering the record set by the McLucas trial. Even with McLucas' conviction, the case against Huggins and Seale was porous. The narrative of events established by all the witnesses including the prosecution's own contradicted the state's case against Seale and Huggins. Kimbro, who testified first, proved unable to tie Huggins to the shooting and acknowledged that he had never seen Seale at the Panther headquarters as Sams had alleged. The defense in the meantime was able to call into question not only Sams' veracity, but also his mental health. Garry was able to show that Seale had expelled Sams, a diagnosed mental patient with a long history of violence, from the Party for beating up several members. In spite of his expulsion, and underscoring the organizational shortcomings of the national Black Panther Party, Sams was still able to pass himself off as a Panther Field Marshall. Shortly before Seale's scheduled arrival in New Haven to deliver a speech at Yale's Battell Chapel on May 19, 1969, Sams and several other emissaries from the national offices showed up on the inspection visit. Testimony for both sides clearly illustrated that Sams initiated the torture of Rackley, and that he ordered it recorded on tape for national headquarters. More importantly, only Sams testified to Seale's alleged directive to kill Rackley.

Prosecutor Markle's attempt to call a New Haven Police detective to the stand to support Sams' claim that Seale entered the headquarters backfired when a diagram displaying where the detective had been parked on the night in question disputed his testimony. The prosecution finally rested in late April. The case went to the jury on May 29. After five days of intense deliberation, the jury reported that it was hopelessly deadlocked 11 to 1 in favor of an acquittal for Seale, and 10 to 2 in favor of an acquittal for Huggins.

As Lonnie McLucas' counsel Michael Koskoff conceptualized the problem, the prosecution's downfall was its attempt to implicate Seale. "They already had a confession from two shooters," Koskoff explained, "They could do no better than that. [State's Attorney] Markle . . . got sucked in by the politics." Citing the prejudicial nature of the publicity generated by both trials, on May 25 Judge Harold Mulvey dismissed the charges against Huggins and Seale. "I find it impossible to believe," he explained in issuing his ruling "that an unbiased jury could be selected without superhuman efforts— efforts which this court, the state, and these defendants should not be called upon to either to make or to endure."[2]

Although the trial ultimately ended in acquittals, the legacy of the New Haven trials is mixed. The trial revealed the vast array of law enforcement techniques and resources used against the Panthers, from paid informants to illegal electronic surveillance.

Celebrated for keeping New Haven calm during May Day, it was later discovered, for example, that the New Haven Police had extensive wiretaps on the Panther headquarters in violation of state and Federal law. More importantly, the New Haven police may have failed to act to prevent the Rackley murder and facilitated the transport of Rackley to the place of his execution via the use of a paid informant's car in the hopes of making a strong case against the Panthers. In the early 1980s, the city settled a massive lawsuit with the victims of the wiretaps including several members of the Black Panther Party.

The legacy of the trial for the Panthers is also mixed. The trial brought national attention to New Haven, and the Panthers committed resources to make New Haven a model chapter, implementing a range of community service programs including a free health clinic that endured beyond the Panther's stay. While in prison awaiting their trials, both Seale and Huggins brought awareness to prisoner abuses. Seale went to work in earnest organizing prisoners at the Montville jail, where he threatened a hunger strike to bring attention to the treatment of those incarcerated there. Huggins likewise used her time in prison to highlight the treatment of female prisoners, especially mothers. Nevertheless, the trial also exposed the problems inherent in the Party's organizational structure and the willingness, even if prodded by informants and agent provocateurs, of members to kill, even one of their own, in the name of advancing their revolutionary aims.

Being able to link the Party with such acts further hurt it in the eyes of the public and provided many opportunities for law enforcement to justify its campaign of harassment that continued to bear deadly fruit. The FBI hunt for George Sams in connection with the Rackley murder, for instance, had set off a series of confrontations between police and the Black Panthers in Chicago that culminated in the December 4, 1969, pre-dawn raid on Party headquarters there. That raid resulted in the police killings of Chicago BPP leaders Fred Hampton and Mark Clark. Police were able to execute the raid with a floor plan of the apartment where the Panthers were staying, drawn by Chicago Minister of Defense, William O'Neal, a paid informant with the FBI.

The reverberations of the Panther trials within New Haven had a significant impact as well. The city for a brief moment captured the national spotlight as the epicenter of radical protest. George Sams, Warren Kimbro, and Lonnie McLucas received sentences for their role in the murder of Alex Rackley. After pleading guilty to second-degree murder and agreeing to turn states evidence, Kimbro ultimately served four years of a life sentence earning time off for exemplary behavior. He dedicated the rest of his life to trying to make a difference through community outreach initiatives. Also paroled after four years, Sams has been in and out of prison for a variety of charges. Granted release on an appeal bond in 1974, McLucas served the longest sentence of all those convicted. With the threat of his bail being revoked in 1977, he refused to denounce his work with the Party. He nevertheless told reporters, "But I deeply regret those three days."[3]

On the positive side, the activities around the trials demonstrated the organizing capabilities of the Panthers and the party's ability to inspire radical change. It also illustrated how the quest for Black Power need not exclude white supporters as black and white activists joined together in a variety of initiatives inspired by the Panther trial to address political inequality, health care, and prisoner's rights issues.

## Notes

1. On the Black Panther Trails in New Haven, see Yohuru Williams, *Black Politics/White Power: Civil Rights, Black Power, and the Black Panthers in New Haven* (Blackwell Press, 2000); Geoffrey Kabaservice, *The Guardians: Kingman Brewster, His Circle, and the Rise of the Liberal Establishment* (New York: Henry Holt and Company, 2004); Paul Bass and Douglas W. Rae, *Murder in the Model City: The Black Panthers, Yale and the Redemption of a Killer* (New York: Basic Books, 2006); Gail Sheehy, *Panthermania: The Clash of Black Against Black in One American City* (New York: Harper & Row, 1971). On New Haven generally in this period, see Williams, *Black Politics/White Power*; Mandi Isaacs Jackson, *Model City Blues: Urban Space and Organized Resistance in New Haven* (Philadelphia: Temple University Press, 2008). See also Yohuru Williams, "No Haven: From Civil Rights to Black Power in New Haven, Connecticut," in *The Black Scholar*, 31, no. 3-4 (Fall/Winter 2001): 54–66; Robert A. Dahl, *Who Governs?* (New Haven: Yale University Press, 1961); Jane Jacobs, *The Death and Life of Great American Cities* (New York: Vintage, 1961); Fred Powledge, *Model City, a Test of American Liberalism: One Town's Efforts to Rebuild Itself* (New York: Simon & Shuster, 1970); Allan R. Talbot, *The Mayor's Game: Richard Lee of New Haven and the Politics of Change* (New York: Harper & Row, 1967); William Lee Miller, *The Fifteenth Ward and the Great Society: An Encounter with a Modern City* (Cambridge: Riverside Press, 1966). On the Black Panther Party as a national organization, see Yohuru Williams and Jama Lazerow, eds., *In Search of the Black Panther Party: New Perspectives on a Revolutionary Movement* (Duke University Press, 2006); Yohuru Williams and Jama Lazerow, eds., *Liberated Territory: Untold Local Perspectives on the Black Panther Party* (Duke University Press 2008). For an account of what was happening elsewhere in Hartford, Connecticut, in this period, see Stacey Close's outstanding essay, "Fire in the Bones: The NAACP, Civil Rights, and Militancy in Hartford, 1943–67," *Journal of Negro History* (Summer 2001).

2. "Unbiased Jury Impossible to Find, Seale Jury," *Eugene Register-Guard* (Eugene, Oregon), May 26, 1971, May 26, 1971, 4a; "Seale Juror Says She Forced Mistrial." *St. Petersburg Times* (St. Petersburg, Florida), May 27, 1971, 12a.

3. McLucas quoted in "Panther Lonnie McLucas still fighting to stay out of prison," *South Mississippi Sun* (Biloxi, MS), October 12, 1977, B-13; see also "McLucas Faces Jail Again in Wake of Court Hearing," *Bridgeport Post* (Bridgeport, CT), October 4, 1977, 3.

# 51 My Dad, Jackie McLean

"Jackie McLean in Connecticut" began in the 1960s. Little did we know at the time that "Jackie McLean in Connecticut" would give birth to two major institutions: The African American Music Department at the Hartt School, University of Hartford (renamed The Jackie McLean Institute of Jazz in 2000), and the Artists Collective, Inc. Both continue to exist today, almost four decades later.

The template for the Artists Collective was formulated throughout the sixties on New York City's Lower East Side, where we lived, and in Harlem. My father became involved with Mobilization for Youth, one of the poverty programs developed by Robert Kennedy during the John F. Kennedy administration. He also worked with the HARYOU ACT, an initiative supported by Congressman Adam Clayton Powell, Jr., to introduce the arts to youth in Harlem. These programs were among several developed nationally in response to the volatile political times of riots, protests, and demonstrations taking place in America's inner-city communities.

My father performed at many of New York City's jazz meccas, including Slug's Saloon, formerly an Armenian bar in our neighborhood. He helped to establish Slug's as a jazz club by initially proposing Sunday afternoon jazz sessions featuring his band. The success of the Sunday events led to sessions throughout the week, and soon the giants of jazz were performing there on a weekly basis.

Jackie McLean's first encounter with Hartford came years earlier when he was a member of Art Blakey's Jazz Messengers. He recalled performing at the Strand Theater. His next Hartford encounter, sometime in the mid-sixties, would come at the invitation of Hartford jazz musician Paul Brown, who hired his band to perform at the Monday Night Jazz concert series offered by the Community Renewal Team.

During this time, my father met Tony Keller, who was the first executive director of the Connecticut Commission on the Arts during the Ella Grasso administration. The meeting would be the beginning of a life-long friendship, and it led to Dad's being invited to become an artist in residence advisor in North Hartford.

During one of my father's performances at a New York club, students attending the University of Hartford, wanting their culture to be better reflected in the curriculum, approached him about teaching a course on African American music. This would be the beginning of the African American Music Department at the Hartt School.

In the beginning, Dad commuted back and forth for his classes, which were held once a week. As time passed, more classes were added, and he began to formalize the African American Music Department with the blessing of Hartt School Founder Dr. Moshe Paranov. Though the two men were from different worlds and generations, they enjoyed intellectual conversations about music, history—and dogs. My father often spoke about Dr. Paranov's beloved pets. Dr. Paranov would succeed each of his dogs with one of the same breed—and the same name. My dad knew them all and loved the concept of renaming multiple dogs of the same breed over a lifetime. When Dr. Paranov retired, my father remained in contact with him, and they worked on special projects until Dr. Paranov's death in 1994 at age 99.

When Dad arrived, the University of Hartford campus was in its infancy; the Hartt School and other initial structures were relatively new. The African American Music Department began in a trailer where the path is now between the Hartt School and the Harry Jack Gray Center. The Gengras Student Union at the time functioned as a cafeteria, game area, bank window, post office, and more. The game area included a pool table, a place my father frequented so he could commune with the students. Often these encounters became counseling sessions about life, lessons he had learned the hard way, and, many times, drug abuse. Counseling was another of my father's callings. He counseled in the New York penal system, in our community, and anyone he thought was in trouble. He continued this avocation when we moved to Hartford.

As my father's Hartford responsibilities grew, he was invited to stay with the Keller family during the week. Conversations about a community arts initiative began.

As time passed, my father and mother Dollie (who was reluctant to move to Hartford) started to consider the idea of moving here. Before the move took place, I was sent on the second phase of the McLean pioneering expedition to Hartford and was enrolled in school. Again, the Kellers extended their home to my dad and me.

We stayed with them during the week and returned to New York on the weekends.

Eventually my father, with the help of Tony Keller, convinced my mother to move to Hartford. My oldest brother was married by this time and not living at home. He and his wife moved into our apartment on the Lower East Side. I am sure my mother really liked this idea—just in case things didn't work out in Hartford. My other brother, who was engaged, did move with us but returned to New York within the year to be married and remained in New York for several years. Eventually he and his wife moved to Hartford.

Living in Hartford, my father continued teaching and developing the African American Music Department at the University of Hartford, which at times was difficult. Until Jackie McLean arrived, Hartt's culture, understanding, and respect embraced only Western classical music traditions. He was also becoming more involved with the North Hartford community and continued drug counseling in addition to performing.

He and Tony Keller began to formulate the idea of a group of artists coming together to teach the arts and to address the perils faced by inner-city youth. With Paul Brown, he enlisted Ionis Martin, Cheryl Smith, and other local artists working in the community. The group began meeting regularly in our living room, and the Artists Collective was born. The Collective began its programming in area schools. My mother became interested in helping. Her work ethic, administrative, artistic, and managerial skills, driven passion, and self-taught business acumen (honed by managing my father's music career) would propel the concept of the Artists Collective into what it is today, the benchmark for community-based programs nationally.

The Artists Collective's first home, in 1973, was at 780 Windsor Street. In 1975, the owners of the building wanted to sell it, and the Collective had to relocate. Nick Carbone, then deputy mayor, and Donald Conrad of the Aetna helped find a new home for the Collective at 35 Clark Street (formerly Saint Michael's School). In 1999, after sixteen years of relentless, driven work by Dollie and others, the Collective was able to commission and build a new building on Albany Avenue designed by Tai Soo Kim.

Jackie McLean touched many people around the world through his art and humanity. All kinds of people from all walks of life recount wonderful stories about my dad, the artist. I am currently communicating with a man from Israel who tells me stories of how he plays Jackie McLean music for his daughter who is five, and how much she loves him. And there's the cab driver who told of being on the verge of suicide due to drug addiction until one fateful encounter with my father, an encounter he credits as saving his life; and the Japanese man who pleaded to come to Hartford to see Jackie McLean just to say thank you because in his youth he had traveled from a remote area in Japan to see my father perform in Tokyo. Once there, he ran out of money, and my father gave him a meal and money to get back home. The gentleman is now an executive at a major Japanese automobile company. I now refer to these wonderful, random communications as postcards from my dad. They keep me connected to him.

## Note

This essay appeared in the Fall 2008 issue of *Connecticut Explored*.

*Charles A. Teale, Sr.*

# 52 My Summers at Camp Courant

When I was a child living in the housing complex known as Bellevue Square in the 1960s, I initially had a very good life. I had all of the resources necessary to be a very happy kid. Then at around the age of six things began to change drastically. My father became very ill and could no longer support our household. The most obvious evidence of this was the lack of food in the house. I can literally recall a time when the only thing in our refrigerator was a bottle of water. We frequently would have to rely on family and neighbors for our meals, which is why some people I knew back then are like family to me even now.

In the midst of all of this were many families of like circumstance. I distinctly recall the first summer that my sister Karen and I spent living under these conditions. We were playing outside one morning when the children of the Jones family passed us by. Two of them were twins, Debra and Dianne, and one of them said, "Hey, Charlie, do you want to go to Camp Courant?" I said "Camp Courant, what's that?" Upon hearing my question she stepped back and looked at me like I had two heads. She then replied, "You don't know what Camp Courant is?"

Now one thing that all of the Jones kids could do was run, so she ran up the four flights of stairs to my mother, and the next thing I knew I was standing in front of the Keney Clock Tower on Main Street, waiting for the bus to go to Camp Courant. Immediately upon entering the bus the children began singing songs that everyone seemed to know but me. I don't think I said a word until we reached the entrance of Camp Courant, which meant that we had to climb a huge hill. At that time I joined in the chant "We've got to make it up the hill," which we repeated until there was no more hill to climb.

When we got off the bus it was like stepping off of a plane and walking into Disneyworld. Because the project I lived in was almost all asphalt and there was no level grassy area to be found, we used to go to the front lawn of Union Baptist Church on Main Street to play football. From time to time someone would kick the ball inaccurately and it would end up in Old North Cemetery. (You could prove how brave you were by just climbing over the fence and retrieving the ball). There was no swimming pool or anything of the sort to be found outside. The basketball court was crowded with teenagers, and a kid of age six wasn't welcome there.

But at Camp Courant I simply followed my friends from one activity to another for hours until I heard someone yell the words "lunch time." As anyone will tell you who went to Camp Courant in the early 1960s, it was time for a glass of milk, two cookies, and a peanut butter and jelly sandwich. After that we had to wait an hour, and then we could go swimming in the pool that still stands in the same location today.

As if days like these weren't exciting enough, there were special days for dignitaries and stars, like Hartford jewelry story owner Bill Savitt (Mr. P.O.M.G., his store's slogan stood for "Peace of Mind Guaranteed") day and Pat Hogan Day. Although Bill Savitt day meant free ice cream, my favorite day was Pat Hogan day. Pat Hogan was the High Sheriff at the time, and he would have people hand out cowboy hats with his name embroidered on them. Walking home from the bus was always interesting on Pat Hogan day because if you were not careful someone would snatch the hat off of your head and the next thing you knew your hat would be on someone else's head.

I was nine years old when we moved from the neighborhood where I used to take the bus to Camp Courant, and it would be another thirty years exactly before I would return to celebrate the 100th anniversary of this institution. With the exception of the maypole (which was gone), everything was exactly the same as I remembered. When it was time for us to eat at this celebration, I was stunned to see that peanut butter and jelly sandwiches were on the dining table. I could not resist the temptation to reminisce about my childhood and made the obvious choice.

In the year 2000, I became chief of the Hartford Fire Department, and Camp Courant was going through major renovations. My wife Helaine and I had the opportunity to participate in this capital improvement project, which transformed the site for the first time in forty years. Now the camp has the same meaning, but the programs offered far exceed those that people of my generation enjoyed.

As I look back on those days before Camp Courant, I remember as a child wondering if anyone cared about me and other children in my neighborhood experiencing the same challenges. I believe this question was answered in the affirmative by the actions of those who made Camp Courant possible, and their contribution helped to instill in me an attitude of service to others. In 2009 I became the first lifetime achievement award recipient in the 115-year history of Camp Courant.

I will always owe Camp Courant a great debt of gratitude.


Note

This essay appeared in the Summer 2010 issue of *Connecticut Explored*.

# PART VII

A Recipe
for the
Future

*Wm. Frank Mitchell*

# 53 My Grandmother's Squash Pie

## *A Regional Discussion of African American Foodways*

People tell their life stories through food . . . They talk about how they did it then, how they do it now. The way they talk tells you who they are.
—DORI SANDERS, *New York Times Magazine*, November 12, 1995

I came to understand that you could tell any story, large or small, through food. The space program, the state of the poor and the state of the rich, life as a soldier, life as a star—all of it could be told through the prism of what was on the table, or what wasn't.
—KIM SEVERSON, *Spoon Fed: How Eight Cooks Saved My Life* (2010)

At any holiday meal in my home in Cleveland during the 1980s my Connecticut grandmother's squash pie was the least welcome guest. More than any green vegetable, more than her famous stewed tomatoes, my cousins and I approached the butternut squash pie with resignation. Duty required eating a little, but it seemed a poor ending to a feast. There were other dessert options at Thanksgiving that we thought ought to replace that pie, but somehow it endured. Though we suffered its presence, we never wondered about its origins. Years later, I found myself wondering how this particular vegetable came to be the pastry of aggravation during our holidays. What was the origin of this recipe, and how far had it traveled to become this commemorative sign for my grandmother? Of course, the question we never considered was, how would our holiday celebrations change when my grandmother, Sarah Taylor Powers, wasn't around to make that pie?

Immediately after their wedding in 1957, my parents John and Betty left Hartford for a honeymoon in California. They made it as far as Cleveland and decided to stay. It wasn't long before my grandparents, my mother's sisters, and their families had all moved to Cleveland. They found a few old friends there—including the

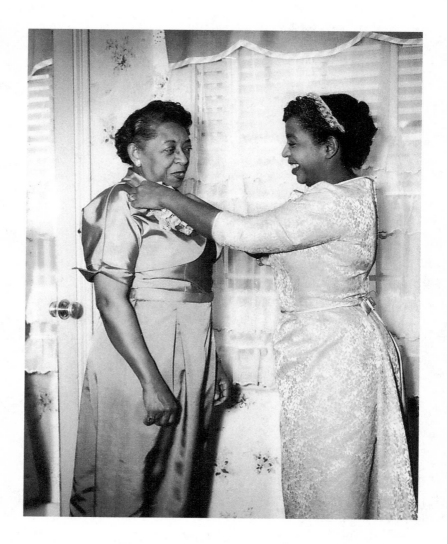

Rev. Emanuel S. Branch, who had moved from Connecticut to lead
a Cleveland church, and they made new friends too.

My grandparents had a more difficult transition to living in the
Midwest. They were Connecticut natives whose life together included residences in Hartford's South End, Bloomfield, and finally
on Tower Avenue in the North End between 1920 and 1960. My
grandmother's family worshipped at Hartford's Union Baptist
Church from its beginnings in the 1870s, but she lived her last years
marooned in the Cleveland suburbs attending a Methodist church.

The Methodist church turned out to be the only compromise
that she would be willing to make. From food, to clothes, to faith,
my grandmother brought with her ideas and customs from Connecticut. She made us a milky, sweet tea she called "cambric." There

was the piece of women's clothing she called a "jumper" that my sister refused to accept. There were the Bible stories, plans for the backyard garden, and opinions on haircuts. But the squash pie was supreme in its idiosyncrasy and effrontery. We didn't know its history, or its journey, but the pie had something to say, and my resolute grandmother continued baking it and bringing it to meals where she knew the more popular sweet potato pie, pumpkin pie, apple pie, and pound cake would be served.

### Pie as Puzzle with Colonial Histories Baked in . . .

My grandmother's stories of her Hartford childhood were so captivating that we looked forward to hearing them on our summer trips to Connecticut. My grandfather, Alfred Powers, shared much less, but there is evidence of his family's existence in mid-nineteenth-century Old Saybrook. Some of the family moved on to Middletown and later fought in the Civil War. They welcomed the new century in Hartford, along with my grandmother Sarah Taylor's parents, who left Virginia's Tidewater area after the Civil War. Virginia's regional culinary culture, though not as celebrated as Louisiana's or South Carolina's, includes distinct Afri-Virginian foodways. Enslaved blacks participated in farming and bartering relationships that allowed them to survive on their rations. Produce from their supplementary gardens fortified the food they were assigned, and some even sold produce from their gardens back to the plantation kitchen. Records of the rations exchange between Thomas Jefferson and Monticello's enslaved blacks show that he purchased potatoes, squash, and other produce for his table from his enslaved workers.[1]

Squash fascinated Jefferson, who sent cymling and potato pumpkin seeds to colleagues and tried cultivating his own hybrids. He praised the potato pumpkin—a favorite with Monticello's black population. In a 1790 letter to Jamaican planter Samuel Vaughn, Jr., Jefferson wondered about the origins of different varieties and their journey from the warmer areas of the South American continent and Mexico to the American colonies. His cousin Mary Randolph included a recipe for the potato pumpkin in her influential 1824 cookbook *The Virginia Housewife*. Along with the native populations who cultivated the vegetable, Jefferson was the most prominent American squash advocate of the period. Some seed historians recognize the cushaw (or Tennessee sweet potato squash) as a green-and-yellow-striped descendant of Jefferson's potato pumpkin that continued to journey across the continent. Pie made with cushaw squash is a traditional favorite appearing in Afri-Virginian cooking, and its use in other areas of the South by the early twentieth century is documented. A version of the pie also appears in Fannie Farmer's 1896 *Boston Cooking-School Cookbook* and Freda DeKnight's 1948 classic *The Ebony Cookbook: A Date with A Dish.*[2]

The great and generative strains of African-American heritage cooking are the product of large and ultimately stationary black communities with some leisure to exploit their shared culinary practices. The foodways of Louisiana and South Carolina are the best-known American examples, but enslaved blacks carried the culinary fundamentals—characterized by a gardening imperative, limited time, and reconstructed recipes drawn from memory—to the North and the South. The transatlantic trade rewarded the Connecticut colony's residents for the advantages of navigable ports and fertile land. Ships sailed south from Connecticut stocked with locally grown provisions and returned with some of the area's earliest black residents.

Many of those black captives would become agricultural workers. Farm skills and culinary expertise brought distinction that helped some navigate life after freedom. These people were participants in the mainstream of Connecticut's economy. Though they were enslaved, their agricultural aptitude and hard-won work experience affirmed a direct connection to the rhythms of antebellum black life that powered the Southern economy. Many of eighteenth- and nineteenth-century Connecticut's most recognized black figures could claim farming in their skill set whether they were ministers, activists, sailors, or skilled tradesmen.

### A Bitter Harvest: Early Black Agricultural Workers

One of the state's earliest documented black residents is Waterbury's Fortune. Enslaved to Dr. Preserved Porter, Fortune and his family of four maintained Porter's seventy-five-acre farm in Waterbury. Fortune's crops included onions, potatoes, apples, buckwheat, oats, and rye. He lived nearby in a small house he owned. Baptized at St. John's Episcopal Church in 1797, Fortune died sometime the following year. After his death, Dr. Porter prepared Fortune's corpse as a teaching skeleton. Recent analysis of Fortune's bones has revealed a great deal about the backbreaking labor required to run an eighteenth-century farm in Connecticut. Fortune, who was in his sixties when he died, suffered over his lifetime from multiple injuries that were common hazards for agricultural workers.

West Hartford residents know Bristow as the name of a local middle school, but this once-enslaved man was also a confident farmer, landowner, and a native of Africa who purchased his freedom in 1775. Afterward, he remained employed by Thomas Hooker's wife Sarah while Hooker fought in the Revolutionary War. Bristow's public reputation as an agricultural expert would have been a product of his ability to acquire knowledge from diverse sources in order to grow and pickle the finest beets, harvest good corn for succotash or pudding, and coax the perfect wheat to make flour for tavern biscuits. Bristow would have learned to anticipate the difficult weather Hartford County residents faced in the late eighteenth century.

Bristow, Fortune, and other captive black farmers such as Adam Jackson of New London mastered the secrets necessary for cultivating Connecticut soil. Records left by John Bartram, Thomas Jefferson, and other gentlemen naturalists, and the account books and diaries of Connecticut farmers may be the best guides to work lives of black agricultural laborers in late eighteenth- and early nineteenth-century Connecticut. Joshua Hempsted (or Hempstead), the eighteenth-century farmer, New London town leader, and Adam Jackson's enslaver, kept a meticulous journal of daily life. He described the workdays he shared with Jackson, who worked Hempsted's land in New London and Stonington for thirty years. Hempsted recorded the picking of fruit in his orchards, chopping wood, fixing fences, harvesting corn, nautical duties, and even Adam's management of other enslaved African workers.[3]

As freedom found the state's enslaved blacks in the early nineteenth century, they made the journey from small-town isolation to the black neighborhoods of the larger cities. These fortified communities sponsored independent black churches and schools in Hartford, Middletown, New Haven, and Bridgeport, supported Prudence Crandall's students and the Amistad captives, and sent men to the Civil War with the Twenty-ninth Connecticut Colored Regiment. But blacks were still a small percentage of Connecticut's population throughout the nineteenth century. Their numbers would soon increase as World War I generated opportunities that would attract young African American laborers from the South. Before long Southern migrants were living with people who'd come from Jamaica, Nevis, and even farther.

By the 1920s the state's black population had grown more ethnically and regionally diverse. Many of the new residents were not only moving from south to north but also transitioning from rural to urban and from agricultural to industrial labor. The new residents had needs, and their neighbors opened rooming houses, lunch counters, little takeout shops, street vendor carts, and other small businesses to serve them. In these new predominantly black neighborhoods filled with poor, working, and professional people, shops that prepared and sold the food that signaled memories of home emerged.[4]

All was not well, however. Before long these neighborhoods became points of concern for social reformers and social scientists who were worried about overcrowding, sanitation, building conditions, and a range of social, cultural, and educational preferences. Some reformers imagined the migrants facing a difficult adjustment to their new urban lives and tried to address all aspects of their lives, from speech, to worship, and even to style of clothing. Cooking and eating elicited special attention. Reformers remembered the example of European immigrants who caused a panic when they tried to feed their "foreign" food to their American children. To combat this peril new residents could take lessons on American cooking at churches, settlement houses, and missions. Reformers need not have worried about Southern migrants' dietary habits, though. Often they were leaving farms and some even had experience with the public health campaigns run by the Negro universities and agricultural extension agents. Ironically, many migrants left situations where they had far more secure food sources that included locally grown produce from their own gardens for a much less certain food situation in the Northern cities.[5]

### Pie Promoter: Migration and a Southern Foodways Muse

Chef, cookbook author, and Southern foodways muse Edna Lewis made the Great Migration journey that defined so many lives in the early twentieth century. She was born in Freetown, Virginia, a town her grandfather helped found after gaining his freedom. Like many families who finally owned land denied them during slavery, Lewis's family found life measured by the seasons of the farm. Preparing, planting, tending, harvesting, and the communal celebrations and work parties that made big chores easier defined the narrative Lewis brought to her career as a New York chef. The promise of World War II's hiring boom lured Lewis to New York. Arriving after the war, she found work and a new life, though others in her cohort would be disappointed by the limited opportunities they found in post-war Waterbury, Bridgeport, Hartford, and New Haven. Lewis took a job in a Brooklyn laundry and later copied designer dresses, which led to her friendship with the antiques dealer John Nicholson. He hired her to cook at his Café Nicholson. Lewis's culinary skills, her reverent appreciation for the seasonal joys of farm life in the early twentieth century, and her ability to transmit that passion made her 1976 cookbook *The Taste of Country Cooking* a classic study of Southern cooking.

The book is organized by season with memories and lessons related to the recipes. The chores and rituals that inspire Lewis's farm memories parallel those of Adam Jackson, Fortune, Bristow, and many others who understood the joys of farming land they owned and eating food they produced as a family. Though separated by region, time, gender, and property rights, the doyenne of Southern cooking and Connecticut's early black agricultural workers were engaged in the same conversation. She couldn't have known how much she might miss those seasonal rhythms or how they would continue to inform her life when she left Virginia for post-WWII New York. She did recognize her good fortune in building a career cooking and promoting Southern foodways when many other migrants felt lucky to find employment in the Northeast's declining factories.

*Cutting the Pie Equitably: Nutrition for a Nation at War*

World War II made nutrition a national concern affecting young men waiting to be drafted, soldiers preparing for war, working mothers, and their school-aged children. The National School Lunch Act standardized the expectations for a healthy lunch and may be the best example of the metamorphosis the 1950s brought to American cooking and eating. Modern refrigerators, convenience foods, and military industrial investment in prepared food producers such as Chef Boyardee and the casual-dining chain Howard Johnson expanded options that made it easier to relinquish traditional foods and cooking methods. For mothers who had war industry jobs and an income, the new convenience foods were souvenirs of their wartime service that would last long after their jobs ended.

The munitions demands at factories in Connecticut's major cities brought new prosperity to black neighborhoods in Waterbury, Hartford, Bridgeport, and New Haven. With the war's end labor needs at Winchester, Chase Brass, and Remington Arms began to slow, but many hopeful migrants still traveled to Connecticut expecting to find manufacturing jobs. The impact of the manufacturing economy's shift was not immediately evident in the neighborhoods. Business at bars, jazz clubs, stores, and restaurants in neighborhoods nourished by the manufacturers remained steady through the 1950s even as the jobs began to disappear.[6]

Major menu changes in local restaurants in the early 1960s co-incided with the general expansion in American appetites; the beginnings of democratization in restaurant dining, the expansion of supermarkets, and the more intense, direct action campaign to expand civil rights. Across Connecticut, NAACP and Urban League officers investigated local civil rights complaints while encouraging members to think nationally, too. In 1960, the dining options in New Haven's Dixwell neighborhood included a restaurant specializing in grilled ribs called the Barbecue Grille. Within the year others would follow and Griff's Restaurant would reopen as Griff's Bar-B-Q. These restaurants were harbingers of the Soul idiom that would soon unite diverse black communities.

### Pie for Breakfast: The New Breakfast Program

Soul suggested the possibility of a summative network of shared cultural experiences that included culinary preferences. A cohesive black community was one of segregation's byproducts. Segregation and related civil rights obstacles defined, organized, and motivated that community. Success meant increased opportunity and choice, which some worried would lead to the fracturing of a previously unified community. Soul Food was an inevitable and comforting response. The dishes that activist writer Amiri Baraka sacralized in his 1960s essay "Soul Food" were the familiar choices. They were foods and styles of preparation that had shed any true regional distinction and moved with black migrants all over the country.[7]

In Connecticut the declining manufacturing economy, the growing population and difficult living conditions, and the nation's incendiary civil rights battles combined to make Hartford, New Haven, and other cities difficult for local and state government to manage. Highway construction and new housing opportunities in the neighboring suburbs lured prosperous white residents, along with shops and services, out of the cities. Without warning the long-suffering direct action activism of sit-ins and marches evolved into an impatiently aggressive political posture that seemed a response to Martin Luther King's 1964 declaration "Why We Can't Wait." In Hartford this transition was so tense that the North End erupted violently in the summers of 1967, 1968, and 1969. Sections of New Haven exploded in the summer of 1967 after a confrontation between a storeowner and a local teen. The destructive impact of such violence on the neighborhood infrastructure was the stunning visualization of the obscured but steady decline in opportunity. A generation that expected to find jobs as their older relatives had realized there would be fewer of those jobs and limited alternatives. Community resources that had made the neighborhoods dynamic and lively places closed or moved as the area's economic strength dissipated. Some essential services left and were replaced by government offices, nonprofits, convenience stores, and the occasional takeout shop or fast food restaurant. Others, especially the modern grocery store chains, skipped these neighborhoods, moving directly to the adjacent suburbs.[8]

Despite the good intentions and very sincere efforts of elected officials and social service staffers, challenges persisted. One of the more creative responses to scarcity was the Black Panther Party's Free Breakfast for School Children Program. After its start in Oakland, the breakfast program quickly spread to other American cities such as New Haven by the early 1970s. This program burnished the bona fides of the youthful self-defense activists by illustrating their concern for families and nutrition. The Panther breakfast—with its serving of rhetoric—stood in stark opposition to previous food programs in the neighborhoods run by reformers hoping to inculcate their mainstream values. A constituency that emerged from Hartford's unrest was an association of low-income mothers that campaigned for increased funding and improved services by foregrounding their status as mothers and their families' nutritional, financial, and economic needs. These groups confidently deployed food as a political symbol, forcing the realization that good nutrition, among other seemingly personal or cultural issues, can be political. Their organizing efforts set the table for future political milestones such as the election of Thirman Milner and John C. Daniels, the first black mayors of Hartford and New Haven, respectively.[9]

The coalitions of neighborhood activists were less successful in addressing the crumbling infrastructure or inspiring a reevaluation of historical or traditional foods that had sustained earlier generations. Fortunately, their environmentally focused peers recognized opportunity in those organizing efforts and used the model to inform their own activism centered on farming, food, and the potential impact on cities. Addressing Hartford's food security issues would be the first challenge. Proposed solutions included community gardens, longer growing seasons, improved relationships with farmers, and additional food processing and bulk-buying opportunities. The Hartford Food System, established in 1978, brought the legacy of direct action together with community organizing, family farming, and healthier living. That organization and others continued to mine neighborhoods for hopeful signs as they encouraged local economic vitality by supporting small health food stores, coop markets, and other ventures that brought nutritional diversity. The success of these initiatives emboldened others to pursue the next wave of urban environmental projects to coordinate better access to fresh and affordable food. Today at farmers' markets, community gardens, cooking demonstrations, and nutrition conversations around New Haven, Hartford, Bridgeport, and other cities, it is not unusual to hear shoppers discussing produce their mother or grandmother grew and the best methods for cooking.[10]

*A Recipe for the Future*

In *The Taste of Country Cooking*, Edna Lewis tells us that,

Over the years since I left home and lived in different cities, I have kept thinking about the people I grew up with and about our way of life. Whenever I go back to visit my sisters and brothers, we relive old times, remembering the past. And when we share again in gathering wild strawberries, canning, rendering lard, finding walnuts, picking persimmons, making fruitcake, I realize how much the bond that held us had to do with food. . . . Although the founders of Freetown have passed away, I am convinced that their ideas do live on for us to learn from, to enlarge upon, and pass on to the following generations. I am happy to see how many young people are going back to the land and to the South. They are interested in natural farming and they seem to want to know how we did things in the past, to learn firsthand from those who worked hard, loved the land, and relished the fruits of their labor.[11]

Cooking up a regional cuisine requires conditions that are impossible to manufacture. Some details about the diet of eighteenth-century blacks in Connecticut may be recovered by archaeological research, and it may be possible to learn more about the variety of foods eaten daily and the preferred cooking methods. Even if more is discovered about what early black residents ate and how they cooked it, their culinary impulses will remain a mystery. Favorite dishes, the instinctive style of preparation—fry, roast, or boil—and the memories and associations conveyed by those dishes; none of that will be recovered from the dirt. It won't be possible to know what sharing Election Day cake meant to celebrants on the eve of the eighteenth-century Black Governor elections. Certain foods symbolized those rare celebrations, but what those foods meant to people who had so little freedom and so few choices is difficult to ascertain without the lore to contextualize the food. There may never be a truly accurate reconstruction of the culinary culture that helped to unite Connecticut's small and disparate black community in the early nineteenth century. But their regional histories, structured by migration and change, belong to a narrative that reaches and reflects the experience of free black residents of Lewis's Freetown as well as that of the enslaved blacks at Jefferson's Monticello or the South Carolina rice plantation Drayton Hall.

The accounts left by the Connecticut narrators James Mars and Venture Smith, and even Hempsted's description of Adam Jackson's workdays, suggest that these men had the autonomy necessary to experiment and to dream. Did they wonder about the taste of vegetables they would one day grow on land they owned as free men? How much more satisfying would that food be? Could they ever convey the significance of a squash, a meal, or a celebration enjoyed under conditions that they created? And would those feelings ever matter to future generations fortunate enough to own land and born with the freedom to enjoy it?

### Traveling Miles: A Good Start

My grandmother's stories didn't go back to the eighteenth century, though sometimes it felt like they might. Though she shared plenty of advice, I find that I'm now like Jefferson writing to friends and strangers seeking guidance on the origins of a recipe. What is missing is the story behind the recipe. Did my grandmother's grandmother make the pie with cushaw or potato pumpkins grown in her garden? Was it the most memorable part of a seasonal celebration and one of the best memories carried North to Hartford? Was the presumably strategic switch to butternut or acorn squash a concession to what was available in New England? I am still not the most enthusiastic advocate of squash pie, but I respect its history, appreciate its inspiration, and accept the challenge to learn more about it. The evolving debate around improved food sources, more healthful eating, and the impact on our lives and planet adds to the urgency of efforts to understand the phenomenon that food historian Michael W. Twitty calls the "Cooking Gene," or the "food-steps" of our enslaved black ancestors' journey to freedom.[12] Cushaw squash shows up at the local farmers market, and the seeds are available through the heirloom catalogues. It hasn't grown perfectly in my garden yet, but I'll keep trying it, and requesting it at the market, and talking about why it matters. And I'll keep looking for the right balance of flavors—sweet, salty, spicy, sentimental, and progressive—to continue the pie's journey.

*Squash Pie*

    1 prepared piecrust
    1 medium sized butternut (or cushaw) squash
        (to yield 2 cups of squash puree)
    Butter or olive oil for roasting the squash
    1 teaspoon cardamom seeds
    2 teaspoons vanilla
    1 teaspoon ground nutmeg
    ½ teaspoon ground cloves
    ¼ cup dark brown sugar
    3 tablespoons honey
    ¼ teaspoon salt
    ¼ teaspoon cayenne
    3 large eggs
    ¾ cup light cream
    2 tablespoons mascarpone cheese

Variations: if you like a sweeter pie add another ¼ cup of sugar. For a little more smoke add a ½ teaspoon of imitation rum flavoring.

Cut squash in chunks brush with butter or oil and sprinkle cardamom, nutmeg, and some vanilla (reserve a little) on the pieces. Roast in 375-degree oven until tender, roughly 45 minutes to an hour. After they have cooled, peel and mash the squash into a chunkier paste and measure 2 cups roughly. Reserve any remaining squash for another dish.

To the squash, mix in spices and honey and stir; in another bowl whisk eggs until blended, add sugar, remaining vanilla, and end with the cream and cheese. Combine the two mixtures and continue stirring until smooth. Pour mix into prepared piecrust and place on cookie sheet to bake in 375-degree oven for forty to fifty minutes—checking regularly.

Notes

1. Leni Sorensen, "Taking Care of Themselves: Food Production by the Enslaved Community at Monticello," *Repast*, vol. 21, no. 2 (Spring 2005): 4. Maria Franklin, "The Archaeological and Symbolic Dimensions of Soul Food: Race, Culture, and Afro-Virginian Identity," in *Race and the Archaeology of Identity*, ed. Charles Orser (Salt Lake City: University of Utah Press, 2001).

2. *William Woys Weaver, Heirloom Vegetable Gardening: A Master Gardener's Guide to Planting, Seed Saving, and Cultural History* (New York: Henry Holt & Co./Owl Publishing Company, 1999). William Woys Weaver, *100 Vegetables and Where They Came From* (Chapel Hill, NC: Algonquin Books, 2000). Merrill D. Peterson, ed. *Thomas Jefferson: Writings, Autobiography, Notes on the State of Virginia, Public and Private Papers, Addresses, Letters* (New York: Library of America, 1984); Gary Paul Nabhan, *Renewing America's Food Traditions: Saving and Savoring the Continent's Most Endangered Foods* (White River Junction: Chelsea Green Publishing, 2008).

3. Pennsylvanians Benjamin Franklin and John Bartram consulted with Jefferson on botanical questions. Bartram published one of the first nursery catalogs and founded the American Philosophical Society with Benjamin Franklin. See www.bartramsgarden.org for more on John Bartram's legacy. For more on Bristow, see Nelson Burr, *From Colonial Parish to Modern Suburb: A Brief Appreciation of West Hartford* (West Hartford: West Hartford Historical Society, 1976); and Noah Webster House & West Hartford Historical Society online exhibition, *Bristow: Putting the Pieces of an African American Life Together*, noahwebsterhouse.org/programs/bristow.htm; Joshua Hempstead, *Diary of Joshua Hempstead of New London Connecticut: Covering a Period of 47 Years from September, 1711 to November, 1758 (1901 New London County Historical Society)* (Whitefish: Kessinger Publishing, 2008); For more on Fortune, see Marilyn Nelson, *Fortune's Bones: The Manumission Requiem* (Brooklyn: Handprint, 2004), and the Mattatuck Museum online exhibition *Fortune's Story*, www.fortunestory.org/fortune/.

4. Warner, *New Haven Negroes: A Social History*.

5. Kathryn J. Oberdeck, *The Evangelist and the Impresario: Religion, Entertainment, and Cultural Politics in America, 1884–1914* (Baltimore: Johns Hopkins University Press, 1999). Stephen Lassonde, *Learning to Forget: Schooling and Family Life in New Haven's Working Class, 1870–1940* (New Haven: Yale University Press, 2005). Tony L. Whitehead, "Sociocultural Dynamics and Food Habits in a Southern Community," in *Food in the Social Order: Studies of Food and Festivities in Three American Communities*, ed. Mary Douglas (New York, NY: Russell Sage Foundation, 1984). Robert T. Dirks and Nancy Duran, "African American Dietary Patterns at the Beginning of the 20th Century," *Journal of Nutrition*, 131, no. 7 (2001): 1881–89.

6. Harvey Levenstein, *Paradox of Plenty: A Social History of Eating in Modern America* (New York, NY: Oxford University Press, 1993); Douglas W. Rae, *City: Urbanism and Its End* (New Haven: Yale University Press, 2003). Geoffrey C. Ward and Ken Burns, *The War: An Intimate History, 1941–1945* (New York: Knopf, 2007).

7. Yohuru Williams, *Black Politics/White Power: Civil Rights, Black Power and the Black Panthers in New Haven* (New York: Wiley-Blackwell, 2000). Douglas W. Rae and Paul Bass, *Murder in the Model City: The Black Panthers, Yale, and the Redemption of a Killer* (New York: Basic Books, 2006). Fred Powledge, *Model City, a Test of American Liberalism: One Town's Effort to Rebuild Itself* (New York: Simon & Schuster, 1970). Mandi Isaacs Jackson, *Model City Blues: Urban Space and Organized Resistance in New Haven* (Philadelphia: Temple University Press, 2008). Dick Cluster, *They Should Have Served That Cup of Coffee: Seven Radicals Remember the '60s* (Cambridge: South

End Press, 1979). Robin D. G. Kelley, *Yo' Mama's Diskfunktional: Fighting the Culture Wars in Urban America* (Boston: Beacon Press, 1998). Vertamae Smart Grosvenor, *Vibration Cooking or the Travel Notes of a Geechee Girl* (New York: Ballantine, 1970). Amiri Baraka (Leroi Jones), *Home: Social Essays* (New York: Morrow, 1966).

8. Alan R. Talbot, *The Mayor's Game: Richard Lee of New Haven and the Politics of Change* (New York: Harper & Row, 1967); also see Powledge.

9. Jessica B. Harris, *High on the Hog: A Culinary Journey From Africa to America* (New York: Bloomsbury USA, 2011).

10. Mark Winne, *Closing the Food Gap: Resetting the Table in the Land of Plenty* (Boston: Beacon Press, 2008), 13–27; Tagan Engel/Cityseed, *New Haven Cooks: A Project of Cityseed* (New Haven: Cityseed, 2010).

11. Edna Lewis, *The Taste of Country Cooking* (New York: Knopf, 1976), xxi.

12. Michael W. Twitty, *Fighting Old Nep: The Foodways of Enslaved Afro-Marylanders, 1634–1864*, Afrofoodways.com, 2010. See also Twitty's website thecookinggene.com, and the D. Landreth Seed Company's African American Heritage Seed Collection, www.landrethseeds.com/catalog/african_american.php.

# 54  Conclusion

*The Charge of Citizenship
for African Americans*

To the free Africans and other free People of Color in the United States.

The Convention of Deputies from the Abolitions Societies in the United States, assembled at Philadelphia, have undertaken to address you upon subjects highly interesting to your prosperity.

We wish to see you act worthily of the rank you have acquired as freemen, and thereby to do credit to yourselves, and to justify the friends and advocates of your color in the eyes of the world . . .

—THEODORE FOSTER, President of the Pennsylvania Society for
Promoting the Abolition of Slavery, the Relief of Free Negroes unlawfully
held in Bondage, and for Improving the Condition of the African Race.
Philadelphia, January 6, 1796

When I entered Yale in 1968, ninety-six black men and women entered with me, the largest group of Afro-Americans ever to arrive on Yale's Old Campus at one time. We were, to a person, caught up in the magic of the moment. Our good fortune was to have been selected, like the few blacks who had preceded us, to be part of the first "large" group of blacks included in Yale's commitment to educate "1,000 male leaders" each year, as Yale's President, Kingman Brewster, declared to our class at the Freshman Assembly. "A thousand male leaders," he had intoned, and two hundred fifty women—for the first time in Yale's 250-year history. But what would becoming a true black leader entail—for ourselves, in the classroom, and for our people outside those hallowed Ivy Walls? What sort of sacrifices and obligations did this special ticket to success bring along with it? We worried about this, and we worried out loud, often, and noisily.

—HENRY LOUIS GATES, Jr., Yale College, class of 1973

Centuries separate Theodore Foster and Henry Louis Gates, Jr. though both recognized the communal responsibility that seemed to be a charge of citizenship for blacks in America.[1] Foster and the men he represented wished enslaved blacks well in the years the abolitionists hoped would bring the end of slavery. These early abolitionists were at the beginning of a long fight for equality that reached a culmination in the years when Gates and other black students entered American universities in large numbers. It is a story that Connecticut's archives, historical societies, and community organizations were well prepared to tell.

In the years after the Revolution, a group of the Northeast's patriotic gentry found abolitionism intriguing. In 1787, Pennsylvanians reorganized a dormant Pennsylvania Society for Promoting the Abolition of Slavery, the Relief of Free Negroes unlawfully held in Bondage, and for Improving the Condition of the African Race. In 1790, Congregational ministers Levi Hart and Jonathan Edwards joined with legislators and educators Simeon Baldwin and Timothy Dwight among other Connecticut state notables to organize the Connecticut Society for the Promotion of Freedom and the Relief of Persons Unlawfully Holden in Bondage. Connecticut's early abolitionists were well represented by the ten-point declaration from the Philadelphia convention that emphasized their guiding doctrine:

1. Accept the responsibility to attend public worship.
2. Literacy is a tool for generational improvement.
3. Developing skills in a useful trade.
4. Recognize the value of diligence, frugality, and simplicity in daily life.
5. Abstinence is a virtue, particularly around alcohol.
6. Remain vigilant against vice especially idleness, frolicking, and dissipation.
7. Embrace legal marriage.
8. Save money and invest in lots, farms, and houses.
9. Maintain a solid public reputation, which will help the community.
10. Serve God and good will follow.[2]

Hart, Edwards, Baldwin, and others truly believed in these principles and as relatively self-made men they had followed these rules and found success. Many had a Yale affiliation and they believed that education, investment in property, and good moral character had been essential to their success. These guiding principles could help the gradually emancipating black community become successful Americans too. The God-centered lifestyle assumes legal marriage, moral behavior, frugality, and the good reputation that follows.

The progressive suggestion to pursue education and self-sufficiency through property ownership was one that many Northeastern blacks —enslaved and free—were ready to hear, but Connecticut's black residents worked toward a different goal than simple personal success. Obtaining an education and securing property were difficult achievements for the recently freed, and those assets were often leveraged for a community benefit like broader civil rights reform.

Not all Connecticut citizens believed their black neighbors were ready to live freely amongst them as a study by The Connecticut Academy of Arts & Sciences at the turn of the nineteenth century revealed. Founded by civic leaders like Hart, Baldwin, and Noah Webster, The Connecticut Academy of Arts and Sciences was created "to promote, diffuse & preserve the knowledge of those Arts & Sciences, which are the support of Agriculture, Manufactures & Commerce, & to advance the dignity, virtue & happiness of a people." In 1800 The Academy sent out a statewide survey requesting information on a range of topics including "free blacks; their number, vices and modes of life, their industry and success in acquiring property; whether those born free are more ingenious, industrious and virtuous, than those who were emancipated after arriving to adult years."

Unfortunately the responses suggested that the abolitionists were far ahead of public opinion in their attitudes about the end of slavery and black residence in Connecticut. While a few respondents reported that their black neighbors were doing well, others were unimpressed and offered harsh assessments of their black neighbors' morality, work ethic, and ambition. Most troubling to the abolitionists was the nearly unanimous absence of property ownership among the freed people. A few responses mentioned black families who managed to secure property but they were exceptions. The CAAS study—a collection of short anecdotal responses from assorted Connecticut towns—helped convince some Society members that neither the state nor its black residents were ready for emancipation and equality.[3]

But emancipation came. It crept in gradually and blacks in Connecticut fought for the basic privileges of freedom. Many followed some version of the puritanical recommendations that emerged from the Philadelphia convention. By fighting for education and trying to pass along property, the state's free blacks nurtured a coherent black community that would welcome their newly emancipated or recently emigrated brothers and sisters. The struggle to establish that community would slowly but surely generate a document trail that would refute CAAS's 1800 collection of doubts and criticisms.

Bitter experience taught Connecticut's earliest black residents lessons on the vagaries of property ownership for blacks. It could help with some forms of independence, but owning property might never translate into freedom: Waterbury's Fortune died enslaved though he owned a home next door to his enslaver. West Hartford's Bristow bought his freedom from Thomas Hart Hooker as Hooker left for the Revolutionary War. The land he managed to acquire in a nearby town went to Hooker's children after Bristow's death. The struggle to maintain property or to leverage the asset to care for family meant it was seldom the solid, dependable, and inheritable asset it seemed to be for whites. One of the state's best known slavery narrators, Venture Smith, saw land, boats, and other assets slip through his hands as he bought family and friends out of slavery, nursed them through illness and misfortune, and suffered through bad investments or robbery. Near the end of his 1798 autobiography he writes:

I have many consolations; Meg, the wife of my youth, whom I married for love, and bought with my money, is still alive. My freedom is a privilege which nothing else can equal. Notwithstanding all the losses I have suffered by fire, by the injustice of knaves, by the cruelty and oppression of false hearted friends, and the perfidy of my own countrymen whom I have assisted and redeemed from bondage, I am now possessed of more than one hundred acres of land, and three habitable dwelling houses. It gives me joy to think that I *have* and that I *deserve* so good a character, especially for *truth* and *integrity*. While I am now looking to the grave as my home, my joy for this world would be full—If my children, Cuff for whom I paid two hundred dollars when a boy, and Solomon who was born soon after I purchased his mother—If Cuff and Solomon—O! that they had walked in the way of their father. But a father's lips are closed in silence and in grief!— Vanity of vanities, all is vanity![4]

Similarly New Haven's William Lanson, a prosperous builder, hotelkeeper, and civic leader, endeavored to keep the land and property he'd acquired in the city's New Township after family illness, poor investments, business expenses, and the machinations of local detractors threatened his achievements. As his fortune slid several public documents appeared in defense of his character and his success. Isaiah Lanson's 1846 pamphlet is a reasoned explication of his father's opportunities and the obstacles he faced while running businesses in nineteenth-century New Haven. He persuasively argues that "If Mr. L. had been a white man, he would have had at least some advantages which he has not had. Some evidence of his would have been taken as good. We have no hesitation in saying that the jury were in a measure prejudiced."[5]

The saga of Connecticut's other noted slavery narrator, James Mars, supports the abolitionists' belief that Connecticut blacks were ready to pursue freedom. Determined beyond his years, the teen-aged Mars ran away from his enslavers and repeatedly rejected the terms of his service. His Christian faith led him to reconcile with his enslaver as he reached the age of emancipation. Mars became a church leader and an activist in Hartford and finally settled with his family in Pittsfield, Massachusetts, where he bought property. When he could no longer farm the land, he moved between Connecticut and Massachusetts selling the short publication that told the story of his early years enslaved in Connecticut. Mars, Lanson, and Smith fought fiercely to improve themselves and the world around them. With all they gained and lost, each could ultimately claim his biography as property and legacy.

Opportunities increased slightly for the next generation. In the early nineteenth century black children attended school with their white peers in larger cities like New Haven, Hartford, and Bridgeport and in smaller towns like Norwich, Litchfield, and Colchester. Often they were not truly welcome and sometimes barely tolerated. There were parents who wanted their children educated but kept them away from these hostile situations. The emergence of independent community schools run by blacks or white allies was a promising alternative to the district schools. These academies solved the problem of integrated schools but they were not always acceptable either.

Sarah Harris' decision to enroll at Prudence Crandall's School in 1833 exemplifies the complications that could accompany the choice to pursue an education. Despite the obstacles, a generation of young blacks would live as freely as possible in Connecticut and expected to continue their education. Harris' family owned a farm, attended church regularly, and had been living without incident in Canterbury until enrolling at the school. Crandall encouraged Sarah even after her affluent white students withdrew from the school. She was determined to teach the African-American young women from Connecticut, Pennsylvania, Rhode Island, and Massachusetts she recruited to replace the other students. Her neighbors violently opposed the school's new mission, and the assistance of William Lloyd Garrison, Lydia Maria Child, and other national figures did not help. The town's impediments included Black Laws enacted to prevent Crandall's new students from attending school, multiple trials, and a violent mob attack that forced the school to close in 1834.

This episode eventually shamed the region's leaders into rethinking positions on integration and education, and the Connecticut legislature finally banned de facto school segregation in 1868. This experience inspired Sarah Harris's commitment to the civil rights activism she would pursue for life. She married George Fayerweather, a blacksmith and activist. They had four daughters and lived first in Connecticut, and later moved to Kingston, Rhode Island, Fayerweather's hometown. Sarah maintained relationships with Crandall, Garrison, and others in her abolitionist network. The Fayerweathers helped fugitives escaping the South and actively encouraged the next generation in the fight to end slavery and gain equality. Sarah never published her story, but she inspired other young black women who would become educators. The University of Rhode Island's Fayerweather Hall is a tribute to her perseverance.

Prudence Crandall's School was the exception. Black community leaders organized small independent schools to educate their children with determination that would have made Simeon Baldwin and Timothy Dwight smile in satisfaction. James Mars, the poet Ann Plato, the photographer Augustus Washington, and the Primus family all worshipped at the Talcott Street Congregational Church, which sponsored a neighborhood school for black children familiarly known as the North African School.

Amos Beman left Middletown to teach at the North African school while he organized the resources needed to complete his theological education. He moved to Hartford in the early 1830s unable to get the Wesleyan education he wanted. Beman ran the North African School until he left to study at New York's Oneida Institute.

Ann Plato, author of the 1841 book *Essays; Including Biographies and Miscellaneous Pieces, in Prose and Poetry*, taught at Hartford's Elm Street Colored School but worshipped at Talcott Street with Rev. James Pennington. Augustus Washington, frustrated in his attempts to finance a Dartmouth education, came to teach at the school in 1844. He planned to return to the college with his savings but the success of his daguerreotype studio funded his emigration plan. In 1853 Washington left America for a prosperous life in Liberia built upon the foundation of his Hartford photographs.

Rebecca Primus, another educator with a Talcott Street affiliation also found a calling outside Connecticut. Hartford's Primus family distinguished itself in the ways the Society abolitionists hoped black residents would. Holdridge and Mehitable Primus owned a home at 20 Wadsworth Street and held jobs as a porter and a seamstress. They conscientiously raised their four children and encouraged their aspirations. Their son Nelson's regional success as a painter led him to venture west where he joined a community of landscape artists that included African-American painter Grafton Tyler Brown. Rebecca taught in Hartford before accepting the Hartford Freedmen's Aid Society's assignment to teach in Royal Oak on Maryland's Eastern Shore in the chaotic years after the Civil War. From Maryland, she exchanged letters with her friend Addie Brown, a Hartford domestic worker. The letters chronicle both women's wartime politicization through the prism of middle-class black life in mid-nineteenth century Hartford. Nelson, like his older sister Rebecca, also wrote home regularly with details of his days in Massachusetts and California.

The Primus family, descendants of an enslaved black who gained his freedom through serving in the Revolutionary War, transferred assets across the generations but ultimately could not hold them. The Primus family is representative of the many black families that successfully owned property, educated their children, and attended church in the years before the Civil War and before blacks could vote. Until slavery ended in America and blacks had full citizenship, assets would always be vulnerable. Holdridge inherited land in Branford from relatives and that land along with the Hartford home went to his wife Mehitable when he died. Mehitable's death in 1899 forced the sale of the family home, and Rebecca, then a widow, her sister Bell, and her husband moved to Adelaide Street where they lived until Rebecca's death in 1932. Education and the support of their family made Rebecca and Nelson Primus's significant contributions to African-American culture possible. As instructors, cultural producers, and managers, they provided and created in addition to receiving.

Nelson Primus's canvases and Augustus Washington's daguerreotypes are documents that represent a transition in generational experience. Mars and Smith self-consciously write themselves into history through memoir. Their narratives look back on their lives and property, and make sense of struggles that could easily become toneless jeremiads. The Primus siblings, Washington, and Ann Plato's documents reflect the moment of their creation and are free of influence from future triumphs or defeats. They clarify the period when these Hartford residents were public figures with sufficient distance from the struggles of daily existence to serve, share, and create. Their activism—not their property—was the legacy they handed down to others. For the most fortunate of these nineteenth-century figures, the compound interest on their achievements would yield an intellectual foundation—cultural and political—that was the bedrock of the twentieth century.

Edward A. Bouchet, the son of free black and previously enslaved parents, attended a community school for black children on Artizan Street near New Haven's Wooster Square. His success there made it possible for him to attend the private Hopkins Grammar School, where he was valedictorian, and to matriculate at Yale College. When he graduated in 1874, the Phi Beta Kappa student became Yale College's first black graduate. He was one of the first Americans to earn a Ph.D. in physics when he completed his dissertation at Yale in 1876. Bouchet was a respected symbol of educational achievement in the high schools for black youth where someone with his education could find teaching opportunities in post Reconstruction America. He taught at Philadelphia's Institute for Colored Youth and ran a high school in Gallipolis, Ohio. Devoted to Yale and New Haven, Bouchet was an inspirational figure to his students encouraging some to attend elite colleges and choose academic careers. But Bouchet is also like the caged bird that Paul Laurence Dunbar described in the 1899 poem *Sympathy*; he is unable to fly into the world that calls him. Bouchet lived his final years in New Haven encouraging another generation in endeavors like the nascent National Association for the Advancement of Colored People.[6] His property, the family home on Bradley Street, may not have traveled across the generations, but within a generation the family members had moved from the object category as slaves listed in the ledgers and wills of their enslavers to paragraphs in the alumni records of several prestigious educational institutions. His educational advocacy may not completely assuage the frustration over the limited opportunities that the early twentieth century afforded him, but Bouchet served many students and his story inspires all.

Anna Louise James had a notable public life as the first African-American woman in Connecticut to be licensed as a pharmacist. Born in Hartford to Anna and Willis James, she was one of nine children. Her father escaped from slavery on a Virginia plantation as a teen. Her mother died young and James moved to Old Saybrook with her sister and brother-in-law Bertha and Peter Lane. After graduation from Saybrook High School in 1905, she followed Peter's example and attended Brooklyn College of Pharmacy to become a licensed pharmacist in 1909. James moved from a Hartford shop back to Old Saybrook in 1911 to join Lane in his pharmacy.

Another generation joined the business when Ann Lane followed her father and her aunt and studied pharmacy at the University of Connecticut. Lane worked with her aunt until she married, moved to New York and began publishing her writing as Ann Petry. Anna James bought out her brother-in-law and ran the pharmacy, a local landmark, until she retired in 1967. The building, known as the James Pharmacy, is now a national historic landmark, and Petry gave her aunt's papers to the Schlesinger Library at Radcliffe. A generation from slavery, Anna James became one of the state's first women pharmacists and ran a beloved business in a shoreline town. Her family archives are housed in an Ivy League library and her shop is a National Historic Landmark.

In a reprise of Augustus Washington's model of higher education financial aid, a small group of World War I era, Morehouse College students worked in the Hartford area to pay for college. And like Washington they fostered a larger migration of black Americans. Summer tobacco work in the Hartford area would become a Morehouse tradition and it brought a teen-aged Martin Luther King, Jr. to the state for two summers during which he enjoyed personal liberties that were unimaginable in Georgia. With National Urban League sponsorship these young men came to the region for summer work in the tobacco fields effectively inventing the Great Migration of southern black workers into labor situations in northern cities. That intervention slowly increased the state's African-American population and diversified the experiences, histories, and resources in the growing black communities of Connecticut's urban centers.

But the student exchange was not limited to Morehouse students heading north. As the communities grew in number and in resources, black students from Connecticut went south to historically black colleges and universities completing this version of a migratory circuit. Middle-class families in black Hartford, New Haven, and other parts of the state sent their daughters south to schools like Howard University, Morehouse, and Bennett College. Greensboro's Bennett College for Women had been sponsored by the Methodist Church and shared some institutional connections to Wesleyan University and other Methodist schools.

Those students who were new to the segregated South could take their liberal arts education along with a political one. Liberties they took for granted in Connecticut were unimaginable in North Carolina leading to some Connecticut representation in planning for the Greensboro 1960 student lunch counter protests. Those graduates returned to Connecticut communities where they found high school aged young people ready to employ direct action tactics in a renewed fight for civil rights.[7]

Their return coincided with the introduction of innovative efforts to balance educational opportunities around the state. A 1965 study of Hartford's segregated schools generated proposals for new integrated middle schools in the city. When that was not warmly received, a one-way busing program emerged as an alternative. Project Concern, a Hartford area one-way busing program, began in 1966–67 allowing hundreds of African-American children to attend school in Farmington and other neighboring suburbs. A small group of children tested the program in 1966, and Project Concern grew from a couple hundred to several thousand students.

New England's independent schools started their own recruitment program in 1963 with Talent Search and A Better Chance. With funding from foundation and government sources, program leaders identified promising students from predominantly black, Latino, or disadvantaged neighborhoods and prepared them to attend prestigious private schools. The program's popularity eased its expansion to include public high schools in wealthy suburbs. By the early 1980s ABC houses in several Connecticut suburbs were "home" for students attending high school far from their actual homes and families through the ABC Public Schools Program.

Admissions policies for independent schools and private colleges adapted too. Glenda Newell-Harris, the first African American student at Farmington's Miss Porter's School, enrolled in 1968. Headmaster Richard Davis agreed to accept Newell believing that Porter's was ready to embrace the civil rights movement.

At Yale, where the occasional black student matriculated in the years after Bouchet, the admissions policy rewarded the university's longstanding constituency until President Kingman Brewster designated Inslee Clark to run admissions. Brewster realized that the university had a significant role to play in the modern civil rights struggle and publicly endorsed the idea with the restructuring of admissions. Clark increased the admissions staff, encouraged public school recruiting visits, and urged Yale's corporation to adopt need-blind admissions in 1966, which made it possible for students with modest family incomes to attend. Clark's efforts made the Class of 1970, the first class he selected in spring of 1966, more varied in school, economic, and racial or ethnic background. The class raised the mean verbal SAT score as well.[8]

Admissions changes at Yale, Wesleyan, and similar institutions had a historically significant impact. Access to the best educational opportunities for a varied student population had immediate and continuous benefits for the campuses, the communities that nurtured the students, and the world they've influenced as alumni. One of the first major community events the cohort of black Yalies organized acknowledged the legacy that made their presence on campus possible. The Black Student Alliance at Yale organized a 1968 conference exploring the realities of African American Studies programs comfortably existing on predominantly white campuses. Students invited a collection of well-known scholars in the field and the group had the support of faculty, administrators, and Ford Foundation funding. The program that emerged was the product of the student-led process.[9] They understood African American Studies as a field of inquiry that could retrieve, organize, and celebrate the scholarship of pioneering black academics while encouraging new research on the very issues they were experiencing and expecting to face in a slowly integrating America. It was a field that would recognize and value the narratives of Venture Smith and James Mars, the advocacy of Sarah Harris Fayerweather, the Primus siblings' creative work, Augustus Washington's photography, and the battles of Lanson, Bouchet, James, and others whose lives ended without a document trail. African American Studies at Yale and many other campuses around the state would be the intellectual home of scholarship that corrects aspects of the past like those responses regarding free blacks collected by the Connecticut Academy of Arts and Sciences. It would make a project like *African American Connecticut Explored* possible. And though the field of study might have been an unimaginable liberty for Simeon Baldwin, Jonathan Edwards, Timothy Dwight, and other Federal era Yalies, they would surely approve of the result.

Connecticut's black population has several centuries of history. Evidence of the fight for freedom dates back to the colony's earliest days, but serious analysis of that material has its beginnings far more recently. The effort unites various disciplines, types of media, and constituencies all committed to recovering and interpreting the stories of African American Connecticut.

## Notes

1. Benjamin Brawley, *A Social History of the American Negro: Being a History of the Negro Problem in the United States*, (New York: Macmillan Co.,

1921), 40–43; Henry Louis Gates Jr., "Two Nations of Black America," 1998, accessed at http://www.pbs.org/wgbh/pages/frontline/shows/race/etc/gates.html.

2. Brawley.

3. Peter P. Hinks, "'A Privilege and Elevation to Which We Look Forward with Pleasure': The Connecticut Academy of Arts and Sciences and Black Emancipation in Connecticut," in *Voices of the New Republic, Connecticut Towns 1800–1832*, ed. Howard Lamar and Carolyn C. Cooper, *Volume II: What We Think*, (New Haven: Connecticut Academy of Arts and Sciences, 2003), 105–16.

4. Venture Smith, 31. For more on Bristow and West Hartford, see past exhibitions section of the Noah Webster House website, www.noahwebsterhouse.org/programs/bristow.htm.

5. Isaiah Lanson, *Isaiah Lanson's Statement and Inquiry: Concerning the Trial of William Lanson before the New Haven County Court.*

6. Yale University Class of 1874, *Biographical Record of the Class of 1874 in Yale College* (New Haven: Tuttle, Morehouse & Taylor, 1879).

> . . . I know why the caged bird sings, ah me,
> When his wing is bruised and his bosom sore,—
> When he beats his bars and he would be free;
> It is not a carol of joy or glee,
> But a prayer that he sends from his heart's deep core,
> But a plea, that upward to Heaven he flings—
> I know why the caged bird sings!
>
> —Paul Laurence Dunbar, from the poem "Sympathy," in *Black Voices: An Anthology of Afro-American Literature*, ed. Abraham Chapman (New York: Mentor Book/New American Library, 1968), 356.

7. Sarah Cardwell, "'I, too, am America': The Founding of Bennett College for Women," *NASPA Journal About Women in Higher Education*, vol. 3, no. 1 (February 2010): 117–39.

8. Glenda Newell-Harris, "Driven to Dream," *Miss Porter's School Bulletin* (Summer 2010): 6–7; Nicholas Lemann, *The Big Test: The Secret History of the American Meritocracy* (New York: Farrar Straus and Giroux, 1999), 147–54; Geoffrey Kabaservice, "Yale's Kingman Brewster and the Early Years of Affirmative Action," *The Journal of Blacks in Higher Education*, vol. 46 (Winter, 2004–2005): 116–23; Richard L. Zweigenhaft and G. William Domhoff, *Blacks in the White Establishment? A Study of Race and Class in America*, (New Haven: Yale University Press, 1991).

9. Farah Jasmine Griffin, *Inclusive Scholarship: Developing Black Studies in the United States: A 25th Anniversary Retrospective of Ford Foundation Grant Making 1982–2007* (New York: The Ford Foundation, 2007).

# Contributor Biographies

KATHERINE J. HARRIS, Ph.D., is a lecturer at Central Connecticut State University. She serves on the State Historic Preservation Council and the site selection committee for the Connecticut Freedom Trail. She is the author of *Pan-African Language Systems: Ebonics and African Oral Heritage* (Karnak House, 2003), *African and American Values: Liberia and West Africa*, The American Values Projected Abroad Series, XVII (University Press of America, 1985) and *Franklin D. Roosevelt's African Diplomacy* (Mellen Press) is due out soon.

STACEY K. CLOSE, Ph.D., is a professor of history at Eastern Connecticut State University. He was project historian for the Hartford African American Heritage Trail and has written numerous journal articles, most recently, Millet, P., Close, S., & Arthur, C., "Beyond Tuskegee: Why African-Americans don't participate in research," in Hampton, R., Crowell, R. & Gullotta, T. (Eds.), *Handbook of African-American Health* (New York: Guilford Press, 2010.)

WM. FRANK MITCHELL, Ph.D., is assistant director & curator of the Amistad Center for Art & Culture.

ELIZABETH J. NORMEN is the publisher of *Connecticut Explored*.

BILLIE M. ANTHONY taught in Connecticut for thirty-eight years. She was the African-American Memorial Project teacher at Hartford's Fox Middle School.

CHRISTOPHER BAKER is a lecturer at the University of Massachusetts. He was the dramaturg at Hartford Stage for fourteen years.

WHITNEY BAYERS was a professional development fellow in historic preservation for the State Historic Preservation Office.

BARBARA J. BEECHING recently earned a Ph.D. at the University of Connecticut. She is co-author of *Connecticut: An Explorer's Guide* (1994).

ANDRA CHANTIM was an intern for *Connecticut Explored*.

JESSICA COLEBROOK was an intern for *Connecticut Explored*.

CHRISTOPHER COLLIER is former Connecticut state historian and professor of history emeritus at the University of Connecticut. He is the author of *Connecticut's Public Schools: a History, 1650 to 2000* (2009).

HILDEGARD CUMMINGS is a former curator of education at The William Benton Museum of Art at The University of Connecticut and author, most recently, of *Charles Ethan Porter, African-American Master of Still Life* (2007).

BARBARA DONAHUE writes local history. Her books include *They Called it the Home for Incurables* (2004), part of which appeared in the February/March/April 2004 issue of *Connecticut Explored*.

MARY M. DONOHUE was the senior architectural historian for the State Historic Preservation Office for more than thirty years and is assistant publisher of *Connecticut Explored*.

NANCY FINLAY is curator of graphics at The Connecticut Historical Society. Her publications include *Picturing Victorian America: Prints by the Kellogg Brothers of Hartford, Connecticut* (2009).

JESSICA A. GRESKO is a reporter for the Associated Press in Washington and an adjunct professor at Catholic University.

CHARLES (BEN) HAWLEY is a Civil War re-enactor with the Fifty-fourth Massachusetts Volunteer Regiment and a Twenty-ninth Connecticut Regiment descendant.

PETER HINKS works in public history and has written extensively on race and slavery in the American North in the eighteenth and nineteenth centuries. His books include *To Awaken My Afflicted Brethren: David Walker and the Problem of Antebellum Slave Resistance* (1997).

GRAHAM RUSSELL GAO HODGES is the George Dorland Langdon, Jr. Professor of History and Africana Studies at Colgate University and author, most recently, of *David Ruggles: A Radical Black Abolitionist and the Underground Railroad in New York City* (2010).

EILEEN HURST is director of the Veterans History Project and associate director of the Center for Public Policy and Social Research at Central Connecticut State University.

DAWN BYRON HUTCHINS is a historian and independent museum consultant.

CAROLYN IVANOFF is a housemaster at Shelton Intermediate School who frequently writes and lectures on American history. She wrote, with Mary J. Mycek and Marian K. O'Keefe *Ebenezer D. Bassett (1833–1908)* (2008).

MARK H. JONES recently retired as state archivist at the Connecticut State Library and is a member of the *Connecticut Explored* editorial team.

JOEL LANG is a retired *Hartford Courant* reporter.

MELONAE' MCLEAN is the marketing and communications coordinator at the Artists Collective, Inc. in Hartford, Connecticut.

HILARY MOSS is associate professor of history and Black Studies at Amherst College.

CORA MURRAY was the senior historian and minority and women's history coordinator in the Historic Preservation and Museum Division of the Connecticut Commission on Culture & Tourism.

ELISABETH PETRY is the author of *At Home Inside: A Daughter's Tribute to Ann Petry* (2009).

CYNTHIA REIK was a teacher at Hartford Public High School for thirty years. She is co-editor of *The Harriet Beecher Stowe Reader* (1992).

ANN Y. SMITH is the former director and curator of the Mattatuck Museum Arts and History Center in Waterbury. She was the project director for the *Fortune's Story* exhibit.

JOHN WOOD SWEET is associate professor of early American history at the University of North Carolina at Chapel Hill and the author of *Bodies Politic: Colonialism, Race, and the Emergence of the American North, 1730–1830* (2003).

CHARLES A. TEALE, SR. retired in 2010 as chief of the Hartford Fire Department, of which he was a member for 28 years.

BARBARA M. TUCKER is professor of history and director of Connecticut Studies at Eastern Connecticut State University.

TAMARA VERRETT was the administrative assistant at Faith Congregational Church.

LIZ WARNER teaches middle-school history at the Independent Day School in Middlefield, Connecticut. She is the author of *A Pictorial History Of Middletown, Connecticut* (1990, 2000).

The late DAVID O. WHITE was an historian and author of *Connecticut's Black Soldiers 1775–1783* (1973).

YOHURU R. WILLIAMS is associate professor of African American history at Fairfield University and is the author of *Black Politics/White Power: Civil Rights, Black Power and Black Panthers in New Haven* (2000).

# Bibliography

"1,200 Call for Freedom in City Rights March." *Hartford Courant*, March 25, 1965.

"1807 List of Freemen of New Haven." New Haven Museum.

"3,000 Leave State to Join Washington Rights March," *Hartford Courant*, August 28, 1963.

"A Fine Chance Tomorrow Afternoon—Good Paintings." *Hartford Daily Times*, Apr. 25, 1887.

"A Grand Christmas Entertainment." the *New Era*, IV (December 30, 1876): 30.

"A Meeting of Congratulation." The *Colored American*, April 17, 1841.

"A White Freeman." *Connecticut Courant*, September 7, 1803.

"Abernathy to Address Rally for Poor in Stamford Friday," *Hartford Courant*, September 26, 1968.

"Abstract of the Proceedings of the Missionary Convention." The *Colored American*, September 4, 1841.

Acomb, Evelyn M. editor. *The Revolutionary Journal of Baron Ludwig von Closen*. Chapel Hill: University of North Carolina Press, 1958.

Adams, Judge Sherman, and Henry R. Stiles. *The History of Ancient Wethersfield, Connecticut*. New York: The Grafton Press, 1904.

"Amistad Freemen." the *Pennsylvania Freeman*, August 18, 1841.

"Amos G. Beman Papers." Beinecke Rare Book and Manuscript Library, Yale University.

"An Artist Who Deserves Fame." *Hartford Daily Times*, September 11, 1879.

Ansel, Patricia Gaffney. "Looking at History Through Architecture." 1, yale. edulynhtil curriculum units/1983/1/83.01.04.

"Appeal Is Made by Marcus Garvey," *Hartford Courant*, February 28, 1924.

Arcari, Anne J. "Freeman in Name Only: The African American in Colonial Farmington, Connecticut." Master of Arts thesis, Trinity College, Hartford, 1998.

"A Racial Isolation in the Public Schools." A Report of the United States Commission on Civil Rights, 1967.

"Art Spirit in Hartford," *Hartford Daily Courant*, Nov. 1, 1904.

Arougheti, Paul, Cristina Change, and Michael Haverland. *Trowbridge Square: Creating an Urban Village*, prepared for Trowbridge Renaissance. New Haven: Yale Urban Design Workshop, 2001.

Asher, Jeremiah. *Incidents in the life of the Rev. J. Asher, pastor of Shiloh (Coloured) Baptist Church, Philadelphia, U.S.* London: C. Gilpin, 1860.

Baldwin, Ebenezer. *Observations on the Physical, Intellectual, and Moral Qualities of Our Colored Population: With Remarks on the Subject of Emancipation and Colonization*. New Haven: L. H. Young, 1834.

"Baldwin Papers." Gov. Raymond. Connecticut State Library Archives.

Baraka, Amiri (Leroi Jones). *Home: Social Essays*. New York: Morrow, 1966.

Barnard, Henry. *First Annual Report of the Board of Commissioners of the Common Schools in Connecticut, together with the "First Annual Report" of the Secretary of the Board*. Hartford: Case, Tiffany, 1839.

Barnes, G. H., and D. L. Dumond, editors. *Letters of T. D. Weld, Angelina G. Weld, and Sarah Grimke, 1822–1844*, 2 vols. New York: Appleton-Century-Crofts, 1934.

Bassett, John S. "Antislavery Leaders in North Carolina." *Johns Hopkins University Studies in Historical and Political Science*, Series XVI: 6 (June 1898).

Battle, Stanley, editor. *The State of Black Hartford*. Hartford: Greater Hartford Urban League, 1994.

Battles, Richard. "That Made the Rally Possible," letter to the editor. *Hartford Courant*, July 31, 1962.

Bayard, Samuel John, editor. *A Sketch of the Life of Com. Robert F. Stockton with Appendix. . . .* New York: Derby & Jackson, 1856.

Beeching, Barbara J. "Great Expectations: Family and Community in Nineteenth Century Black Hartford." PhD diss., University of Connecticut, 2010.

Bemis, Samuel Flagg. *John Quincy Adams and the Union*. New York: Knopf, 1956.

Bennett, Lerone. *The Shaping of Black America*. Chicago: Johnson Pub. Co. Inc., 1975.

"Billy Winters Dead." *Deep River New Era*. Deep River: Deep River Historical Society (Friday, November 22, 1900).

Binder, Frederick M. *The Color Problem in Early National America As Viewed by John Q. Adams, Thomas Jefferson, and Andrew Jackson*. The Hague: Mouton, 1968.

Birney, Catherine H. *The Grimke Sisters: Sarah and Angelina Grimke: The First American Women Advocates of Abolition and Women's Rights*. Westport: Greenwood Press, 1969 [1885].

"Births, Marriages, Deaths, I, 1706–1840." Canterbury Town Hall, Canterbury Land Records, Book 7, 19, 127.

"Black Face Boys Star at Poli's." *Hartford Courant*, April 13, 1917.

"Black Governors." *Connecticut Courant*, February 22, 1851.

"Black Muslim Minister Sees U.S. a Sinking Ship." *Hartford Courant*, July 24, 1962.

Bolton, Charles Knowles. *The Private Soldier under Washington*. New York: C. Scribner's Sons, 1902.

Bontempts, Arna, editor. *Five Black Lives*. Middletown: Wesleyan University Press, 1971 and 1988.

Borders, William. "Hartford Is Calm As Patrols Go On." *New York Times*, July 15, 1967.

Brawley, Benjamin. *A Social History of the American Negro: Being a History of the Negro Problem in the United States*. New York: Macmillan Co., 1921.

"Break Ground Today: 3 Georgia Churches Rise Again from Ashes," *Hartford Courant*, February 3, 1963.

Briggs, Jon, and Thomas D. Williams. "Arrest Triggered First Bombs." *Hartford Courant*, July 14, 1967.

Brister Baker Probate, 1793 #532. Connecticut State Library.

"Bristow: Putting the Pieces of an African American Life Together," http:// noahwebsterhouse.org/programs/bristow.htm

Brooke, Edward W. *Bridging the Divide: My Life*. New Brunswick: Rutgers University Press, 2007.

"Brother Ray—please acknowledge." The *Colored American*, January 2, 1841.

Brown, Barbara W., and James M. Rose. *Black Roots in Southeastern Connecticut, 1650–1900*. New London: New London County Historical Society, Inc., 2001.

Brundage, W. Fitzhugh. *Lynching in the New South: Georgia and Virginia, 1880–1930*. Urbana: University of Illinois Press, 1993.

Burgesson, John. "Hundreds Turn Out for MLK Celebration," www.ctpost .com/local/article/Hundreds-turn-out-for-MLK-celebration.

Burkett, Randall. "The Reverend Harry Croswell and Black Episcopalians in New Haven 1820–1860." the *North Star*, vol. 7, no. 1 (Fall 2003).

Burpee, Charles W. *The Story of Connecticut*. New York: The American Historical Co. Inc., 1939.

Burr, Nelson. *From Colonial Parish to Modern Suburb: A Brief Appreciation of West Hartford*. West Hartford: West Hartford Historical Society, 1976.

"Business and land owner Isaac Glasko 1823." Public Records of State of Connecticut. Box 2: Folder 3.

"Busload of Sympathizers Due Back This Evening," *Hartford Courant*, August 12, 1962.

Cable, Mary. *Black Odyssey*. New York: Viking, 1971.

Cameron, Diane. "Circumstances of Their Lives: Enslaved and Free Women of Color in Wethersfield, Connecticut, 1648–1832." *Connecticut History* (Fall 2005): 249.

"Canterbury Connecticut, Land Records, 1831–1850." Canterbury, Town Clerk's Office.

"'Can't Happen Here' Resident Thought." *Hartford Times*, July 14, 1967.

Cardwell, Sarah. "'I, too, am America': The Founding of Bennett College for Women," *NASPA Journal About Women in Higher Education*, vol. 3, no. 1 (February 2010).

Carrington, Karlynn. "Building on a Lost Heritage," *Hartford Courant*, October 18, 1982.

Carson, Clayborn, Emma Lapsansky-Werner, and Gary Nash. *The Struggle for Freedom*. New York: Prentice Hall, 2007, 2011.

Carter, Holland. "Ellis Ruley," *New York Times*, April 5, 1996.

Castle, Henry Allen. *The History of Plainville 1640–1918*. New Britain: Hitchcock Printing and Distribution Services, 1966.

Catlin, Roger. "Hartford Activist Honored." *Hartford Courant*, November 16, 1986.

Caulkins, Frances Manwaring. *A History of Norwich, Connecticut. . . .* Norwich: The Author, 1866.

"Census Finds Blacks Leaving State." *The New York Times*, April 16, 1978.

"Charles Ethan Porter: Short Sketch of a Bright and Versatile Artist—Promising and Rising Painter." *Plain Dealer* (Detroit, MI), Mar. 17, 1893.

Chastellux, Marquis De. *Travels in North America in the Years 1780, 1781, and 1782, II*. Translated by Howard C. Rice, Jr. Chapel Hill: University of North Carolina Press, 1963.

Child, Lydia M., editor. *The Oasis*. Boston: Benjamin C. Bacon, 1834.

*Church History of Walters Memorial African Methodist Episcopal Zion Church*. Bridgeport: Walters Memorial African Methodist Episcopal Zion Church, 2002.

"Citizens Council Re-Organize." *Hartford Chronicle*, November 2, 1946.

"City School Board Will Act Today on Robeson Concert." *Hartford Courant*, November 13, 1952.

Close, Stacey K. Interview with local leaders at home of Mr. and Mrs. Gladys Fisher. April 7, 2000.

———. Interview with Mayor Thurman Milner. July 29, 1998.

———. "Black Hartford's Print Protest: *Hartford Chronicle, Connecticut Chronicle*, and *New England Bulletin*." *The Griot*, vol. 22, no. 1 (Spring 2004).

———. "Black Southern Migration, Black Immigrants, Garveyism, and Transformation of Black Hartford, 1917–1922." *The Griot*, vol. 23 no.1 (Spring 2004).

———. "Fire in the Bones: Hartford's NAACP, Civil Rights, and Militancy, 1943–1969." *Journal of Negro History*, vol. 86, no. 3 (Summer 2001).

———. "Historical Impact of Brown II on Black Hartford 1954–71." *Illinois Schools Journal*, vol. 84, no. 2 (Spring 2005).

Cluster, Dick. *They Should Have Served That Cup of Coffee: Seven Radicals Remember the '60s.* Cambridge: South End Press, 1979.

Cockerham, William. "World War II Set Stage for Blacks to Activate Civil Rights Efforts." *Hartford Courant*, September 28, 1992.

Cogswell, James. *"God, the Pious Soldier's Strength & Instructor: A Sermon Deliver'd at Brooklyn in Pomfret, to the Military Company, Under the Command of Capt Israel Putnam, on the Thirteenth Day of April, 1757."* Boston: Draper, 1757.

Cohen, Jeffrey B. "Angry After King's Death Left Lasting Mark on Hartford's North End," hartfordinfo.org/issues/documents/history/htfd_courant _040608.asp.

Collier, Christopher. *Connecticut's Public Schools: A History, 1650–2000.* Orange: Clearwater Press, 2009.

"Colored People Await Report of NY Convention." *Hartford Courant*, August 5, 1922.

"Comments on the Reed Pastorate." *Hartford Courant*, August 25, 1919.

"Commission on Human Relations Set Up to Promote Racial Harmony." *Hartford Courant*, November 30, 1963.

Connecticut State Archives, Miscellaneous, II: 33.

———. Revolutionary War, II, IV: 1a.

———. Revolutionary War, II, IV: 101–2.

———. Revolutionary War, II, V: 163–68.

———. Revolutionary War, III, III: 66–68.

Connecticut Historical Society collections, XII: 58.

*Connecticut Journal*, September 13, 1831. Beinecke Library, Yale University

*Connecticut War Record*, June 1864. New Haven: Peck, White & Peck (monthly newspaper, can be accessed at the Connecticut State Library).

Conniff, Michael L., and Thomas J. C. Davis. *Africans in the Americas: A History of the Black Diaspora.* New York: St. Martin's Press, 1994.

Connors, Daniel J. *Deep River: The Illustrated Story of a Connecticut River Town.* Stonington: Pequot Press Inc. and The Deep River Historical Society, 1966.

Cooley, Timothy Mather. *Sketches of the Life and Character of the Rev. Lemuel*

*Haynes, A.M. for Many Years Pastor of a Church in Rutland, Vt., and Late of Granville, New-York*. New York: J.S. Taylor, 1839.

"Correspondent at Washington." The *Colored American*, November 14, 1840.

Costello, A. E. *History Of The Police Department of New Haven From the Period of the Old Watch in Colonial Days to the Present Time. Historical and Biographical. Police Protection: Past and Present. The City's Mercantile Resources Illustrated*. New Haven: The Relief Book Publishing Co., 1892.

Courtney, Steve. "Ann Plato Showed Talent Was Colorblind." *Hartford Courant*, August 4, 2002.

Craig, John "Dr. King Blames Wallace for Violent Atmosphere," *Hartford Courant*, October 21, 1963.

———. "Wesleyan Baccalaureate Is Delivered by Dr. King," *Hartford Courant*, June 8, 1964.

Cruz, Jose. *Identity and Power: Puerto Rican Politics and the Challenge of Ethnicity*. Philadelphia: Temple University Press, 1998.

Cummings, Hildegard. *Charles Ethan Porter: African-American Master of Still Life*. New Britain: New Britain Museum of American Art, 2007.

Cunningham, Charles E. *Timothy Dwight, 1752–1817. A Biography*. New York: MacMillan, 1942.

Dahl, Robert A. *Who Governs?* New Haven: Yale University Press, 1961.

Davis, Charles H. S. *History of Wallingford, Conn., from its Settlement in 1670 to the Present Including Meriden and Cheshire*. Meriden: Charles H.S. Davis, 1870.

Davis, Leroy. *A Clashing of the Soul: John Hope and the Dilemma of African American Leadership and Black Higher Education in the Early Twentieth Century*. Athens: University of Georgia Press, 1998.

DeBoer, Clara Merritt. *Be Jubilant My Feet: African American Abolitionists in the American Missionary Association, 1839–1861*. New York: Garland Publishing, Inc., 1994.

Deep River Land Records 44/256–8/20/1898, 43/281–5/25/1899, 48/280–5/17/1919, 48/279–5/17/1919.

Dickinson, James. *A Sermon, Delivered in the Second Congregational Church, Norwich*. Norwich: The Anti-Slavery Society, 1834.

Diop, Cheik Anta. *Precolonial Black Africa: A Comparative Study of the Political and Social Systems of Europe and Black Africa, from Antiquity to the Formation of Modern States*. New York: Lawrence Books, 1987.

Dirks, Robert T., and Nancy Duran. "African American Dietary Patterns at the Beginning of the 20th Century," *Journal of Nutrition*, vol. 131, no. 7 (2001): 1881–89.

"Display Ad, Edward Countryman-bey," *Hartford Courant*, June 2, 1980.

Donahue, Barbara, and the Farmington Historical Society Research Team. *Speaking for Ourselves: African American Life in Farmington, Connecticut*. Farmington: Farmington Historical Society, 1998.

"Dr. King Mourned in the Northeast," *Hartford Courant*, April 5, 1968.

"Dr. King Says U.S. Prestige at Lowest Ebb," *Hartford Courant*, March 14, 1961.

Driscoll, Theodore. "Negroes Split on Riot Cause." *Hartford Courant*, July 17, 1967.

Du Bois, W. E. B. *The Autobiography of W.E.B. Du Bois*. New York: International Publishers, 1997.

———. *The Souls of Black Folk* (1903), with Introduction by Dr. Nathan Hare and Alvin F. Poussaint, MD. New York: Signet Classic, 1969.

Duberman, Martin Baum. *Paul Robeson*. New York: Alfred A. Knopf, 1988.

Dunbar, Paul Laurence. "Sympathy," in *Black Voices: An Anthology of Afro-American Literature*, edited by Abraham Chapman. New York: Mentor Book/New American Library, 1968.

"Education–An Appeal to the Benevolent." *Philadelphia Chronicle*, September 5, 1831.

"Education Association Board Supports 'Project Concern.'" *Hartford Courant*, September 27, 1967.

Ellis Ruley obituary, *Norwich Bulletin*, January 17, 1959.

Engel, Tagan, and Cityseed. *New Haven Cooks: A Project of Cityseed*. New Haven: Cityseed, 2010.

Engers, Rachel. "Anatomy of an Insurrection." *Yale Medicine* (Spring 2002).

"Equality Is Seen Ahead for Negro." *Hartford Courant*, January 3, 1933.

"Extracts from a Letter from the Editor." *Liberator*, June 18, 1831.

Farrow, Anne, Joel Lang, and Jenifer Frank. *Complicity: How the North Promoted, Prolonged, and Profited from Slavery*. New York: Ballantine Books, 2005.

"FEPC Considered Unimportant." *Hartford Chronicle*, January 25, 1947.

"Five State Clergymen Jailed in Prayer Vigil," *Hartford Courant*, August 29, 1962.

Foner, Phillip S. *History of Black Americans: From the Emergence of the Cotton Kingdom to the Eve of the Compromise of 1850*. Westport: Greenwood Press, 1983.

Foote, George, and Richard Silocka. *Maritime History and Arts*. New Haven: Yale University Teachers' Institute.

"For the Colored American." The *Colored American*, November 20, 1841.

Forten, James to William Lloyd Garrison, October 20, 1831. Anti-Slavery Collection, Boston Public Library.

"Forten, James to William Lloyd Garrison, July 28, 1832," in *The Black Abolitionist Papers*. Ed. George E. Carter, C. Peter Ripley, and Jeffrey Rossback. Chapel Hill: University of North Caroline Press, 1991.

*Fortune's Story*, www.fortunestory.org/fortune/

Fowler, William Chauncey. *History of Durham, Connecticut*. Hartford: Wiley, Waterman and Eaton, 1866.

Franklin, John Hope, and Evelyn Higginbotham. *From Slavery To Freedom: A History of African Americans*. New York: McGraw-Hill, 2011.

Franklin, John Hope, and Alfred A. Moss Jr. *From Slavery To Freedom: A History of African Americans*. New York: McGraw Hill Inc., 1994.

Franklin, Maria. "The Archaeological and Symbolic Dimensions of Soul Food: Race, Culture, and Afro-Virginian Identity," in *Race and the Archaeology of Identity*, edited by Charles Orser. Salt Lake City: University of Utah Press, 2001.

"Free Man's Charge," in *New Haven's Settling in New-England And Some Lawes For Government: Published for the Use of that Colony*. London: M.S. for Livewell Chapman, 1673.

*Freedom's Journal*, May 11, 1827, November 23, 1827.

Fuller, Grace Pierpont. *An Introduction to the History of Connecticut as a Manufacturing State*. Northampton: Smith College, 1915.

Garvey, Marcus. *Philosophy and Opinions of Marcus Garvey*, edited by Amy Jacques Garvey. New York: Athenaeum, 1969.

Gates, Henry Louis, Jr. "Two Nations of Black America," accessed at www.pbs.org/wgbh/pages/frontline/shows/race/etc/gates.html, 1998.

Gates, Henry Louis, Jr., and Gene Andrew Jarrett. *The New Negro: Readings on Race, Representation, and African American Culture, 1892–1938*. Princeton: Princeton University Press, 2007.

*Geer's Hartford City Directory*, 1902, 1936, 1938. Hartford History Center, Hartford Public Library.

"G. Grant Williams: Speaks on 'Barbering as a Profession,' His Address Before the National Negro Business League." *Hartford Courant*, August 28, 1902.

"George Goodman Blasts Critics," *Hartford Chronicle*, March 11, 1946.

Gill, Jonathan. *Harlem: The Four Hundred Year History from Dutch Village to Capital of Black America*. New York, NY: Grove Press, 2011.

"Go Get 'em Rogers." *Hartford Courant*, January 18, 1917.

Goldfield, David, et al. *American Journey: A History of the United States*. Boston: Pearson, 2004/2011.

"Golf Club Rejects Him, Jackie Robinson Claims," *Hartford Courant*, May 11, 1958.

Goodwin, Mary. "Education Board Sticks to Stand on Robeson; Concert Will Be Held." *Hartford Courant*, November 14, 1952.

"Gospel Singer, Dr. King Boost Cause of Equality," *Hartford Courant*, October 29, 1962.

Grant, Ellsworth Strong. "The Ill-Fated Farmington Canal." *Connecticut Explored*, vol. 6, no. 2 (Spring 2008).

Grant, Ellsworth Strong, and Marion Hepburn Grant. *The City of Hartford, 1784–1984: An Illustrated History*. Hartford: Connecticut Historical Society, 1986.

Grant, Steve. "Sisters Trace Black Ancestors to 1700s in Litchfield County." *Hartford Courant*, March 3, 2002.

———. "William Lanson: The Slave Who Helped Build New Haven." *The Hartford Courant*, September 16, 2001.

Green, Adam. *Selling the Race: Culture, Community, and Black Chicago, 1940–1955*. Chicago: University of Chicago Press, 2007.

Green, Constance Belton. "Three Black Women Lawyers in Connecticut: Reflections." Unpublished manuscript, 2012.

Greene, Lorenzo Johnston. *The Negro in Colonial New England, 1620–1776*. New York: Columbia University Press, 1942.

Griffin, Farah Jasmine, ed. *Beloved Sisters and Loving Friends: Letters of Rebecca Primus of Royal Oak, Maryland to Addie Brown of Hartford, Connecticut, 1854–1868*. New York: Alfred A. Knopf, 1999.

Griffin, Farah Jasmine. *Who Set You Flowin'? The African–American Migration Narrative*. New York: Oxford University Press, 1995.

———. *Inclusive Scholarship: Developing Black Studies in the United States, a 25th Anniversary Retrospective of Ford Foundation Grant Making 1982–2007*. New York: The Ford Foundation, 2007.

Griffith, Jean. "King's Ties to Wesleyan Leave a Mark," *Hartford Courant*, January 16, 1984.

Grosvenor, Vertamae Smart. *Vibration Cooking: or, the Travel Notes of a Geechee Girl*. New York: Ballantine, 1970.

"Group Prayers at Capitol for Integration Leaders," *Hartford Courant*, July 31, 1962.

Hamilton, Charles V. *Adam Clayton Powell, Jr.* New York: MacMillan, 1991.

Hansen, Karen V. "No Kisses Is Like Youres': An Erotic Friendship Between Two African-American Women During the Mid-Nineteenth Century." *Gender and History*, vol. 7 (July, 1995).

Harlan, Louis. *Booker T. Washington: The Wizard of Tuskegee, 1901–1915*. New York: Oxford University Press, 1983.

Harper, Douglas. "Slavery in Connecticut." *Slavery in the North* (2003): http://www.slavenorth.com/connecticut.htm.

Harris, Evelen Rosenfeld. "The Transformation of the Bridgeport, Connecticut, Schools: A Study of the Process of Educational Change, 1876–1880." Dissertation, New York University, 1983.

Harris, Jessica B. *High on the Hog: A Culinary Journey from Africa to America*, New York: Bloomsbury USA, 2011.

Harris, Joseph E. *Africans and Their History*. New York: Penguin Books, Revised Edition, 1987.

Harris, Katherine J. *William Lanson: The Triumph and Tragedy Entrepreneur, Political and Social Activist, Black King (Governor), Contractor on Long Wharf and the Farmington Canal Projects*. New Haven: The Amistad Committee Inc. of New Haven, 2012.

"Hartford Minister Plans Month Working in South," *Hartford Courant*, July 21, 1965.

"Hearing Is Continued on Stamford Bias Plan," *Hartford Courant*, February 3, 1962

Hempstead, Joshua. *Diary of Joshua Hempstead of New London Connecticut: Covering a Period of 47 Years from September, 1711 to November, 1758 (1901 New London County Historical Society)*. Whitefish: Kessinger Publishing, 2008.

Highsmith, Gary. "New Haven's African King." Yale Teacher's Institute. www .yale.edu/ynhti/curriculum/units/1997/4/97.04.04.x.html

Hileman, Maria. "A Former Slave's Odyssey." *The Day* (December 24–29, 2000): A 5–6.

Hill, Robert, editor. *The Marcus Garvey and UNIA Papers*, vol. 7. Berkeley: University of California Press, 1989.

Hine, Darlene Clark, Elsa Barkley Brown, and Rosalyn Tearborg-Pen, eds. *Black Women in America*. Bloomington: Indiana University Press, 1994.

Hine, Darlene Clark, and Kathleen Thompson. *A Shining Thread of Hope: The History of Black Women in America*. New York: Broadway Books, 1998.

Hinks, Peter P. "'A Privilege and elevation to which we look forward with pleasure': The Connecticut Academy of Arts and Sciences and Black Emancipation in Connecticut," in *Voices of the New Republic, Connecticut Towns 1800–1832*, edited by Howard Lamar and Carolyn C. Cooper, *Volume II: What We Think*. New Haven: Connecticut Academy of Arts and Sciences, 2003.

*Historical and Archaeological Survey: Long Wharf Pier Structure*. New Haven: 2008.

"Historical Sketch of the Schools of Bridgeport prior to consolidation."
  Bridgeport Board of Education, Fourth Annual Report, 1880. Connecticut
  State Library.

*History of Walters Memorial African Methodist Episcopal Zion Church.* Bridgeport: Walters Memorial African Methodist Episcopal Zion Church, 2002.

Hoadly, Charles. *The Public Records of The Colony of Connecticut From May,*
  *1717, to October, 1725.* Hartford: Press of Case, Lockwood & Brainard, 1872.

Hoadly, Charles J. *Records of the Colony and Plantation of New Haven, from*
  *1638 to 1649 transcribed and edited in Accordance With A Resolution of The*
  *General Assembly of Connecticut, With Occasional Notes and An Appendix.*
  Hartford: Case, Tiffany and Company for the editor, 1857.

Hodges, Graham Russell Gao. *David Ruggles: A Radical Black Abolitionist*
  *and the Underground Railroad in New York City.* Chapel Hill: University
  of North Carolina Press, 2010.

———. *Roots & Branch: African Americans in New York and East Jersey,*
  *1613–1863.* Chapel Hill: University of North Carolina Press, 1999.

Holmberg, David. "Mount Olive Pastor to Attend Conference," *Hartford*
  *Courant,* May 29, 1966.

Hudson, Barbara. "Connecticut Freedom Trail Documentation for Bristol,
  Connecticut." Bristol Historical Society, Bristol, CT, 2012.

Hughes, Arthur H., and Morse S. Allen. *Connecticut Place Names.* Hartford:
  Connecticut Historical Society, 1976.

Hummel, Ruth S. *The Farmington Canal in Plainville, Connecticut: New*
  *England's Longest Canal in One of Connecticut's Smallest Towns Circa*
  *1828–1848.* Plainville: Plainville Historical Society, Inc., 2007.

Humphreys, Frank Landon. *The Life and Times of David Humphreys 1752–1818:*
  *Diary of David Humphreys.* New York: G.P. Putnam, 1917.

Huntington, Elijah B. *History of Stamford, Connecticut from its Settlement in*
  *1641 to the Present Time, Including Darien, Which Was One of its Parishes*
  *until 1820.* Stamford: the author, 1868.

Hurst, Ryan. "William H. Ferris." www.blackpast.org/?q=aah/ferris-william
  -henry-1874–1941.

"Independents Win on School Board." *Hartford Courant,* November 7, 1951.

*International Encyclopedia of the Social Sciences.* New York: Gale, 1968.

"Jackie Robinson Gets Task of Calming Buffalo Youth," *Hartford Courant,*
  July 1, 1967.

"Jackie Robinson Joins Brooklyn Team Today," *Hartford Courant,* April 11,
  1947.

"Jackie Robinson Jr. Dies In Car Crash," *Hartford Courant,* June 18, 1971.

"Jackie Robinson Pleads for North End Project," *Hartford Courant,* January
  31, 1953.

"Jackie Robinson Shuns Militants," *Hartford Courant,* May 1, 1969.

"Jackie Robinson to Speak Friday at Weaver Rally," *Hartford Courant,*
  January 29, 1953.

"Jackie Robinson to Take Part in NAACP Benefit," *Hartford Courant,* May
  14, 1958.

Jackson, Mandi Isaacs. *Model City Blues: Urban Space and Organized Resistance in New Haven.* Philadelphia: Temple University Press, 2008.

Jacobs, Jane. *The Death and Life of Great American Cities.* New York:
  Vintage, 1961.

Janick, Herbert. *A Diverse People: Connecticut 1914 to Present*. Chester: Pequot Press, 1975.

Jarvis, Monique. "Conscience of the Community: Art Johnson." *Hartford Inquirer*, September 8, 1999.

Jefferson, Thomas. *Notes on the State of Virginia*. 1782.

Jeffries, John W. *Testing the Roosevelt Coalition: Connecticut Society and Politics in the Era of World War II*. Knoxville: University of Tennessee Press, 1979.

"John Cotton Smith Papers." *Collections*. Vol. VI. 229. Hartford: Connecticut Historical Society.

Johnson, Arthur. "Progressive Politics in Hartford." In *State of Black Hartford*, edited by Stanley Battle. Hartford: Greater Hartford Urban League, 1993.

Johnson, Charles S. *The Negro Population of Hartford, Connecticut*. New York: National Urban League, 1921.

Johnson, Curtis S. *Raymond E. Baldwin: Connecticut Statesman*. Chester: Pequot Press, 1972, 83–84.

Johnson, Malcolm. "Urban League Shuns Demonstrations to Stress Education, Director Says." *Hartford Courant*, March 19, 1965.

Jones, Howard. *Mutiny on the Amistad*. New York: Oxford University Press, 1987.

Jones, Mark H. "When Hartford Almost Segregated Its Schools." *The Hartford Courant*, November 6, 1994.

———. "'To Tell Our Story': Mary Townsend Seymour and the Early Years of Hartford's Branch of the National Association for the Advancement of Colored People, 1917–1920." *Connecticut History*, vol. 44, no. 2 (Fall 2005).

Jones, Richard Michael. "Stonington Borough: A Connecticut Seaport in the Nineteenth Century." Dissertation, City University of New York, 1976.

"Juliette Phifer Burstermann Collection, 1929–1992." Willimantic: University Archives, J. Eugene Smith Library, Eastern Connecticut State University.

Kabaservice, Geoffrey. *The Guardians: Kingman Brewster, His Circle, and the Rise of the Liberal Establishment*. New York: Henry Holt and Company, 2004.

———. "Yale's Kingman Brewster and the Early Years of Affirmative Action," the *Journal of Blacks in Higher Education*, vol. 46 (Winter, 2004–2005).

Kelley, Robin D. G. *Yo' Mama's Diskfunktional: Fighting the Culture Wars in Urban America*. Boston: Beacon Press, 1998.

Kenney, Michael. "Boycott Urged to Win Visible Jobs for Negroes." *Hartford Courant*, July 14, 1963.

King, Coretta Scott. *My Life with Martin Luther King, Jr.* New York: Holt, Rinehart, and Winston, 1969.

"King Stirred State Audiences." *Hartford Courant*, April 5, 1968.

"King's Brother Greets Sympathizers from State," *Hartford Courant*, March 19, 1965.

"King's Death Pleases Leader of Minutemen," *Hartford Courant*, April 5, 1968.

"Land owner Pero Moody 1823." Public Records of State of Connecticut, Box 2: Folder 3. State Archives, Connecticut State Library

"Lane, Bertha to Anna Louise James, October 28, 1906." Beinecke Rare Book and Manuscript Library, Yale University.

Lang, Joel. "Discovering Ellis Ruley." *Northeast Magazine/The Hartford Courant*, September 8, 1996.

Lanson, Isaiah. *Isaiah Lanson's Statement and Inquiry Concerning the Trial of William Lanson, Before the New Haven County Court.* November Session, 1845. New Haven: 1846 Yale Law School.

Lanson, William. "Notice," *Columbian Register*, March 14, 1829. Lanson Papers, New Haven Museum; also available at www.yale.edu/glc/citizens/stories/module3/documents/lanson_statement.html.

Lanson, William. *William Lanson's Statement of Facts Addressed To The Public.* New Haven: Self published, 1850, New Haven Museum.

Lapsansky, Emma. "Since They Got Them Separate Churches: Afro Americans and Racism in Jacksonian Philadelphia." *American Quarterly*, 32 (Spring, 1980): 54, 75.

Lassonde, Stephen. *Learning to Forget: Schooling and Family Life in New Haven's Working Class, 1870–1940.* New Haven: Yale University Press, 2005.

Lathrop, Arthur. *Twentieth-Century Norwich, Connecticut.* Salem: Higginson Book Co, 2007.

Lemann, Nicholas. *The Big Test: The Secret History of the American Meritocracy.* New York: Farrar Straus and Giroux, 1999.

"Letter from Charles Jacobs. The Connecticut Sons of the American Revolution, to the author," November 23, 1971.

Levenstein, Harvey. *Paradox of Plenty: A Social History of Eating in Modern America.* New York: Oxford University Press, 1993.

Lewis, David Levering. *W.E.B. DuBois: Biography of A Race, 1868–1919.* New York: Holt, 1994.

Lewis, Edna. *The Taste of Country Cooking.* New York: Knopf, 1976.

"Lewis Tappan Papers." Library of Congress, reel #6.

*Life of James Mars, a Slave Born and Sold in Connecticut. Written by Himself.* Hartford: Case Lockwood Company, 1868.

Lincoln, C. Eric and Lawrence Mamiya. *The Black Church and the African American Experience.* Durham: Duke University Press, 1990.

Lindsey, DeLois C., and Sheila L. Traynum. *A Promise to My Mother: The Saga of the Ellis Walter Ruley Family.* San Diego: Black Forest Press, 2003.

Litchfield, Norman, and Sabina Connolly Hoyt. *History of the Town of Oxford, Connecticut.* Oxford, Connecticut: N. Litchfield, 1960.

Litwack, Leon F. *North of Slavery. The Negro in the Free States, 1790–1860.* Chicago: University of Chicago Press, 1961.

"Local Group Leaves for Albany, Ga. . . ," *Hartford Courant*, August 9, 1962.

Loewenberg, Bert James, and Ruth Bogin. *Black Women in Nineteenth-Century American Life.* University Park and London: Pennsylvania State University Press, 1976.

Logan, Rayford, and Michael R. Winston. *Dictionary of American Negro Biography.* New York and London: Norton and Co., 1982.

Long, Michael G. ed., *First Class Citizen: The Civil Rights Letters of Jackie Robinson.* New York: Times Books, 2007.

Lowenfish, Lee. *Branch Rickey: Baseball's Ferocious Gentleman.* Lincoln: University of Nebraska Press, 2009.

Lyman, Dean B., Jr. *An Atlas of Old New Haven or "Nine Squares" as shown on various early Maps.* New Haven: Chas. W. Scranton & Co., 1929.

"Mahalia Jackson, Dr. King to Be Seen at Bushnell," *Hartford Courant,* October 20, 1962.

Main, Jackson Turner. *Society and Economy in Colonial Connecticut.* Princeton: Princeton University Press, 1983.

"Malcolm X at U of H: Muslim Leader Warns of Racial Bloodshed." *Hartford Courant,* October 30, 1963.

"Malcolm X Visited City 3 Times in Recent Years." *Hartford Courant,* February 22, 1965.

"Malcolm X States Creed Of Muslims at Bushnell." *Hartford Courant,* June 5, 1963.

Marable, Manning. *Black Liberation in Conservative America.* Boston: South End Press, 1997.

"Martin Luther King Coming Here Sunday," *Hartford Courant,* March 10, 1967.

McCain, Diana Ross. *To All on Equal Terms: The Life and Legacy of Prudence Crandall.* Hartford: Connecticut Commission on Arts, Tourism, Culture, History and Film, 2004.

———. *Black Women of Connecticut: Achievement Against the Odds.* Hartford: Connecticut Historical Society, 1984.

"McGlannan files." Mattatuck Museum Collection Records, Waterbury, Connecticut.

"McLucas Faces Jail Again in Wake of Court Hearing," *Bridgeport Post,* October 4, 1977, 3.

McManus, Edgar J. *Black Bondage in the North.* Syracuse: Syracuse University Press, 1973.

"Meeting in [*sic*] Behalf of the Amistad Africans." The *Colored American,* February 6, 1841.

"Meetings of the Liberated Africans." The *Colored American,* May 22, 1841.

Menschel, David. "Abolition Without Deliverance: The Law of Connecticut Slavery 1783–1848." *The Yale Law Journal,* vol. 3 (September 24, 2001): 183, 189, 193.

Middletown Board of Education, *Fourth Annual Report,* 1861, Connecticut State Library.

Middletown Board of Education, *Annual Report,* 1864. Connecticut State Library

Miles, William. "'Freedom' Bus Welcomed Back from Albany, Ga.," *Hartford Courant,* August 13, 1962.

Miller, William Lee. *The Fifteenth Ward and the Great Society: An Encounter with a Modern City.* Cambridge: Riverside Press, 1966.

"Minister Say Events at Ole Miss Aid Reds," *Hartford Courant,* October 6, 1962.

*Minutes and Proceedings of the First Annual Convention of the People of Color.* Philadelphia, 1831. http://ia700208.us.archive.org/12/items/ minutesproceedin66/minutesproceedin66.pdf

Moore, George H. *Historical Notes on the Employment of Negroes in the American Army of the Revolution.* New York: C.T. Evans, 1862.

"More Than 3,000 March Down Main Street to Pay Tribute to Dr. Martin Luther King," *Hartford Courant,* April 8, 1968.

Morse, Gardner. "Recollections of New Haven." In *Papers of the New Haven Colony Historical Society*, Volume 5, 1887.

Moss, Hilary. "Education's Inequity: Opposition to Black Higher Education in antebellum Connecticut." *History of Education Quarterly*, vol. 46, no. 1 (Spring 2006).

Motley, Constance Baker. *Equal Justice Under Law*. New York: Farrar, Straus, Giroux, 1998.

N.A.A.C.P. *Black Heroes of the American Revolution 1775–1783*. New York: NAACP, [n.d.].

N.A.A.C.P. *Minutes of the Meeting of the Board of Directors*. New Haven: Southern Connecticut State University, November 12, 1917, and December 10, 1917.

N.A.A.C.P. "Papers of, Bridgeport-Stratford, Annual Report of Branch Activities, 1964, Branch Files, Part 25, Series B, Regional Files and Special Report, 1956–65." Middletown: Wesleyan University, Olin Library.

"NAACP Leader Against Proposed Parking Garage." *Hartford Courant*, November 1, 1967.

Nabhan, Gary Paul. *Renewing America's Food Traditions: Saving and Savoring the Continent's Most Endangered Foods*. White River Junction: Chelsea Green Publishing, 2008.

Nappier, Connie, Jr. interviewed by Eileen Hurst, Veterans History Project, Central Connecticut State University, March 15, 2006 and February 26, 2010.

*National Intelligencer*, December 24, 1816, December 31, 1816 and January 3, 1817. Ithaca: Rare Book Room, Cornell University.

"NECAP Commended by National Movement." *Hartford Courant*, July 19, 1963.

"NECAP Shuns Warning Its Picketing Is Illegal." *Hartford Courant*, July 21, 1963.

"NECAP Warned Not to Break Law." *Hartford Courant*, July 20, 1963.

"NECAP to File Charges Against Windsor Police." *Hartford Courant*, July 14, 1963.

"NECAP to Seek Hiring Negotiations with 'Well-Known' Hartford Bank," *Hartford Courant*, August 8, 1963

"NECC Makes Annual Report." *Hartford Chronicle*, January 5, 1947.

Negri, Sam. "Slum Landlords Blasted at Walter Court Rally." *Bridgeport Telegram*, January 14, 1963.

"Negro College and City Meeting." *Columbian Register*, September 13, 1831.

"Negro Leader to Give Third Keller Lecture," *Hartford Courant*, May 3, 1959.

"Negro Leader Speaks at Bushnell Tonight," *Hartford Courant*, July 14, 1961,

"Negro March Ends in Vandalism." *Hartford Couran*, September 19, 1967.

"Negro Ministers Set Day of Prayer Here March 28," *Hartford Courant*, March 7, 1956.

"Negro Rights Crusader to Speak at Bushnell," June 29, 1961.

Nell, William C. *The Colored Patriots of the American Revolution*. Boston: R.F. Wallcut, 1855.

Nelson, Marilyn. *Fortune's Bones: The Manumission Requiem*. Brooklyn: Handprint, 2004.

"New Dickinson Play on Its Way Here." *Hartford Courant*, January 20, 1917.

"New Haven." *Connecticut Journal*, October 11, 1831.

"New Haven County Bar Hits Alabama Arrests," *Hartford Courant*, February 2, 1956.

*New Haven Directory*. New Haven: James M. Patten, 1856, 1857.

*New Haven Directory*. New Haven: Price, Lee, 1890.

*New Haven Register*, February 15, 1872.

"New Haven Voting Rights Petition." 1850.

Newell-Harris, Glenda. "Driven to Dream." *Miss Porter's School Bulletin* (Summer 2010.)

Neyer, Constance. "John B. Stewart Sr. Dies: A Forceful Voice for Blacks." *Hartford Courant*, April 1, 1996.

"Niantic History." www.dickshovel.com/nian.html.

"Nixon Ticket Rapped by Jackie Robinson," *Hartford Courant*, August 12, 1968.

Noel, Jr., Don. "The Negro in Hartford: The Politician." *Hartford Times*, November 26, 1963.

———. "The Negro in Hartford: Americus, Ga.—Segregated 'Sister City." *Hartford Times*, November 26, 1963.

———. "The Negro in Hartford: First War Brought Southern Influx." *Hartford Times*, November 26, 1963.

———. "John Rogers: You were a good boy if you came from an old family," *Hartford Times*, November 26, 1963.

"North Side Regains Calm." *Hartford Times*, July 15, 1967.

Northrop, Birdsey N. *Report of the Secretary to the Board of Commissioners of Education*. 1874.

"Not Guilty, Says Black Caucus—Violence Was Already There." *Hartford Courant*, September 21, 1967.

Oberdeck, Kathryn J. *The Evangelist and the Impresario: Religion, Entertainment, and Cultural Politics in America, 1884–1914*. Baltimore: Johns Hopkins University Press, 1999.

*Office of the Public Records Administrator and State Archives Finding Aid To African Americans and Native Americans 1808—1869*. General Assembly State Archives Record Group No. 2, Connecticut State Library, Hartford, 2001.

"On Way to Selma from State," *Hartford Courant*, March 9, 1965.

O'Neill, Helen. "A Life That Sang of Pure Courage, Career Never Colored Convictions for Paul Robeson." *Hartford Courant*, February 11, 1996.

O'Neill, Molly, "Talking Turkey," *New York Times Magazine*, November 12, 1995.

Orcutt, Samuel. *History of the Town of Wolcott*. Waterbury: American Printing Co., 1874.

Orcutt, Samuel and Ambrose Beardsley. *The History of the Old Town of Derby, Connecticut, 1642–1880: With Biographies and Genealogies*. Springfield: Press of Springfield Printing Company, 1880.

Osofsky, Gilbert. *Harlem: The Making of a Ghetto*. Chicago: Ivan R. Dee, 1996.

Osterweis, Rollin G. *Three Centuries of New Haven, 1638–1938*. New Haven: Yale University Press, 1953.

Ovington, Mary White. *Half a Man*. New York: Hill and Wang, 1969.

Owens, William. *Slave Mutiny: The Revolt on the Schooner Amistad*. New York: Plume, 1997 reprint [1953].

Pagliuco, Christopher. "Ivoryton." *Connecticut Explored*, Fall 2008.

"Panther Lonnie McLucas Still Fighting to Stay Out of Prison," *South Mississippi Sun* (Biloxi, Mississippi), October 12, 1977.

Papers of the NAACP. John Bracey, Sharon Harley, and August Meier, general editors, Selected Branches File, 1940–55, reel 2, Group II, Box c-24, Hartford, CT Branch, microfilm, University Publications, 2000.

Papirno, Elissa. "State's Newest Holiday Is Marked by Confusion," *Hartford Courant*, January 15, 1977.

Patterson, Orlando. *The Ordeal of Integration: Progress and Resentment in America's Racial Crises*. New York: Basic Civitas, 1998.

Pawlowski, Robert E. *How the Other Half Lived: An Ethnic History of the Old East Side and South End of Hartford*. West Hartford: R. E. Pawloski, 1973.

Payne, Les. "The New Crisis." *Magazine of Opportunities and Ideas* (January/ February 2001).

Pennington, James W. C. *The Fugitive Blacksmith; or, Events in the History of James W. C. Pennington Pastor of the Presbyterian Church, New York*. London: Charles Gilpin, 1850.

The People's Forum, "The Housing Bill Should Be Supported," *Hartford Courant*, February 6, 1959.

Pessen, Edward. *Jacksonian America Society, Personality, and Politics*. Champagne: University of Illinois Press, 1969.

"Peter White an African by birth who died owning a $200 to $300 estate." Public Records of the State of Connecticut, Box 7, doc. 56 (1826). Connecticut State Library.

Peterson, Merrill D., ed. *Thomas Jefferson: Writings, Autobiography, Notes on the State of Virginia, Public and Private Papers, Addresses, Letters*. New York: Library of America, 1984.

"Petition of Prince Goodin to the Connecticut General Assembly, Colonial Wars, 1675–1775, French War." Connecticut Archives, Connecticut State Library, 147–148.

"Petition to the General Assembly for the Franchise, by Amos Beman" (1841). Connecticut State Library, 1841.

"Petition for Tax Exemption to Compensate for lack of Franchise." Connecticut State Library.

"Petition for Trial for fugitive slaves, from New Haven to Legislature of the State of Connecticut" (July 1838). Connecticut State Library.

Petry, Ann. *The Narrows*. New York: Kensington Publishing Corporation, 2008.

———. Journal and other undated notes, unpublished.

Petry, Elisabeth, ed. *Can Anything Beat White? A Black Family's Letters*. Jackson: University Press of Mississippi, 2005.

———. *At Home Inside: A Daughter's Tribute to Ann Petry*. Jackson: University Press of Mississippi, 2008.

Pfarrer, Donald. "Segregation a 'Cancer,' Says Rev. Mr. King," *Hartford Courant*, January 15, 1962

Piersen, William D. *Black Yankees: The Development of an Afro-American Subculture in Eighteenth-Century New England*. Amherst: University of Massachusetts, 1988.

Platt, Orville H. "The Negro Governors." In *Papers of the New Haven Colony Historical Society* VI. New Haven: Tuttle Morehouse and Taylor Co. 1900.

"Postscript." The *Colored American*, March 13, 1841.

Powell, Richard J. "Cinqué: Antislavery Portraiture and Patronage in Jacksonian America." *American Art*, vol. 11, no. 3 (Autumn 1997).

Powledge, Fred. *Model City, a Test of American Liberalism: One Town's Effort to Rebuild Itself.* New York: Simon & Schuster, 1970.

"Prayer Day to Be Asked by Negroes," *Hartford Courant*, March 13, 1956.

"Preparatory Convention." the *Union Missionary Herald*, January 1842.

Preserved Porter's estate inventory, 1804. Collection of the Connecticut State Library, State Archives.

Primus Family Papers, 1853–1924. Connecticut Historical Society Library, Hartford.

*Proceedings of the Connecticut State Convention of Colored Men: held at New Haven, on September 12th and 13th, 1849.* New Haven: William H. Stanley, 1849.

Quarles, Benjamin. *The Negro in the American Revolution.* Chapel Hill: Institute of Early American History and Culture, 1961.

———. *Black Abolitionists*, 2d ed. London: Oxford University Press, 1977.

"Race, Ethnic Shifts Shown." *New York Times*, April 19, 1981.

Rae, Douglas W. *City: Urbanism and Its End.* New Haven: Yale University Press, 2003.

Rae, Douglas W., and Paul Bass, *Murder in the Model City: The Black Panthers, Yale, and the Redemption of a Killer.* New York: Basic Books, 2006.

Rampersad, Arnold. *Jackie Robinson: A Biography.* New York: Alfred A. Knopf, 1997.

Ray, Florence, and Henrietta Ray. *Sketch of the Life of Rev. Charles B. Ray.* New York: J. J. Little & Co., 1887.

*Record of Service of Connecticut Men in the War of the Revolution, War of 1812, Mexican War.* Hartford: The Case, Lockwood & Brainard Company, 1889.

*Register of the Inhabitants of the Town of Litchfield, Conn.* Hartford: The Case, Lockwood & Brainard Company, 1900.

Reik, Cynthia. Interview with John Gale, 2011.

———. Interview with Ann Uccello, 2011.

———. Interview with David Rhinelander, 2011.

———. Interviews with Donna and Denise Nappier, 2011.

———. Interview with Constance Price, 2011.

Renner, Gerald. "City Honors A Pastor of Legend." *Hartford Courant*, June 21, 1986.

"Report of Connecticut Inter-Racial Commission to His Excellency Raymond Baldwin, Governor of Connecticut." In Governor Raymond Baldwin Papers, RG-5, Box 463, IRC Folder, Hartford: CSL Archives, September 8, 1944.

*Report of The Joint Select Committee on African Colonization*, 130A-130H Connecticut General Assembly. Hartford: Connecticut State Library.

"Rev. Dr. King to Appear at Mt. Olive Ceremony," *Hartford Courant*, January 23, 1964.

"Rev. R. A. Battles Dies; Rights Activist," *Hartford Courant*, June 23, 1980.

Revolutionary War Pay Book, Fourth Connecticut Regiment, 9–10/1782. New Haven Colony Historical Society.

Revolutionary War Service Records. Pension S17244. National Archives (as noted in White, David O. *Connecticut's Black Soldiers 1775–1783*. Chester, CT: Pequot Press, 1973).

————. Service of Pomp Edore. National Archives (and as noted in David O. White. *Connecticut's Black Soldiers 1775–1783*. Chester, CT: Pequot Press, 1973).

————. Service of Thomas Sackett. National Archives (and as noted in David O. White. *Connecticut's Black Soldiers 1775–1783*. Chester, CT: Pequot Press, 1973).

"Robinson Buys Home in Stamford," *Hartford Courant*, December 13, 1953.

Robinson, Jackie. *I Never Had It Made*. New York: Harper Collins, 1995.

"Robinson's Son is Arraigned," *Hartford Courant*, August 27, 1968.

Rogers, John E. *Inner City Bicentennial Booklet 1776–1976*. West Hartford: University of Hartford, 1975.

Root, Jesse. *Reports of Cases Adjudged in the Superior Court and Supreme Court of Errors, from July A.D. 1789 to January A.D. 1798 . . . with a Variety of Cases Anterior to that Period . . . I.* Hartford: Hudson and Goodwin, 1798.

Rose, James M., and Barbara W. Brown. *Tapestry: A Living History of the Black Family In Southeastern Connecticut*. New London: New London County Historical Society, 1979.

Rose, James M., Ph.D., and Alice Eichholz, Ph.D., CG. *Black Genesis: A Resource Book for African-American Genealogy*. Baltimore: Gale Research Co. and Genealogical Publishing Co. Inc., 2005.

Sakamoto, Dean. Greenway Preliminary Research Inventory Study, July 2009. New Haven, Connecticut

Sappol, Michael. *A Traffic of Dead Bodies*. Princeton: Princeton University Press, 2002.

Schenck, Elizabeth Hubbell. *The History of Fairfield, Fairfield County, Connecticut*. New York: J.J. Little and Company, 1905.

Schmoke, Kurt. "The Dixwell Avenue Congregational Church 1829 to 1896." *New Haven Colony Historical Society Journal*, vol. 20, no. 1 (1971).

Schoonrock, Keith. "Bowles Would End Guard Segregation." *Hartford Courant*, January 8, 1949.

Scott, Emmett J., and David Kinley, editors. *Negro Migration During the War*. New York: Arno Press, 1969.

"Seale Juror Says She Forced Mistrial." *St. Petersburg Times*, May 27, 1971.

Sernett, Milton. *Bound for the Promised Land*. Durham: Duke University Press, 1997.

Severson, Kim. *Spoon Fed: How Eight Cooks Saved My Life*. New York: Penguin, 2010.

Sheehy, Gail. *Panthermania: The Clash of Black Against Black in One American City*. New York: Harper & Row, 1971.

Shelton, Jane De Forest. "The New England Negro: A Remnant." *Harper's New Monthly Magazine* (March 1894): 536.

Shepherd, Earl. *Ancestor Book: The Wards, Countryman, Pertillar, Shepherd, Williams, Sherman, Swans, Richardson, Moore, Boone, Stewart*. Hartford: Unpublished, August 2000.

Simpson, Frank. "They Seek Equality for All People." *Hartford Courant Magazine*, September 14, 1952.

Simpson, Stan. "Art Johnson's Past Shaped an Activist's Rich Life." *Hartford Couran*, September 8, 1999.

Simpson, Stan. "Work Camp in Simsbury Was a Haven to Student Tobacco Workers," *Hartford Courant*, January 21, 1991.

*Simsbury, Connecticut Births, Marriages and Deaths.* Transcribed from the Town Records and published by Albert C. Bates. Hartford, 1898.

*Sketch of The Baptist Churches in Saybrook, Connecticut, with the Summary of Belief Covenant, and Catalogue of Members of the Deep River Baptist Church.* Hartford: Press of Case, Lockwood & Brainard, 1870.

Smith, Glenn Robert, and Robert Kenner. *Discovering Ellis Ruley: The Story of an American Outsider Artist.* New York: Crown Publishers, 1993.

Smith, Venture. *A Narrative of the Life and Adventures of Venture, a Native of Africa: But Resident above Sixty Years in the United States of America.* New London: Charles Holt 1798.

Smith-Rosenberg, Carroll. "The Female World of Love and Ritual: Relations Between Women in Nineteenth-Century America." In *Disorderly Conduct: Visions of Gender in Victorian America.* New York: Oxford University Press, 1985.

Sorensen, Leni. "Taking Care of Themselves: Food Production by the Enslaved Community at Monticello," *Repast*, vol. 21, no. 2 (Spring 2005).

Sorin, Gerald. *The New York Abolitionists: A Case Study of Political Radicalism.* Westport: Greenwood Publishing Corp, 1971.

"Southampton Affair." *Columbian Register*, September 13, 1831.

Spivey, Donald. "Point of Contention: The Historical Perspective of the African American Presence in Hartford." In *The State of Black Hartford*, edited by Stanley Battle. Hartford: Greater Hartford Urban League, 1994.

"Spurred by Albany, GA: Rallies, Voter Drive Set for City Negroes." *Hartford Courant*, September 2, 1962.

Stacom, Don. "Renaissance Man Revival in Enfield." *Hartford Courant*, December 1, 1997.

Stamford Genealogical Society. *Bulletin*, 13 (September 1970): 9–10.

Starr, Edward C. *A History of Cornwall, Connecticut: A Typical New England Town.* New Haven: Tuttle, Morehouse and Taylor, 1926.

"Stars to Perform for Rights Units," *Hartford Courant*, September 8, 1963.

"State FEPC Presents Bill." *Hartford Chronicle*, February 1, 1947.

*Statement of Facts Respecting the School for Colored Females in Canterbury, Connecticut, Together with a Report of the Late Trial of Miss Prudence Crandall.* Brooklyn: Advertiser Press, 1833.

Stetler, Henry G. *Attitudes Toward Racial Integration in Connecticut.* Hartford: Commission on Civil Rights, 1961.

Stewart, James Brewer. *Holy Warriors: The Abolitionists and American Slavery.* New York: Hill and Wang, 1976.

———. "The New Haven Negro College and the Meanings of Race in New England, 1776–1870." *New England Quarterly*, 76 (September 2003).

Stone, Frank Andrews. "African American Connecticut: African Origins, New England Roots." *The Peoples of Connecticut Multicultural Ethnic Heritage Series*, 99. Storrs: University of Connecticut, 1991.

"Strangers Pay Woman's Way to Sister's Funeral." *Hartford Courant*, September 18, 1963.

Sullivan, George. *Black Artists in Photography 1840–1940.* Dutton, New York: Cobblehill Books, 1996.

Swift, David E. *Black Prophets of Justice: Activist Clergy Before the Civil War*. Baton Rouge and London: Louisiana State University Press, 1989.

Talbot, Alan R. *The Mayor's Game: Richard Lee of New Haven and the Politics of Change*. New York: Harper & Row, 1967.

"The Amistad Africans. Farewell Meetings and Embarkation." The *Colored American*, December 25, 1841.

"The Attack on Black Citizenship in Connecticut." Historic Transcripts. The Gilder Lehrman Center for the Study of Slavery and Resistance, New Haven, 2007. cmi2.yale.edu/citizens all/stories/Module3/documents/lanson_statement.html.

The *Colored American*, September 14, 1839, September 28, 1839, August 8, 1840, September 19, 1840, May 15, 1841, December 21, 1841.

*The Hartford Courant*, July 1, 1847, October 27, 1985, February 3, 1991

"The Colored People Who Live in Hartford." *Hartford Courant* [part three], October 24, 1915.

The Hartford Negro Interest Group. "Making Acquaintance with Hartford's Negro Groups." Hartford Collection, Hartford Public Library.

"The Farmington Canal." *Connecticut Herald*, September 20, 1831, vol. XXVIII, No. 43, Whole No. 1456.

"The Low Black Schooner Captured." *New York Journal of Commerce* (evening edition), August 28, 1839.

"The Low Black Schooner Captured." *Charleston Courier*, September 2, 1839.

*The Morning Herald*, New York, October 4, 1839, quoted in "Amistad—A True Story of Freedom" at the Connecticut Historical Society.

*The Pennsylvania Freeman*, November 5, 1840, July 16, 1841.

"The Slaver." *New York Morning Herald*, August 28, 1839.

"The Suspicious Looking Schooner Captured and Brought Into This Port." *The New London Gazette*, August 28, 1839. Reprinted in the *Emancipator*, September 6, 1839

*The Valley Drummer*. Derby: Archives of the Derby Historical Society, January 15, 1987.

Thomas, Herman E. *James W.C. Pennington: African American Churchman and Abolitionist*. New York: Garland Pub., 1995.

Thomas, Herman Edward. "An Analysis of the Life and Work of James W. C. Pennington, a Black Churchman and Abolitionist." Unpublished dissertation, Hartford Seminary Foundation, 1978.

"Three State Freedom Riders to Appear at Rally Here," *Hartford Courant*, July 4, 1961.

Town of New Haven *Register of Deeds*, vol. 55, 1804–1807. Microfilm Connecticut State Library, Hartford.

"Townsend, Amos to Lewis Tappan, October 3, 1841." *American Missionary Association Papers*. Amistad Research Center, Tulane University, New Orleans, Louisiana

Trapp, Patricia. "Silent Voices and Forgotten Footsteps: A Chronicle of the Early Black Culture of Glastonbury, 1693–1860." M.A. Thesis, Wesleyan University, 1996.

"Treaty between Robert F. Stockton and Eli Ayres, and chiefs of Mesurado." In Jehudi Ashmun's Papers. Ministry of Foreign Affairs, Republic of Liberia, December 15, 1821.

Trotter, Joe W. & Earl Lewis, editors. *African Americans in the Industrial Age: A Documentary History, 1915–1945.* Boston: Northeastern University Press, 1996.

Trout, Amy. "The Story of the Farmington Canal." New Haven Colony Historical Society, 1995, reprinted in *Yale Alumni Magazine* (October 2001): 1–20.

Trowbridge, T. R. "History of Long Wharf in New Haven." In *Papers of the New Haven Historical Society*, 1. New Haven: New Haven County Historical Society, 1863.

Trumbull, J. Hammond. *Memorial History of Hartford County, Connecticut, 1633 to 1884*, 2 vols. Boston: Edward L. Osgood, 1886.

Tucker, Jean. "Dr. King Shared Peace Prize Credit with Aides, Rev. Battles Reports," *Hartford Courant*, December 15, 1964.

———. "Restraint, Expectations Gave March Its Power," *Hartford Courant*, August 30, 1963.

———. "Weakening of Rights Bill Is Feared by Dr. King," *Hartford Courant*, March 12, 1964.

Twitty, Michael W. *Fighting Old Nep: The Foodways of Enslaved Afro-Marylanders, 1634–1864.* Afrofoodways.com, 2010.

"Two Charming Pictures." *Hartford Daily Times*, Sept. 9, 1884.

"Two Church Burnings in Georgia," *Hartford Courant*, September 10, 1962.

"Unbiased Jury Impossible to Find, Seale Jury," *Eugene Register-Guard* (Oregon) May 26, 1971, May 26, 1971.

"Very Interesting Correspondence." The *Colored American*, May 22, 1841.

*Vital Records Book.* Deep River: Deep River Historical Society.

Walls, William Jacob. *African Methodist Episcopal Church: Reality of the Black Church.* Charlotte: A.M.E. Zion Publishing House, 1974.

Wansey, Henry. *The Journal of an Excursion to the United States of North America in the Summer of 1794.* New York: Johnson Reprint Corp., 1969.

"Want Negroes to Return to the South." *Hartford Courant*, February 22, 1918.

Ward, Geoffrey C. and Ken Burns, *The War: An Intimate History, 1941–1945.* New York: Knopf, 2007.

Warner, Robert Austin. *New Haven Negroes: A Social History.* New York: Arno Press, 1969.

Warner, Robert A. "Amos Gerry Beman: 1812–1874; a Memoir on a Forgotten Leader." *Journal of Negro History*, vol. 22, no.2 (April 1973).

Warshauer, Matthew. *Connecticut in the American Civil War: Slavery, Sacrifice, and Survival.* Middletown: Wesleyan University Press, 2011.

Weaver, William Woys. *100 Vegetables and Where They Came From.* Chapel Hill: Algonquin Books, 2000.

———. *Heirloom Vegetable Gardening: A Master Gardener's Guide to Planting, Seed Saving, and Cultural History.* New York: Henry Holt & Co./ Owl Publishing Company, 1999.

Webber, Christopher L. *American to the Backbone: The Life of James W. C. Pennington, the Fugitive Slave Who Became One of the First Black Abolitionists.* New York: Pegasus Books, 2011.

Welch, Vicki S. *And They Were Related, Too.* Self published, Xlibris Corporation, 2006.

Wentworth, Erastus. "The Freedmen of Sixty Years Ago." *Ladies' Repository: a monthly Periodical, devoted to Literature and Religion* (March 1876): 36.

Wetherell, Ellen F. *In Free America or Tales from North and South.* Boston: Colored Co-Operative Publishing Company, 1901. Available at http://www.archive.org/stream/infreeamerica00weth#page/n7/mode/2up.

White, Alain C. comp. *The History of the Town of Litchfield, Connecticut 1720–1920.* Litchfield: Enquirer Print, 1920.

White, David O. *Connecticut's Black Soldiers 1775–1783.* Chester: Pequot Press, 1973.

———. "Addie Brown's Hartford." *Connecticut Historical Society Bulletin*, 41 (April 1976).

———. "The Fugitive Blacksmith of Hartford: James W. C. Pennington." *Connecticut Historical Society Bulletin*, 49 (1984).

White, Shane D. "It Was a Proud Day: African Americans, Festivals, and Parades." *The Journal of American History*, vol. 81, no. 1 (June 1994).

Whitehead, Tony L. "Sociocultural Dynamics and Food Habits in a Southern Community." In *Food in the Social Order: Studies of Food and Festivities in Three American Communities*, edited by Mary Douglas. New York: Russell Sage Foundation, 1984.

"William Lanson and Bias Stanley's Petition to General Assembly for the right to Vote, 1814." Hartford: Connecticut State Library, 1814.

Williams, Austin F. letter to Lewis Tappan. August 18, 1841. Amistad Research Center, Tulane University, New Orleans, Louisiana. (Copies at Farmington Library)

Williams, George Washington. *History of the Negro Race in America from 1619 to 1880* I. New York: G.P. Putnam's Sons, 1883.

Williams, Thomas D. "City Stores Hit by Bricks, Fire." *Hartford Courant,* July 13, 1967.

Williams, Yohuru. "No Haven: From Civil Rights to Black Power in Connecticut." *The Black Scholar*, vol. 31 no. 3–4 (Fall/Winter 2001).

———. *Black Politics/White Power: Civil Rights, Black Power and the Black Panthers in New Haven.* New York: Wiley-Blackwell, 2000.

Williams, Yohuru and Jama Lazerow, eds. *In Search of the Black Panther Party: New Perspectives on a Revolutionary Movement.* Duke University Press, 2006.

———. *Liberated Territory: Untold Local Perspectives on the Black Panther Party.* Duke University Press, 2008.

Willis, Deborah, ed. *Picturing Us: African American Identity in Photography.* New York: New Press, 1994.

———. *Reflections in Black: A History of Black Photographers 1840 to the Present.* New York: W.W. Norton & Co., 2000.

Winch, Julie. *A Gentleman of Color: The Life of James Forten.* New York: Oxford University Press, 2002.

Winne, Mark. *Closing the Food Gap: Resetting the Table in the Land of Plenty.* Boston: Beacon Press, 2008.

Woodson, Carter G. *The Education of the Negro Prior to 1861.* New York: G. P. Putnam's, 1915.

Woodson, Carter Godson. *The Mis-Education of the Negro.* New York: SoHo Books, 2012 [1933].

Woodward, Carl R. "A Profile in Dedication, Sarah Harris and the Fayer-weather Family." *The New England Galaxy*, 15 (Summer 1973).

"Would Fight Plan to Establish Jim Crow School Here." *Hartford Courant*, November 27, 1917.

"Yale Dean Takes Part in March," *Hartford Courant*, March 10, 1965.

Yale University Class of 1874, *Biographical Record of the Class of 1874 in Yale College*. New Haven: Tuttle, Morehouse & Taylor, 1879.

Yetman, Dr. C. Duncan to Cynthia Reik, 2011.

Young, Nedda. "Dr. King Tells of '2 Americas' at Dinner Honoring Minister," *Hartford Courant*, March 13, 1967.

Zaiman, Jack. "Cronin Elected City's Mayor; CCC Barely Controls Council." *Hartford Courant*, November 7, 1951.

Zaiman, Jack. "First Negro in History on Council." *Hartford Courant*, November 9, 1955

Zweigenhaft, Richard L. and G. William Domhoff. *Blacks in the White Establishment? A Study of Race and Class in America*. New Haven: Yale University Press, 1991.

# Index

Page numbers in *italics*
refer to the illustrations.

# Garnet Books

Titles with asterisks (*) are also in the Driftless Connecticut Series

THE BOOK TEAM (left to right) Elizabeth J. Normen, Katherine J. Harris, Wm. Frank Mitchell, Stacey K. Close, Olivia White. *Photo by John Groo.*

ELIZABETH J. NORMEN is the publisher of *Connecticut Explored*, the magazine of Connecticut history. STACEY K. CLOSE is a professor of history at Eastern Connecticut State University. KATHERINE J. HARRIS was an adjunct professor at Central Connecticut State University. WM. FRANK MITCHELL is assistant director and curator of the Amistad Center for Art & Culture. Also pictured is OLIVIA WHITE, who was the executive director of the Amistad Center for Art & Culture and a member of the book development team.